CATHAY
AND THE WAY THITHER

CATHAY
AND THE WAY THITHER

BEING A COLLECTION OF
MEDIEVAL NOTICES OF CHINA

TRANSLATED AND EDITED

BY

COLONEL SIR HENRY YULE, R.E., C.B.,
K.C.S.I.
CORR. INST. FRANCE

NEW EDITION, REVISED THROUGHOUT IN THE LIGHT OF
RECENT DISCOVERIES

BY

HENRI CORDIER, D. LITT., HON. M.R.A.S.,
HON. COR. M.R.G.S., HON. F.R.S.L.
MEMBER OF THE INSTITUT DE FRANCE
PROFESSOR AT THE ECOLE DES LANGUES ORIENTALES
VIVANTES, PARIS

VOL. I
PRELIMINARY ESSAY
ON THE INTERCOURSE BETWEEN CHINA AND THE WESTERN
NATIONS PREVIUOS TO THE DISCOVERY OF THE CAPE ROUTE

GYAN

Published by

Gyan Publishing House
5, Ansari Road
Daryaganj, New Delhi-110002
Phone: 011-47034999, 9811692060
E-mail: books@gyanbooks.com

Distribution Network
gyanbooks.com
India, USA, Canada, UK, Australia, France

ISBN : 978-81-212-3198-5 (Set)
ISBN : 978-81-212-4817-4 (HB)
First Published, London, 1915

2nd Impression 2020

Printed at: Gyan Press, Delhi.

Cathay and the Way Thither Vol. I
Author: Colonel Sir Henry Yule

WORKS ISSUED BY

The Hakluyt Society

CATHAY AND THE WAY THITHER

VOL. I

SECOND SERIES

No. XXXVIII

ISSUED FOR 1915

COUNCIL

OF

THE HAKLUYT SOCIETY.

SIR HENRY YULE.

From the third edition of his "Marco Polo" by permission of Miss A. F. Yule.

Reproduced for the Hakluyt Society by Donald Macbeth, London. *Frontispiece.*

CATHAY
AND THE WAY THITHER

BEING A COLLECTION OF
MEDIEVAL NOTICES OF CHINA

TRANSLATED AND EDITED

BY

COLONEL SIR HENRY YULE, R.E., C.B., K.C.S.I.
CORR. INST. FRANCE

NEW EDITION, REVISED THROUGHOUT IN THE LIGHT
OF RECENT DISCOVERIES

BY

HENRI CORDIER, D.LITT., HON. M.R.A.S.,
HON. COR. M.R.G.S., HON. F.R.S.L.
MEMBER OF THE INSTITUT DE FRANCE
PROFESSOR AT THE ÉCOLE DES LANGUES ORIENTALES VIVANTES, PARIS

VOL. I

PRELIMINARY ESSAY

ON THE INTERCOURSE BETWEEN CHINA AND THE WESTERN
NATIONS PREVIOUS TO THE DISCOVERY OF THE CAPE ROUTE

LONDON:
PRINTED FOR THE HAKLUYT SOCIETY
MDCCCCXV

"Sed si aliqua scribimus propter noticiam legentium quæ in partibus vestris nesciuntur, non debetis propter hoc nos appellare mendaces, qui vobis referimus illa quæ ipsi vidimus vel ab aliis pro certo audivimus quos esse credimus fide dignos. Imò est valdè crudele ut homo propter bonum quod facit ab aliis infametur."—*Joannis de Plano Carpini Prologus.*

——"Such also is the case with Geography. For the experience of ages confesses that many of the outlying tracts of the earth remain excluded from the bounds of accurate knowledge, owing to the difficulty of penetrating regions of such vast extent; whilst some countries are very different from the descriptions that have been given of them on the faith of travellers' tales too uncritically accepted, and others, through the partial operation of revolutions and catastrophes, are no longer what they used to be. Hence it is needful, as a general rule, to abide by the most recent accounts that we possess, keeping an eye, however, all the while, upon the statements of older authors, and on what can be critically educed from their narratives, so as to form some judgment as to what is worthy of credit and what is not."—*The Geography of Claudius Ptolemy*, i, 5.

"Wherefore the task we have undertaken is a double one: first, to preserve the opinions of our author in their integrity, so far as they call for no correction; secondly, where he has failed in making things clear, to set forth the correct view to the best of our ability from the narratives that are accessible to us, and from the data afforded by more accurate maps."—*Id.*, i, 19.

"VELLERAQUE VT FOLIIS DEPECTANT TENVIA SERES
En Vergyl: Soe from Folioes of olde Travells
Ye Scrybe his slender China Yarnes unravells
And rudelie webeth them with Notes and Queries."

ANON.

DEDICATION AND PREFACE.

TO

SIR RODERICK IMPEY MURCHISON, Bart., K.C.B.,

ETC. ETC. ETC.

PRESIDENT OF THE HAKLUYT SOCIETY.

Dear Sir Roderick,

I am happy to be allowed to inscribe to you, from whom I have experienced no little kindness, this book, which endeavours to throw some light on the medieval geography of Asia. The subject, at least, needs no apology to one who is the honoured President of the Geographical as well as of the Hakluyt Society; for he has the best right of any man to say, "*nihil geographicum a me alienum puto.*"

The work was originally designed to embrace only the story of Friar Odoric, and perhaps of one more traveller; but seeing how much light the various fragments of minor medieval writers concerning China threw upon one another and upon Marco Polo, and how little known several of them were to English readers, it seemed desirable to gather all into one collection, edited as thoroughly as my capacities admitted. I never ventured to think of introducing Marco himself into the group. There is room enough, probably, for a new English edition of that prince of medieval travellers; but he claims an orbit for himself, and has no place among these asteroids. What is aimed at in these volumes is a work that shall bear some such relation to Polo as the collections of the lesser Greek geographers bear to Ptolemy.

When this task was entered on, I was more within reach of necessary aids than circumstances known to you have of late permitted, or it would scarcely have been attempted. All the reading accessible to me has, indeed, been directed to the illustration of my authors; but Palermo is not London or Paris; and the absence of some capital authority has often stopped me short in the investigation of a difficulty, just as a traveller, in projecting a complex journey, is stopped short by a black bar in the columns of his railway-guide.

I am painfully sensible also, that, in regard to many subjects dealt with in the following pages, nothing can make up for the want of genuine oriental learning. A fair familiarity with Hindustani for many years, and some reminiscences of elementary Persian, have been useful in their degree; but it is probable that they may sometimes also have led me astray, as such slender lights are apt to do.

Of the authors dealt with, ODORIC, IBN BATUTA, and GOËS are already more or less accessible to English readers; the first from old HAKLUYT'S version, the second from LEE'S translation of an Arabic abridgment, and the third from the narrative in ASTLEY'S collection.

Since the last work was published, however, a hundred and twenty years have past, and our knowledge of the regions traversed by the gallant Jesuit, though still exhibiting considerable gaps, has been greatly extended; whilst the other two travellers have never, so far as I know, been systematically edited; *i.e.*, with some endeavour to accompany their narratives with a commentary which should aim at identifying the places visited by them, and at the elucidation or condemnation of their statements.

In regard to Ibn Batuta, "mine Arabike," as John BUNYAN says of his Latin, "I borrowe"; not, however, from Lee, but from the unabridged travels as rendered into French by MM. DEFRÉMERY and SANGUINETTI. Though the version is thus borrowed, the commentary is not; and it is certainly my belief that by it some new light is thrown on this curious traveller.

Of the other authors here laid under contribution the vain and garrulous but truthful JOHN DE' MARIGNOLLI is the most conspicuous. He has been incidentally cited by Sir Emerson TENNENT, whom little escapes; but otherwise he is, I believe, almost unknown in England.

Each of the authors, however, will present his credentials in the proper place, before telling his story; and it is not needful to say more here regarding them individually.

For repetitions occurring in the text, I need not apologise; they are inevitable in what is a collection, not a selection. But it is to be feared that repetitions occur also sometimes in the notes, and for these I beg indulgence. In addition to my great distance from the printer, circumstances rendered it necessary to send the first sheets to the press many months before the later sections were ready; and thus it has been impossible to give the whole work a consistent revision.

Several kind friends have taken trouble in making references for me, or in answering questions bearing on the work. I beg all to accept my warm thanks; but I will only name here Mr. MAJOR and Mr. MARKHAM, who have also in turn been good enough to see the revised proofs through the press.

I trust that my own labour, which has been considerable, may not have been in vain. I have tried to present pretty fully one special aspect of a great subject which in all ages has had a peculiar fascination. We can see that the ancients felt something of this charm attaching to the dim legends which reached them across the length of Asia about the SERES dwelling in secluded peace and plenty on the shores of the Eastern Ocean. The vast multiplication of manuscripts and translations of Polo and Odoric, and of Odoric's plunderer MANDEVILLE, shows how medieval Christendom experienced the same attraction in the tales which those travellers related of the vast population, riches, arts, and orderly civilisation of CATHAY. The charm rekindled when the Portuguese discoveries revealed CHINA, and many marvelled with an eccentric Jesuit why God had bestowed such bounties on a hive of pagans[1]; a charm which nearly three centuries of partial knowledge scarcely quenched. Familiarity of late years has had something of its proverbial result; and closer examination of a civilisation in decay has discerned how much rottenness now exists at the core of the vast and fantastic structure.

When we see communities that have long passed the zenith of their civilisation and genius going down simultaneously in population and in moral power, there seems little of mystery in their future. But in regarding a country like China, in which moral and intellectual decay and disorganization have been accompanied by an increase of population so vast as to amount to nearly a third of the world's inhabitants, the field of speculation as to its destiny is dark indeed. Though under forms sometimes doubtless most imperfect, the influences of Christianity, the Divine Regenerator of the nations, have

[1] "Cur Deus tot bonis infidelem sibi Chinam beaverit?" Kircher, *China Illustrata*, p. 165.

entered China on at least three several occasions. Twice they appear to have been choked and extinguished; on another occasion we have seen them perverted to the purposes of a vast imposture. The future is with God. Of the clouds that are gathering round the world's horizon China has its share. The empire which has a history coeval with the oldest of Chaldæa seems to be breaking up. It has often broken up before and been reconsolidated; it has often been conquered, and has either thrown off the yoke or absorbed its conquerors. But *they* derived what civilisation they possessed from the land which they invaded. The internal combustions that are now heaving the soil come in contact with new and alien elements of Western origin. Who can guess what shall come of that chemistry?

I am,

Dear Sir Roderick,

Yours with much regard,

H. YULE.

PALERMO,
July 23rd, 1866.

PREFACE TO SECOND EDITION

Cathay and the Way Thither issued in 1866 in two volumes was the second work edited by Sir Henry YULE for the HAKLUYT SOCIETY. A few years before (1863) Yule had given an annotated translation of the MIRABILIA DESCRIPTA by Friar JORDANUS. Both works have been for a long time out of print and *Cathay* commands exorbitant prices when copies rarely appear in a bookseller's catalogue. I have not to praise a work which has been for a long time the vade-mecum of all those engaged in the study of the Far East in Ancient and Middle Ages. All agree in considering it as *the* indispensable guide of all those interested in the historical geography not only of China, not only of Central Asia, but also of Asia at large. At the time of its appearance, it included well nigh all that was then known regarding the history of the East, notwithstanding the title showing the modesty of the learned editor: *A Collection of Medieval Notices of China.* Since 1866, Science, especially geography, owing to discovery of new lands and travel in hitherto insufficiently studied countries, has rapidly progressed; Yule himself in his great work on *Marco Polo* first printed in 1871 had brought a great deal of fresh material in this new work, leaving *Cathay* far behind. It was therefore necessary to give a new edition of *Cathay* embodying all the more recent information. As the editor of the third edition of the *Book of Ser Marco Polo,* I was supposed to possess special qualifications for performing this new task. My old and learned friend, Sir Clements R. MARKHAM, President of the Hakluyt Society, asked me to undertake this edition of *Cathay*. I gladly accepted the offer as an opportunity of marking my deep esteem for the man, and of my admiration for the geographer whom I had known in the person of Yule.

I might repeat here what I said in the Preface of the third edition of the *Book of Ser Marco Polo*: "I have suppressed hardly any of Sir Henry Yule's notes and altered but few, doing so only when the light of recent information has proved him to be in error, but I have supplemented them by what I hope will be found useful, new information." As far as possible, I have adhered to these principles in this edition of *Cathay*, but, besides numerous additional notes, it has been found necessary to add in the Preliminary Essay a new chapter on Central Asia founded on recent researches and also a few Supplementary Notes; the beginning of the chapter on the Chinese Knowledge of the Roman Empire has been entirely recast. Indeed the new information has increased the bulk of the work to such an extent that it has been found necessary to print four volumes instead of two[1].

To the works mentioned in the Preface of the *Book of Ser Marco Polo* should be added the narrative of the Travels and Discoveries of Sir Aurel STEIN in Central Asia, the learned book on the Western Turks by my colleague and friend, Prof. Ed. CHAVANNES, the numerous and valuable notes given to me by that young and brilliant scholar, Prof. Paul PELLIOT. I might name a good many other works but they will be found indicated in the foot-notes or in the list appended to the fourth volume.

[1] My own additions are placed between brackets [ ].

My thanks are due not only to the COUNCIL and the HON. SECRETARY of the HAKLUYT SOCIETY, who have done me the great honour of selecting me to supervise this new edition of *Cathay*, but also to Miss Amy Frances YULE for the authorization to reproduce her father's portrait from the third edition of the *Book of Ser Marco Polo*, and to the CAMBRIDGE UNIVERSITY PRESS for the care taken in the printing of the work.

HENRI CORDIER.

PARIS, 8 RUE DE SIAM,
December, 1914.

TABLE OF CONTENTS

V. INTERCOURSE WITH ARMENIA AND PERSIA, ETC.

VI. NESTORIAN CHRISTIANITY IN CHINA.

VII. LITERARY INFORMATION REGARDING CHINA PREVIOUS TO THE MONGOL ERA.

VIII. CHINA, KNOWN UNDER THE MONGOL DYNASTY AS CATHAY.

IX. CATHAY PASSING INTO CHINA. CONCLUSION.

Supplementary Notes.

LIST OF ILLUSTRATIONS

VOL. I.

VOL. II.

VOL. III.

VOL. IV.

PRELIMINARY ESSAY.

NOTES ON THE INTERCOURSE OF CHINA AND THE WESTERN NATIONS PREVIOUS TO THE DISCOVERY OF THE SEA-ROUTE BY THE CAPE.

"On se formeroit des notions peu exactes sur la Chine, et l'on n'auroit qu'une idée imparfaite des avantages qu'on peut obtenir en étudiant l'histoire de ce pays, si l'on se représentoit un empire isolé, pour ainsi dire, à l'extrémité de l'Asie, séparé du reste du monde, dont l'entrée auroit toujours été interdite aux étrangers, et dont les relations au dehors se seroient bornées à quelques communications passagères avec les peuples les plus voisins de ses frontières."—*Abel Rémusat.*

I. EARLIEST TRACES OF INTERCOURSE. GREEK AND ROMAN KNOWLEDGE OF CHINA.

1. THAT spacious seat of ancient civilisation which we call CHINA has loomed always so large to western eyes, and has, in spite of its distance, subtended so great an angle of vision, that, at eras far apart, we find it to have been distinguished by different appellations according as it was regarded as the terminus of a southern sea-route coasting the great peninsulas and islands of Asia, or as that of a northern land route traversing the longitude of that continent.

In the former aspect the name applied has nearly always been some form of the name SIN, CHIN, SINAE, CHINA. In the latter point of view the region in question was known to the ancients as the land of the SERES; to the middle ages as the empire of CATHAY.

2. The name of Chin has been supposed, like many another word and name connected with the trade and geography of the far east, to have come to us through the Malays, and to have been applied by them to the great eastern monarchy from the style of the dynasty of Ts'IN, which a little more than two centuries before our era enjoyed a brief but very vigorous existence, uniting all the Chinese provinces under its authority, and extending its conquests far beyond those limits to the south and the west.

There are reasons however for believing that the name of CHINA must have been bestowed at a much earlier date, for it occurs in the laws of Manu, which assert the *Chinas* to have been degenerate Kshatriyas, and in the Mahabharat, compositions many centuries older than the imperial dynasty of Ts'in[1]. The indications of the geographical position of the nation so called are indeed far from precise, but in the absence of positive evidence to the contrary it seems reasonable to believe that the name *China* meant to the Hindus then what it means still; whilst there is also in a part of the astronomical systems of the two nations the strongest implication of very ancient communication between them, so ancient as to have been forgotten even in the far-reaching annals of China[2].

Whether the Chinese were known at all to the Hindus

[1] Lassen, i, 857–8; Pauthier, *M. Polo*, p. 550. The latter author says: "I shall take another occasion to establish that the statement in the Laws of Manu is partially true, and that people from India passed into Shen si, the westernmost province of China, more than one thousand years before our era, and at that time formed a state named *Thsin*, the same word as China." It is remarkable that, as the same scholar notices, the name of *China* is used in the Japanese maps (*Ib.* 449).

[2] See Lassen, i, 742 *seqq.* ["Ibn al-Kalbī says after Aš-Širkī, that China is called *Čin* because Čin and Baghar are the two sons of Baghbar ibn Kamād ibn Yāfath (Japhet)." Yākūt, in Ferrand, *Textes*, p. 207.]

in remote antiquity, and whether they were known by the name of Chinese, are of course two different questions. But if it be established that they must have known one another, the probability becomes strong that the name China in the writings of the one people indicated the other. And this name may have yet possibly been connected with the Ts'in, or some monarchy of like dynastic title; for that dynasty had reigned locally in Shen si from the ninth century before our era; and when, at a still earlier date, the empire was partitioned into many small kingdoms, we find among them the dynasties of the *Tsin* and the *Ching*[1].

[Sir Henry Yule has raised again the question of the name of *China* in *Hobson-Jobson*, pp. 196–7:

"The European knowledge of this name in the forms *Thinae* and *Sinae* goes back nearly to the Christian era. The famous mention of the *Sinim* by the prophet Isaiah would carry us much further back, but we fear the possibility of that referring to the Chinese must be abandoned, as must be likewise, perhaps, the similar application of the name *Chinas* in ancient Sanskrit works. The most probable origin of the name—which is essentially a name applied by *foreigners* to the country—as yet suggested, is that put forward by Baron F. von Richthofen, that it comes from *Jih-nan*, an old name of Tongking, seeing that in Jih-nan lay the only port which was open for foreign trade with China at the beginning of our era, and that that province was then included administratively within the limits of China Proper (see Richthofen, *China*, i, 504–510; the same author's papers in the *Trans. of the Berlin Geog. Soc.* for 1876; and a paper by one of

[1] The Tsin reigning at Fung chau in Shan si, endured from B.C. 1106 to 676 and longer under other titles; the Ching, in Ho nan, from B.C. 1122 to B.C. 477 (see Deguignes, i, 88, 102, 105: also Lassen, i, 857; St. Martin, *Mém. sur l'Arménie*, ii, 51).

the present writers in *Proc. R. Geog. Soc.*, November, 1882).

"Another theory has been suggested by our friend M. Terrien de Lacouperie in an elaborate note, of which we can but state the general gist. Whilst he quite accepts the suggestion that Kiao-chi or Tongking, anciently called *Kiao-ti*, was the *Kattigara* of Ptolemy's authority, he denies that *Jih-nan* can have been the origin of Sinae. This he does on two chief grounds: (1) That Jih-nan was not Kiao-chi, but a province a good deal further south, corresponding to the modern province of *An* (*Nghé Ane*, in the map of M. Dutreuil de Rhins, the capital of which is about 2° 17′ in lat. S. of Hanoi). This is distinctly stated in the Official Geography of Annam. *An* was one of the twelve provinces of Cochin China proper till 1820–41, when, with two others, it was transferred to Tongking. Also, in the Chinese Historical Atlas, Jih-nan lies in Chen-Ching, *i.e.* Cochin-China. (2) That the ancient pronunciation of Jih-nan, as indicated by the Chinese authorities of the Han period, was *Nit-nam*. It is still pronounced in Sinico-Annamite (the most archaic of the Chinese dialects) *Nhut-nam*, and in Cantonese *Yat-nam*. M. Terrien further points out that the export of Chinese goods, and the traffic with the south and west, were for several centuries B.C. monopolised by the State of *Tsen* (now pronounced in Sinico-Annamite *Chen*, and in Mandarin *Tien*), which corresponded to the centre and west of modern Yun-nan. The *She-ki* of Sze-ma Ts'ien (B.C. 91) and the Annals of the Han Dynasty afford interesting information on this subject. When the Emperor Wu-ti, in consequence of Chang-Kien's information brought back from Bactria, sent envoys to find the route followed by the traders of Shuh (*i.e.* Sze-chu'an) to India, these envoys were detained by Tang

Kiang, King of Tsen, who objected to their exploring trade-routes through his territory, saying haughtily: 'Has the Han a greater dominion than ours?'

"M. Terrien conceives that as the only communication of this Tsen State with the Sea would be by the Song-Koi R., the emporium of sea-trade with that State would be at its mouth, viz. at Kiao-ti or Kattigara. Thus, he considers, the name of *Tsen*, this powerful and arrogant State, the monopoliser of trade-routes, is in all probability that which spread far and wide the name of *Chīn*, *Sīn*, *Sinae*, *Thinae*, and preserved its predominance in the mouths of foreigners, even when, as in the 2nd century of our era, the great Empire of the Han has extended over the Delta of the Song-Koi.

"This theory needs more consideration than we can now give it. But it will doubtless have discussion elsewhere, and it does not disturb Richthofen's identification of Kattigara."]

Mr William Crooke, the new editor of *Hobson-Jobson*, has added the following note:

[Prof. Giles regards the suggestions of Richthofen and T. de Lacouperie as mere guesses. From a recent reconsideration of the subject he has come to the conclusion that the name may possibly be derived from the name of a dynasty, *Ch'in* or *Ts'in*, which flourished B.C. 255–207, and became widely known in India, Persia, and other Asiatic countries, the final *a* being added by the Portuguese.]

We should now add:

[Professor Paul Pelliot (*Bul. Ecole Franç. Ext. Orient.*, iv, 1904, pp. 144 *seq.*) does not accept Richthofen's theory; he shows that Jih nan was the most southern of the three provinces into which Tung King was divided under the Han dynasty: Kiao chi, Kiu chen and Jih nan;

in Kiao chi, *i.e.* the estuary of the Red River, was established the chief government and there probably landed the envoys of Mark Aurel; the pronunciation of Jih nan was then *ñit-nam*, in which it is impossible to find the *Sinae* of Ptolemy; the Indian *Cīna* or *Chinas* when they were exactly known were no doubt regarded as Chinese. With regard to Terrien's theory, Pelliot says that there is nothing to show that the kingdom of Tien was in communication *by sea* with the Red River; he thinks that Padre Martini's theory of the name of China being derived from the first Ts'in dynasty (249–207 B.C.) is still the more probable and it seems to agree with China's own tradition.]

[Some time ago, Prof. Hermann Jacobi in his paper *Kultur-, Sprache- und Literarhistorisches aus dem Kauṭiliya* (*Sitz. K. Preuss. Akad.*, xliv, 1911, p. 961) came to the conclusion that: "The name *Cīna* is secured as a designation for China in B.C. 300, so that the derivation of the word China from the dynasty of the Ts'in (B.C. 247) is definitely exploded. On the other hand, this notice is of interest also as proving the export of Chinese silk into India in the 4th century B.C." This conclusion is based upon the fact that in the *Kauṭiliya*, Prof. Jacobi finds a mention of China, more specifically the record of the fact that silken ribbons are produced in the country of China. As the author of this work was the famous minister of King Čandragupta who seized the reins of government between B.C. 320 and 315, the composition of the work must be dated around B.C. 300 and several years earlier rather than later according to Prof. Jacobi, who says that it affords a sure chronological basis. Mr. Berthold Laufer, of Chicago, adopting Prof. Jacobi's views, has come to the conclusion that "it may not be impossible that *Cīna* has been the ancient (perhaps Malayan) name adhering to the coast of Kuang-tung Province and the coast-line farther to the south, in times anterior to the settlement of the Chinese in those regions" (*T'oung pao*, Dec. 1912). Prof. Pelliot shows (*Ibid.*) that even under the Han Dynasty the Hiung Nu called the Chinese "Men of Ts'in"; Ts'in was the name given to China by the people west of the empire in ancient time; China was known after as Ταυγάστ (Theophylactus Simocatta, 7th cent., Tabγač of the Turkish Inscriptions of the same period), and at the time of the K'i tan or Leao (916–1125) as K'i tai. I believe we may, till further evidence is produced, adhere to the traditional etymology of the name of China being derived from the Ts'in dynasty.]

3. Other indications of ancient communication are found in the annals and traditions both of the Chinese and of western nations. Thus in the reign of T'ai Wu or T'ai Mou (B.C. 1634) ambassadors accompanied by interpreters, and belonging to 76 distinct kingdoms, are reported to have arrived from remote regions at the court of China[1].

At a far earlier period, under the reign of Hwang Ti, the [third of the Five Rulers of the Legendary Period] (B.C. 2697), the Chinese historians allege that the inventors of sundry arts and sciences arrived from the western kingdoms in the neighbourhood of the Kwen lun mountains[2]. In the time of Yao (B.C. 2356) there came the envoys of a race called Yué-shang shi, arriving from the south, and presented to the emperor "a divine tortoise, one thousand years old," having on its back inscriptions in strange characters resembling *tadpoles*, in which was

[1] *Chine Ancienne*, p. 76. [Terrien has, *Chinese Civilization*, p. 383: "*c.* 1538 B.C. In Tai Mou's twenty-sixth year arrivals from a western state near Karashar. Wang-Mêng was sent there with presents, and also to the West Wang-mus to get some of their famous balsam."]

[2] *Ch. Anc.*, p. 29.

related the history of the world from its beginning. Yao caused these to be transcribed, and they were known thereafter as the *Annals of the Tortoise.* The same nation sent a new embassy to China in B.C. 1110 [under the reign of Ch'eng Wang][1]. As *Yue-shang-shi* signifies "a people with long training robes" (like those of the Assyrian monuments), and as the tadpole form ascribed to the characters is suggestive of the cuneiform writing; as the commentators likewise say that the country of these people was reached in a year, after passing by Fu nan[2] and Lin Yi[3] (or the modern Siam), Pauthier has conjectured that the envoys came from Chaldaea[4].

4. Absolute tradition in countries west of India however is found of an exceedingly early communication with China, and this is singularly confirmed by the annals

[1] [Neither the *Shu King* nor Sze-ma Ts'ien mentions this embassy in B.C. 1110 from Kiao chi (Cochin-China); it is mentioned in the *Ts'ien Han Shu* and the *Han Han Shu*; the invention of the compass [south pointing chariot] by Chau Kung is connected with this legendary embassy. Cf. Legge, *Chinese Classics*, III, ii, pp. 536–7; Pelliot, *Fou-nan*, pp. 58–9.]

[2] [Fu nan was in the Khmer country and was conquered by Tchen la (Cambodia). See Pelliot, *Le Founan* (*Bul. Ecole Ext. Orient.*, April-June, 1903).]

[3] [Lin Yi, kingdom of Champa.]

[4] *H. des Relations Politiques de la Chine*, etc., pp. 5–7. [Terrien de Lacouperie has spent a great deal of labour and ingenuity to prove that the Chinese civilisation had its origin in western Asia and more particularly from Babylonia and Elam. Sinologists have not accepted his theories, at times rather wild, though Terrien has thrown light on some particular points. He has collected a number of his papers under the title of the *Western Origin of the Early Chinese Civilization from* 2300 B.C. *to* 200 A.D., Lond., 1894. Terrien placed the arrival from the west of Hwang-ti, the first leader of the civilised Bak Sings, upon the banks of the Loh where he sacrificed, *c.* 2282 B.C., in the fiftieth year of his reign. *L.c.*, p. 381. With reference to the so-called Bak see C. De Harlez, *T'oung pao*, 1895, p. 369.] If I remember rightly, some of the Chaldean inscriptions mentioned in Rawlinson's *Ancient Monarchies* are considered to go back to B.C. 2000 or earlier, but I have not the book to refer to. [New researches permit us to go back *at least* 3000 years B.C.: witness the inscription of Naram Sin.]

of the latter country. Thus the legendary history of the Persians relates that their ancient king, the famous Jamshid, had two daughters by a daughter of Máhang or Mahenk, king of Máchin (or Great China)[1]. It has been suggested [without any foundation] that his name indicates *Mu Wang*, of the Chau dynasty, who reigned from B.C. 1001 to 946, dying in the latter year in the 104th year of his age, and who is related in the Chinese annals to have made in the year 985 a journey into the remote countries of the west, and to have brought back with him skilled artizans and various natural curiosities[2].

Indeed China is often mentioned in the ancient legends of Persia, but as these seem to be chiefly known through the poetry of Ferdusi, probably little stress can be laid upon such allusions. Thus however Jamshid is pursued through India and China by the agents of Zohak; Feridun bestows upon his second son, Tur, Tartary and part of China; Siawush, the son of Kaikobad, marrying [Feringees] the daughter of Afrâçiâb, receives in dowry China [Chinese Tartary?] and Khotan; Kai Khusru (Cyrus) is sent in his youth by Afrâçiâb beyond the sea of China, and Jiv seeks him all through that country amid wonderful adventures; in the wars of Kai Khusru

[1] [Jamshid "eut de Peritchehreh, fille du roi du Zaboulistan, un fils nommé Tour; et de Mahenk, fille du roi de Madjin, deux autres appelés Betoual et Humayoun." (Jules Mohl, *Modjmel al-Tewarikh*, *Journ. Asiat.*, fév. 1841, p. 155.) I need not insist on the legendary character of this story.]

[2] *Ib.* pp. 14–15, and *Chine Ancienne*, pp. 94 *seqq.* [The legendary voyage of Mu Wang to the West has been related in the *Mu T'ien tze chuen*, translated by Eitel in the *China Review*, xvii, pp. 223–240, 247–258. On this legend of Mu and of Si Wang Mu, see Chavannes, *Se-ma Ts'ien*, ii, pp. 6–8 note, and Terrien de Lacouperie, *Chinese Civilization*, pp. 35, 77, 384. Terrien, under the date of *c.* 986 B.C., notes the "Journey of Tchou Muh Wang, to Turfan, Karashar, the Yulduz plateau and further west, perhaps as far as Kashgar. He brought back with him several clever artificers, the arts of inlaying metal and of making paste-gems, etc., some jade from Khotan-Yarkand, amber through Wakhan, etc., marionettes, and other things."]

and Rustum with Afrâçiâb Rustum captures the Emperor of China on his white elephant; Lohrasp, the successor of Kai Khusru, exacts homage from the sovereigns of Tartary and China; Gushtasp (Darius Hystaspes) makes war on Arjasp, King of Tartary, pursues him to his capital and slays him there[1].

5. Under the third year of Ch'eng wang (B.C. 1113) there is a curious and obscure tradition of the arrival at the court of men from the kingdom of *Nili*, who had come by sea, and in whom Pauthier again suggests that we have visitors from the banks of the Nile[2]. This notion might have derived some corroboration from the Chinese porcelain phials alleged to have been found in Egyptian tombs as old as the eighteenth dynasty; but I understand that Dr. Birch has demolished their claims to antiquity[3].

6. Some at least of the circumstances which have been collected in the preceding paragraphs may render it the less improbable that the SINIM of the Prophet Isaiah, a name used, as the context shows, to indicate some nation of the extreme east or south, should be truly interpreted as indicating the Chinese[4].

[1] Malcolm's *H. of Persia*, i, 1815, pp. 21, 46 *seq.*

[2] *Chine Ancienne*, p. 85. [Terrien de Lacouperie remarks that "Stan. Julien proposed afterwards an identification [of Nīlē] with the Indian town of *Nala*, but this town was founded by Asoka, thus eight centuries after the event reported in the text, and its name is differently transcribed in Chinese." Terrien has proposed to identify *Nili*, *Nĕlĕ* or *Nĕrĕ* with the old country of Norai, on the west side of the Irawadi, between Manipuri, and Momien of S.W. Yun nan, afterwards the Shan state of Mogaung. (*Early Chinese Civilization*, pp. 39–41.)]

[3] [It has been proved by Stanislas Julien and G. Pauthier in France, W. H. Medhurst Jr. and Harry S. Parkes in China (*Trans. China Br. R. As. Soc.*, Pt. III and IV) that the inscriptions on the porcelain bottles found in Egyptian tombs in 1834 belong to poems of the T'ang and Sung dynasties, *i.e.* to a period of several centuries after Christ.]

[4] "Behold, these shall come from far; and, lo, these from the north and from the west; and these from the land of SINIM" (xlix, ver. 12). See article *Sinim*, in *Smith's Dict. of the Bible*.

7. The name of China in this form was late in reaching the Greeks and Romans, and to them it probably came through people of Arabian speech, as the Arabs, being without the sound of *ch*[1], made the *China* of the Hindus and Malays into *Sín*, and perhaps sometimes into *Thín*. Hence the *Thin* of the author of the Periplus of the Erythraean Sea, who appears to be the first extant author to employ the name in this form[2]; hence also the *Sinae* and *Thinae* of Ptolemy, who doubtless derived them from his predecessor Marinus of Tyre, the loss of whose work, with the details into which it seems to have entered to a much greater extent than Ptolemy's, is so much to be regretted[3].

[The question of *Sinim* is still opened. See H. Cordier, *Bibliotheca Sinica*, col. 1919.—Terrien de Lacouperie writes: "There is no probability of doubt that these *Shinas* of ancient and modern times on the slopes of the Hindu-Kush, were the remote populations referred to in the expression *land of Sinim* of the Book of Isaiah. Such will be the conclusion of my enquiry." (*Babylonian Record*, Jan. 7, 1887.) I should say that there *is* probability of doubt in Lacouperie's theory.]

[1] [This is not exact for the ancient Arabic pronunciation. See G. Ferrand, *Textes relatifs à l'Extrême Orient*, i, p. 9.]

[2] That is if Müller's view be right in ascribing the work to the first century.

[3] Though the latest scholars have abandoned that reading of Strabo which ascribed the use of the name *Thinae* to Eratosthenes (the passages which speak of the parallel passing through *Thinae*—διὰ Θινῶν—being shown to read correctly δι' Ἀθηνῶν; see Müller's Edition, p. 945 and the various passages referred to there); it is rather singular that the name should not have been known before the end of the first century, supposing such to be the fact. For Shi Hwang-ti the great Emperor of the Ts'in is said to have sent an army of three hundred thousand men into Tartary, whilst Ptolemy Euergetes about the same time carried his conquests to Bactria. The expedition of the latter may probably, however, have preceded that of the Chinese prince. Ptolemy reigned B.C. 247–222, Shi Hwang-ti from 246 as king of Ts'in, but only from 221 as sovereign of the whole empire. M. Reinaud, in his *Relations Politiques et Commerciales de l'Empire Romain avec l'Asie Orientale*, a book which contains some ingenious suggestions and useful references to which I am indebted, but which is in the main an example of building pyramids on the apex, says that Ptolemy used the term Sinae "*pour se donner un air d'érudition*"; but why he should say so it is hard to perceive, even if it be an error to date the Periplus before Ptolemy.

8. Since the reaction from the sentiment of those days succeeding the revival of literature which ascribed all knowledge to the Greeks, it has often been doubted and denied that the Sinae of Ptolemy indeed represented the Chinese. But compare the statement of Marcianus of Heraclea (who is in this as in most other parts of his work, merely condensing and popularising the results of Ptolemy's definitions), when he tells us that the " nations of the *Sinae* lie at the extremity of the habitable world, and adjoin the eastern Terra Incognita," with that of Cosmas a century or two later in speaking of *Tzinista*, a name which no one [save Baron Walckenaer, who maintained it to be Tenasserim (see *N. Ann. des Voyages*, vol. 53, 1832, p. 5), and Mr Beazley[1]] has questioned to indicate China, that " beyond this there is neither habitation nor navigation." Who can doubt that the same region is meant by these two authors ? The fundamental error of Ptolemy's Indian geography, I mean his notion that the Indian Sea was entirely encompassed by the land, rendered it *impossible* that he should do other than misplace the Chinese coast, and thus no doubt it is easy to perplex the question to any extent over his latitudes and longitudes. But considering that the name in the same shape has come down among the Arabs as applied to the Chinese from time immemorial ; considering that in the works of Ptolemy and his successors whatever else may be said about the name it certainly represented the furthest east of which they had any cognisance ; and considering how inaccurate are Ptolemy's configurations and longitudes in a region so much further within his horizon as the peninsula of Hither India, to say nothing of the Mediterranean, it seems almost as reasonable to deny that

[1] [Tzinista "is probably only a dim notion of Malaya or Cochin-China." (C. R. Beazley, *Dawn of Modern Geog.*, 1897, p. 197 *n.*)]

Ptolemy's India contained Hindus as to deny that his *Sinae* were Chinese.

9. As far as I can collect, the names *Sinae* or *Thinae* are mentioned by only two ancient authors besides Ptolemy, viz., by the author of the Periplus of the Erythraean Sea, who, as we have already mentioned, uses the term Θὶν, keeping still closer to the original form, and by Marcianus, whom we have just quoted. Whilst Ptolemy assigns to the nation in question a position so far to the south[1], the author of the Periplus places them beyond Transgangetic India indeed, but far to the *north*, under the very *Ursa Minor*, and touching on the frontiers of the further regions of Pontus and the Caspian[2].

10. Marcianus is lauded by Lassen for his superior knowledge of South Eastern Asia, but it is by no means clear that the praise is well deserved[3]. His statements with regard to that quarter of the earth appear to be merely an abstract and popularisation of those of Ptolemy, of whom he speaks as the most godlike and wisest of men. He brings out in his compacter statements still more distinctly the erroneous notion that the Indian Sea was an enclosed basin terminating beyond the Gulf of the *Sinae*. Here the *Terra Incognita* that lay east of the *Sinae*, and the *Terra Incognita* that ran south of the Indian Sea in prolongation of Ethiopia, met and formed an angle. But the *Sinae* themselves were the remotest denizens of the habitable world. Above them to the north and

[1] The Metropolis *Thinae* is placed by him in long. 180°, lat. 3° *south*.

[2] The passage of the Periplus regarding *Thin* and *Thinae*, and those of Ptolemy regarding *Sinae* and *Serice*, will be found in Supplementary Notes I and II at the end of this essay.

[3] See Lassen, iii, 287 *seqq.*, and especially 290. Müller treats the pretensions of Marcianus in a very different fashion, and with more justice. (See his *Prolegomena to Geog. Græci Minores*, pp. cxxix *seqq.*)

north-west lay the Seres and their metropolis ; all east of these two nations was unknown land full of reedy and impenetrable swamps[1].

11. If we now turn to the SERES we find this name mentioned by classic authors much more frequently and at an earlier date by at least a century[2]. The name indeed is familiar enough to the Latin poets of the Augustan age[3], but always in a vague way, and usually with a general reference to Central Asia and the farther east[4].

[1] All this is merely abstracted from Ptolemy. See the passages of the latter in Note II.

[2] There are two mentions of the Seres which *may* be much earlier. One is in a passage ascribed to Ctesias, which speaks of the Seres as people of portentous stature and longevity. The passage, however, is found in only one MS. (of the *Bibliotheca* of Photius), and is attended by other circumstances which cause doubt whether it is really from Ctesias (see Müller's *Ctesias*, pp. 86 *seq.*, and his *Geog. Gr. Minores*, ii, 152). ["It is said that the Seres and the Northern Indians are so tall, that one meets men 13 cubits high ; they live more than two hundred years. In a certain part of the river Gaïtros (Γαΐτρου), there are men like beasts, having a skin similar to that of the hippopotami and consequently impenetrable to arrows. In India, in the remote part of an island situated in the sea, it is said that the inhabitants have long tails, such as those ascribed to satyrs." (See Müller's *Ctesias*, pp. 86–7.)] The other mention is found in a passage, or rather two passages, of Strabo. These also allude only to the longevity of the Seres, said to exceed two hundred years, and Strabo at the time seems to be quoting from Onesicritus (Müller's *Strabo*, xv, i, 34 and 37). The date of Ctesias is about B.C. 400 ; Onesicritus was an officer of Alexander's (d. B.C. 328.) *Smith's Dictionary of Gr. and Rom. Geography*, article *Serica*, would lead one by its expressions to suppose that Aristotle had spoken of that country, which of course he does not. The reference is to that passage where he speaks of βομβύκια being wound off from a certain insect in the Island of Cos. See the passage quoted in Note IV at the end.

[3] [See Supplementary Note II.]

[4] Seneca is still more indefinite, and will not commit himself to *any* view of their locality :

"Et *quocunque loco* jacent
Seres vellere nobiles" (*Thyestes*, 378) ;

whilst Lucan *does* commit himself to the view that they were somewhere at the back of Ethiopia. For, apostrophising the Nile, he says :

"Teque vident primi, quærunt tamen hi quoque, Seres"
(x, 292).

We find, however, that the first endeavours to assign more accurately the position of this people, which are those of Mela and Pliny, gravitate distinctly towards China in its northern aspect as the true idea involved. Thus Mela says that the remotest east of Asia is occupied by the three races, the Indians, the Seres, and the Scythians, of whom the Indians and the Scythians occupy the southern and northern extremities, the Seres the middle. Just as in a general way we might say still that the extreme east of Asia is occupied by the Indies, China, and Tartary, the three modern expressions which answer with tolerable accuracy to the India, land of Seres, and Scythia of the Ancients[1].

12. Ptolemy first uses the names of SERA and SERICE, the former for the chief city, the latter for the country of the Seres, and attempts to define their position with a precision beyond what his knowledge justified, but which was the necessary result of the system of his work. Yet even his definition of Serice is quite consistent with the view that it indicated the Chinese Empire in its northern aspect, for he carries it eastward to the 180° of longitude; which is also according to his calculations, in a lower latitude, the eastern boundary of the *Sinae.* In one especial point he is inferior in the justness of his views to his predecessors, for whilst Mela and Pliny both recognise the position of the Seres upon the Eastern Ocean which terminates Asia, no such ocean is recognised by Ptolemy (so far as I can discover) in any part of his work. The Ravenna Geographer denounces as an impious error the idea that there is in the extreme east an ocean passing from south to north.

13. Ammianus Marcellinus devotes some paragraphs to a description of the Seres and their country. It is no

[1] See Extracts from Mela and Pliny in Notes III and IV.

more than a conversion of the dry statements of Ptolemy into fine writing, with the addition of some more or less fabulous particulars about their mode of growing silk and carrying on commerce, which are similar to those given by Pliny. One passage indeed of the geographical description of Ammianus is startling at first sight in its seeming allusion to the Great Wall; and in this sense it has been understood by Lassen, and apparently also by Reinaud[1]. But a comparison of the passage with Ptolemy's chapter on Serice from which it is derived will show, I think, convincingly that he is speaking merely of an encircling rampart of lofty mountains within which the spacious and happy valley of the Seres is conceived to lie.

14. If, however, we try to fuse into one general description the ancient notices of the Seres and their country, omitting anomalous and manifestly fabulous statements, the result will be something like the following[2]: "The region of the Seres is a vast and populous country, touching on the east the Ocean and the limits of the habitable world, and extending west nearly to Imaus and the confines of Bactria. The people are civilised men, of mild just and frugal temper, eschewing collisions with their neighbours, and even shy of close intercourse, but not averse to dispose

[1] See Lassen, ii, 536, and Reinaud's translation of the passage in *Rel. Pol. et Commerc. de l'Empire Romain*, etc., p. 192. The original words run: "Ultra hæc utriusque Scythiæ loca, contra orientalem plagam in orbis speciem consertæ celsorum aggerum summitates ambiunt Seras, ubertate regionum et amplitudine circumspectos" [Lib. xxiii]. The whole of the passage from Ammianus will be found translated in Note VI. In a previous page he speaks of Serica as a province of Persia!

[2] It must be acknowledged, however, that apart from the exceptional statement of Pausanias (see § 17) the serious notices of the Seres reduce themselves to two, viz., that given by Pliny and that given by Ptolemy. For it will easily be seen by comparing the extracts in the notes, (1) that the notices of Mela and Pliny are either the one copied from the other, or both copied from a common source, and (2), that, as has been already observed, the statements of Ammianus are copied from Ptolemy and Pliny.

of their own products, of which raw silk is the staple, but which include also silk stuffs, furs, and iron of remarkable quality."

Now the Chinese Empire had during the century before our era, and again about a century after that date, just the extension which such a description would imply[1], whilst the other characteristics all have a distinct basis in the character of the nation. Their reputation for integrity and justice, in spite of much that might be said against it, must have had some solid foundation, for it has prevailed to our own day among their neighbours in parts of Asia most remote from each other[2]. The silk, silk-stuffs, and furs of China preserve their fame to our own day also ; and their iron to which Pliny assigns the palm was probably that fine cast-iron, otherwise unknown to the ancients, which is still one of the distinguishing manufactures of China[3].

[1] Strabo, in the only passage in which he seems to speak *proprio motu* of the Seres, says of the kings of Bactria that "they extended their rule to the frontier of the Seres and the Phryni." [καὶ δὴ καὶ μέχρι Σηρῶν καὶ Φρυνῶν ἐξέτεινον τὴν ἀρχήν.] (Müller's *Strabo*, book xi, p. 443.)

[2] Thus Wood quotes the testimony regarding the Chinese of a travelled Mullah in Badakshan : "Like every other native of those countries with whom I conversed on the subject, he praised their probity and good faith" (p. 279). Burnes heard that "their commercial regulations are just and equitable. The word of a Chinese is not doubted, nor does the tea ever differ from the sample" (iii, 195). And on the remote frontier of Burma and Siam, "all the travellers whose journals I have consulted speak in unconscious unison of the bitter feeling with which the Burmese are regarded by all the alien tribes which are in any way subject to their authority. And they speak with a like unanimity of the high character which was ascribed to the Chinese for justice, moderation, and good faith" (*On Geog. of Burma*, etc., in *J.R.G.S.*, xxvii).

[3] "Ex omnibus autem generibus palma Serico ferro est. Seres hoc cum vestibus suis pellibusque mittunt" (xxxiv, 41) "We found cast-iron pots and pans of remarkable quality to form a chief item among the miscellaneous 'notions' (apart from the silk which is the staple) imported by the Chinese into Ava by the Yun nan Road. The art of iron casting is, like most Chinese arts, a very old one ; and we find that in the first century B.C. the

15. Of actual diplomatic communication with the Seres I believe there is only one obscure trace in Roman history; this is in the representation of the historian Florus that among the numerous missions from remote nations that sought the footstool of Augustus there came envoys also from the Seres[1]. [The Seres who are mentioned by Florus may have visited Rome as private individuals, merchants, etc., but certainly not on a diplomatic mission. "The Chinese Annals clearly insinuate that Kan Ying (A.D. 98) was the first Chinese who ever penetrated as far west as T'iao chih" (Hirth, *l.c.* p. 305[2]).]

people of Ta wan or Farghânah acquired the new art of casting iron tools and utensils from Chinese deserters (Julien, quoted by Lassen, ii, 615). There is mention of Chinese iron in a passage of the Arabian geographer Ibn Khurdadhbah, quoted below (§ 83).

[1] "Even the rest of the nations of the world which were not subject to the imperial sway were sensible of its grandeur, and looked with reverence to the Roman people, the great conqueror of nations. Thus even Scythians and Sarmatians sent envoys to seek the friendship of Rome. Nay the Seres came likewise, and the Indians who dwelt beneath the vertical sun, bringing presents of precious stones and pearls and elephants, but thinking all of less moment than the vastness of the journey which they had undertaken, and which they said had occupied four years. In truth it needed but to look at their complexion to see that they were people of another world than ours. The Parthians also, as if repenting for their presumption in defeating the Romans, spontaneously brought back the standards which they had captured in the catastrophe of Crassus. Thus all round the inhabited earth there was an unbroken circle of peace or at least of armistice." ["Omnibus ad Occasum et Meridiem pacatis gentibus, ad Septemtrionem quoque, duntaxat intra Rhenum atque Danubium, item ad Orientem intra Cyrum et Euphratem, illi quoque reliqui, qui immunes imperii erant, sentiebant tamen magnitudinem, et victorem gentium populum Romanum reverebantur. Nam et Scythæ misere legatos, et Sarmatæ, amicitiam petentes. Seres etiam, habitantesque sub ipso sole Indi, cum gemmis et margaritis, elephantes quoque inter munera trahentes, nihil magis, quam longinquitatem viæ imputabant, quam quadriennio impleverant; et tamen ipse hominum color ab alio venire cælo fatebatur. Parthi quoque, quasi victoriæ pœniteret, rapta clade Crassiana ultro signa retulere." Florus, Lib. iv, 12.]

[2] ["The only official mission [226] which might have gone forward from China to Ta-Ts'in direct is that of Ts'in-lun, a Syrian merchant, who had come to some port in Cochin China and was sent [from Kiao chi] on to the emperor of Wu [Nan king],

16. That Greek and Roman knowledge of the true position of so remote a nation should at best have been somewhat hazy is not to be wondered at. As the circle of their knowledge widened its circumference from the central shores of the *Mare Nostrum*, it also became of course, in something like quadruple ratio, fainter and less definite; a fact that seems to have been forgotten by those who, in dealing with the identity of *Sera* and *Thinae*, have attached as much precision to the expressions of partial knowledge hovering on the verge of ignorance, as if these had been the expressions of precise but fragmentary knowledge such as our geographers possessed of the Antarctic Coasts, or of the Nyanza Lakes. Yet how very vague this knowledge was we may see in comparing the positions of *Thinae* as assigned respectively by Ptolemy and the author of the Periplus, or in observing the wholesale corrections which Ptolemy applied to the data of Marinus in determining the distance in longitude of Sera from the Stone Tower and of the Stone Tower from the Euphrates. Moreover it is natural in such a state of imperfect knowledge both that the name of the remoter but dominant nation should sometimes be applied to its nearest subject races, and that the characteristics of these nearest races should sometimes be transferred to the governing nation. Something in a degree analogous has taken place in our own specific application of the term DUTCH only to our own neighbours of the Netherlands. Still more in point is the fact that in the days of the T'ang dynasty, when the Chinese power extended to Transoxiana, Arab, and Armenian writers sometimes spoke of Farghânah by the name of China; and the

one of the three states contending for the supremacy during the third century A.D., Sun-ch'üan, *alias* Ta-ti (A.D. 222–252)" (Hirth, *l.c.* p. 306).]

Armenians sometimes gave the name of Chinese even to the Khazars and other races north of the Caspian[1].

17. We shall also find presently that the view entertained by the Chinese themselves of the Roman Empire and its inhabitants had some striking points of analogy to those views of the Chinese which are indicated in the classical descriptions of the Seres. There can be no mistaking the fact that in this case also the great object was within the horizon of vision, yet the details ascribed to it are often far from being true characteristics, being only the accidents of its outer borders towards the east.

18. The name of Seres is probably from its earliest use in the west identified with the name of the silkworm and its produce, and this association continued until the name ceased entirely to be used as a geographical expression[2]. Yet it was long before the Westerns had any correct conception of the nature of the article which they imported at so much cost. Virgil tells how the Seres

[1] St. Martin, *Arménie*, ii, 19, 20. An author quoted by Ibn Haukal places the frontiers of *Sín* close to Mâ-warâ-n-Nahr, and an Arab poet speaks of Kutaybah, the conqueror of Transoxiana for the Moslem, as being interred in the land of *Sín*, whilst it is known from other testimony that this was in Farghânah. (Rémusat, in *Mém. de l'Ac. des Insc.*, viii, 107.)

[2] The Chinese *See* and *Szu*, Silk, is found in the Corean language or dialect in the form *Sir*, in Mongol *Sirkek*, in Manchu *Sirghé*. Klaproth supposes this word to have given rise to the Greek σήρ, the silk-worm, and Σῆρες, the people furnishing silk, and hence *Sericum*, silk. (*Mém. rel. à l'Asie*, iii, 265.) Looking to the Tartar forms of the word the idea suggests itself that *Sericum* may have been the first importation, and that Sēr and Seres may have been formed by inverse analogy from that word taken as an adjective. Deguignes makes or borrows a suggestion that the work *Sherikoth*, which occurs in the Hebrew of Isaiah, xix, 9 ("They that work in fine flax and they that weave net-works shall be confounded"—Deguignes by mistake quotes *Ezekiel*) means silk, and he refers to the Arabic *Saraqat*. This, according to Freytag, means a long piece of white silk, sometimes silk in general. (*Mém. de l'Acad. des Insc.*, xlvi, 575.) Pardessus, in the modern *Mém. de l'Acad. des Insc.*, xv, p. 3, says *Sir* is Persian for silk, but I cannot discover the authority. *Sarah*, connected with the Arabic word just quoted, is "a stripe of white silk." (F. Johnston's *Dict.*)

combed out from the leaves of the forest the fleecy staple of their trade; and poet after poet echoes the story down to Claudian[1]. Pliny knows no better, nor does Ammianus, three centuries later than Pliny[2]; yet in the interval a juster idea of the facts had been published by Pausanias, who knew that silk was spun by insects which the Seres tended for the purpose. Either there was sounder knowledge on the subject afloat in the mercantile world which the poets ignored, sticking to the old literary tradition of the fleecy leaves as they did to the Descend O Muse; or Pausanias must have had some special source of information. The former solution of the difficulty would be the most probable, if the error were confined to the poets, but when we find a sober historian like Ammianus adopt the tale, we seem forced upon the latter. M. Reinaud thinks that Pausanias must have come in contact with a Roman visitor of China in the days of Marcus Aurelius, respecting whom we shall have to speak further on. I may observe, however, that among the Ancients, and indeed down to the time when the invention of the press had had time to take effect, the *fluctuation* of knowledge in regard to geographical truth in general, and to the

[1] A specimen from Silius Italicus is worth quoting, as it shows a correct idea of the position of the Seres on the shores of the remotest eastern sea:

"Jam, Tartessiaco quos solverat æquore, Titan
In noctem diffusus equos, jungebat Eoïs
Littoribus, primique novo Phæthonte retecti
Seres lanigeris repetebant vellera lucis" (opening of book vi).

In another passage an audacious hyperbole carries the ashes of Vesuvius to that distant land:

"Videre Eoï (monstrum admirabile!) Seres
Lanigeros cinere Ausonio canescere lucos" (xvii, 600).

[2] Even in the middle ages Jacques de Vitry, writing about 1213, and believing in his Virgil, says: "Quædam etiam arbores sunt apud Seres, folia tanquam lanam ex se procreantes, ex quibus vestes subtiles contexuntur" (Deguignes in *Mém. de l'Acad. des Insc.*, xlvi, 541). Probably, however, this writer did not think of silk (which he must have known well enough) as the Seric vestment in question.

Far East in particular, is very noticeable; chiefly due no doubt to the absence of efficient publication and the difficulties of reference. Familiar instances of this are seen in the false notion of the Caspian entertained by Strabo, and the opposite error in regard to the Indian Sea held by Ptolemy, as compared with the correct ideas on both subjects possessed by Herodotus[1]. We find a like degeneration in the Arabian knowledge of India in comparing Al Biruni with Edrisi; and other examples will occur in the allusions to China which we shall have to cite.

1 [We may add the following information from various authors:

"Qua ab Scythico oceano et mari Caspio in oceanum eoum cursus inflectitur, ab exordio huiusce plagæ profundæ nives: mox longa deserta: post Anthropophagi gens est asperrima: dein feris spatia obsita ferme dimidiam itineris partem impenetrabilem reddiderunt. quarum difficultatum terminum facit iugum mari imminens, quod Tabim barbari dicunt: post quae adhuc longinquae solitudines. sic in tractu eius orae, quae spectat aestivum orientem, post inhumanos situs primos hominum Seras cognoscimus, qui aquarum aspergine inundatis frondibus vellera arborum adminiculo depectunt liquoris et lanuginis teneram subtilitatem humore domant obsequium. hoc illud est sericum in usum publicum damno severitatis admissum et quo ostendere potius corpora quam vestire primo feminis, nunc etiam viris luxuriæ persuasit libido. Seres ipsi quidem mites et inter se quietissimi, alias vero reliquorum mortalium coetus refugiunt, adeo ut ceterarum gentium commercia abnuant. primum eorum fluvium mercatores ipsi transeunt, in cuius ripis nullo inter partes linguae commercio, sed depositarum rerum pretia oculis æstimantibus sua tradunt, nostra non emunt." (C. J. Solinus, *Polyhistor*, Mommsen's ed., Berlin, 1864, p. 201.) Cf. Pliny—"Seres à proprio oppido nomen sortiti sunt, gens ad Orientem sita, apud quos de arboribus lana contexitur: de quibus est illud, Ignoti facie, sed noti vellere Seres." (*S. Isidori Hisp. Episcopi Opera omnia*, Parisiis, 1601, *Origin.* Lib. ix, cap. ii, *de gentium vocabulis*, p. 117.)

And again:

"Seres oppidum orientis, à quo & genus sericum & regio nuncupata est. Hæc à Scytico Oceano & mari Caspio ad Oceanum orientalem inflectitur, nobilibus fertilis frondibus, à quibus vellera decerpuntur, quę cæteris gentibus Seres ad vsum vestium vendunt." (*Ibid.*, Lib. xiv, cap. iii, *De Asia*, p. 187.)]

["Sericum dictum, quia id Seres primi miserunt. Vermiculi enim ibi nasci perhibentur, à quibus haec circum arbores fila ducuntur. Vermes autem ipsi Graecè βόμβυκες nominantur." (*S. Isidori Hisp. Episc. Opera omnia*, Parisiis, 1601, *Orig.* Lib. xix, cap. xxvii, *De lanis*, p. 266).]

19. The Chinese annals tell us that the people whom they call the *Asi* (supposed by Julien and others to be the Parthians)[1] were the intermediate traders who carried silk from the east to the west, and they inform us that these Asi threw every obstacle in the way of direct communication between the Chinese and the Romans. The latter, we are assured, were exceedingly desirous of such communication, but the Asi, who were very inferior to the people of the Roman empire in the arts of weaving and the quality of dyes, feared to lose the profits of agency and manufacture entirely unless they retained a monopoly of the trade. The statement is no doubt incorrect that *all* silk was passed on to the Romans in a manufactured state, or if true, could only have been so for some brief period, but the anxiety of the Romans to rid themselves

[1] The name *Asi* is however said by Rémusat to have been applied by the Chinese almost promiscuously to the nations between the Jaxartes and Oxus, as far south as Samarkand; and in one of his quotations it is applied to people of Khojand, and in another to people of Bokhara. In the extracts from Menander (Note VIII at the end) the *Sogdians* appear as intermediaries in the silk trade, *i.e.*, the people of the country whose centre is Samarkand. [*An-hsi*, *An-si* is Parthia. The *Ts'ien Han Shu* says: "The king of the country of An-hsi rules at the city of P'an-tsu; its distance from Ch'ang-an is 11,600 li. The country is not subject to a tu-hu [a Chinese governor in Central-Asiatic possessions]. It bounds north on K'ang-chü, east on Wu-i-shan-li, west on T'iao-chih.... It lies on the banks of the Kuei-shui [Oxus]." And again: "When the emperor Wu-ti [B.C. 140–86] first sent an embassy to An-hsi [Parthia], the king ordered a general to meet him on the eastern frontier with twenty thousand cavalry. The eastern frontier was several thousand li distant from the king's capital. Proceeding to the north one came across several tens of cities, the inhabitants of which were allied with that country. As they sent forth an embassy to follow the Chinese embassy, they came to see the country of China. They offered to the Chinese court large birds' eggs, and jugglers from Li-kan, at which His Majesty was highly pleased." (Hirth, *China and the Roman Orient*, pp. 141, 36.) Notices of An-si are also to be found in the *Shi ki*, in the *Hau Han Shu*, etc. Hirth adds, p. 141: "There can be no doubt that the Hekatompylos of Greek and Roman writers, being the chief capital of the Empire, is identical with the city of P'an-tou (Parthura ?) mentioned in the *Ch'ien-han-shu* and with the city of Ho-tu (old sound Wodok ?) mentioned in the *Hou-han-shu*."]

of dependance on the nations of Persia for the supply of silk is fully borne out by the story which Procopius and others relate as to the introduction of the silkworm into the Byzantine territories by two monks in the time of Justinian (circa 550)[1]. The country from which the monks brought their precious charge is called by Theophanes simply that of the Seres, but by Procopius *Serinda*. China may be intended, but of this there can be no certainty. Indeed it is possible that the term was meant to express a compound like our *Indo-China*, some region intermediate between Serica and India, and if so not improbably Khotan[2].

20. There are among the fragments of the Greek historians other curious notices of intercourse with the Turkish tribes of Central Asia in the days of Justinian's immediate successors, which, though they do not bring up mention of the Chinese under any denomination, are in a degree relevant to our subject, because they show the Byzantine empire in contact and intercourse with nations which occupy a prominent place in the Chinese annals, and introduce the names of some princes who are to be recognised in those also[3].

We have, however, in this (6th) and the following century, from Greek writers, two remarkable notices of China, in the comparison of which we still may trace the duplicate aspect of this great country to which we have referred in the opening of this Essay. For Cosmas, the

[1] See extracts in Note VII.

[2] D'Anville suggests that Serinda may be a compound name, but identifies it with *Sirhind* in North Western India. This name I presume however to be Persian, and to date from comparatively late times. Gosselin will have it to be Srinagar in Kashmir. The Ravenna Geographer puts *India Serica* in the North of India on the Ganges and Acesines (*Rav. Anon. Cosmog.* Berlin, 1860, pp. 45, 48).

[3] See a sample of these narratives in Note VIII.

first of these authors, recognises it chiefly on its southern or maritime side, the other, Theophylactus, solely on its land side, and without knowledge of any other. The evidence of both goes to show that the name of Seres had been now practically almost, if not entirely, forgotten.

21. COSMAS, called from his maritime experiences *Indicopleustes*, apparently an Alexandrian Greek, who wrote between 530 and 550[1], is the first Greek or Roman writer who speaks of China in a matter-of-fact manner, and not as a land enveloped in half mythical haze. He speaks of it also by a name which I suppose no one has ever disputed to mean China[2].

This writer was a monk when he composed the work which has come down to us, but in his earlier days he had been a merchant, and in that capacity had sailed on the Red Sea and the Indian Ocean, visiting the coasts of Ethiopia, and apparently also the Persian Gulf and the western coasts of India, as well as Ceylon[3].

His book was written at Alexandria, and is termed a *Universal Christian Topography*[4], the great object of it being to show that the Tabernacle in the Wilderness is a pattern or model of the universe. The earth is a

[1] Dates deduced by Montfaucon from different parts of his work show that parts of it were written in 535, and other parts at least twelve years later. The work bears tokens of having been often altered and expanded. Five books only were at first published; six and a fraction more were added gradually to strengthen arguments and meet objections. (See preface in Montfaucon's *Collectio Nova Patrum et Script. Græc.*, ii, which contains the work; extracts were also previously published in Thévenot's Collection of Travels.) [A new edition and translation of Cosmas has been brought out by Mr. J. W. McCrindle for the Hakluyt Society, 1897.]

[2] See page 12.

[3] Sir J. E. Tennent (*Ceylon*, i, 542) says that Cosmas got his accounts of Ceylon from Sopatrus whom he met at Adule, and Lassen ascribes all Cosmas says of India to the same authority (ii, 773). But I have not found the ground of these opinions. One anecdote is ascribed to Sopatrus, no more.

[4] Χριστιανικὴ Τοπογραφία περιεκτικὴ παντὸς τοῦ Κόσμου.

rectangular plane, twice as long as it is broad. The heavens come down to the earth on all four sides like the walls of a room; from the north wall to the south wall, at an undefined height, a semicircular waggon-vault is turned, at the level of the springing of which lies the firmament, like a flat ceiling. All below this firmament is this world; the upper story is Heaven, or the world to come. In fact one of those enormous receptacles, which carry the dresses of female travellers in our day, forms a perfect model of the Cosmos of Cosmas.

In the middle of the rectangular surface of this world lies the inhabited earth encompassed by the Ocean. Beyond the Ocean, bordering the edges of creation, is the unvisited transoceanic land, on which, in the far east, lies Paradise. Here, too, on a barren and thorny soil, without the walls of Paradise, dwelt man from the fall to the deluge. The ark floated the survivors of the human family across the great ocean belt to this earth which we inhabit, and which, in comparison with that where Noah and his fathers dwelt, is itself almost a Paradise. The earth rises gradually from the south towards the north and west, culminating in a great conical mountain, behind which the sun sets.

Again and again this crotchety monk sputters with indignation against those who reject these views of his, "not built," he says, "on his own opinions and conjectures, but drawn from Holy Scripture, and from the mouth of that divine man and great Master, Patricius[1]." Those wretched people who chop logic, and hold that the earth and heavens are spherical, are mere blasphemers, given

[1] [This appears from Assemani to be the translated name of *Mar-Aba*, Patriarch of the Nestorian Church from 536 to 552 (see ii, 412; iii, 73–6; iii, pt. ii, 406). The same author says that Cosmas, in his expositions of Scripture and his system of the World, closely follows two chief Nestorian Doctors, Theodorus of Mopsuestia and Diodorus of Tarsus (405).]

up for their sins to the belief of such impudent nonsense as the doctrine of Antipodes[1]. The sun, instead of being larger than the earth, is only of the diameter of two climates (18° of latitude) on the earth's surface[2].

Altogether the book is a memorable example of that mischievous process of loading Christian truth with a dead-weight of false science, which has had so many followers. The book as a whole is what Robert Hall called some dreary commentary, "a continent of mud," but there are a few geographical fossils of considerable interest to be extracted from it[3]. These have been dug

[1] See pp. 125, 185, 191, etc., and the drawing in ridicule of the doctrine of Antipodes.

[2] P. 264.

[3] [Mr. J. W. McCrindle in his edition of Cosmas writes: "Since the *Topography* had for its main design the exposition of these views, it has been compared by Yule to 'a mere bank of mud, but remarkable on account of certain geographical fossils which are found imbedded in it.' This comparison, however, we venture to think, does less than justice to the work, for besides the geographical there are many other 'fossils' to be found in the mud, of different kinds and generally of more or less interest and value. A list of these—but not pretending to be complete—has been given by Montfaucon in his Introduction. Among others may be specified the indication of Clysma as the place of the passage of the Red Sea; the wares brought by merchants to the Israelites when they sojourned in the wilderness; the seat of the terrestrial Paradise; the worship of Mithras by the Persians; the rite of baptism; the date of the Nativity; the question of the canonicity of the Catholic Epistles; the exposition of the prayer of Hezekiah; the inscriptions on the rocks found in the desert of Sinai; the state of Christianity in Socotra, Ceylon and India; the extent to which Christianity had spread over the heathen world; the interpretation of the prophecies of Daniel; extracts from Pagan writers and Fathers of the Church preserved only by Cosmas; and his views on the destiny of children who die in the womb or in infancy. The portion, moreover, of the *Topography* which is the 'mud bank' of the comparison is not without some value. It is a specimen of a once prevalent and not yet quite extinct mode of Scriptural exegesis; it reveals what were some of the main currents of thought which permeated the Christian world at the beginning of the Middle Ages; it discloses to what a lamentable degree, as Monotheistic Christianity rose to the ascendant, triumphant alike over the Persian Dualism of the Manichaeans, and the Greek Pantheism of the Neo-Platonists, the light of Hellenic learning and science had faded from Christendom before as yet Islam, which was destined to receive and preserve that

out accordingly, and will be found in Note IX, at the end of this Essay.

22. It will be seen from one of these extracts that Cosmas had a very correct idea of the position of China, as lying on the extreme eastern coast of Asia, "compassed by the ocean running round it to the left just as the same ocean compasses Barbary (Somâli Land) round to the right." He knew also that a ship sailing to China, after running east for a long way, had to turn to the north at least as far as a ship bound for Chaldaea would have to run up from the straits of Hormuz to the mouths of the Euphrates; and that thus it was intelligible how China by the overland route lay much nearer to Persia than might have been thought from the length of the sea-voyage thither.

23. The form of the name which he gives the country is remarkable, *Tzinitza,* as it reads in the 2nd extract, but as it occurs further on (5th extract) more correctly TZINISTA, representing the Chinasthána of the old Hindoos, the Chinistan of the Persians, and all but identical with the name given to China in the Syriac inscription of Si-ngan fu, of which we shall speak further on, viz., TZINISTHAN[1]. Cosmas professes no knowledge of geographical details between Ceylon and China, but he is aware that the clove country lies between the two, which is in itself a considerable step in geography for the sixth century. Silk, aloes-wood, cloves, and sandal-wood are the chief exports that came westward to Ceylon from China and the intermediate countries.

light, had appeared in the world; and while it exhibits the attitude in which Theology and Science in those days stood to each other, it illustrates the signal danger of regarding Scripture as a storehouse of divine communications which may be turned to account in defending or in oppugning scientific speculations" (pp. xx–xxi).]

[1] See Pauthier, *L'Inscript. de Singanfu,* p. 42.—[Tzinista, Greek transcription of Sanskrit Cīnasthāna.]

24. The other Greek notice of China, which has been alluded to above, is to be found in the History of THEOPHYLACTUS SIMOCATTA, a Byzantine writer of the early part of the seventh century. This author appears to have acquired, through some exceptional source, a knowledge of wars and revolutions that had been going on among the Turkish nations of Central Asia, and some curious fragments of the history of their relations with one another and with their neighbours, which he introduces into his book without much relevance to the thread of his narrative. Among these fragments is a notice of a great state and people called TAUGAS, which he describes as very famous over the east, originally a colony of the Turkish race, now forming a nation scarcely to be paralleled on the face of the whole earth for power and population. Their chief city was at a distance of 1500 miles from India[1]. After treating of some other matters, the historian returns to the subject, and proceeds[2]:—

25. "The ruler of the land of the Taugas[3] [Ταυγάς] is called *Taïssan*, which signifies, when translated, the *Son of God*[4]. This kingdom of Taugas is never disturbed

[1] *Theoph. Simoc.*, vii, 7. The main subject of the history of Theophylactus is the reign of Maurice. Gibbon calls this author "a vain sophist," "an impostor," "diffuse in trifles, concise in the most interesting facts."

[2] *Ib.*, vii, 9.

[3] The name of China which this probably represents will be shown below. In the Latin version in the *Corpus Hist. Byz.* and in the Bonn edition it is *Taugast*, as also in the Ecclesiastical History of Nicephorus Callistus, who copies largely from Theophylactus (Lang's Lat. Version, Francf., 1588, book xviii, ch. 30).

[4] This is supposed by Klaproth to represent the Chinese *Thiantsé*, "Son of Heaven." It is curious, however, that the name of the emperor reigning in the latter years of Theophylactus, and a very celebrated sovereign in Chinese history, was *T'ai Tsung*. He came to the throne in 626. The last addition *known* to have been made to the history of Theophylactus is an allusion to the death of Chosroes, King of Persia, which occurred in 628. Smith's *Dict. of Greek and Roman Biography* says that the historian is supposed to have died in the following year, but there does not

by disputed successions, for the authority is hereditary in the family of the chief. The nation practises idolatry, but they have just laws, and their life is full of temperate wisdom. There is a law binding on these people which prohibits the men from ever wearing ornaments of gold, although they derive great wealth in gold and silver from their commerce, which is both large and lucrative. The territory of Taugas, of which we are speaking, is divided in two by a river[1], which in time past formed the boundary between two very great nations which were at war with one another. These nations were distinguished from one another by their dress, the one wearing clothes dyed black, the other red. In our own day, however, and whilst Maurice wielded the Roman sceptre, the nation of the black-coats crossed the river to attack the red-coats, and having got the victory over them they thus became supreme over the whole empire[2].

seem to be any authority for this ; and it is *possible* that at a later date the name of T'ai Tsung might have reached him. [What renders the change of *Thiantsé*, says Yule in an additional note, or some similar term into *Taissan* more probable than it seems at first sight, is the fact that Ssanang Ssetzen calls the title by which the Chinese Emperor, Ying Tsung, ascended the throne for the second time (A.D. 1457) *Taissun*, the real title being *T'ien Shun*, "Favoured by Heaven." (See Schmidt, p. 293, and *Chine Ancienne*, p. 405.)]

[1] ["Le Wei choui coule au nord de cette ville, et s'y divise en deux bras, qui se rejoignent après l'avoir parcourue. Ce sont les deux rivières dont Théophylacte parle. Le récit de cet auteur donne une preuve de son exactitude, et témoigne en faveur de la véracité des Annales chinoises." Klaproth, *J. As.*, viii, 1826, pp. 227–230.]

[2] The great river is the Kiang, which divided the Empire of the Sui, whose capital was at Ch'ang-ngan or Si-ngan fu, from that of the Ch'en whose Emperor resided at Nan king. The sovereign of the Sui crossed the Kiang as here related in the year 589, and therefore in the reign of Maurice at Byzantium (582–602). The Ch'en Emperor threw himself into a well ; the tombs of his ancestors were violated and their bodies thrown into the Kiang. The Sui thus became masters of the United Empire as Theophylactus relates. (Klaproth, *Mém.*, as below, and see Deguignes, vol. i, 51, 52.) The characteristic black clothing of the people of Shen si, in which lay the capital of the Sui, is noticed by Hajji Mahomed in the extracts given in Note XVIII.

"And this city of Taugas they say was founded by Alexander the Macedonian, after he had enslaved the Bactrians and the Sogdianians, and had consumed by fire twelve myriads of barbarians.

"In this city the king's women go forth in chariots made of gold, with one ox to draw them[1], and they are decked out most gorgeously with gold and jewels of great price, and the bridles of the oxen are gilt. He who hath the sovereign authority hath 700 concubines[2]. And the women of the chief nobles of Taugas use silver chariots.

"When the prince dies he is mourned by his women for the rest of their lives, with shaven heads and black raiment; and it is the law that they shall never quit the sepulchre.

"They say that Alexander built a second city at the distance of a few miles, and this the barbarians call KHUBDAN[3].

"Khubdan has two great rivers flowing through it,

[1] In *Chine Ancienne,* I see a plate from a Chinese drawing which represents Confucius travelling in a carriage drawn by one ox (Pl. 30).

[2] The Emperor T'ai Tsung above mentioned, is said to have dismissed three thousand women from the imperial establishment. (*Ch. Anc.*, p. 286.)

[3] This is sufficient of itself to show that the Taugas of the Greek writer is China. For *Khumdan* was the name given by the Turkish and Western Asiatic nations to the city of Ch'ang-ngan—now represented by Si-ngan fu in Shen si—which was the capital of several Chinese dynasties between the 12th century B.C., and the 9th century A.D. The name Khumdan appears in the Syriac part of the Si-ngan fu inscription repeatedly; in the Arab *Relations* of the 9th century published by Renaudot and by Reinaud; in Mas'udi; in Edrisi (as the name of the great river of China); and in Abulfeda. What is said in the text about the two rivers running through the city is substantially correct (see Klaproth as quoted below). I have here transposed two periods of the original, to bring together what is said of Khubdan. Pauthier takes Khumdan for a western transcription of *Ch'angan,* whilst Neumann regards it as a corruption of *Kong-tien,* court or palace. Both of these explanations seem unsatisfactory. [Khumdan=Khamdan=Khan t'ang, the court of the Emperor=Si-ngan fu. See Hartmann, *Chine* in *Encyclop. de l'Islam,* p. 863.]

the banks of which are lined with nodding cypresses, so to speak.

"The people also have many elephants; and they have much intercourse for trade with the Indians. And these are said to be Indians who are white from living in the north.

"The worms from which the silk filaments are produced are found among these people; they go through many alternations, and are of various colours. And in the art of keeping these creatures the barbarians show much skill and emulation."

26. The passing remarks of some scholars have identified the Taugas of this curious passage with some of the tribes of Turkestan, but there can be no reasonable doubt that it refers to the Chinese, though there is no allusion by Theophylactus to Sinae or Seres, and it is pretty clear that he was repeating what some well-informed person had told him without himself at all understanding where the country lay of which he spoke. Deguignes first showed that the passage referred to China. Gibbon accepted this view, and Klaproth has expounded it in the same sense, apparently unaware that he had been anticipated[1]. And yet he does not explain the name applied to the Chinese or their capital.

Deguignes explained it as indicating the *Ta-göei*, great Göei, or Wei dynasty[2], which preceded the Sui, but there can be little doubt that it represents the obscure name of

[1] Gibbon, ch. cxl, notes; Klap., *Mém. Rel. à l'Asie*, iii, 261–4; [*Journ. Asiatique*, viii, 1826, pp. 227–230].

[2] [Pelliot (*T'oung pao*, Oct. 1912, p. 732) adopts Deguignes' theory: "From 386 to 556 the north of China was occupied by a foreign dynasty coming from eastern Mongolia which took the Chinese name *Wei*; its capital was for a long time in Shan si, then in Ho nan. But the Chinese historians have kept the native name of these invaders with the transcription T'o pa (Thak-bat)." It is possible that Tabγač has been derived from T'o pa, Thak-bat.]

TAMGHAJ, once applied vaguely to China or some great country lying in the mists of the Far East by the western nations of Asia, and by old Arabian and Persian writers. Thus in 1218, when Mahomed, Sultan of Khwarizm, received envoys from Chinghiz Khan, at Bokhara, he sent by night for one of those envoys who was a native of his own territories, and asked him if it was really true that Chinghiz Khan had conquered Tamghaj[1]?

[1] D'Ohsson, i, 203. That author refers in a note to the Taugas of Theophylactus. So also Albiruni terms the city of Yangju in China "the Residence of the Faghfur, who has the title of *Tamghâj Khan*" (Sprenger's *Post- und Reise-route des Orients*, p. 90). Abulfeda says the same, quoting the "*Qanun*," which I believe is Albiruni's work—"the Faghfur of China, who is called Timghaj Khan, and who is the Great King, according to the history of Al-Niswy, where in his account of Khwarizm Shah and the Tartars, it is stated that the name of the King of the Tartars in China is *Tooghaj*." I take this from MS extracts of Abulfeda kindly translated for me by Mr Badger. ["On lit dans le *Qânoûn* : Yandjoû est le capitale du Faghfoûr de la Chine. Il porte le nom de Tamghâdj-khân : c'est leur grand roi. On lit dans la chronique de Nasawi, laquelle est consacrée à l'histoire des rois du Khârizm et des Tatars : La capitale du roi des Tatars en Chine se nomme Toûghâdj." Aboulfeda, II, 2e partie, p. 123.—Guyard's translation.] I do not know how the last word is written in the Arabic, and its closer correspondence to the Taugas of Theophylactus is almost certainly due to accident. The Niswy or Nessawi quoted by Abulfeda was secretary to Sultan Jalaluddín of Khwarizm, and no doubt the allusion is to the anecdote told in the text from D'Ohsson.

Mas'udi says the King of China when addressed was termed Tamgama Jabán [and not *Bagbour*] (qu. Thamgaj ?) (*Prairies d'Or*, i, 306).

Clavijo says: "The Zagatays call him (the Emperor of China) *Tangus*, which means Pig Emperor" (!). See Markham, pp. 133–4. ["Los Chacatays lo llaman Tangus, que han por denuesto, que quiere decir Emperador Puerco." (P. 152, *Vida del gran Tamorlan por Ruy Gonzalez de Clavijo*, Madrid, 1782.)] In the Universal History it is mentioned (probably after Sharifuddín) that in 1398 envoys came to Timur from *Tamgaj Khan*, Emperor of Cathay. ["In Ili are found the Chinese called *T'ao-hua-shi*. Palladius supposes that this is designed to render the word *tamgaj*, applied in ancient times by the Mohammedans in China." Bretschneider, *Med. Researches*, i, p. 71.]

The following examples are more doubtful. "We call this region China, the which they in their language name *Tame*, and the people *Tangis*, whom we name *Chinois*" (*Alhacen, his Arabike Historie of Tamerlane*, in *Purchas*, iii, 152).

Tangtash, Tangnash, Taknas, occur repeatedly in the translation of Sadik Isfahani and of the *Shajrat ul Atrák* as synonymous

27. I am not aware of any other mention of China in a Greek writer till we get to LAONICUS CHALCONDYLAS in the latter half of the fifteenth century. We need not be surprised at the vagueness of the site ascribed to Taugas by Theophylactus when we find this author, who wrote from one to two centuries after the travels of Polo, Odoric, and Ibn Batuta, describing Cathay in one passage as somewhere near the Caspian, in another as in India, between the Ganges and Indus[1].

with Machín, or a great city therein. But these words are perhaps corrupt readings of *Nangiás*, which was a name applied by the Mongols to Southern China. (See D'Ohsson, i, 190–1; Quat., *Rashideddin*, p. lxxxvi.)

The name can scarcely have any reference to the *T'ang* dynasty, for they did not attain the throne till the latter years of Theophylactus, and he mentions Taugas in connexion with a Khan of the Turks in the time of the Emperor Maurice. It should be mentioned, however, that the title *Thangáj* is found on a coin of a Turkish Khakan of A.D. 1043–44 (see Fræhn's remarks on this in Meyendorff's *Voyage d'Orenbourg à Bokhara*, p. 314 *seqq.*; see also *D'Herbelot* in v. *Thamgaj*). The geographer Bakui also defines *Thamgaj* as a great city of the Turks' country, near which are many villages between two mountains, and only approached by a narrow defile. (*Not. et Extr.*, ii, 491.)

[1] "Hence he (Timur) directed his march against the Chataides, threatening them with destruction. This people are believed to be the same with the ancient Massagetæ, who crossed the Araxes (Jaxartes ?) and took possession of an extensive region adjoining that river, in which they settled." (*De Rebus Turcicis*, iii, p. 67.) Again: "Chataia is a city towards the east of Hyrcania, great and flourishing in population, and surpassing in wealth and all other attributes of prosperity all the cities of Asia except Samarkand and Memphis (Cairo). By the Massagetæ it was established with excellent laws in olden time." (*Ib.*) Somewhat later (p. 86) he puts *Chatagia* in India, as mentioned above. Indeed geography for a Greek writer must have been in a state of very midnight at this time, when a historian who ventured to treat of Timur and Shah Rukh (Σαχρούχος) was fain to say of *Cheria* (Herat): "in what part of Asia it was situated, whether in the land of the Syrians or the land of the Medes, he could not ascertain. But some thought that anciently Cheriah was Ninus (Nineveh) as Pagdatine (Baghdad) was Babylon." (*Ib.*, p. 68.)

II. CHINESE KNOWLEDGE OF THE ROMAN EMPIRE.

28. Having thus set forth such indications as we can of acquaintance with China from Greek and Roman writers, we shall now collect such notices of the Greek and Roman territories as we are able to find in translations from Chinese sources.

It was under the Emperor Wu Ti, of the Han dynasty (B.C. 140–87), that the Chinese first had relations with the countries west of the Bolor mountains, and even the *discovery* of those regions is ascribed by Chinese writers to this period, though the correctness of that idea may well be questioned. ["The thirty-six kingdoms then opened up became afterwards gradually subdivided into more than fifty; all lying to the west of the Hiong-nu, and south of the Wu-sun. Along the north and south run great mountains, and through the centre flows a river [Tarim]....On the west it is limited by the Ts'ong-ling mountains[1]."]

[In the third century before our era, two rival peoples were fighting for supremacy in the north of China, then divided into states under the power, more and more nominal, of the princes of the State of Chau; they were the Hiong Nu, extending from the north of the Shan si Province to lake Barkul, and the Yue chi settled in the region forming the present province of Kan Su. The Hiong Nu, at first subject to the Yue chi, vanquished these a first time at the end of the third century and a second time in B.C. 177. The Yue chi, expelled from Kan Su, their cradle, in 165, went to Ku cha, arrived in the country of the Ili river and of its two southern tributaries, the

[1] [A. Wylie, *Notes on the Western Regions*, translated from the "Tsëën Han Shoo," Bk 96, Pt I (*Journ. Anth. Inst.*, Aug. 1880).]

Tekes and the Konges where the Wu sun were established; the newcomers defeated the Wu sun, and passed beyond the Issik-kul; the Yue chi split into two branches: the little Yue chi who mixed with the K'iang or Tibetans, and the great Yue chi who took Kashgar at the expense of the Sakas (B.C. 163). The Yue chi, defeated again by the Hiong Nu, protecting the Wu sun, were compelled to march towards the south, pushing the Sakas before them, and after some intermediate halts, they arrived first in Ta wan (Farghânah), and then subjugated the kingdom of Ta Hia, or Bactriana, whose capital was Lan She, south of the Oxus, in Badakhshan, northern part of Tokharestan; in B.C. 120 the Yue chi destroyed the Greek dynasty and took in the same year the saka kingdom of Soter Megas. The Sakas or Sak, whom Herr von Le Coq thinks of Iranian stock, fled to the N.W. of India, settled in Sindh and Pendjab, and finally mixed probably with the Yue chi. Later on the Yue chi made the conquest of Kashmír and, after seeing their Indian Empire fall into pieces in the hands of the Hindú princes, disappeared in the fifth century of our era before the White Huns. The part played by the Yue chi, Tokharians or Indo-Scythians, has been considerable, and they were probably the intermediaries between China and the West, and it is certainly by them that buddhism was known to the Celestial Empire. According to Prof. F. W. K. Müller, of Berlin, one of the "unknown" languages brought to light by the recent excavations in Central Asia is the language of the Tokharians, Indo-Scythians or Yue chi, of the Indo-Germanic group of languages.]

[The Chinese Emperor Wu being desirous of opening communication with the Ta Yue chi in order to excite a diversion against the Hiong Nu, the constant disturbers of the Chinese frontier, ignoring that these Yue chi had already left the Ili valley and fled south, sent for this purpose an officer called Chang K'ien with about one hundred people (A.D. 138). Chang K'ien had hardly left by the north-western route before he was caught by the Hiong Nu and kept a prisoner for about ten years. Chang K'ien then escaped with some of his comrades, but adhering to his mission succeeded in reaching Ta wan (Farghânah), where he was well received by the people who were acquainted by fame with the powers and riches of China, though they had never had any direct communication with that country. The Yue chi were north of the Oxus, but having conquered Ta Hia (Tokharestan), they went south to occupy their capital Lan She, and Chang K'ien followed them thither, passing through K'ang kiu, but failed to induce them to quit their new seat upon the Oxus to return to their eastern deserts and battle with the Hiong Nu. Thus unsuccessful, after a stay of one year (A.D. 128) with the Yue chi, Chang K'ien tried to return to China by way of Tibet, but was again taken by the Hiong Nu and detained for some time; he managed to escape in 126, and at last this adventurous man got back to China with a Turkish wife and a single follower out of the hundred who had started with him. He was able to report, from personal knowledge, of the countries on the Jaxartes and Oxus, and, from the information he had collected, on other countries of the west. He had noticed bamboos and cloths forwarded from Yun Nan and Sze ch'wan through Shen tu (India) and Afghanistan, and suggested that a new route be taken through India to go westward instead of crossing the Hiong Nu country, and henceforward the emperor Wu acted upon this advice[1].]

One of the consequences of Chang K'ien's voyage was

[1] [Chavannes, *Se-ma Ts'ien*, i, pp. lxxi–lxxiii.]

a desire of the Emperor Wu to open a route to the west through the Turkish and Tibetan tribes; this he was able to do after the victory of General Ho K'iu-ping in A.D. 121 and the conquest of Kan chau and Leang chau which formed the commandry of Ts'iau ts'iuan with a governor (*t'ai chau*) at the place now named Su chau; this commandry was subsequently divided into three: Wu wei (Leang chau), Chang ye (Kan chau) and Tun hwang. The Great Wall built by Ts'in Shi Hwang Ti in A.D. 214, and uniting the various walls erected against the Hiong Nu by the Northern States, was pushed on to the west through the desert after the second expedition of Li Kwang-li against Ta wan in A.D. 101 and 102[1].]

[The Yue chi had fled before the Wu sun of the Ili valley; Chang K'ien gave the advice to make an alliance with these Wu sun against the Hiong Nu, thus securing a free access to the West. Chang K'ien was again sent in A.D. 115 with 300 men to the country of the Wu sun, too weak to show openly their hostility to the Hiong Nu. However Chang K'ien was well received and was able to send agents to Farghânah and Zarafshân. Chang K'ien has the merit of having opened up the road to the countries in the north-west.

The Chinese envoys had reported "that Ta wan had excellent horses in the city of Urh-sze; but they refused to show them to the envoys.... The Emperor forthwith despatched the sturdy yeoman, Chay Ling, and others, on a mission to the king of Ta-wan, with 1000 ounces of gold, and a golden horse, to prefer a request for some of the famous horses in the city of Urh-sze...the demand of the Chinese envoy was met by an absolute refusal. The envoy was enraged, and gave way to unguarded

[1] [Chavannes, *Documents chinois découverts par* A. Stein, pp. v–vi.]

utterances, hammered the golden horse into a shapeless mass, and left (Wylie, *Notes on the Western Regions*, p. 53)." The envoy was murdered at Yau ch'eng and the Emperor, who had already chastised Lau lan, in a fury sent against Ta wan (B.C. 104) Li Kwang-li who was utterly defeated; but in 102 the Chinese general was more successful, reached Ta wan and Yau ch'eng, punished the kings, and returned to China in the following year.]

[Another consequence of Chang K'ien's voyage was the endeavour of the Chinese to find in the south a route to Ta-hia, *viâ* India. To the east were the kingdoms of Tong Hai (Che Kiang) and of Min Yue (Fu Kien); to the south, Chao T'o had founded the kingdom of Nan Yue with Canton as its capital; to the west had been established the kingdom of Tien (Yun Nan); the Chinese were badly received in 122 by the chief of Tien and in 112 they sent an army against Nan Yue. Having established their power in the south by wars in B.C. 111 and 110, the Chinese were able to bring all their forces against the Hiong Nu. The Emperor Wu died in B.C. 87.]

About the same time the Chinese began to take vigorous measures against the Hiong Nu, and to extend their frontier westward. By B.C. 59 their power reached all over what is now Chinese Turkestan; a general government was established for the tributary states; and about the time of our era, fifty-five states of western Tartary acknowledged themselves vassals of the empire, whilst the Princes of Transoxiana and Bactriana are also said to have recognised its supremacy.

29. [During part of the first century the power of China decayed; in 99 the Emperor Wu sent general Li Kwang-li to fight the Hiong Nu near Lake Barkul; another general, Li ling, at first victorious, was crushed

south of Hami; the Hiong Nu recovered some of their ascendancy and during the period *yong p'ing* (A.D. 58–75) they twice attacked Tun hwang, but they were repelled. At the end of this period, the Chinese entered into communication with the western countries. In A.D. 83, Pan Ch'ao, one of the most illustrious commanders in the Chinese annals, born in 32, at P'ing ling (Shan si province), who had appeared in the field some years previously, was appointed commander of the troops. He took advantage of the feuds between the various countries of Central Asia, Su-le (Kashgar), K'ang kiu (Sogdiana), Shan Shan (South of Lob Nor), Yu t'ien (Khotan), Kiu mi (Uzun Tati), Ku mo (Aqsu), Sh'e ch'eng (Uch Turfan), So kiu (Yarkand), the Yue chi, the Wu sun (Ili) to turn them against K'iu tze (Kucha). In 88 the Yue chi, who had helped the Chinese in attacking Kiu she (Turfan), sent them a tribute of jewels and lions and asked in marriage for their king a princess of the Han family; their ambassador was put under arrest by Pan Ch'ao and sent back; the Yue chi, very angry at the treatment of their envoy, sent an army of 70,000 men under the command of Sie, through the Ts'ong ling (Pamir) to attack Pan Ch'ao; Sie tried to gain to his cause K'iu tze (Kucha), but his emissaries were stopped by Pan Ch'ao, their chief was put to death, and Sie frightened retired; from this time the Yue chi sent a yearly tribute to the Chinese. From A.D. 89 to 104, all the western countries had submitted to the empire, but the K'iang (Tibetans) revolted then and the west was again cut off from China. In 91 Pan Ch'ao was appointed General Protector (*tu hu*) after K'iu tze (Kucha), Ku mo (Aqsu) and Wen Su (Uch Turfan) had submitted. After attacking Yen k'i (Karashahr), Pan Ch'ao took Kiu she (Turfan) and, according to the Chinese historians, then crossed the Ts'ong ling (Pamir), but this is doubtful. It is not, however, doubtful that he did not push his conquests to the Caspian, nor did he have a way open to the shores of the Indian Ocean, though "we are told that in the year 97 he despatched one of his officers called Kan Ying to make his way by sea to TA TS'IN or the Roman Empire" (Yule[1]). In 100 he asked to be relieved of his command and he died in A.D. 102 at the age of 71 years. He was replaced by his son Pan Hiong who had a military camp of 300 men established at Tun hwang; during the period *yong p'ing* (A.D. 58–75), a Chinese official had already been stationed at Tun hwang and another one at Kiu she (Turfan)[2].]

30. Notices of the TA TS'IN region are found in the geographical works of the time of the latter Han (A.D. 56–220)[3], in the annals of the Ts'in (265–419), and of the T'ang (618–905). But references are also made by the Chinese editors to the same country as having been known in the days of the first Han dynasty (from B.C. 202) under the name of LIKAN or LIKIEN, a name which Pauthier with some probability refers to the empire of the Seleucidæ of Syria, whose conquests at one period extended to the regions of the Oxus[4].

[1] [Yule says in 102; it is a mistake.]—Rémusat, in *Mém. de l'Acad. des Ins.* (new), viii, 116–125. Klaproth, *Tab. Hist.*, p. 67, etc.; see also Lassen, ii, 352 *seq.*

[2] Ed. Chavannes, *Trois généraux chinois de la dynastie des Han orientaux.* (*T'oung pao*, May, 1906, pp. 210–269.)

[3] [See A. Wylie, *Notes on the Western Regions*, translated from the "Tsëën Han Shoo," Bk 96, Pt I (*Journ. Anthrop. Inst.*, Aug. 1880.)]

[4] Pauthier, *De l'Authent.*, pp. 34, 55 *seqq.*; Klap., *o.c.*, p. 70. [" We are told in records as old as the *Hou Han Shu* and the *Wei lio* that Ta Ts'in and Li-kan are one and the same country, and it is clear that Li-kan is the older name of the two. It apparently first occurs in the *Shih-ki* (ch. 123). When Chang K'ien had negotiated his treaties with the countries of the west, the king of An-hsi (Parthia) sent an embassy to the Chinese court and presented large birds' eggs, probably ostrich eggs, and jugglers from Li-kan." (Hirth, *l.c.*, pp. 169–170.)]

The name *Ta Ts'in* (*Great China*), we are told, was applied to those western lands on account of the analogy of its people to those of the Middle Kingdom. Some even alleged that they had sprung originally from China. But this was probably a puerile perversion, and we may suppose that the name was given from some perception that those Greek and Roman countries bore to the west the same relation that China and its civilisation bore to Eastern Asia.

From this we gather, among other things, that the Chinese in the time of Pan Ch'ao recognised the term *Ts'in* as a name by which they were known, at least to foreigners. Indeed Fa Hian the Buddhist traveller (early in the fifth century) repeatedly speaks of his native land under this name[1], though perhaps with a restricted reference to the ancient territory of the Ts'in which was the province of his birth.

31. Ta Ts'in, according to the earlier of these notices, is otherwise called the kingdom of the Western Sea [*Hai si*]. It is reached from the country of the *T'iao chi* (Tajiks, or Persians, according to Pauthier and others)[2],

[1] *E.g.*, pp. 7, 333.

[2] [Visdelou identifies *T'iao chi* with Egypt, Deguignes with Persia. According to Hirth, *China and the Roman Orient*, p. 144, it is Babylonia. Under the Han, it was a western kingdom; it became a government under the T'ang; see Chavannes, *Tou kiue*, p. 368.

It would be more exact to say that T'iao chi corresponds to Mesene, *i.e.* the country between the Tigris and the Euphrates, near their confluence, and Babylonia and the sea; it was annexed in 225 to their possessions by the Sassanid sovereigns and finally was part of the Khalifate of Baghdad.

The earliest mention of T'iao chi appears in the *Ts'ien Han shoo* (B.C. 206–A.D. 23) and the *Shi ki*, Hirth, *l.c.*, p. 144.

"My interpretation of these (Chinese) records leads to the conclusion that the ancient country of Ta-ts'in, called Fu-lin during the middle ages, was not the Roman Empire with Rome as its capital, but merely its oriental part, viz., Syria, Egypt and Asia Minor; and Syria in the first instance." (Hirth, *China and the Roman Orient*, p. vi.)

"The length of the sea-route from T'iao-chih to Ta-ts'in,

by traversing the sea obliquely for a distance of 2000 miles and is about 8000 miles distant from Ch'ang ngan or Si-ngan fu. The name of the capital is ANTU[1]. The *An si*, and people of India, drive a great and profitable trade with this empire by the way of the Great Salt Sea, and merchants sailing thither are obliged to provide themselves with necessaries for three years. Hence there are few who succeed in reaching so remote a region[2]. The extent of the empire is 2000 miles from east to west, and as much from north to south[3], and it has 400 cities of the first class. The coinage is stated to be of gold and silver, ten pieces of silver making the value of one piece

i.e., from a port on or near the mouth of the Euphrates (Babylon, Velogesia, Hira, Orchoë, Charax Spasinu ?) to Aelana, the sea-port of Petra or Rekem, is described as measuring over 10000 li." ... "We have to interpret this expression [10,000 li]... as meaning an indefinite large number." (Hirth, *China and the Roman Orient*, p. 164.)

"We may conclude from the hints contained in the earlier Chinese histories, that this route (Central Asia, Hekatompylos, Acbatana, Ktesiphon, Hira, mouth of the Euphrates, Persian Gulf, Indian Ocean, Red Sea, Aelana and Petra with its bifurcation to Gaza along the Phoenician coast and to Bostra, Damascus, etc.) was the principal channel of trade between China and Syria as the representative of the Far West from the beginning of commercial relations till up to the year A.D. 166." (Hirth, *China and the Roman Orient*, p. 169.) It will be seen hereafter that the sea-route was known before the year A.D. 166.

Dr. Hirth has given the translation and the text of various notices of Ta Ts'in from Chinese works in *China and the Roman Orient*; in the Supplementary Notes will be found the notice from Chau Ju-kua's *Chu-fan-chi*, translated also by Hirth in 1912, pp. 102–4.]

[1] Antioch, probably, as Pauthier supposes; and, if so, it shows that the information came from a date earlier than the time of Pan Ch'ao. [With reference to this name, apparently indicating *Antioch*, it is curious to read in Mas'ūdī that at the time of the Musulman conquest there remained of the original name of the city only the letters *Alif*, *Nún*, and *Tá* (*Ant* or *Anta*, see *Prairies d'Or*, iii, 409).]

[2] So, conversely, the author of the *Periplus* says, "It is not easy to get to this Thin, and few and far between are those who come from it."

[3] The extract at p. 36 of Pauthier (*De l'Authent.*) has 1000 li (200 miles); but this is evidently a mistake for 10,000, as given in another extract at p. 43.

of gold[1]. There follows a variety of what read to us as vague or puerile notices of the constitution and productions of the country, including, however, a detailed and apparently correct enough account of the coral fisheries of the Mediterranean[2].

32. In the annals of the T'ang we are told that the country formerly called Ta Ts'in has in later days been called FU LIN (πόλιν, = Byzantium, see Note to Ibn Batuta, vol. IV, *infra*)[3]. Many of the trivialities in the

[1] In the Byzantine coinage, however, *twelve* of the ordinary silver coin (*miliaresion*) went to the piece of gold (*nomisma*).

[2] Pauthier, *De l'Auth.*, pp. 34–40; Klap., p. 68.

[3] ["The texts of the T'ang dynasty speak of 'Fu-lin, that is the ancient Ta-ts'in,' or of 'Tats'in, also called Fu-lin,' and it appears that the two names were interchangeable. From the Chinese point of view the question would, therefore, be simple enough. If Ta-ts'in is Syria, Fu-lin must be Syria....My present view... is briefly this: Ta-ts'in is the Roman empire with all its grandeur emanating from Rome, its capital; but the detail placed on record in the contemporaneous texts is confined to its Asiatic provinces, for which reason, not Rome but Antioch is described as the capital city. Its relations to China were of a commercial kind. Fu-lin is the Eastern empire of Byzantium, but as in the case of Ta-ts'in, the Chinese accounts are confined to certain Asiatic portions of it, and its relations to China were chiefly ecclesiastical." (F. Hirth, *The Mystery of Fulin*, 1910, p. 1.) Prof. Chavannes after accepting this view has abandoned it in his *Notes additionnelles sur les Tou-kiue* (*T'oung pao*, 1904, p. 37, note 3). Hirth has thus resumed the arguments of Chavannes, *l.c.*, p. 2, who refers to Yule's notes in *Cathay*, p. 402:

"1. The name Fu-lin represents the Greek accusative πόλιν in εἰς τὴν πόλιν, Istán-polin, according to Mas'udi the origin of Istambul.

2. The name Fu-lin appears in Chinese literature previous to the arrival of the Nestorians in China.

3. It may have been brought to China during the Sui period by the Western Turks, who had been visited by Byzantine ambassadors in 568 and 576 A.D.

4. The king of Fu-lin who sent ambassadors to China in 643 was called *Po-to-li*. By substituting [one character for another], the name would appear as *Po-si-li*, which may stand for βασιλεύς.

5. The Arab general *Mo-i*, who was sent to effect the siege of Fu-lin, may be identical with Muawia's son 'Yézid ben Muawia,' one of the three emirs who attacked Constantinople.

6. The king of Fu-lin who sent an embassy to China in 1081 *Mié-li-i-ling-kai-sa* may have been identical with the pretender Nicephorus Melissenus." However, Prof. Hirth maintains his view and identifies Fu-lin with Bethlehem, *l.c.* p. 17, and in a

older accounts of Ta Ts'in are repeated, with some circumstances that are new. And among the peculiarities ascribed by the Chinese to the Roman empire it is curious to recognise not a few that nearly or entirely coincide with things that have been described by ancient or mediæval writers as peculiarities of China, or the adjoining countries. Such are the eminently peaceful and upright character of the people; the great number of cities and contiguous succession of populated places; horse-posts; the provision made for the conveyance and maintenance of foreign ambassadors; the abundance of gold and gems, among which are some in the form of tablets that shine in the dark[1]; pearls generated from the saliva of golden pheasants (!), tortoise-shell, rare perfumed essences, asbestos stuffs that are cleaned by fire, cloths of gold brocade and damask silk; remarkable capons, rhinoceroses, lions, and vegetative lambs[2]. Jugglers and conjurors are also seen who perform amazing things[3].

new paper in the *Journ. Amer. Orient. Soc.*, xxx, 1909, and xxxiii, 1913.

I never accepted the derivation of Fu-lin from Bethlehem, an obscure place for the Chinese; phonetically it cannot come from πόλιν. M. Blochet has suggested that *Fu-lin* is derived from *Rûm* but adduced no proof of the fact, while M. Pelliot has quite recently brought forward a number of linguistic facts confirming this view. The word Fu-lin is found for the first time in a Chinese work of the middle of the sixth century, but it is quite possible that it was known a century before, according to Pelliot, under the forms *Pu-lan* and *Pu-lam*.]

[1] Benjamin of Tudela says that the lustre of the diamonds on the emperor's crown at Byzantium was such as to illumine the room in which they were kept (p. 75).

[2] The obscure extracts in Pauthier (*op. cit.* pp. 39, 47), as to certain lambs found to the north of the kingdoms dependent on Fu lin, which grow out of the ground, and are attached by the navel to the soil, appear to refer to the stories of the Lamb-Plant of the Volga countries (see *Odoric*, p. 241), and not, as Pauthier supposes, to the fat-tailed sheep of Western Asia. [Cf. Chavannes, *T'oung pao*, May, 1907, p. 183 *n.*; and Hirth, *China and the Roman Orient*, p. 261.]

[3] See traces of this juggling skill in a passage of one Italian version of Odoric, at p. 338 of *Appendix*. In the Byzantine

33. If such trivialities as most of these were all on which to build, the identification with the Roman empire would not be very satisfactory. But in addition to the name of *Fu lin*, and the position ascribed to the kingdom as lying N.W. of Persia, others of the details, though the mention of some of them has a dash of the whimsicality of Chinese taste, appear to be genuine touches from the reports of those who had visited Constantinople. The accounts of the coral fishery and the horse-posts have already been alluded to, as well as the desire ascribed to the kings of Ta Ts'in for a direct communication with the Middle Kingdom, which has its counterpart in the statements of Procopius and Menander about the silk trade. The compass of 100 *li* or 20 miles, ascribed to the capital of Fu lin, nearly corresponds with that estimated by Benjamin of Tudela, and by popular opinion in the city itself[1]. It stands upon the shore of the sea; the houses are very lofty, and built of stone; the population extends to 100,000 fires (say 500,000 souls); the adjoining boroughs, villages, and houses are in such numbers as to form an almost unbroken succession[2]. The palaces and

History of Nicephorus Gregorias, there is a curious account of some Blondins of those days, whose itinerancies extended from Egypt through Constantinople to Cadiz, and who, in their funambulistic exhibitions, shot arrows standing on the rope, and *carried boys on their shoulders* across it at a vast height from the ground, etc. (viii, 10).

[1] Benjamin says eighteen miles (p. 74). According to Gibbon, it was really between ten and eleven. "Ambitus urbis non attingit tredecim milliaria...si ejus situs collinus in planitiem explicaretur, in ampliorem dilataretur latitudinem, attamen nondum ad magnitudinem *quam vulgo Byzantini ei attribuunt, videlicet duodeviginti milliariorum*." (*Pet. Gyllius de Topog. Constant.* in Banduri, *Imp. Orientale*, Venet., 1729, i, 284; see also Ducange, *Const. Christiana.*) [According to the *Sin T'ang Shu*, translated by Hirth, *l.c.*, p. 57: "The capital [of Fu lin] is built of [granite] stone; the city is eighty li broad."]

[2] When King Sigurd sails into Constantinople, he steers near the shore, and sees that "over all the land there are burghs, castles, country towns, the one upon the other without interval." (*The Saga of Sigurd—Early Travels in Palestine*, p. 59.)

other great houses of the capital had colonaded porticoes, and parks with rare animals; there were twelve principal ministers, distinguished by titles of honour, who directed the administration of the empire[1]. One great gate of the city towards the east is 20 *chang* (about 200 feet) high, and is covered with gold-leaf from top to bottom[2]; another of the gates has a golden steelyard over it, and also a clock showing the twelve hours of the day by means of the golden figure of a man who drops a golden ball at every hour[3]; the houses have flat terraced roofs, over which, in hot weather, water is discharged from pipes; the costume of the sovereign, his jewelled collars and cap, his silken robe embroidered with flowers, and without any opening in front, are all in accordance with particulars

[1] The Empire, whilst entire, was divided into *thirteen* dioceses; but of the administrators there were *twelve* vice-prefects, a number likely to adhere in popular accounts. Gibbon also says: "The successive casualties of inheritance and forfeiture had rendered the sovereign proprietor of many stately houses in the city and suburbs, of which *twelve were appropriated to the ministers of state*" (ch. liii). Gibbon is, perhaps, here building on Benjamin of Tudela, whose words closely corroborate the popular view as exhibited in the Chinese notices: "Twelve princely officers govern the whole empire by (the emperor's) command; each of them inhabiting a palace at Constantinople, and possessing fortresses and cities of his own" (p. 74).

[2] *The Saga of Sigurd*, quoted above, says: "The Emperor Alexius had heard of King Sigurd's expedition, and ordered the City Port of Constantinople to be opened, which is called the GOLD-TOWER, through which the emperor rides when he has been long absent from Constantinople, or has made a campaign in which he has been victorious" (p. 59). The Golden Gate stood towards the south end of the western wall of the city, not on the east as said in the Chinese reports. "The western side of the city is towards the land," says Mas'ūdī, "and there rises the Golden Gate with its doors of bronze." (*Prairies d'Or*, ii, 319.) It was built by Theodosius, and bore the inscription, "*Hæc loca Theudosius decorat post fata tyranni; Aurea Sæcla gerit qui portam construit auro.*" (*Insc. Constant.*, in Banduri, i, p. 156.)

[3] Pauthier quotes passages from Codinus about a brazen *modius*, etc., over the arch of Amastrianus; but they do not seem to afford any real corroboration of this account. See Banduri, at pp. 18, 73–74; and Ducange, p. 170. The latter, indeed, speaks of a *golden horologe* in the Forum of Constantine; but this is a slip, for the original, which he cites, has χαλκοῦν (p. 134).

to be observed in effigies of the Byzantine emperors[1]. But the most convincing proof that the Chinese authors had real information about the empire of Constantinople, is found in a notice which they give of a somewhat obscure passage in the Byzantine History :—

34. " The *Ta shi* (or Mohamedan Arabs), after having overrun and forcibly taken possession of kingdom after kingdom, at last sent their general-in-chief, MOI, to lay siege to the capital city of Fu lin. YENYO, who was the negociator of the peace which followed, made it one of the conditions that the *Ta shi* should every year pay a tribute, consisting of gold and silk-stuffs[2]."

In this passage is commemorated the remarkable fact that the Khalif Moawiyah, after having (A.D. 671–678) for seven successive summers renewed the endeavour to take Constantinople, at length felt himself under the necessity of sending envoys to sue for peace from the Emperor Constantine IV Pogonatus. The latter agreed, and sent the patrician *Ioannes* Petzigaudias (the *Yenyo* of the Chinese) to Damascus to conduct the negociation with the Arabs. The result was that the latter pledged themselves to a thirty years' peace, and to pay to the

[1] The Chinese story ascribes wing-like appendages to the emperor's cap. Pauthier refers to medals as showing these; but I have not been able to verify this. The wings attached to the cap are rather an ancient Hindu feature, and are remarkably preserved in the state costume of the kings of Burma and the sultans of Java. [I suppose that these so-called wings are the flaps or fanions flowing from the tiara or cap of the sovereign; examples of these flaps may be seen on the coins of Tigranes I the Great (97–56 B.C.), king of Armenia.]

[2] Pauth., *De l'Auth.*, p. 49. ["Since the Ta Shih [Arabs] had conquered these countries they sent their commander-in-chief, Mo-i, to besiege their capital city; by means of an agreement, they obtained friendly relations, and asked to be allowed to pay every year tribute of gold and silk; in the sequel they became subject to Ta Shih [Arabia]." *Kiu T'ang Shu*, translated by Hirth, *l.c.*, pp. 55–6; this passage has been mistranslated by Pauthier and Bretschneider; cf. Phillips, *China Review*, vii, p. 412.]

empire every year 3000 pieces of gold, fifty slaves, and fifty horses[1].

35. In a later work, called the *History of the Barbarous Nations*, some of the particulars ascribed to Ta Ts'in appear to belong to Syria under the Ayubite sultans, but with these also are mixed up circumstances, both old and new, which really point to the Roman empire. Thus it is said, with that confusion of Christianity with Buddhism of which we have elsewhere quoted various instances (Benedict Goës, *infra*) :—" On the recurrence of every seventh day people assembled from all directions to offer their devotions in the chapels, and to adore Fo."

In all these notices we see much that is analogous between the fragmentary views of the great seats of western civilisation under the names of Ta Ts'in and Fu lin, taken in the Far East, and those of the great eastern civilisation under the names of Sinæ and Seres taken in the west. In both we see the same uncertainty in degree as to exact position, the same application of facts belonging to the nearer skirts of the half-seen empire as descriptive of the whole; and in that isolated chance record in the Chinese books of a real occurrence in the history of Byzantium we have a singular parallel to the

[1] See *Niceph. Patriarch. Breviarium Historic.*, in the 1st volume of the *Corpus Byzant. Histor.*, pp. 21–2; also, *Theophanis Chronographia*, in the same coll., p. 295, and Gibbon, ch. lii. Pauthier seems to think that the circumstances are passed over entirely by Gibbon and other modern historians; but this is a mistake. Gibbon does not name the Greek envoy; but he mentions his going to Damascus, and the result. He also relates how the tribute was greatly augmented a few years afterwards, when the Khalifate was in difficulties; but finally repudiated by the Khalif Abdulmaliq in the time of Justinian II. The circumstances, with the name of the Patrician, are also detailed in St. Martin's edition of Lebeau (*Hist. du Bas Empire*, xi, 428). Silk-stuffs are not mentioned here as part of the tribute; but "gold and silk-stuffs" do frequently appear as the constituents of tribute exacted in the early Saracen wars. See Gibbon, ch. li, *passim*. I believe no *Mahomedan* writer records this transaction.

like fragment of Chinese history which had been picked up and entered in his narrative by Theophylactus. The form given in the Chinese fragment to the name of the Khalif [Moawiyah] is nearly the same as that (*Maui*) which we find in an Armenian writer [1], and this little circumstance may possibly indicate the people who furnished the Chinese annalists with some of their scraps of knowledge.

36. After this short view of the Chinese ideas of the Roman empire we may return to Kan Ying, the officer whom General Pan Ch'ao commissioned at the end of the first century [2] to open communication with those western regions, whether in view to trade or to conquest [3]. This officer proceeded to take ship, it would seem on the Persian Gulf [in T'iao chi]. "But the ship's company said to him, 'When out at sea a multitude of things will occur to make you sigh for what you have left behind. He who occupies his business in the great waters is liable to regret and repentance for. what he has undertaken. If the envoy of the Han has no father, no mother, no wife or children to pine after, then let him go to sea—not otherwise." They also represented that with a fair wind it would take two [4] months at least to cross the sea to Ta Ts'in, and if the wind were adverse it might take two years to make the return voyage, so that adventurers

[1] Michael the Syrian, translated by Dulaurier in *Journ. Asiat.*, sér. iv, tom. xiii, p. 326.

[2] [Under the emperor Ho, the 9th year (97 A.D.) *yong yuan*.]

[3] Klaproth says that Pan Ch'ao entertained a scheme for *invading* the Roman Empire, but that the general to whom this was confided was better advised, and retraced his steps. (*Tabl. Hist. de l'Asie*, p. 67.) The extract, however, given by Pauthier from the Annals of the Tsin, as cited in the Encyclopædia of the Emperor K'ang Hi says Kan Ying was despatched as *envoy*. (Pauth., p. 38.) Probably he was sent to reconnoitre.

[4] [Chavannes translates *three* months from the *Hau Han Shu*; cf. *T'oung pao*, May, 1907, p. 178.]

bound for Ta Ts'in were accustomed to lay in stores for three years[1]. Such at least were the excuses made by the chicken-hearted Kan Ying, who was certainly not the man to conquer the Roman empire; he therefore thought better of it, and retraced his steps. Hence at this time no contact occurred between the representatives of the two great seats of civilisation[2].

36 *bis*. [One of the consequences of Chang K'ien's voyage and the search for a road southward towards India, was the conquest of the country of the Kiao chi (Tong King) which under the Anterior Han (B.C. 206–A.D. 24) and the Posterior Han (A.D. 25–220) was annexed to China (B.C. 111–A.D. 39 and A.D. 42–186) and divided into three parts: Kiao chi (Ha-noi), Kiu chen (Thanh hoa?) and Ji nan (Kwang binh). Tong King became the terminus of the sea route instead of Tiao chi. Canton took the place of Tong King after some hard competition; the pilgrim Yi Tsing embarked at Canton. When Annam became independent in 968, Tong King was abandoned by the Chinese and Canton remained up to the nineteenth century the great emporium of China, except during the Mongol period when Zaitùn seems to have been the important trading port of China. However from the second century until the end of the sixth century, *i.e.* before the Tibetan invasion, the Turkestan route was taken in preference.]

37. Sixty years later, however (A.D. 166), in the reign of Hwan Ti[3] of the Han, an embassy came to the court of China from ANTUN, king of Ta Ts'in (the Emperor M. Aurelius ANTONinus). This mission had no doubt made

[1] This may have referred rather to the difficulty of obtaining provision suited to Oriental tastes. Governor Yeh, when a captive bound for Fort William, laid in seven years' provision of *eggs*!

[2] Pauthier, *u.s.*; Rémusat, *op. cit.*, p. 123.

[3] [Ninth year *yen-hi*.]

the voyage by sea, for it entered China by the frontier of Ji nan or Tong King, bringing presents of rhinoceros horns, ivory, and tortoiseshell. This is not precisely the sort of present we should have looked for, and indeed the Chinese annals say that it was believed the ambassadors had purloined the rarer objects of their charge; just the accusation that was brought against Friar John of Montecorvino eleven hundred years later. It seems likely enough that they had lost their original presents by shipwreck or robbery, and had substituted in the east such trumpery as they were told the Chinese set a value upon. The historians also observe that the embassy came by this southern route, and not by the northern route, which, it is implied, they might have followed; a route which was doubtless debarred to them by Parthian hostility[1].

[With regard to this embassy, which evidently was not sent by Marcus Aurelius and was headed by some Syrian merchant, we shall remark that the same route to Kiao chi was followed in 159 and 161 A.D. under the same emperor Hwan Ti by ambassadors from *T'ien tchu* (India). Already in 120 A.D. musicians and jugglers

[1] Klap., 68–9; Pauthier, *De l'Auth.*, p. 32; *Id.*, *Hist. des Relations*, etc., p. 20; Deguignes in *Mém. de l'Acad.*, xxxii, 358. Reinaud supposes that Pausanias may have got his information about the production of silk from the members of this embassy (*supra*, p. 21). ["The sea route from the Persian Gulf to Rekem, it appears from what we may gather, was the principal channel for the silk trade up to the time of the Parthian war conducted under Marcus Aurelius Antoninus by Avidius Cassius during the years A.D. 162 to 165; whereas the bulk of oriental articles which had nothing to do with further treatment (dyeing, embroidering, re-weaving) in Phoenicia, probably went to Alexandria, for distribution over the Roman Empire. It is probably not an accidental coincidence that just at the conclusion of this war, which terminated with the capture of Seleucia and Ktesiphon by the Romans in A.D. 165, a mission went forward from Ta-ts'in by sea to the Far East which arrived at the court of China in October, A.D. 166. Up to this time the Parthians had monopolised the trade between China and Ta-ts'in as we learn from the *Hou Han-shu*, the *Wei lio* and other records." (Hirth, *l.c.*, pp. 173–4.)]

from Ta Ts'in had arrived in Burmah, showing that relations by sea existed between the Roman Empire and the Far East[1]. The first relations between China and Southern and Western Asia through Burmah took place at the beginning of the 2nd century of our era, when king Yung-yau-tiao was reigning in the country of Shan; Yung had received in 97 some sort of imperial investiture, and he was the prince who sent the Ta Ts'in jugglers to China in 120[2].]

About the same time [*c.* 164], and perhaps by means of this embassy, the Chinese philosophers were made acquainted with a treatise on astronomy, which had been brought from Ta Ts'in; we are told that they examined it, and compared it with their own[3].

38. Some intercourse would seem to have been kept up after this of which no precise record has been preserved. For we are told that early in the third century the Sovereign of Ta Ts'in sent to the Emperor T'ai Tsu[4], of the Wei dynasty which reigned in Northern China, articles of glass of a variety of colours, and some years later a person who had the art of "changing flints into crystal by means of fire," a secret which he imparted to others, and by which the fame of the people of the west was greatly enhanced in China[5].

A new embassy came from Ta Ts'in in the year 284, bringing *tribute*, as the presents are termed on this occasion, with the usual arrogant formula of the Chinese. This

[1] [Chavannes, *Les Pays d'Occident* d'après le *Heou Han Chou*, *T'oung pao*, May, 1907, p. 185.]

[2] [Pelliot, *Deux Itinéraires*, p. 132.]

[3] Deguignes in *Mém. de l'Acad.*, xlvi, 555.

[4] *Ibid.* [There is something wrong in this passage from Deguignes as there is no T'ai Tsu of the Wei dynasty.]

[5] Klaproth, *op. cit.* Pauthier, probably by an alternative translation, calls the presents "glasses of a red colour, stuffs of azure silk figured with gold, and the like" (p. 49).

must have been despatched by the Emperor Carus (282-283), whose short reign was occupied with Persian war[1].

A long suspension of intercourse seems to have followed, enduring till the 7th century. In the time of the *Sui* the Emperor Yang Ti (605–617) greatly desired to open communication with Ta Ts'in, now called Fu lin, but he could not succeed in his object. In 643 however, during the reign of T'AI TSUNG, the second emperor of the T'ang dynasty, and one of the greatest monarchs in Chinese history, whose power was acknowledged south of Hindu Kush and westward to the Caspian, an embassy came from Fu lin bringing a present consisting of rubies, emeralds, etc. This embassy is alleged to have been sent by the King of Fu lin called POTOLI or PHEITOLI. The emperor deigned to address a gracious and conciliatory letter in reply to this mission[2]. Considering that the

[1] ["During the T'ai-k'ang period of the emperor Wu-ti (A.D. 280–290) their king [Ta Ts'in] sent an envoy to offer tribute."] *Chin-shu*, tr. by F. Hirth, *China and the Roman Orient*, p. 45.

[2] It is difficult to guess who is meant by the *Wang Pheitoli*, who sent this embassy. Heraclius died in February 641; his son Constantine three months later. Heracleonas was then proclaimed; but speedily displaced by Constans, son of Constantine, at the age of eleven. Klaproth ascribes this embassy to *Theodorus*, the brother of Heraclius, whose name might be represented in Chinese as *Potoli*. But he appears to have been killed in 638. Pauthier adopts the name, but applies it to *Pope Theodorus*, who might have sent this embassy to China after his accession to the Pontifical throne in November 642; a desperately improbable hypothesis. May not *Wang Pheitoli* represent the *Prætorian* Prefect during the infancy of Constans? St. Martin thinks the name represents *Valentine* Cæsar, whose revolt put Constans on the throne. (On Lebeau's *Hist. du Bas Empire*, xi, 306.) [With regard to *Potoli*, Hirth, *l.c.*, p. 294, remarks: "The old pronunciation of this name was probably *Bat-da-lik* (the modern Cantonese sound is *Po-to-lik*); and this, in default of any prominent personage being mentioned under a similar name in that period of the history of Syria, I consider as the Chinese form of Arabic *Bathric*. D'Herbelot (*Bibl. Orient.*, vol. i, p. 380), says: "*Bathrik* et *Bathrirah*, dont le pluriel est *Batharekah*, signifie en Arabe, Persien et Turc, le Patriarche des Chrétiens de chaque Secte et de chaque Église." It is further stated by d'Herbelot that, at the council of Constantinople held under Theodosius the Great in A.D. 381, the rank of the patriarchs,

Musulmans had in the seven preceding years wrested Syria from the Roman Empire and Persia from the Sassanian kings; that Yezdegerd, the last of these latter, had sent (as we shall see hereafter) envoys to China to seek support, and that the suzerainty of T'ai Tsung was acknowledged in Farghânah, Bactria, and a part at least of Afghanistan and Khorassan, it seems not improbable that the object of the Byzantine mission also was to stir up a Chinese diversion against the terrible new enemy.

39. Another embassy from Fu lin, mentioned without particulars under the year 711, must have been despatched under Justinian II, who was slain in that year. In 719 arrived another embassy from the ruler of Fu lin, who is termed on this occasion, not king, but YENTHUHOLO, *of the rank of Premier Functionary of the Empire*, bringing presents of lions and great sheep with spiral horns. The emperor at this time was Leo the Isaurian. Possibly the mission, whatever its object, may have been despatched before he was established on the throne (717)[1].

the spiritual rulers over large countries, was fixed, and that the patriarch of Antioch was to rank fourth amongst five (*viz.*, those of Rome, Constantinople, Alexandria, Antioch, and Jerusalem." J. Edkins writes: "My own suggestion in regard to *Pa-ta-lik* is that it was the title of the Nestorian patriarch....Dr. Hirth introduces the Arabian word *Bathrik* from d'Herbelot as the medium by which the word Patriarch was introduced to the Chinese. But the Chinese at that time had both *p* and *b* in their syllabary, and so had the Greeks, and of course the Syrians also. It is better to pronounce *pa* as the syllabic spelling requires." (*Journ. China Br. R. As. Soc.*, xx, 1885, p. 283.) Chavannes thinks that *Po-to-li* is a transcription of the word *basileus*. Cf. *T'oung pao*, Dec. 1913, p. 798.]

[1] Pauthier translates the appellation in the Chinese record, "*Patrice, ou chef supérieur des fonctionnaires de l'empire*" (p. 50). Leo is termed, at the time of his election to the empire, *Leo the Patrician* (*Niceph. Constant.*, p. 34). I suppose the name Λέοντος τοῦ Ἰσαύρου might become in Chinese organs something like *Yenthuholo*.

[From the *Kiu T'ang shu* quoted by Hirth, *l.c.*, p. 295, we gather the following facts:

In 742 came, bringing presents, another mission from Fu lin, but this time composed of *priests of great virtue*[1]. Leo (717–741) was still reigning when this party must have been despatched from Byzantium, if from Byzantium they came. But we shall find that the Christian inscription of Si-ngan fu records the arrival in 744 of a priest of Ta Ts'in, *Kiho* by name, who, "observing the stars and the sun, came to the court to present his respects to the august emperor." Kiho is immediately afterwards styled "*Of great virtue.*" Probably therefore the same event is alluded to, and it may appertain rather to the missions of the Nestorian Church than to the political relations of the Eastern Empire with China.

40. Another long interval then occurs; the Mahomedan power now forming a wide and dense barrier between the Empires. But in 1081, during the reign of Chên Tsung of the Sung dynasty, whose capital seems to have been still at Ka'i-fung fu, an embassy arrives from Fu lin, despatched by the King MILI-I-LING (or MIKIALING) KAISA. This is supposed by Klaproth and Pauthier to indicate the Emperor *Michael* Ducas, who, indeed, was compelled to resign the purple some three years before (1078), but whose envoys, in the uncertainties of Asiatic travel, might have been detained long upon the way[2].

1. The emperor Yang-ti wishes to communicate with Fu lin A.D. 605–617.
2. An embassy is sent to China in A.D. 643.
3. The capital of Fu lin is besieged by the Arabs, and finally submits to Arab rule.
4. An embassy is sent to China in A.D. 667.
5. An embassy is sent in A.D. 701.
6. An embassy is sent in A.D. 719.]

[1] Klap., p. 70; Pauthier, pp. 32, 50. The extract in the last reference appears to mix up the missions of 719 and 742.

[2] The name of the Byzantine Cæsar appears to be read by Pauthier himself, as it has been by Deguignes, *Mi-li-iling*. Klaproth makes it *Mikialing*, but probably with some forcing, as Pauthier, though adopting this reading in a later work, says "*Mikia-i-ling* comme Klaproth *a cru pouvoir lire*." (Klap.,

Another mission is mentioned without particulars in the year 1091, which would fall in the reign of Alexius I Comnenus. And the last distinct record of a communication from the Byzantine Empire is found in 1371 under Hong Wu of the Ming dynasty, a few years after the expulsion of the House of Chinghiz, when there came to the court an envoy from Fu lin called *Kúmín Nikúlún.* This person received presents, and an imperial letter in reply to the requests which he had submitted[1]. Other envoys from this country, it is vaguely added, came with tribute. I cannot throw any light upon the identity of this Nicholas Comanus, or whatever his name was.

II*. COMMUNICATION WITH CENTRAL ASIA.

[We have already seen what were the conquests of General Pan Ch'ao in Central Asia.

The decline of the Chinese power in Central Asia dates from the beginning of the second century of our era under the emperor Ngan Ti (A.D. 107–125) of the Posterior Han.

p. 70; Deguignes, i, 67; Pauthier, *De l'Auth.*, p. 33; *Do., Hist. des Relations*, etc., p. 22.) If Michael be not accepted, I suppose the name of the competitor for the empire, *Bryennius Cæsar*, would be the only alternative; but why either should have sent a mission to China I cannot venture to suggest. [Hirth thinks that *Mi-li-i-ling Kai-sa* must be the title of a Seldjuk underking; it stands "for the words 'Melek-i-Rûm Kaisar,' *i.e.*, 'underking of Rûm and Caesar.' King of Rûm was, indeed, the title of Soliman, whose residence was at Iconium in Asia Minor." *L.c.*, p. 300.]

[1] Pauth., 51. This is cited from the Supplement to the Literary Encyclopædia of Ma Twan-lin. The Great Imperial Geography, also quoted by Pauthier (p. 54), gives a somewhat different account. "Towards the end of the dynasty of the Yuen (a parenthesis says in 1341, but the fall of the Yuen was in 1368) a man of Fu lin named Nikúlún came for purposes of trade to the middle kingdom. In the fourth year of Hung Wu of the Ming this merchant of Ta-Ts'in was invited to appear at court. The emperor ordered presents to be made to him, and an imperial letter was entrusted to him to be delivered to his king when he should return to his own country, and relate what he had witnessed. In consequence of this an embassy came to China with tribute." [On Nikúlún, see *Cathay*, iii, p. 12 *n.*]

During the third century, the emperor Wu Ti (265–290), of the Western Tsin, had once more secured the unity of China, which had been divided into three kingdoms during the *San kwo chi* period; he tried to re-establish Chinese influence in the valley of the Tarim and built adjoining the old Great Wall another wall with watch-towers beyond Su chau.

During the First Han there were four routes to the west; (1) Tun hwang, south of Lob Nor, Charchan and Khotan; (2) Tun hwang, north of Lob Nor, Kurla south of Karashahr, Kucha, Aqsu; (3) Hami, Turfan, Kucha, where it met the second route; (4) Hami, towards lake Barkul and the northern slopes of the T'ien Shan.

The great power of Central Asia from the first half of the sixth century to the middle of the seventh century were the Western Tu Kiue (Turks).

The Turks or *Tu Kiue* were subject to the Juan Juan during the first half of the sixth century of our era. In 546, the Tölös, of whom the Uighúrs were a branch, attacked the Juan Juan but were defeated by the Tu Kiue; the Juan Juan having refused to reward the victorious party, the chief of the Tu Kiue, T'u men (Bu min), son of the great jabgu T'u Wu, turned against his lord who was crushed in 552. The Turks were divided into two branches: the Northern, Eastern or Orkhon Branch and the Western Branch; the two branches were distinct from the middle of the sixth century, but their political separation due to the intrigues of the Chinese dates from 582. The chief of the Northern Turks bore the title of *qagan* while the head of the Western Turks or Turks of the Ten Tribes was the *jabgu*. T'u-men's brother, She-tie-mi (Istämi), is the ancestor of the Western Tu Kiue. After the downfall of the Juan Juan, the Turks became the neighbours of the Hephthalites who were the enemies of the Persians.

Khosru Naoshirwan, taking advantage of the disaster that had befallen the Juan Juan, made an alliance with the conqueror and married the daughter of the qagan She-tie-mi (Dizabul, Silzibul); the Hephthalites were subjugated between 563 and 567 and the Oxus became the boundary between the Turks and the Persians; later on, availing themselves of the weakness of the Sassanids, the Turks annexed the whole of the possessions of the Hephthalites. The agreement between Turk and Persian did not last long. The Sogdians, who were the chief intermediaries in the silk trade and had passed from the rule of the Hephthalites to that of the Turks, with the help of their new lords, wished to push their trade into Persia and, being unsuccessful there, they sent—with the approval of the Turks—an embassy to Justin II, at Byzantium, hoping to find in the Roman Empire a market for their trade. The intrigues of the Turks brought on a war between the Romans and the Sassanids (571–590) which weakened the two countries, now unable to stand against the rising power of the Arabs whose victory at Yarmuk (20th August 636) gave them Syria. The Arabs then turned against the Persians and their king Yezdijerd. The decline of the Turks began about 630. The T'ang Emperor, T'ai Tsung, having defeated the Northern Turks, had now his hands free and turned against the Western Turks. The Chinese allied themselves with the Uighúrs, and finally the Tu Kiue were subjugated in 659[1].

The Karluk (*Ko lo lu*) seem to have taken the place in political importance of the Western Tu Kiue in the middle of the eighth century; originally they were but one of the clans of the Tu Kiue, living to the N.W. of Pei t'ing across the Black Irtysh (Pu ku chen). They apparently were the ancestors of the Boghra Khân dynasty established at

[1] [Ed. Chavannes, *Doc. sur les Tou kiue* (*Turcs*) *occidentaux*.]

Balaçâcâghun (Balāsāghūn)[1]. The Boghra Khans (Ilak Khans) in the eighth century were the dominant power in Semiriechie and Kashgar, though these countries were then in the hands of the Tu Kiue. Afrâçiâb is supposed to be their ancestor. Probably on the suggestion of the Sassanids, in the middle of the tenth century, Satok Boghra Khan who was reigning over the country from Issik-kul to Kashgar (Urdukand) embraced Islạm and captured Bokhara; his capital was Kashgar, but after his death in 993, it was transferred to Balāsāghūn and his descendants took the title of Ilak Khan; the last of them was killed by Mohamed Khwariszm Shah who was himself defeated by Chinghiz Khan[2].

The Boghra Khans were the allies of the Tibetans, but when these lost their power, the Khans were at the mercy of their enemies the Uighúrs. To the causes of the decline of Chinese influence in Central Asia must be added the enterprise of the Tibetans. Under the Han, the tribes scattered throughout Tibet were known as the *Ki'ang*; under the T'ang and the Sung it was called *T'u fan*=*T'u po* =*T'u bod*; the Leao called it *T'u po t'è*. The historical period of Tibet begins at the end of the sixth century A.D. when the first king, Lunt sang, made inroads to India. Srong btsan sgam po, Lunt sang's son, married Bribtsun, daughter of Ançuvarman, sovereign of Nepal in 639, and

[1] [The exact site of Balāsāghūn in Central Asia is not known; Grenard thinks it is Tokmak; Barthold says it must be looked for in the Russian territory of Semiriechie, probably on the Chu, where many ruins are seen to-day; astronomical calculations would seem to show that B. was situated to the N.W. of Awliya-Ata, formerly Tarāz on the Talas river; in the year 1218, B. was captured without any resistance by Jebe Noyon, one of the generals of Chinghiz Khan, and the Mongols gave it the name of Ghūbāliq; it was in ruins in the fourteenth century. (Grenard, *La légende de Satok Boghra Khan*, *J. As.*, Jan.–Fév. 1900; V. Bartold, *Encyclop. de l'Islam*.)]

[2] [Elias-Ross, *Tarikh-i-Rashidi*, p. 287 *n.*; Bretschneider, *Med. Res.*, i, pp. 252–3.]

in 641 the princess of Wen ch'eng, daughter of the Chinese Emperor T'ai Tsung, whose court he had visited in 634; under their influence he introduced Buddhism into his states, and founded in 639 Lha dan (Lhásá); the power of the Tibetans increased yearly. In 663 they conquered Ku ku nor from the T'u yu huen, of Sienpi race; for the first time they took in the first year, 4th month of the period Hien Hêng (670), the Four Garrisons of the Protectorate of Ngan-si, and they took possession of Kashgaria (670–692), thus cutting the road of the Chinese to the West.

The destruction by the Chinese (658–659) of the Empire of the Western Tu Kiue had extended the power of the Son of Heaven beyond the Oxus, to the Indus; it is the epoch of its greatest extension towards the West, but internal difficulties during the reign of the Empress Wu Hau, the conquests of the Arabs, and the occupation of Kashgar by the Tibetans, closed the road of the Pamir to the invader from the East, and rendered illusory the domination of China in these distant countries, notwithstanding the victorious expedition led in 747 by general Kao Sien-chi beyond the Pamir, through the Baroghil and Darkot passes to Gilgit, to stop the advance of the Tibetans.

Being the allies of the Arabs, whom they supported in the valley of the Jaxartes; the Tibetans in return received their help in Kashgaria. They dominated in Kan Su, Sze chw'an, Yun Nan and penetrated even into Ch'ang ngan, the capital of the T'ang Emperors. Taking advantage of the struggle of the Chinese and of the Tibetans, P'i-lo-ko, in the eighth century, founded the kingdom of Nan chao with Ta-li as its capital; the new kingdom declined after the ninth century; the Chinese were too busy elsewhere to look after it, but in 1253 the Mongols subjugated the kingdom of Ta-li which had replaced Nan chao.

In 692, the Chinese retook their Four Garrisons (Karashahr, Kucha, Kashgar, Khotan) of Central Asia. " During the reign T'cheng yuen, 785–804 A.D., the black-coated Ta shi began a war with T'u fan (Tibet), and the Tibetans were obliged every year to send an army against the Ta shi. On this account the Chinese frontier enjoyed more peace [1]." The two most ancient historical edicts of Tibet have been found by Dr. L. A. Waddell upon a lofty pillar of victory which stands at the foot of Potala Hill, under the castles of the ancient kings, now incorporated in the palace of the Dalai lama; they date between A.D. 730 and 763, are the earliest documents hitherto discovered, and throw a side-light on the ancient history and geography of China. The eighth century is the culminating point of Tibetan power, which was destroyed when the Uighúrs became the masters of the whole country between Pei t'ing and Aqsu.

The Uighúrs were of Turkish race; their ancestor was a descendant of the Hiong nu; at the time of the Posterior Wei, they were called *T'iele* (Tölös) and were subject to the Tu Kiue; they lived on the banks of the Selenga; in the middle of the seventh century their chief P'u sa rebelled against the northern Tu Kiue, defeated their chief Hie-li qagan, and in 646 they sent an embassy to China. Under T'ai Tsung, the Uighúr tribe became the Han hai Prefecture, and the chief T'u mi tu was appointed commander of the region. Their power went on increasing from the beginning of the eighth century; at first they were called by the Chinese *Hwei ho* and later *Hwei hu* and *Wei wu eul*; the Tibetans appear to have named them *Dru gu*.

The expansion of the religion of Mo-ni (Mani), Manichæism, is intimately connected with the history of the

[1] From the History of the T'ang (Bretschneider, *Arabs*, p. 10).

Uighúrs; the discovery of documents made in Central Asia and at Tun hwang by Stein, Grünwedel, von Le Coq, Pelliot, and the researches of F. W. K. Müller, have thrown new and unexpected light on Manichæism, its dogma and its art, believed to be lost; the pictures on stone brought to Berlin by von Le Coq give a high idea of this art. Though the contemporary Chinese savant Tsiang Fu is of opinion that Manichæism was introduced into China as early as the time of the Northern Chau (A.D. 558–581) and of the Sui (A.D. 581–618) dynasties, it appears that its first pilgrim came to China from Ta Ts'in only in 694; Manichæism seems to have been mentioned for the first time in Chinese books by Hiuen Tsang in his Memoirs (seventh century); a Manichæan astronomer arrived in China in 719; Manichæism had henceforth a great deal of influence on Chinese astronomy. However an imperial edict of Hiuan Tsung in 732 declared the religion of Mo-ni a perverse doctrine taking falsely the name of Buddhism. Circumstances soon allowed Manichæism to take a more important place. The emperor Hiuan Tsung, who had chastised the Uighúrs guilty of murdering the commander of Liang chau (713–714) and stopped the traffic on the road to Ngan-si, died on the 3rd May, 762; his successor Su Tsung mounted the throne on the 16th May following; troubles arose, and during the rebellion which ensued, the Uighúrs entered Lo Yang on the 20th Nov. 762, pillaged it and left it in November 763. At Lo Yang the Uighúr qagan, having met some Manichæans, was converted to their faith and when he left this capital he took with him four of their priests. In 768 and 771 the Uighúrs of the Manichæan faith were ordered to build temples called *Ta yun kwang ming*. We note that some Manichæans were among the members of the Uighúr embassy sent to China in 806. But the influence of Manichæism declined with the power of the Uighúrs. In 840 the Kirghiz, who claimed to be originally descended from the Chinese general Li Ling captured by the Hiong nu in 99 B.C., took the Orkhon capital of the Uighúrs and killed the qagan. The Uighúrs were scattered to the south and to the south-west towards Turfan and Karashahr and to the west towards Kucha; however thirteen Uighúr tribes elected in 841 Wu-kiai as their qagan; Wu-kiai led a wandering life, and finally was killed in 847 in the Altai. After the fall of the Uighúrs, the property of the Manichæans was confiscated and their temples were closed. The remaining Uighúrs settled at Kan chau, in Kan Su, and at Kao ch'ang, east of Turfan. Their religion lasted in Chinese Turkestan until the thirteenth century; in China proper it was concealed under the cover of Buddhism and Taoism till it disappeared finally [1].

The capitals of the Uighúrs were Kao ch'ang, Khotcho or Idiqut Shahri, near Turfan, and Kara Balgasún [2] on the left bank of the Orkhon. An inscription in Chinese, Turki and Sogdian found at Kara Balgasún, devoted to the qagan who died in 821, throws a good deal of light on Manichæism [3]. The Uighúr writing, from which is derived the Manchu script, is itself derived probably from the Sogdian and not from the Estranghelo, its parent writing.]

III. COMMUNICATION WITH INDIA.

41. We have seen, in the early part of this Essay, that reason exists for believing in very early intercourse

[1] [Bretschneider, *Mediaeval Res.*, i, pp. 236 *seq.*; Chavannes, *Tu Kiue*, pass.; Chavannes et Pelliot, *Un traité manichéen retrouvé en Chine*, *J. As.*, ii, 1912; i, 1913.]

[2] [A plan of this city has been given by Radloff in his *Atlas der Alterthümer der Mongolei*, 1892–6.]

[3] [See the bibliography in *Bibliotheca Sinica*, col. 2732–3.]

between India and China; but the Chinese annals appear to have lost all sight of this, for their first mention and knowledge of India is referred to B.C. 122, when Chang k'ien, returning from his adventurous expedition to Bactriana, brought back intelligence about various regions in the West. When in that country he observed among the articles exposed for sale certain canes, which struck him as being like those grown in the mountains of Kiong shan, and cloths also which he recognised as the production of the country of *Shu*, *i.e.* Ch'eng tu fu in Sze ch'wan. On inquiry he was told that these articles had been purchased by merchants in the country of SHEN TU, otherwise called T'IEN CHU (Sind or India). This country lay some thousand *li* to the south-east of Ta Hia or Bactriana, and from all that he could gather could not be far distant from the province of Sze ch'wan, which accounted for the importation of the articles which he had seen for sale. There were three roads by which Shen tu might be reached from China; one, leading by the Kiang, very dangerous and difficult; a second by the north and through the lands of the Hiong Nu, who would certainly obstruct attempts at communication; and a third, which would be the safest, by Sze ch'wan. The emperor, pleased with the hope of adding to the list of his tributaries in those western countries, sent Chang k'ien to attempt to enter India by the way of Kien wei (Siu chau fu in Sze ch'wan), and others by different roads. Indeed some ten attempts in all were made, but they were all as unsuccessful as Colonel Sarel's late attempt to follow in the steps of Chang k'ien[1].

[1] See De Mailla (I can only refer to the Italian translation, vol. vii); Julien in *J. As.*, sér. IV, tom. x, 91–2; Deguignes in *Mém. de l'Acad.*, xxxii, 358. The Italian translation of De Mailla is a curiosity. The editor, finding that the Chinese names were distasteful to the readers of his earlier volumes, changes them all into a more pleasing form. Thus Kúblái figures as *Vobalio*, Wang Khan as *Govannio*, Ilchiktai as *Chitalio*. [See the title of this translation in H. Cordier's *Bibliotheca Sinica*, col. 586–7.]

42. In the succeeding century, however, relations must have been opened, for in A.D. 65 the Emperor Ming Ti, in consequence of a dream, sent ambassadors to T'ien chu to obtain instruction in the doctrines of Buddha, and to bring back images of him, a step which brought upon that emperor's memory the execrations of the orthodox Confucian *literati*, and which led to very peculiar relations between the two countries for many centuries[1].

Under the Emperor Ho Ti (A.D. 89–105) Indian sovereigns several times sent tribute (presents) to the court of China, and again in 159 under Hwan Ti, the same emperor that received the mission supposed to have come from Marcus Aurelius.

43. Throughout the greater part of the third and fourth centuries political intercourse between India and China seems to have been interrupted[2], though it may

[1] [The authenticity of this story is very doubtful. From the study of some newly discovered texts, it appears that Buddhism was introduced into China at the beginning of the Christian era, and that at the very time the two bonzes are supposed to have been brought back from India by Ming Ti's envoys, some Buddhist monks and laymen were living in China with a brother of the Emperor. Prof. Henri Maspero, of Hanoi, who made a careful study of the texts, has come to the conclusion that the traditionary history of the introduction of Buddhism in China is based entirely on some pious legends of the second century. H. Maspero, *Le songe et l'ambassade de l'empereur Ming, Bul. Ecole Ext. Orient.*, Jany.–March, 1910, pp. 95–130. In B.C. 2 the king of the Yue chi was a fervent Buddhist and tried to develop his religion in China; it is probably from him and through the ambassadors of Ngai Ti that the Chinese knew Buddhism.]

[2] [Chavannes has given as an appendix to his translation of Sung Yun (*Bul. Ecole franç. Ext. Orient.*, July–Sept., 1903) a list of various works relating to India published in China before the time of the T'ang. According to the *Leang Shu*, during the Period of the Three Kingdoms, a sovereign of Wu (A.D. 222–280) sent in the middle of the third century K'ang Tai and Chu Ying as ambassadors to Fan Siun, king of Fu Nan (Cambodia); they learned that some years previously, Fan Shan, king of Fu Nan, had sent a mission to Central India whose sovereign sent back with them a certain Ch'en sung who was seen by K'ang Tai, to whom he gave some information on India recorded in the *Leang Shu*.] [" At the time of the Wei and Tsin (220–419) the relations between China and India were interrupted, and they were not

be gathered from the history of Fa Hian's travels that a sea-trade between China and India existed at the end of the latter century, as it probably had done for some time previously. Its commencement, however, perhaps does not ascend beyond the early years of the Eastern Tsin (residing at Nan king, 317–420) as the first intercourse between China and Ceylon is ascribed to their time. Ceylon was famed for its figures of Buddha, and these often were sent as presents to the Chinese court. The first embassy from Ceylon arrived in 405[1], having come apparently overland, as it was *ten years* upon the road. It brought a Jade image of Buddha, exquisite in material and workmanship. In the course of the same century came four more Singhalese embassies; one in 428, when the King *Chacha Mohonoan* (Raja Mahanaama, reigned 410–432) sent an address to the emperor, together with a model of the shrine of the Sacred Tooth; one in 430, one in 435, and a fourth in 456, composed of five priests, of whom one was Nanté, a famous sculptor, and who brought a threefold image of Buddha. During the sixth century the kings of Ceylon acknowledged themselves vassals of China, and in 515 Kumara Dás, on succeeding to the throne, sent an envoy to China to announce the event, and who reported that the king had been desirous to go himself, but was afraid of the sea. Embassies are also recorded under the years 523, 527, 531[2].

resumed for a long time." *Pien-yi-tien*, quoted by Sylvain Lévi, *Mélanges Charles de Harlez*, p. 176.]

[1] [The first embassy from Ceylon came to China under the reign of Hiao Wu-ti (373–396) of the Tsin. With regard to the embassy of 428 sent by King *Ts'a-li Mo-ho-nan* (Kṣatriya Mahānāman), see S. Lévi, *Wang Hiuen-t'se*, p. 413.—According to the *Mahāvaṃsa*, Mahānāman reigned from 412 to 434; during his reign Buddhagosa came from Magadha to Ceylon.]

[2] Tennent's *Ceylon*, 2nd ed., i, 590–1; 596. Sir Emerson Tennent was supplied with unpublished translations of extracts from Chinese authors for his work. The authorities are given by him.

44. In 428 also the King of Kapila (the birth-place of Buddha in the present district of Gorahkpúr) by name *Yuei-ai* or "Loved of the Moon," *i.e. Chandragupta*, sent an ambassador carrying a diamond ring, a gold bracelet, red and white parrots, etc., to the Emperor Wu Ti. In 466 came another mission from the same court, and again in 500–504 bringing a trained horse.

In 441, 455, 466, and 473 other Buddhist kingdoms in or adjoining India sent tribute. In 502 *Kioto* (or Gupta), a king of India, sent one Chulota to present to the emperor a letter, a spittoon of lapis-lazuli, perfumes, cotton-stuffs, etc. This king's territory adjoined the great river *Sinthao* (Indus) with its five branches. Rock-salt like crystal, it is observed, is found there[1].

In 605 Yang Ti of the Sui dynasty, the same whose desire had been to open relations with the Roman empire, having formed some ambitious projects, sent to try and induce the kingdoms of Tibet and India to render him homage, but those of India refused, which much enraged the emperor.

Two years later we find one Chang-tsuen, "Director of the Military Lands," sent on an embassy to Ceylon[2].

45. In 641 the King of Magadha (Behar, etc.) sent an ambassador with a letter to the Chinese court. The emperor (the great T'ai Tsung) in return directed one of his officers to go to the king with an imperial patent and to invite his submission. The King *Shiloyto* (Çīladītya) was all astonishment. "Since time immemorial," he asked his officers, "did ever an ambassador come from MOHOCHINTAN?" "Never," they replied. The Chinese author remarks that in the tongue of the barbarians the Middle Kingdom is called Mohochintan (*Mahachinas-*

[1] Julien, *u.s.*, pp. 99–100.
[2] Tennent, i, 583.

thana)[1]. This led to a further exchange of civilities extending to 646[2]. But the usurping successor of Çīladītya did not maintain equally amicable relations, and war ensued, in the course of which the Chinese, assisted by the Kings of Tibet and Nepal, invaded India. Other Indian kings lent aid and sent supplies; and after the capture of the usurper *Alanashun*, and the defeat of the army commanded by his queen on the banks of the *Khientowei* (Gandhara), 580 cities surrendered to the Chinese arms, and the king was carried prisoner to China[3]. A magician, who accompanied the Chinese general from India, was employed to treat the Emperor T'ai Tsung, who was very ill, but with no success. Wang Hiuen-ts'e, the envoy who had gone on the mission which resulted in this war, wrote a history of all the transactions in twelve books, but it is lost[4].

1 [In 643, 17th year of the period Cheng kwan, Li I-piao with Wang Hiuen-ts'e as his second, was sent to Magadha to take back a Brahman; according to the History of the T'ang he was the bearer of a reply of the Chinese Emperor to King Harṣa Çīladītya. Sylvain Lévi, *Wang Hiuen-ts'e, Journ. Asiat.*, xv, 1900, pp. 298–9, 320–1.]

2 [In 646 Wang Hiuen-ts'e was sent again to Magadha with thirty horsemen. Harṣa Çīladītya having died was replaced by his usurping minister Na-fu-ti O-lo-na-shoen, who had the Chinese escort massacred and Wang, taking refuge in Tibet where Srong-btsan Sgam-po was reigning, gathered a troop of 1200 Tibetans and 7000 Nepalese horsemen, fell upon Magadha, captured the king and brought him back as a prisoner to China (648). Sylvain Lévi, *l.c.*, pp. 300–1. In 657 Wang was sent again on a mission to the western countries.]

3 [" K'ien-t'o-wei ramène à Gandavatī ou Gaṇḍavatī, une des formes possibles du nom de la Gaṇḍakī (cf. grec Κονδοχάτης). C'est donc dans la région entre Pāṭaliputra, situé au confluent de la Gaṇḍakī et du Gange, et le Népal d'où sort la Gaṇḍakī, qu'il faut chercher la ville de Tch'a-pouo-ho-lo," captured by Wang Hiuen-ts'e. Sylvain Lévi, *l.c.*, p. 307 *n*.]

4 [See Sylvain Lévi, *Wang Hiuen-ts'e, J. As.*, xv, 1900.] Julien, pp. 107–110. The Çīladītya of this account is known from Hiuen Tsang to have been one of the great kings of Indian history. His empire extended from the sea-coast of Orissa at least as far north-west as Kanauj, which was his capital, and possibly to the frontiers of Kashmír (see Lassen, iii, 673 *seqq.*). Lassen, as far

In 667–8 it is asserted the Kings of the five Indies all sent to offer homage; and this homage was repeated in 672 and 692. These kings are named in the Chinese Annals—(1) the King of Eastern India, named *Molopama*; (2) the King of Western India, called *Shiloyito*; (3) the King of Southern India, called *Chilukhipalo*; (4) the King of Northern India, called *Nana*; (5) the King of Central India, called *Timosina*[1].

In 670 King Datopiatissa of Ceylon sent a memorial to the Emperor with a present of native productions. Another Ceylonese embassy came in 711[2].

46. In 713 an embassy came to the Emperor Hien Tsung from Chentolopiti (*Chandrapida*), King of Kashmír, acknowledging allegiance, and some years later a patent of investiture was granted to this prince. A successor and brother called *Mutopi* (*Muktopida*) also offered homage and requested the Emperor to send troops into Kashmír, offering to quarter them on the banks of the Lakė Mahapadma in the centre of that valley. Tribute continued to be paid regularly by Kashmír for some time. The pressure of the rising power of Tibet probably induced this state to seek Chinese protection[3].

Between 713 and 731 repeated missions are reported from the different kingdoms of India, one of which begged aid against the Arabs and the Tibetans, and requested the

as I can discover, says nothing as to this Chinese invasion of India, or the usurper Alanashun. Nor is the chronology consistent with his (from Hiuen Tsang), which continues Çīladītya's reign to 650; whilst the account followed in the text makes him already dead in 646. The Emperor T'ai Tsung died in 650.

[1] *Chine Ancienne*, p. 301.

[2] Tennent, i, p. 597. [The King of Ceylon in 670 was Hatthadaṭha or Dāṭhopatissa II (664–673).]

[3] Rémusat, *u.s.*, p. 106; *Chin. Anc.*, 311; Reinaud in *Mém. de l'Acad.*, xvii, p. 190. There is a King Chandrapida in the Kashmír Annals, but he is killed in 691. The king reigning 695–732 was Laladītya, a great conqueror. He seems to have had a brother Muktopida (see Lassen, iii, 993, 997).

Emperor to bestow an honorific title upon the Indian monarch's army. The Emperor perhaps found this the most convenient part of the petition to comply with, and decreed it the title of "the Army which cherishes virtue[1]."

In 742 foreign merchants who had arrived in China by the Sea of the South brought a number of precious articles from the kingdom of Lions (*Sinhala* or Ceylon) to be presented to the Emperor on behalf of *Shiloshukia* their king[2]. Other embassies came from the same island in 746, 750, 762. There is then an interval of many

[1] See Julien, *u.s.*, and compare *Chine Ancienne*, pp. 309, 310. About this time there is frequent mention in the Chinese Annals of relations with two kingdoms called *Great and Little Poliu*, which lay between Kashgar and Kashmír. The king of Little Poliu dwelt in a city called *Nieito*, near a river called *Soï*. The Great Poliu was more to the east; this country was occupied by the Chinese forces in 747 (Rémusat, in *Mém. de l'Acad.* as above, pp. 100–2). Rémusat renders Poliu *Purut*; but there can be no doubt that the kingdoms in question are Ladakh and Balti, which continued to a late date to be known as *Great and Little Tibet*. These titles will be found in Tavernier I think, and in the letters of the Jesuit Desideri (1716), and indeed the term Little Tibet for Balti is scarcely yet obsolete. Ladakh is probably "the city of Tibet, built on an eminence over a river" of Edrisi (i, 492). In Meyendorff we find the cities of Great and Little Tibet still spoken of at Bokhara. The Georgian Danibeg went from Kashmír to the "city of Tibet" in twenty days. It was three months from Lhásá. And the Tajik route given by Meyendorff speaks of reaching by the Karakorum pass "Tibet, a city on the *croupe* of a mountain, with the governor's residence at the top," a description which applies perhaps equally well to Ladakh and Balti. The latter is perhaps the name concealed in the Poliu of the Chinese, and the Soï may be the *Shayok* (Meyendorff, pp. 122, 339). ["Pulu is the modern Balti. At this time it was divided into two states, Greater and Lesser. The Greater Pulu is described in the T'ang History as being due west of T'ufan, contiguous to the Small Pulu, and bounded on the west by the Northern Indian State, Wuch'ang (Udyâna). They sent several missions with tribute to China from the year 696, but were finally conquered by the Tibetans in 734." Bushell, *Early History of Tibet*, *J. R. As. Soc.*, N.S., xii, p. 530.—Kao Sien-chi was the Chinese general in command in 747. The Soï or Soyi River is no doubt the Shyok River.]

[2] *Ch. Anc.*, p. 312. This is not mentioned by Tennent. The king reigning at Anurajapura at this time was Aggabodhi III or Akbo.

centuries before Ceylon is again heard of in the Chinese Annals[1].

47. Towards 758–760, China, it is said, having lost the country of *Holong*, the Kings of India ceased to send homage[2]. I do not know what country is indicated, whether *Khulum* in the valley of the Oxus or some region on the Yun nan frontier. The former is probable, as the narratives of the Buddhist pilgrims show that the long route by Kashgar and Badakhshan was that generally followed between India and China.

The Tibetans at this time were becoming powerful and troublesome neighbours, insomuch that about 787 the Emperor Te Tsung, by the advice of one of his ministers, applied to the Uighúrs, the Princes of India, and the Khalif to join in a league against them[3].

After this, for a long time no political intercourse is heard of; but a few more missions from Indian kingdoms are recorded under the later years of the tenth century and the beginning of the eleventh as visiting the Court of the Northern Sung. With the exception of one in 1015 from the country of *Chulien*, which is supposed by Deguignes to be the Chola Kingdom of Southern India, I suspect these embassies to belong rather to the Archipelago than to India Proper[4].

48. Throughout this period, however, there are frequent notices either of the visits of Indian Buddhist devotees to the Court of China or of leave obtained from

[1] Tennent, *ib.*, p. 597.

[The embassies of 742 and 746 and probably also those of 750 and 762 were sent by Aggabodhi VI Sīlamegha (741–781). S. Lévi, *l.c.*, p. 428.]

[On the relations between Ceylon and China see the translations from the *Pien-yi-tien*, by Sylvain Lévi, *Journ. Asiat.*, Mai–Juin, 1900, pp. 411–418.]

[2] Julien, p. 111.

[3] *Ch. Anc.*, p. 321.

[4] Deguignes, i, pp. 66 *seqq.* *Tanmoeilieu*, one of the kingdoms named, is perhaps Tana-Malayu, the Malay country.

the Emperor by Chinese Buddhists to visit India for religious objects[1]. One of the parties from India is related to have been accompanied by the son of an Indian king, by name Mañjuçri, a very zealous Buddhist, who was treated with great favour by the Emperor. The monks were jealous of this, and as he did not understand Chinese they made him believe that the Emperor had ordered his departure. He went off in much indignation to the southern coast to embark in a merchant vessel for India[2]. These religious visitors to China became very frequent after 975, perhaps a sign that by that time Buddhism was becoming oppressed in India. In 986, however, a monk of I chau (Kamul) returning from India brought a letter from a king who is called *Mosinang*, written in terms of humblest reverence, which are preserved

[1] The route of one of these parties is described as carrying them by Kan chau, Sha chau, I chau (Kamul), Karashahr, Kucha, Khotan, Khulum, Peshāwar, and Kashmír.

[2] Julien, pp. 111–114. This Mañjuçri appears in the traditions of the Newars of Nepal as the Buddhist Apostle of their country (see Lassen, iii, 777 *seqq.*, quoting from B. H. Hodgson). [The Bodhisattwa Mañjuçri, Mañjughosa-Bissōchtma, called at times Vâgîçvara, "Lord of the Voice," came to Nepal from Maha Čina (Great China); the disciples who accompanied him were the first colonists; they also came from Maha Čina; he gave a king to the country, the Chinese Dharmâkara who himself had as his successor another Chinaman Dharmâpala. The Newars are the companions of Mañjuçri who returned to China when his task was finished; he is more particularly venerated at the Wu t'ai shan (*Pañča cîrṣa parvata*) in the Shan si Province. Mañjuçri appears to have been a Hindu by birth and the Sanskrit sources of Târanâtha make him live under the reign of Čandragupta, King of Orissa, a short time after the reign of Mahâpadma, about the epoch of the Macedonian invasion.—S. Lévi, *Népal*, i, pp. 320, 340. With regard to the relations of China with Nepal it is said that King Çaktisiṃha sent presents to China and that the Emperor was so pleased with them that he in his turn sent a seal bearing engraved the name of Çaktisiṃha with the title of Râma, and an official letter, in the year of China (Čīnâbda) 535. Relations were resumed under the Ming; Hung Wu sent in 1384 a bonze to Nepal to bring to the king a seal conferring upon him the official investiture; these relations continued under Yong lo. (Sylvain Lévi, *Le Népal*, ii, pp. 227, 228.)]

by the Chinese authority, and transmitting relics of Sakya[1].

49. Indeed, for many centuries subsequent to the introduction of Buddhism in China, the intercourse between its devotees in the two countries was frequent, and the narratives of Chinese pilgrims who spent years in studying the Buddhist doctrines in their original country and in visiting the sacred sites and monastic establishments of India, form a curious and valuable part of Chinese literature. Of these works several have been translated into European languages, as the Travels of Fa Hian (399–414);

[1] Julien, pp. 115–116. This letter was translated by one Shihu, an Indian ecclesiastic, who also communicated some information about the kingdoms of India. Besides Central India (here Magadha) there were in the north the kingdoms of *Utiennang* (Udyana, according to Julien), west of that *Khientolo* (Gandhara), *Nanggolokialo* (Nagarahara), *Lanpo* (Lamghan, now generally called Laghman), then *Gojenang* (probably *Ghazni*), and then Persia. Three days' journey west of Magadha was *Alawei* (*Rewa ?*), then Karana Kiuje (*i.e. Kanya Kubja* or Kanauj), Malwa, Ujjayani, *Lolo* (Lara, according to Julien), Surashtra, and the Western Sea. Southern India was four months' journey from Magadha, and ninety days west of it was Konkana.

Gandhara mentioned above [is the valley of Peshāwar, the Pu-lu-sha-pu-lo of the Chinese Pilgrim Hiuen Tsang, Puruṣapura, the Purushavar or Purshavar of Al-birûni, the Pershavar or Peishavar of Abul Fazl. (A. Foucher, *l.c.*, p. 327.) The capital of Gandhāra was Peshāwar (Puruṣapura)]. It is the *Kandahâr* of Al-biruni and other early Arab writers, the capital of which was *Waihand*, which stood on the west of the Indus north of the Kabul River's confluence. This is supposed to be the *Utakhanda* of Hiuen Tsang, and has been identified with Ohind or Hûnd about fifteen miles above Attok. Udhyana lay *west* of Gandhara, the country on the Upper Swat and eastern part of the modern Kafiristan. [The Swat valley and neighbourhood constitute the principal portion of the old province of Udyāna, and the capital was Mungali, or Mung-kie-li, identified by General Sir A. Cunningham (*Ancient Geog. of India*, p. 82) with Minglaur=Mingaur, or Mingora. Major Deane accepts Mungali=Minglaur, but makes a separate place of Mingaur. Foucher has Mung-kie-li =Mangalapura, some distance from the left bank of the Swat River. (H. A. Deane, *Note on Udyāna and Gandara, Journ. R. As. Soc.*, 1896, p. 655. A. Foucher, *Notes sur la Géog. ancienne du Gandhāra, Bul. Ecole franç. Ext. Orient.*, 1901, pp. 322 *seq.*).] Nanggolokialo or *Nagarahara* appears to have been near the present Jalalabad. See Reinaud in *Mém. de l'Acad.*, xvii, 108, 157, etc.; Lassen, iii, 137 *seq.*; V. St. Martin in *N. Ann. des Voyages* for 1853, ii, 166.

of Hiuen Tsang (travelled 628–645); and of Hwei Sing[1], who set out in 518. One of the latest of these travellers was Khinie[2], who journeyed (964–976) at the head of a body of 300 monks whom the Emperor despatched to India to seek relics of Buddha and collect books of palm-leaves. Fragments of descriptions of the western countries are cited from a work of one of these pilgrims older even than Fa Hian, the monk Shi-tao-an who died in 385. It does not seem to be known if the work is extant[3].

These pilgrimages must have become more unfrequent as the indigenous Buddhism of India gradually perished, but perhaps they had not altogether ceased even in the middle of the fourteenth century. For at that date we find the Emperor of China asking leave from Mahomed Tughlak to rebuild a temple near the base of the Himalaya, which was much visited by his subjects[4].

50. In the thirteenth century we find revived indications of communication with Ceylon[5]. Singhalese writers mention imports from China at this time; and in 1266 Chinese soldiers are mentioned as taking service in the army of the Ceylonese King. We hear, also, during the

[1] [Companion of Sung Yun.]

[2] [Khinie is properly named to-day Ki-ye; his itinerary has been translated with the name of Wang-nieh by G. Schlegel in the *Mémoires du Comité sinico-japonais*, xxi, 1893, pp. 35–64, and again by the late Edouard Huber in the *Bulletin de l'Ecole d'Extrême-Orient*, ii, July, 1902, pp. 256–9. Prof. Chavannes has added some valuable notes to the itinerary in the same periodical, Jan.–March, 1904. The itinerary was printed in the first chapter of the Wu ch'wan lu; it was written by Fan Ch'eng-ta, who obtained his notes from Ki-ye, then living near the O-mei shan in the Sze ch'wan Province. Ki-ye died eighty-four years old.]

[3] Julien, *op. cit.*, pp. 272–294, and Preface to *Vie de Hiouen Thsang*. The Chinese bibliographer quoted by Julien observes of Fa Hian that he applies the term *Chong Kouo* or Middle Kingdom to *India* instead of China. This error he observes is a fashion of the Buddhist monks, and is not worth the trouble of refutation! I suppose the Buddhists used it as a translation of *Madhyadesa*, the classical name which the Burmese still apply to Gangetic India.

[4] See Ibn Batuta, *infra*, Vol. IV.

[5] Tennent, i, 497–8.

Mongol reign in China of the occasional despatch by the Emperors of officers to Ceylon to collect gems and drugs; and, on three occasions, envoys were sent to negotiate the purchase of the sacred alms-dish of Buddha. Such missions are alluded to by Polo and Odoric.

51. As late as the beginning of the fifteenth century, under the Ming dynasty, the Chinese made a remarkable and last attempt to renew their former claims to honorary allegiance in the maritime countries of the west. In 1405 a mission from China, which had come to Ceylon bringing incense and offerings to the Shrine of the Tooth, was maltreated by the reigning King Wijayabahu VI [1398–1410], who was a native of *Solli*[1] or the Peninsula, and an oppressor of Buddhism[2]. The Emperor Ch'eng Tsu [had dethroned his nephew Kien wen (Hwei Ti) who disappeared when his capital, Nan King, was captured and his palace invaded in 1402, and was] indignant at the outrage, and anxious to do something for the re-establishment of the declining prestige of China, despatched [the eunuch] Cheng Ho, [commonly known as San Pao T'ai kien, a native of the Yun nan province and] a soldier of distinction, with a fleet of sixty-two ships, and a force [of more than 37,000 soldiers], and armed with credentials and presents, to visit the western kingdoms[3]. He touched

[1] ["The King is of the *Soli* race, a most earnest believer in the Buddhist religion, and one who treats elephants and cows with a feeling of veneration." (Ma Huan, *Journ. China B. R. As. Soc.*, 1885, p. 212.)]

[2] [S. Lévy, *l.c.*, p. 437, remarks that the king who treated rudely Cheng Ho at the time of his first visit to Ceylon A lie ku na eul (A-le-ko-nar) is the prince named in the royal list Bhuvaneka Bahu V, who was known under the name of Alagakkonāra before his accession to the throne; this king was of origin Coḍa, the Sinhalese word for Soli.]

[3] [The Emperor Yong lo, fearing that his predecessor Hwei Ti "was concealing himself in some country over the sea, wanted to trace him, and at the same time to display his military force in foreign countries, in order to show that China was rich and strong. In the sixth month of the year 1405, he ordered Chêng Ho, his companion Wang Ching-hung, and others, to go as envoys to the

at Cochin China, Sumatra, Java, Cambodia, Siam, and other places, proclaiming at each the imperial edict and conferring imperial gifts. If any of the states refused to acknowledge the Emperor's supremacy they were subdued by force; and in 1407 the expedition returned to China accompanied by envoys from the different nations. Cheng Ho being sent again next year on a like mission, the Singhalese King tried to entrap and capture him, but Cheng Ho avoided the snare, caught the king, his whole family and officers of state, and carried them prisoners to China. In 1411 the Emperor set the prisoners free, but deposed the misdemeanant king, and appointed another of the party in his place, who was sent back to Ceylon accompanied by a Chinese commissioner to invest him as a royal vassal of the empire. This new king is named by the Chinese *Pulakoma Bazae Lacha*, which identifies him as Parakkāna Bahu Raja VI, whose reign according to the Ceylonese annals extended from 1410 to 1462. Tribute was paid regularly by Ceylon for fifty years; apparently therefore throughout the long reign of this prince and no longer. During that time the king

kingdoms in the western ocean. They took with them 30,000 soldiers and a large quantity of gold and silks. The fleet consisted of 62 ships, most of them of large tonnage, some measuring 440 feet long and 180 feet broad. They sailed from Liu-kia-kiang, an inlet of the Yang-tze, situated a little to the north of Wu sung, the entrance of the Shanghai River. They touched on their way south at Woga, at the mouth of the Min, from which place they sailed to Cochin China, and so on to the various countries in the Straits and India, making known at each place the orders from the Emperor. They gave presents to the princes and chiefs, and those who would not submit were compelled to do so by force. Ma Huan has left us an account of twenty of the kingdoms visited by the expedition." (Ma Huan's work is named *Ying-yai-shêng-lan*; Ma Huan was an Interpreter and a Mohamedan. Cf. Geo. Phillips, *Journ. R. As. Soc.*, 1895, pp. 523 *seq.*) The King of Ceylon visited by Ma Huan was Parakkāna Bahu VI, second successor to Bahu V (1410–1462). Recently, in the town of Galle, Ceylon, a tablet has been found bearing inscriptions in Chinese, Tamil and Persian; it refers to the second visit to Ceylon of Cheng Ho and bears a Chinese date (7th year Yong lo) corresponding to the 15th Feb. 1409.—*Spolia Zeylanica*, June, 1912; *J. North China B.R.A.S.*, 1914, pp. 171–2.]

is asserted to have been on two occasions the bearer of it in person[1]. Other circumstances mentioned appear to imply that a Chinese Resident was maintained on the island who superintended the administration. The last tribute was paid in 1459. Chinese influence was thus a matter of recent memory on the arrival of the Portuguese in the beginning of the following century, and they found many traces of it remaining.

Those events are of course very differently represented in the Ceylonese annals. According to their account the King of Mahachina landed in the island with an army under the pretence of *bringing tribute*; the King of Ceylon was then treacherously taken and carried captive to China, etc.[2]

52. As regards warlike relations between India and China in the middle ages we may mention the Mongol invasion of Bengal "by way of Cathay and Tibet" during the reign of Alauddin Musaüd King of Delhi; the only invasion of Bengal from that quarter distinctly recorded in history. This took place about 1244, and was defeated by the local officers. Firishta in speaking of it says it is supposed that they entered by the same route which was followed by Mahomed Bakhtiyar Khilji when he invaded Cathay and Tibet from Bengal[3]. This refers to the

[1] [The work *Ts'ien Wen ki* written by Chu Yun-ming, quoted by W. F. Mayers, *China Review*, iii, 329, contains a note entitled "The Voyages to the West," with particulars of an undertaking in the reign of Siuen Teh (1426–1435); the members of the expedition included: Officers, soldiers, purveyors, steersmen, leadsmen, interpreters, clerks, accountants, doctors, blacksmiths, carpenters, and other artificers, sailors, and landsmen; in all, 27,550 souls! The expedition left Lung Wan (near Nan King) on the 6th day of the intercalary 12th moon of the 5th year of Siuen Teh (about the beginning of A.D. 1431), visited Sumatra and the Malay Peninsula and sailed to Ceylon (6th of 11th moon, 7th year), Calicut, Ormuz (26th of 12th moon); sailed on return voyage (18th of 2nd moon of 8th year) via Pulo Condor, Chan ch'eng and reached Nan King on the 6th of the 7th moon.]

[2] Tennent, pp. 601–2.

[3] Briggs's *Firishta*, i, 231.

expedition some forty years before, to which allusion is made at Note E, Ibn Batuta, Vol. IV of the present work. It is very possible that Bakhtiyar Khilji's ambition dreamt even of a raid upon China, but it is difficult to gather from the account extant how far he had really got when forced to retreat; perhaps not beyond the Assam valley[1]. In the still more disastrous enterprise of Malik Yuzbek in 1256–57 aims more distant than Kámrúp are not alluded to. The mad expedition of Mahomed Tughlak in 1337 was, according to Firishta's account, directed against China. Of the force, which both that historian and Ibn Batuta[2] estimate at one hundred thousand horse besides infantry, scarcely any returned to tell the tale, except the few who had been left to garrison posts in rear of the army. It is difficult to guess by what point this host entered the Himalaya, nor have I been able to identify the town of *Jidiáh* at the base of the mountains, mentioned by Ibn Batuta, which would ascertain the position.

53. We ought not to omit in the record of relations between China and India, the two embassies mentioned by the author last named, viz., that sent by the Mongol Emperor Shun Ti or Togan Temur to the Court of the same Mahomed Tughlak in 1341–42, and the unlucky return embassy entrusted to the Moorish traveller himself, which has furnished this collection with one of its chief items.

An embassy from Bengal is mentioned in the time of Ch'eng Tsu of the Ming (1409), but from what sovereign, Hindu or Musalman, does not appear[3]. It was, perhaps,

[1] See Stewart's *History of Bengal*, pp. 45–50.

[2] Ibn Batuta, iii, 325.

[3] *Chine Anc.*, p. 402. [Phillips says that most of the facts of "Mahuan's account of Bengala are to be found endorsed in the records of Foreign countries, to be met with in the Ming Dynasty histories. In one account I find that Gai-ya-szu-ting, the king of Bengala, sent, in 1409, an embassy with presents to the Chinese Court; another king of Bengala, by name Kien-fuh-ting, sent a

one of those complimentary missions which General Cheng Ho went cruising to promote, as mentioned on p. 76.

And in 1656, though the date is beyond the field of our notices, we find that the Dutch envoy Nieuhoff was presented at Peking along with an ambassador from the Great Mogul, at that time Shah Jahan[1].

54. Returning to earlier days, we find that in the time of the Mongol emperors an ample trade by sea existed between China and the ports of Malabar. To this Polo, Odoric, Marignolli, and Ibn Batuta bear witness. The rise of this trade, so far as we know about it, will be more conveniently related under the head of Chinese intercourse with the Arabs. Ibn Batuta alludes to the Chinese merchants residing at Kaulam[2], and such residents are

letter to the Emperor of China, written on gold leaf, and accompanied by a present of a giraffe. The first embassy, viz. that of Gai-ya-szu-ting, is said to have come to China in the sixth year of Yong-lo's reign, which corresponds with 1409 of our era. The Bengal king reigning at that time appears to have been Shihab-ad-din Bayazid Shah, who only came to the throne in that year. A former king, Ghiyas-ad-din, who reigned from 1370–1396, comes very near the Chinese name Gai-ya-szu-ting, but he had ceased to reign ten years before the embassy is said to have arrived in China. Possibly the Chinese dates are wrong. In the twelfth year of Yong-lo, 1415, the time assigned by the Chinese chroniclers to the arrival of the second embassy to China, Jalál-ad-din was king of Bengal. To make his name agree with the Chinese Kien-fuh-ting is somewhat difficult, but I think no other can be meant." (*J.R.A.S.*, 1895, p. 534.)

Mr. John Beames, *l.c.*, p. 900, makes the following remark on the subject: "As to the identification of Gai-ya-szu-ting with Ghiyas-uddin, the Chinese date seems to be wrong, as there are no coins or inscriptions of this king later than A.H. 799, corresponding to A.D. 1396. But the other king may, perhaps, be identified as follows: In A.D. 1415 (=A.H. 817–818) Jaláluddin was king, but his reign did not commence till A.H. 818, the end of March, 1415. In the former part of the year 1415 his father, the Hindu Raja Káns, was apparently still alive. Might it not, therefore, be possible that the Chinese historian has mixed up the two, and made out of Káns and Jaláluddin a joint name, Káns uddin, which he represents by Kien-hut-ding. A Chinese would not be aware of the incongruity of a mixed Hindu and Musulman name." This seems to me far-fetched.]

[1] Pauth., *Relations Polit., etc.*, p. 49.

[2] iv, p. 103.

also alluded to in ancient Malabar documents[1]. I have already suggested that Marignolli's mention of "Tartars" in connection with the tomb of St Thomas at Mailapúr (III, p. 251, *infra*) may indicate that Chinese traded, perhaps were settled, also on the Coromandel Coast. But Ritter's idea that CHINAPATAM, one of the native names of the town of Madras, is a trace of ancient Chinese colonisation here, is not well founded. That name, properly Chennapatam or Chennapapatam, was bestowed on the site granted to the British in 1639 by the Naik of Chingleput, in honour of that chief's own father-in-law, *Chennapa* by name[2]. It is curious, however, in connection with such a suggestion, that Gasparo Balbi in the sixteenth century, speaking of certain Pagodas seen in making Negapatam after rounding Ceylon (apparently the monolithic temples at Mahabalipuram, commonly known still as the Seven Pagodas) observes that they were called the *Sette Pagodi de' Chini*, and were attributed to ancient Chinese mariners[3].

[1] See *Madras Journal* for 1844, p. 121.

[2] Ritter, v, 518, 620; *Madras in the Olden Time*, by J. T. Wheeler, Madras, 1861, i, p. 25. ["In honour of the local Naik's father Chennappa, the settlement, as distinct from the town of Madras itself, was called Chennappapattanam, but the natives now apply the name Chennapattanam to the whole city." (*Imp. Gaz. India*, xvi, pp. 368–9.)]

[3] It is worth noting that the Catalan Map of 1375 has in this position a place called *Setemelti*; qu. an error for *Sette templi*? [See note in *Marco Polo*, ii, p. 336.] [We read in the *Tao yi chi lio* (1349) that "T'u t'a (the eastern stupa) is to be found in the flat land of Pa-tan (Fattan, Negapatam ?) and that it is surrounded with stones. There is a stupa of earth and brick many feet high; it bears the following Chinese inscription: 'The work was finished in the eighth moon of the third year *hien chw'en* (1267).' It is related that these characters have been engraved by some Chinese in imitation of inscriptions on stone of those countries; up to the present time, they have not been destroyed." Hien chw'en is the *nien hao* of Tu Tsung, one of the last emperors of the Southern Sung Dynasty, not of a Mongol Sovereign. I owe this information to Prof. Pelliot, who adds that the comparison between the Chinese Pagoda of Negapatam and the text of the *Tao yi chi lio* has been made independent of him by Mr. Fujita in the *Tōkyō-gakuhō*, November 1913, pp. 445–6.]

55. We hear from Marco Polo of some part of the intercourse which Kúblái Khan endeavoured to establish with western countries of Asia, and his endeavours are also specially mentioned in the Chinese annals. Unfortunately he and his officers seem to have entertained the Chinese notion that all intercourse with his empire should take the form of homage, and his attempts that way in Java and Japan had no very satisfactory result. But he is said to have been more fortunate in 1286 with the kingdoms of MAPAEUL, SUMUNTALA, SUMENNA, SENGKILI, MALANTAN, LAILAI, NAVANG, and TINGHOEUL. Of these the first four are almost certainly Indian. Maabar[1], (Dwara) Samundra[2], Sumnath[3], are not difficult to recognize; the fourth, Sengkili, is probably the Shinkali of Abulfeda, the Singuyli of Jordanus, the Cynkali of Marignolli, *i.e.* Cranganor[4]. The rest of the names probably belong to the Archipelago[5].

[1] See *infra*, p. 141; II, 67, etc.

[2] The kingdom of the Bilal Rajas immediately north of Ma'bar, and constantly coupled with it in the Mahomedan histories.

[3] See *Marco Polo*, pt. III, ch. 32.

[4] See *infra*, p. 133; II, 249.

[5] Thus Malantan, Navang, Tinghoeul may be compared with the names of the actual Malay states or provinces of Kelantan, Pa hang, and Sungora. Pauthier introduces the list (which he gives as Siumenna,Senghili, Nanwuli, Malantan, Tingkorh, Maparh, and Sumuntala) as that of "ten maritime kingdoms of the Indian Archipelago," but that is merely an opinion of his own. It is possible, certainly, that Sumuntala may represent Sumatra, as it appears to do in passages quoted from Chinese geographies by M. Pauthier. Some of these, indeed, appear to be derived from European sources; others do refer to the Chinese Annals as far back as the tenth century, and if these can be depended on as showing that the island or a kingdom on it was called Sumatra at so early a date, the circumstance is remarkable. In the absence of more distinct evidence, I should doubt if the name is so old. The Malay traditions, quoted by Dulaurier, ascribe the foundation of the city called Sumatra to the father of the king reigning in Ibn Batuta's time.

The list of names in the text is from Gaubil (see G., *Hist. de Gentchiscan*, p. 205; Pauthier's *Polo*, p. 572; also Baldelli Boni's *Il Milione*, ii, 388).

I may observe that in an old Chino-Japanese map described

IV. INTERCOURSE WITH THE ARABS.

56. This likewise, in all probability, goes back to an earlier date than is to be learned from any existing history, as the forms in which the name of China reached the Greeks have already suggested to us[1].

The earliest date to which any positive statement of such intercourse appears to refer is the first half of the fifth century of our era. At this time, according to Hamza of Ispahan[2] and Ma'sudi, the Euphrates was navigable as high as Hira[3], a city lying south-west of

by Klaproth and Rémusat, the kingdoms of *Sumenna*, *Kylantin*, *Mapoeul*, and *Tinghoeul*, are placed far to the west beyond the Arabs. (*Not. et Ext.*, vol. xi, and Klap., *Mém.* ii.) This, however, only shows that the author of the map did not know where to put them.

[1] [" Mahomet n'a point ignoré le nom de la Chine, car il recommanda à ses disciples d'acquérir la science, dussent-ils aller la chercher en Chine. Il avait eu quelque notion de ce vaste empire, soit par Selman Farsy ou par les membres des colonies persanes établies sur les côtes de l'Arabie, soit par les gens des ports du Yemen qui étaient en rapports fréquents avec les villes du littoral du golfe Persique où abordaient les navires naviguant dans les mers des Indes, de la Malaisie et du sud de la Chine." Ch. Schefer, *Relat. des Musulmans avec les Chinois*, p. 2.]

[2] [Martin Hartmann says (*Chine* in *Encyclopédie de l'Islam*): " Reinaud ne devrait pas citer, au sujet des navires de Chine à Hīra, Hamza-al-Iṣfahānī, p. 102: il est dit seulement: 'Hira était alors le pays riverain (*sāḥil* n'est pas la bordure littorale) de l'Euphrate; car la mer (lire *al-baḥr* au lieu d'*al-furāt* que Gottwaldt traduisit par inadvertance; cette faute de transcription s'explique par la présence du mot *al-furāt* un peu plus haut) pénétrait alors loin dans les terres (littér. se trouvait plus près de la bordure septentrionale de la plaine côtière babylonienne) et arrivait même jusqu'à Nadjaf.' Cette addition fantaisiste a fait ensuite naître dans la tête de Richthofen le beau tableau suivant (*China*, i, 520): 'Suivant le témoignage de Masudi et de Hamza d'Ispahan, les navires chinois venaient chaque année (!) jeter l'ancre à côté des navires hindous devant les maisons de Hīra.' "]

[3] [" Less than a league south of Kûfah are the ruins of Ḥîrah, which had been a great city under the Sassanians. Near by stood the famous palaces of As-Sadîr and Al-Khawarnaḳ, the latter built, according to tradition, by Nu'mân, prince of Ḥîrah, for King Bahrâm Gûr, the great hunter. The palace of Khawarnaḳ with its magnificent halls had mightily astonished the early Moslems when they first took possession of Ḥîrah on the conquest of Mesopotamia." (G. Le Strange, *Lands of the Eastern Caliphate*, p. 75.)]

ancient Babylon, near Kufa[1], (now at a long distance from the actual channel of the river), and the ships of India and China were constantly to be seen moored before the houses of the town[2]. Hira was then abounding in wealth, and the country round, now a howling wilderness, was full of that life and prosperity which water bestows in such a climate. A gradual recession took place in the position of the headquarters of Indian and Chinese trade. From Hira it descended to Obolla[3], the ancient Apologos, from Obolla it was transferred to the neighbouring city of Basra, built by the Khalif Omar on the first conquest of Irak (636), from Basra to Siraf[4] on the northern shore

[1] [" The city of Al-Kûfah was founded immediately after the Moslem conquest of Mesopotamia, at the same time as Baṣrah was being built, namely, about the year 17 (638), in the Caliphate of 'Omar. It was intended to serve as a permanent camp on the Arab, or desert side of the Euphrates, and occupied an extensive plain lying above the river bank, being close to the older Persian city of Al-Ḥîrah. Kûfah rapidly increased in population, and when in the year 36 (657) 'Alî came to reside here the city during four years was the capital of that half of Islam which recognised 'Ali as Caliph. In the mosque at Kûfah 'Ali was assassinated in the year 40 (661)." (G. Le Strange, *Lands of the Eastern Caliphate*, p. 75.)]

[2] Reinaud, *Relations*, etc., I, xxxv; Tennent's *Ceylon*, i, 541; Mas'ūdī in *Prairies d'Or*, i, 216 *seqq*. The passage in Mas'udi, as translated by Barbier de Meynard and Pavet de Courteille, is not so precise in its evidence as I should have gathered from Reinaud and Tennent. I have not access to Hamza. [Yule in a note says: " The facts stated in Sir H. Rawlinson's paper in vol. xxvii of the *J.R.G.S.*, p. 185, seem to throw very great doubt upon the allegation that Hira could have been a haven for eastern trade at the time indicated, if *ever* it was so."]

" Hira was the seat of a race of kings who had embraced the Christian religion, and reigned above six hundred years under the shadow of Persia " (Gibbon, ch. li).

[3] [Al-Ubullah=Apologos, " dated from Sassanian or even earlier times, but it lay on the estuary and was feverish, and the Moslems when they founded their new city, Baṣrah, built this further inland near the desert border." (G. Le Strange, *Lands of the Eastern Caliphate*, p. 47.)]

[4] [" Further up the coast, to the north-west of Nâband, was the port of Sirâf, the chief emporium of the Persian Gulf in the 4th (10th) century, prior to the rise of Ḳays island into pre-eminence. Sirâf, Iṣtakhrî says, nearly equalled Shîrâz in size and splendour; the houses were built of teak wood brought

of the gulf, and from Siraf successively to Kish[1] and Hormuz[2].

from the Zanj country (now Zanzibar), and were several storeys high, built to overlook the sea." (G. Le Strange, *Lands of the Eastern Caliphate*, p. 258.)]

[" Aujourd'hui cette ville [Killah] est le rendez-vous général des vaisseaux musulmans de Siraf et d'Oman, qui s'y recontrent avec les bâtiments de la Chine; mais il n'en était pas ainsi autrefois. Les navires de la Chine se rendaient alors dans le pays d'Oman, à Siraf, sur la côte de Perse et du Bahrein, à Obollah et à Basrah, et ceux de ces pays naviguaient à leur tour directement vers la Chine. Ce n'est que depuis qu'on ne peut plus compter sur la justice des gouvernants et sur la doctrine de leurs intentions, et que l'état de la Chine est devenu tel que nous l'avons décrit, qu'on se rencontre sur ce point intermédiaire." Mas'ūdī, i, p. 308.]

[1] [" The country of Ki-shï [Island of Kish] is on a small island in the sea, in sight of the Ta-shï (coast), which is distant from it a half day's journey. There are very few towns (in this region....Every year the Ta-shï send camels loaded with rose-water, gardenia flowers, quicksilver, spelter, silver bullion, cinnabar, red dye plants, and fine cotton stuffs, which they put on board ships on arriving in this country to barter with other countries." (Chau Ju-kua, pp. 133-4.)

" The island of Ḳays, or as the Persians wrote the name, Kîsh, which in the course of the 6th (12th century) became the trade-centre of the Persian Gulf after the ruin of Sîrâf." (G. Le Strange, *Lands of the Eastern Caliphate*, p. 257.)]

[2] [" Old Hurmuz, or Hurmuz of the mainland, lay at a distance of two post-stages, or half a day's march from the coast, at the head of a creek called Al-Jîr, according to Iṣṭakhrî, 'by which after one league ships come up thereto from the sea,' and the ruins of the town are still to be seen at the place now known as Minâb, vulgarly Minao. In the 4th (10th century) Old Hurmuz was already the seaport for Kirmân and Sijistân, and in later times, when New Hurmuz had been built on the island, this place supplanted Ḳays, just as Ḳays had previously supplanted Sîrâf, and became the chief emporium of the Persian Gulf....At the beginning of the 8th (14th) century—one authority gives the year 715 (1315)—the king of Hurmuz, because of the constant incursions of robber tribes, abandoned the city on the mainland, and founded New Hurmuz on the island aforesaid called Jîrun (or Zarûn), which lay one league distant from the shore. (Le Strange, *l.c.*, pp. 318–319.) In one of the itineraries of Kia Tan (between A.D. 785 and 805) we read: 'Now the Fu-li-la river of the realm of the Ta-shï flows southward into the sea. Small boats ascend it two days and reach the country of Mo-lo, an important market of the Ta-shï.' Rockhill says: 'Molo I am disposed to identify with old Hurmuz,' and adds: 'Assuming that the identification of Mo-lo with Hormuz is correct, it is interesting to note that this is the only reference in Chinese works to this great port of the Persian Gulf. This is another proof that the Chinese cannot have taken any personal part in the sea trade

57. Chinese Annals of the T'ang dynasty [618–907] of the seventh and eighth centuries, describe the course followed by their junks in voyaging to the Euphrates from Kwang chau (Canton). After indicating the route and the times occupied as far as Ceylon[1], we are told that they passed in front of MOLAI (Malé of Cosmas, Malabar), after which they coasted ten small kingdoms towards the north-west, and after two days' sail to the north-west across sea (Gulf of Cambay) they reached TIYU (probably Diu). Ten days' further voyage carried them past five small kingdoms to another TIYU, near the Great River MILAN or SINTEU[2]. In twenty days more they came to the frontiers of another country, where there was a great lighthouse in the sea[3]; one day more brought them to Siraf, and thence they reached the mouth of the Euphrates.

with Persia in the eighth century, as Geo. Phillips (*J.R.A.S.*, 1895, 525) thinks they did.'" (Chau Ju-kua, p. 14 *n.*)]

[1] All which, strange to say, is omitted by Deguignes, from whom this is quoted (*Mém. de l'Acad. des Insc.*, xxxii, 367). The passage does not seem to have been reproduced by later Chinese scholars. It also speaks, as may be gathered from Deguignes in another essay, of the different places in Asia whither the goods taken to the Gulf were carried for sale, and indicates places of commerce on the coast of Africa. (*Mém.*, as above, xlvi, 547.)

[2] The *Milán* or *Sinteu* is the *Sindhu* or *Indus*, called by the Arabs *Mehrán*. *Tiyu* is probably, as suggested by Deguignes, the port of Diul, Dewal, or DAIBUL, which lay to the west of the Indus mouths and cannot have been far from Karáchi. Edrisi speaks of it specifically as frequented by Chinese ships. Daibul was besieged and taken by the Mahomedans before the end of the seventh century. The district at the mouths of the Indus appears to have retained the name long after the decay of the port, for Barbosa calls this territory *Diul* (Jaubert's *Edrisi*, i, 161; Gildemeister, p. 170, but the reading of Ibn Haukal here which places Daibul on the *east* of the Indus appears to be erroneous; *Barbosa* (Lisbon ed.), p. 266; Reinaud in *Mém. de l'Acad.*, xvii, p. 170).

[3] Probably at the Straits of Hormuz. I do not find any light there mentioned, but Mas'ūdī mentions that at the terminus of this voyage at the entrance of the roadstead near Obollah and Abadan (*i.e.*, off the mouth of Euphrates) there were three great platforms on which beacons were lighted every night to guide ships coming in. (*Prairies d'Or*, i, 230.)

The ships of China, according to some authorities, used to visit Aden as well as the mouths of Indus and Euphrates[1]. I do not think that either Polo or any traveller of his age speaks of them as going further than Malabar, the ports of which appear to have become the *entrepôts* for commercial exchange between China and the west, nor does it appear what led to this change. Some time in the fifteenth century again they seem to have ceased to come to Malabar, nor can it be positively gathered from Abd-ul-Razzak or Conti whether Chinese vessels continued to frequent that coast in their time (*circa* 1430–42)[2]. We read, however, that Ch'eng Tsu of the Ming dynasty (1402–24) despatched vessels to the islands and countries of India, Bengal, Calicut, Ceylon, Surat, the

[1] See *Ibn el Wardī*, in *Not. et Extraits*, ii, 43. Edrisi says that, from Aden ships sailed for Hind, Sind, and China (i, 51). He gives a list of the wares brought from China by these ships, but except iron, sword-blades (perhaps Japanese), shagreen, rich stuffs and velvets, and various vegetable tissues, the articles rather belong to the Archipelago.

["In the nineteenth year of Yong-lo (1422), an Imperial envoy, the eunuch Li, was sent from China to this country [Aden] with a letter and presents to the king. On his arrival he was most honourably received, and was met by the king on landing and conducted by him to his palace. During the stay of the embassy the people who had rarities were permitted to offer them for sale. Cat's eyes of extraordinary size, rubies, and other precious stones, large branches of coral, amber, and attar of roses were among the articles purchased. Giraffes, lions, zebras, leopards, ostriches, and white pigeons were also offered for sale." (Mahuan's *Account of Aden*. Geo. Phillips, *Journ. R. As. Soc.*, 1896, p. 348.)—"It is stated in the History of the Ming, that the first embassy from Aden to China was sent in 1427 and that they subsequently were often repeated." (Bretschneider, *Arabs*, p. 18.) In the same year, 1427, an envoy arrived at the Chinese court from Mu ku tu su [Magadoxo, on the east coast of Africa. (*Ibid.* p. 21.) Chu pu which lies not far from Magadoxo sent also an envoy to China during Yong-lo's reign. (*Ibid.*, p. 22.)]

Baroch is also mentioned as a port visited by ships of China (Edrisi, i, 179); and Suhár in Oman (the Soer of Polo), as a port from which Arab vessels traded to China (*Id.*, i, 152).

[2] Abdul Razzāk, however, does mention merchants and maritime people of China among those who frequented Hormuz in his time (1442). He does not distinctly say that ships of that country came, and the passage is perhaps too general to build upon. (*Ind. in XV Cent.*, p. 56.)

Persian Gulf, Aden, and the Red Sea, expeditions to which reference has been made in a previous page, and which do not seem to have been in any degree commercial. This, however, is the last notice with which I am acquainted of Chinese vessels visiting Malabar and Western Asia[1].

57 *b*. [The Arabs were known by the Chinese as the *Tazi* or *Ta shi* (*Ta shi* is but a transcription of the Persian *Tazi* تازی or *Tajik* تاجیك ; the Arabs were then made known to the Chinese by the Persians ; this fact seems to prove the priority of the travels of the Persians. Cf. Ferrand, *Textes*, pp. 2–3) ; from the Sung Dynasty (960–1279), when no less than twenty embassies from the Ta shi are reckoned, the Mohamedans are known as the *Hwei Hwei*, also *Hwei Ho* or *Hwei Hu*, the very names given to the Uighúrs during the T'ang dynasty. We do not know the exact date of the entrance of the Mohamedans into China: there is an inscription in the mosque of Si-ngan fu dated 742 from which it appears that the doctrine of Mahomet penetrated into China during the period K'ai hwang (581–600), Sui dynasty; the date of Hegira being 622, it is difficult to believe that Islam was known in China some years previously ; the inscription is no doubt apocryphal[2]. For a long time the inscription of the mosque (*Hwei Sheng sze*) of Canton (1st day 8th month 10th year *Che cheng*=2 Nov. 1350) was considered as the most ancient in China, but the inscription of the mosque of *Ts'iuan chau* (1310–11)[3] is older. Now a Sino-Arabic document has been found in Japan whither it was sent from *Ts'iuan chau* in 1217 by a Japanese bonze; this is so far the oldest known Arabic document found in China[4].]

[1] Deguignes, i, 72.
[2] H. Cordier, *Journal des Savants*, Jan. 1913, p. 31.
[3] Arnáiz and Van Berchem. (*T'oung pao*, VII, 1896.)
[4] Pelliot in *J. Asiat.*, Juillet–Août 1913, pp. 177 *seq.*

58. The Arabs at an early date of Islam, if not before[1], had established a factory at Canton, and their numbers at that port were so great by the middle of the eighth century that in 758 they were strong enough to attack and pillage the city, to which they set fire and then fled to their ships[2]. Nor were they confined to this port. The city now called Hang chau fu, the Quinsai and Khansa of the middle ages, but known in those days to the Arabs as KHANFU[3], was probably already frequented by them; for, one hundred and twenty years later, the number of foreign settlers, Musulman, Jew, Christian, and Gueber, who perished on the capture of that city by a rebel army, is estimated at one hundred and twenty

[1] ["In the year 651 A.D. the king of the Ta-shi, by name *Han mi mo mo ni* [Emir al mumenin], sent for the first time an envoy with presents to the Chinese court, and at the same time announced in a letter, that the house Ta-shi had already reigned thirty-four years and had three kings." (From the History of the T'ang, Bretschneider, *Arabs*, p. 8.)]

[2] Deguignes, i, 59, ii, 503; also in *Mém. de l'Acad.*, xlvi, 545. In the latter essay, Deguignes attributes this outbreak to the Arab auxiliaries mentioned further on.

["The history of the T'ang states finally, that in the year 758 the Po ssu, following on the path of the Ta shi (Arabians), invaded unexpectedly *Kuang chow* (Canton), destroyed the town by fire, and returned to their country by sea. This appears to me to be the last time that the Persians are mentioned under the name of *Po ssu* in Chinese history." (Bretschneider, *Notes and Queries on C. and J.*, iv, p. 57.)]

[3] *Khanfu* was properly only the port of Hang chau or Khansa, called by the Chinese KAN P'HU (a name still preserved as that of a town half a league north of the old site), and by Marco Polo *Ganfu* (ii, 189). The place is mentioned as a coasting port in Chinese Annals under A.D. 306; as the seat of a master attendant in 706; and as that of a marine court under the Mongols. (Klap., *Mém. rel. à l'Asie*, ii, 200 *seqq.*). The name of the port seems to have been transferred by the early Arabs to Hang chau; for there seems no reason to ascribe to Kan p'hu itself the importance here assigned to *Khanfu*. Indeed, Abulfeda says expressly, "*Khanfu*, which is known in our days as Khansa." [Pelliot proposes to see in Khanfu a transcription of Kwang-fu, an abridgement of Kwang chau fu, prefecture of Kwang chau (Canton). Cf. *Bull. Ecole franc. Ext. Orient.*, Jan.–June 1904, p. 215 *n.*, but I cannot very well accept this theory. See *Marco Polo*, ii, 199.]

thousand, and even two hundred thousand[1]! Of course we must make large deductions, but these contemporary statements still indicate a large foreign population.

59. In the eighth century also the Arabs began to know the Chinese not only as *Sinæ*, but as *Seres*, *i.e.* by the northern land route. The successes of Kutaiba, who in the time of Khalif Walid overran Bokhara, Samarkand, Farghânah, and Khwarizm, and even extended his conquests across the Bolor to Kashgar, brought the two powers into dangerous collision[2]; and the Emperor of China seems to have saved himself from an Arab invasion, only by the very favourable reception which he gave to an embassy from Kutaiba, composed of twelve Mahomedans, whom he sent back loaded with presents for the Arab general[3].

This was no doubt the embassy to the Emperor Hwen Tsung (*circa* 713), of which the Chinese annals relate that the envoys demanded exemption from the *kotow*, and in consequence were put upon their trial and pronounced worthy of death. The emperor, however, graciously pardoned them[4]!

[1] Reinaud, *Relations*, etc., i, p. 64; Mas'ūdī, *Prairies d'Or*, i, 304.

[2] Hajáj, the Viceroy of Irak, sent messages to Kutaiba and to Mahomed Ibn Kassim in Sind, urging both to press forward to the conquest of China, and promising that the first to reach it should be invested with the government. This induced Kutaiba to advance to Kashgar, and Mahomed to press towards Kanauj. But the death of their patron and of the Khalif put an end to their schemes and brought destruction upon both. (Reinaud in *Mém. de l'Acad.*, xvii, 186).

[3] De Sacy in *Not. et Extraits*, ii, 374–5.

[4] Rémusat, *Mélanges Asiat.*, i, 441–2. ["In 713 A.D. an Envoy appeared from the Ta shi, bringing as presents beautiful horses and a magnificent girdle. When the Envoy was presented to the Emperor, he refused to perform the prescribed obeisance, saying: 'In my country we only bow to God never to a Prince.' At first they wanted to kill the Envoy: one of the ministers however interceded for him, saying that a difference in the court etiquette of foreign countries ought not to be considered a crime.

"In the year 726 A.D. an Envoy, by name *Su li p'u*, came from

The emperors seemed to have entertained a correcter apprehension of the character of the new enemy than their successors have exhibited in later days when coming in contact with European nations, and consequently they were very cautious in their answers to the many applications that were made to them for aid against the irresistible Arabs. Yet collisions were not entirely avoided. Indeed according to one Mahomedan historian[1] the end of the year 87 of Hegira (A.D. 709) had already witnessed the glorious defeat of two hundred thousand Tartars who had broken into the Mahomedan conquests under the command of *Taghabun*, the Chinese Emperor's nephew. And at a later date, about 751, we find the Chinese troops under their general Kao Sien-chi engaging those of the Khalif near Taraz or Talas and entirely routed[2]. A few years afterwards (757–8), when the Emperor Su Tsung was hard pressed by a powerful rebel, he received an embassy from the Khalif Abu Jafar al Mansúr, accompanied by auxiliary troops. But even these ministers of timely aid are related in the Chinese annals to have been compelled to perform the *kotow* in spite of their strong remonstrances. Uighúr and other western troops also joined the emperor's standard, and the rebel was completely defeated in the immediate neighbourhood of Si-ngan fu [A.D. 757]. These auxiliaries seem to have been found very unmanageable; the eastern capital, Lo yang, was pillaged by them, and, as we have seen, one account ascribes to them, on their

Ta shi to the court. He made the required obeisance before the Emperor and received a purple robe and a girdle as presents." From the History of the T'ang; Bretschneider, *Arabs*, p. 8.] So in turn ten Chinese envoys are said to have been murdered at the Burmese court in 1286, because they insisted on appearing in the royal presence with their boots on. (*Mission to Ava*, p. 79.)

[1] Tabari, quoted in *Ch. Anc.*, p. 310.

[2] *Ib.*, 311; Deguignes, i, 58. [Kao Sien-chi was routed by the Arabs (*Ta shi*) allied to the Karluk near Talas in the 9th year *t'ien-pao* (750). See Chavannes, *Tou-Kiue*, p. 142.]

way to embark for the west, the sack of Canton which occurred at this time[1].

Mention has been made in a preceding page how about 787 the emperor applied to the khalif to join in a league against the Tibetans. Some years later (798) the celebrated Khalif Harún Al Rashíd sent three ambassadors to the Court of China, and it is recorded of them that they performed, apparently without remonstrance, the ceremonies to which the former Arab envoys, like ours in modern times, had so strongly objected[2].

An embassy from the khalif is said to have also reached the Chinese Court in 974, and another to have visited the Northern Sung in 1011[3].

V. INTERCOURSE WITH ARMENIA AND PERSIA, ETC.

60. Besides that communication by land and sea with Arabia, and with the various states of India, of which illustrations have been given, there existed from an old date other and obscurer streams of intercourse between China and Western Asia, of which we have but fragmentary notices, but which seem to indicate a somewhat fuller mutual knowledge and freer communication than most persons probably have been prepared to recognise.

[1] See *Mém. de l'Acad.* (old), xvi, p. 254, and *supra*, p. 89. ["*A po lo pa* [Ab'ul Abbas, 750–754, the first Khalif Abbasid] was chosen king and his territories were henceforward called *Hei yi Ta shi*, or black coated Ta shi. After his death his brother *A p'u ch'a fo* [Abu Jafar, 754–775] ascended the throne. In the year 756 the king sent an Embassy to China. The Emperor retook, with the help of his (the caliph's) army, both capitals of China." From the History of the T'ang. Bretschneider, *Arabs*, p. 9.]

[2] Rémusat, *u.s.*

[3] Deguignes, in *Acad.*, xlvi, 544; *H. des Huns*, i, 66, *seqq.* ["The History of the Sung dynasty, 960–1280, has a long article on the Ta shi (Arabs), yet I have found but little of interest in it. Mention is made of twenty Embassies from the Ta shi having come to China in ships during this past period. But it seems that most of them bore no official character and have to be reduced to mercantile expeditions." Bretschneider, *Arabs*, p. 11.]

Thus, China appears to have been well known from an early period to the Armenians. Moses of Chorene, who wrote a little after A.D. 440, and who probably drew from earlier authors, speaks of JENASDAN (*i.e. Chinistàn* or China) as a great plain country, east of Scythia, at the extremity of the known world, and occupied by a wealthy and civilised people of character so eminently pacific as to deserve to be called not merely *friends of peace* but *friends of life*. Their country furnished an abundance of silk, insomuch that silk dresses, so rare and costly in Armenia, were there common to all classes. It also produced musk, saffron, and cotton. Peacocks were found there. Twenty-nine nations were comprised within its bounds; and not all of equal civilisation, for one was addicted to cannibalism[1]. The king, whose title was *Jenpagur*, had his residence in the city of *Siurhia* towards the Terra Incognita. The country of the *Sinae* adjoined Jenasdan and embraced seven nations; it contained many rivers and mountains, and extended likewise to the Unknown Land[2]. According to the same historian, in the reign of Tigranes VI (A.D. 142–178) several bodies of foreign settlers, and amongst others Chinese, were placed in Gordyene or Kurdish Armenia, for the defence of the country[3].

[1] Compare Ptolemy, vi, 16; and *Marco Polo*, ii, 225, 228 *n*.

[2] St. Martin, *Mém. sur l'Arménie*, ii, 22, 23, 377. The *Jenasdan* of Moses of Chorene is perhaps the Empire of the Wei dynasty which ruled in Northern China with varying power from the fourth to the sixth century, and whose authority in Tartary was very extensive. Their capitals were various; *Lo yang* was one of them. I do not know if this could be identified with Siurhia; but it may be observed that in the Syriac of the Si-ngan fu inscription Lo yang is supposed to be meant by *Saragh*. The *Sinae* would perhaps represent the Tsin reigning at Nan king. [Yule adds: "Some clue to the origin of this name [Siurhia] may perhaps lie in the circumstance that the Mongol Ssanang Ssetzen appears to give Daitu or Peking, as the capital of the Great Khan, the appellation of *Siro-Khaghan*. The meaning of the title is not explained by Schmidt. (See his work, p. 127.)"]

[3] St. Martin, ii, 47.

To more than one great Armenian family a Chinese descent was attributed. One of these families was that of the Orpelians, which in Georgia was known by the name of *Jenpakuriani* from their supposed ancestor the Jen-pakur or Emperor of China[1]. Another family was that of the Mamigonians, one which plays an important part in Armenian history. Their story is told by Moses of Chorene, who refers their establishment in Armenia to a date two hundred years before his own time, and therefore to the first half of the third century. He relates that, in the latter days of Ardeshir, the founder of the Sassanian dynasty (who died in 240), a certain Arpog was King of China, one of whose sons, Mamkon by name, fled from home on account of a charge brought against him, and took refuge in Persia. The Chinese threatening war on account of the shelter afforded him, he was obliged to retire to Armenia, where he was received by the King Tiridates, who eventually bestowed the province of Daron upon him and his Chinese followers. From this Mamkon came the family of the Mamigonians, whose Chinese descent is spoken of by all the Armenian historians[2].

About the same time we find it stated that the Emperor of China offered to mediate between Ardeshir, King of Persia, and Khosru I of Armenia; whilst Suren, a brother of St. Gregory of Armenia, is represented as taking refuge in China. All these circumstances imply some familiarity of relation. The authority quoted for them is Zenob, a

[1] St. Martin says that *Pakur* is the Faghfur of the Mahomedan writers, the generic name applied to the Emperors of China. See note under § 85, *infra*.

I notice, however, that *Pakor* forms a part of the name or title of many of the Georgian kings in Deguignes's list.

[2] There appears to be some chronological hitch in this account; for Tiridates, who was carried off as an infant to the Romans, was not established on the throne till the beginning of Diocletian's reign (284), forty-four years after the death of Ardashir. (Smith's *Dict. of Greek and Rom. Biog.*)

Syrian, who wrote in Armenian in the beginning of the fourth century. And he says that they were derived from a history of China written in Greek by one Parta or Barta of Edessa[1].

61. The offer at mediation between Persia and Armenia just referred to is apparently unknown to the Chinese Annals. Their first notice of Persia[2] is the record of an embassy to the court of the Wei in 461; succeeded by a second in 466[3]. In the year 518–519 an ambassador came from *Kiuhoto* (Kobád), king of that country, with presents and a letter to the emperor. The Chinese annalists profess to give the literal terms of the letter, which uses a tone of improbable humility[4].

In the reign of Naoshirwan, the celebrated son of Kobád, an embassy came to the Persian court from the Emperor of China, bringing splendid presents. Among these are mentioned a panther formed of pearls with eyes of rubies; a silk robe of ultramarine blue of extraordinary splendour on which was represented in gold the Persian monarch with his courtiers round him; and a golden box to contain this robe and also a female figure, whose face was veiled with her long hair, through

[1] St. Martin, 29.

[2] ["The country *Po ssu* is mentioned for the first time in Chinese Annals in 519 A.D., when the king of *Po ssu* sent an Embassy with presents to the court of the Northern Wei (386–558). The sending of such embassies was often repeated. The Sui dynasty (589–618) received also embassies from *Po ssu*, and during the reign of the emperor Yang Ti (605–617) a Chinese Envoy was sent to *Po ssu*." (Bretschneider, *Notes and Queries on China and Japan*, iv, p. 54.)]

[3] Deguignes, i, 184. [See above in Communication with Central Asia, p. 59.]

[4] "To the Son of Heaven, the Sovereign of the Great Realm, whom Heaven hath caused to exist and hath placed at the sunrising to reign eternally over the empire of the Han; the King of Persia, Kobád, presents his respectful homage a thousand and ten thousand times and prays his Imperial Majesty to accept it." (Pauthier, *De l'Auth.*, p. 60.)

which her beauty shone like a ray of light through the darkness[1].

In the same reign (567) is mentioned that the King of Persia sent an embassy to Wu Ti, Emperor of the Chau dynasty, perhaps to engage his aid against the Turks who had then become formidable upon the Bactrian frontiers, as we see in the extracts from Menander, in Note VIII[2].

In 638, Yezdijerd III, the last of the Sassanid kings, when hard pressed in the uttermost corners of his dominions by the Saracens, sent an envoy to seek help from the Emperor of China, now the great and powerful T'ai Tsung. The Persian prince, obliged to retire into Turkestan [after his defeat at Nehāwend (642)], met in Sogdiana his messenger returning with T'ai Tsung's refusal of assistance. This embassy is mentioned both by Chinese and Arabian historians; by the former the unfortunate king is styled *Yisséssé*[3]. The son of this king, called by the Chinese Pi lou ssé, *i.e.*, Perozes or Firúz, established himself in Tokharistan, apparently under some subordination to the Chinese Government. In 661 he reported to China that the Arabs were again pressing him hard, and some years later (670–673) he took refuge at the Chinese court, where he received a high nominal command, [built a Mazdean

[1] Malcolm's *History of Persia*, i, 144–5; Ma'sūdī, *Prairies d'Or*, ii, 201. In the latter's version the long-haired beauty is not a picture, but a living damsel who carried the casket.

[2] Deguignes, ii, 385.

[3] Rémusat, *L'Acad.*, viii, p. 103; St. Martin, ii, 19; Klap., *Tab. Hist.*, p. 208; Pauth., *De l'Auth.*, pp. 17, 61. The reply of the Chinese Emperor is thus represented by the Arab historian, Tabari: "It is just that kings should help one another; but I have gathered from your own ambassadors what manner of men are these Arabs, what their habits, their religion, and the character of their leaders. People who have such a faith and such leaders will carry all before them. Try, then, to make the best of things by gaining their good graces." (*Not. et Extraits*, ii, 365.)

temple in 677, at Ch'ang ngan], and died soon after[1]. After his death, his son, called by the Chinese *Ni ni ssé* or *Ni nici ssé* (Narses ?), took the oath of allegiance to the emperor. In 679 a Chinese general, with a body of troops, was ordered to escort this prince to his paternal dominions; but the general seems to have descried serious obstacles to the completion of this duty; for he turned back from the frontier near Taraz "because of the length of the way and the fatigue of the journey," as the Chinese annalist quaintly puts it. The prince betook himself to Tokharistan where he was hospitably received; but, whatever efforts he may have made to recover his throne, he found them fruitless at last; for, in 707 we find him again presenting himself at the Chinese court, where, like his father, he was consoled with a sounding military title, and did not long survive. But here we must look back a little[2].

[1] *Firuz*, as the name of a son of Yezdijerd, the last Sassanid king, is mentioned by Mas'udi, *Prairies d'Or*, ii, 241. [Yezdijerd III died in 651 at Marv.]

[2] ["The following historical facts with regard to Po ssu are stated in the history of the T'ang.

"Towards the end of the reign of the Sui dynasty (589–618), the Khan of T'u K'üe devastated the kingdom of Po ssu and killed the king K'u sa ho. His son Shi li was appointed as successor by the victors, who gave him a Vice-regent as assistant. Later, the daughter of K'u sa ho was murdered. After the death of Shi li, his son Tan ko fang was forced to take refuge in Fo lin, but was subsequently recalled. His nephew *Yi t'su ssu* became king after the death of Tan ko fang. This king sent, in the year 638, an Envoy, *Mo ssu pan*, with presents to the Chinese Court. Yi ts'u ssu was dethroned on account of several crimes,—he fled to Tokharestan—but was slain on the road by the Ta shi (Arabs). His son *Pi lu ssu* came to Tokharestan and sent off an Envoy to the Emperor Kao Tsung (650–684) to ask for assistance to redress his wrongs. The Emperor declined all interference, saying that Po ssu was a country situated too far from his own. In the year 661 he again implored the Emperor and complained especially against the Arabians. The Emperor at last sent an Official to Po ssu and created a seat of Government in the town of *Tsi ling*, at the head of which Pi lu ssu was appointed. On the death of Pi lu ssu the Emperor was desirous to enthrone *Ni nie shi* (son of Pi lu ssu) as king of Po ssu, but the Chinese armies, which were to uphold him, did not reach Po ssu and were obliged to return. Ni nie shi lived for 20 years as a guest with the king of Tokharestan. In the year 707 he came again to the court of China, where he

62. In the days of Yang Ti of the Sui dynasty (605–617) China had begun to regain that influence over the states of Central Asia which it had enjoyed in the great days of the Han, preceding and following the Christian era, and under T'ai Tsung of the T'ang (627–650) that influence was fully re-established and the frontiers of the empire were again carried to the Bolor and even beyond it to the borders of Persia. In these remoter provinces the actual administration remained in the hands of the native princes who acknowledged themselves the vassals of the emperor. But from him they accepted investiture, Chinese seals of office, and decorations as lieges of the empire. Their states were divided after the Chinese manner into departments, districts, and cantons (*fu*, *chau*, and *hien*), each of which received a Chinese name by which it was entered in the imperial registers; whilst Chinese camps were scattered over the whole territory. The tributary states west of the Bolor formed sixteen *fu* and seventy-two *chau*, over which were distributed a hundred and twenty-six Chinese military posts. The list of the sixteen districts of the first class has been published by Rémusat, and, though doubts attach to the localities of some, enough has been made out to show that this Chinese organisation extended, at least in theory, over Farghânah and the country round Tashkand, over the eastern part at least of Mâ-warâ-n-Nahr, the country on the Oxus from Balkh upwards, Bamian and other districts adjoining the Hindu Kush, with perhaps Sejistan and part of Khorasan[1].

died. There now remained only the Western Branch as rulers. They sent in the beginning of the eighth century ten embassies to the Court of China, which brought as presents valuable carpets, also a throne made of agate." (Bretschneider, *Notes and Queries on China and Japan*, iv, p. 57.)]

[1] Rémusat, *u.s.*, pp. 81 *seqq.* This author considers Kandahar and Kabul to be included in the Chinese distribution of provinces; but see Reinaud, *Mém. sur l'Inde* in *Mém. Acad.*, xvii, 167–8.

One of the Chinese *Fús* is termed *Pussé*; *i.e.*, "Persia,"

The states of Turkestan and Khorasan were probably desirous to place themselves under Chinese protection in the vain hope of finding it a bulwark against the Saracen flood, and may themselves have originated this action of the Chinese Government. Besides the states which were thus organised on a Chinese model, others occupying a wider circle sent occasional embassies of compliment which the Chinese represent as bearing tribute, and among these are found the Khans of Khwarizm and the Khazars. The kings of Samarkand for several generations are alleged to have received investiture from China, but it does not appear that their territory was organised in the Chinese fashion.

The orders for that organisation were issued in 661, and it must remain very doubtful how far they were

which should be at least on the borders of that country. The chief city of this department was called *Tsi ling*. Now, it seems not improbable that this department of *Persia* was really part of SEJISTAN, the chief city of which in early Mahomedan times was called ZARANJ (compare the *Drangiane* and *Zarangiane* of the Greeks), a name which might be well represented by the Chinese *Tsi ling*. This is the more probable, as near Zaranj stood the ancient city of *Fars* (Farrah ?), the traditional capital of Rustum, which might suggest the Persia or Pussé of the Chinese (see Edrisi, i, 445). M. Pauthier suggests *Shiraz* as the identification of Tsi ling. But it would have been a bold step surely in 661 to name Shiraz as the seat of a Chinese Government (see *De l'Auth.*, p. 61). ["H. Yule, dans son *Cathay*, t. i, p. lxxxvii, identifie Tsi-ling à Zaranj, ville près de laquelle se trouve l'ancienne cité de Fars (Farrah), la capitale traditionnelle de Roustoum, qui pourrait expliquer le Pars (P'o sse) des Chinois. Il me parait impossible que l'administration des Chinois ait pénétré aussi loin de leur domaine, qui avait alors pour confins, encore plus fictifs que réels, les quatre places de guerre (Talas, K'outché, Kachgar et Ouch)." Devéria, *Origine de l'Islamisme en Chine*, p. 307 *n*. This argument is not to the point; the Chinese organisation may not have been carried out and still Firúz may have taken a refuge at Zaranj or Tsi ling. The following works on Seistan do not throw any light on the question: *Journal from Bunder Abbass to Mash'ad by Sistan, with some account of the last-named Province*. By Major-General Sir F. J. Goldsmid. (*Proc. R. Geog. Soc.*, xvii, 1872–73, pp. 86–92); *Notes on Seistan*. By Major-General Sir H. C. Rawlinson. (*Journal Roy. Geog. Soc.*, 1873, pp. 272–294, map); *The Frontiers of Baluchistan*. By G. P. Tate, Lond., 1909.]

ever carried out, considering that in that very year, as we have seen, the Sassanian Prince Firúz was beginning to find Tokharestan too hot to hold him. The highest point of this tide of the Chinese power must have been then reached, but several of the states west of the Bolor are represented as continuing to send tribute to China with wonderful persistence for years after the conquests of Kutaiba, and well into the middle of the eighth century[1].

The Chinese Annals represent indeed that some small districts of Persia maintained their independence against the Arabs for a considerable time, and between 713 and 755[2] sent ten separate embassies to the court of China. A prince of Tabaristan is especially mentioned as sending one of these missions; his country is correctly described as surrounded on three sides by mountains and on the north by the Little Sea (the Caspian). The capital was called SARI[3]. In the time of the Kings of Persia this had been the seat of an officer called the Great General of the East. This officer had refused to submit to the Arabs, and in 746 he (or rather a successor) sent envoys to the Emperor of China and received a title of honour. Eight years later he sent his son to China, and the Emperor conferred high military rank upon him. The father perished at the hands of the Arabs.

One more embassy is reported from Persia in 923.

[1] See Rémusat, to p. 102. He says the Chinese power really extended to the Caspian in the latter half of the seventh and first half of the eighth centuries. But how can this be reconciled with the Mahomedan conquests?

[2] [The Chinese priest Kan shin (Kien chen) from Yang chau in 748 mentions the existence of a very large Persian village in the island of Hai-nan. (Takakusu in *Premier Congrès int. des Études d'Ext. Orient*, Hanoi, 1903, p. 58.)]

[3] An old city of Mâzandarân, which is celebrated in the legends of Afrasiab. There are, or were in the last century, still to be seen at Sari four ancient circular temples, each thirty feet in diameter and one hundred and twenty feet high. (Malcolm, i, p. 261.)

The greater part of Persia seems at that time to have been under the Samanid dynasty at Bokhara, with whom intercourse was carried on and a marriage alliance took place some twenty years later, if we can depend on the Arabian traveller Ibn Muhalhil (see § 84).

63. In this part of our subject we may also mention as worthy of note, though without being able to throw any light upon it, the tradition of the Druzes of Syria that China is the land of their forefathers, and the happy country to which good Druzes revert beyond the grave[1].

VI. NESTORIAN CHRISTIANITY IN CHINA.

64. The traditions of the eastern churches take back the preaching of the Gospel in China to a very old date indeed. Not St. Thomas only is asserted to have carried so far his indefatigable missionary journeys[2], for the apostle Bartholomew is related by a Syro-Arabian writer to have gone preaching to India and further China[3].

[1] Mr. Cyril Graham in *Journ. R. Geog. Soc.*, vol. xxvii, pp. 262-3.

[2] The Chaldæan breviary of the Malabar Church in its office of St. Thomas contains this passage :

"By St. Thomas were the errors of idolatry banished from among the Indians;

"By St. Thomas were the CHINESE and the Ethiopians converted to the truth;

"By St. Thomas did they receive the Sacrament of Baptism and the adoption of children;

"By St. Thomas were they brought to believe in the Father, the Son, and the Holy Ghost;

"By St. Thomas when they had gotten the Faith they did maintain it;

"By St. Thomas hath the brightness of the doctrine unto life arisen over all the Indies;

"By St. Thomas hath the Kingdom of Heaven taken unto itself wings and passed even unto CHINA."

And again in an anthem :

"The Hindus and the CHINESE and the Persians, and all the people of the Isles of the Sea, and they who dwell in Syria and Armenia, in Javan and Romania call Thomas to remembrance and adore Thy Name, O Thou our Redeemer." (Assemani, pp. 32, 516.)

[3] Ditto, p. 576.

Apart from these legends, a Christian author of the third century speaks of the Seres with the Persians and Medes as among the nations who had been reached by the power of the Word[1]. On this we cannot build as evidence that Christianity had then extended to China; but that it was in the following century already widely diffused over Mesopotamia and Persia is shown by the number of Bishops and Presbyters who are named as martyrs or otherwise in connexion with the persecutions of Sapor[2]; whilst the existence of an episcopal see at Marv and Tús in 334, raised to metropolitan dignity in 420, shows how early the church had established itself also in Khorasan[3].

65. After the condemnation and banishment [in 431] of Nestorius, his opinions nevertheless spread extensively in Persia and throughout the eastern churches. The separation from Byzantine orthodoxy and influence (formally accomplished about 498) rather recommended

[1] That new power which has arisen from the works wrought by the Lord and his Apostles "has subdued the flame of human passions, and brought into the hearty acceptance of one faith a vast variety of races, and nations the most different in their manners. For we can count up in our reckoning things achieved in India, among the SERES, Persians, and Medes; in Arabia, Egypt, Asia, and Syria; among the Galatians, the Parthians, and the Phrygians; in Achaia, Macedonia, and Epirus; in all the islands and provinces which the rising or the setting sun looks down upon." ["Virtutes sub oculis positae, et inaudita illa vis rerum, vel quae ab ipso fiebat palam, vel ab ejus praeconibus celebrabatur in orbe toto: eas subdidit appetitionum flammas, et ad unius credulitatis assensum mente una concurrere gentes et populos fecit, et moribus dissimillimas nationes. Enumerari enim possunt, atque in usum computationis venire ea, quae in India gesta sunt, apud Seras, Persas, et Medos: in Arabia, Ægypto, in Asia, Syria, apud Galatas, Parthos, Phrygas: in Achaja, Macedonia, Epiro: in insulis et provinciis omnibus, quas sol oriens, atque occidens lustrat..."] (Arnobius, *Adversus Gentes*, in ii, 448, *Max. Biblioth. Patrum*, 1677).

[2] As., pp. 52–3, 415.

[3] Ditto, 477, 479. ["Tûs, in the 4th (10th century), was the second city of the Naysâbûr quarter of Khurâsân." Cf. Le Strange, *Eastern Caliphate*, pp. 388–390. "Great Marv, in the middle ages, was called Marv-ash-Shâhijân, to distinguish it from Marv-ar-Rûd, Little Marv." *Ibid.*, p. 398.]

the Separatists to the Kings of Persia, though their treatment by those princes constantly fluctuated between favour and persecution. And much the same may be said of their condition under the Arabian khalifs. At first they seem to have been treated by the Mahomedans with some amount of good will[1]. They found employment with the khalifs, especially as secretaries and physicians, and in the latter capacity many of them acquired a wide eastern fame. Still they were always liable to be treated with capricious outbursts of severity, and too often the heavy hand of Islam was brought down upon them through their own internal rivalries and factions.

66. Whatever may have been the faults of the churches, there seems to have been a strong missionary spirit among them in the seventh and eighth centuries, as shown both by positive historical statements[2], and by the extension eastward of the metropolitan sees. Such were constituted at Herat, Samarkand, and in CHINA in the first quarter of the eighth century, and no doubt these must have existed as ordinary bishoprics for some time before[3]. Under the patriarchate of Timothy again (778–820) we find the record of the appointment of one David

[1] The Patriarch Jesujabus (650–660) in a letter given by Assemani, deplores a falling away of thousands of Christian people in the province of Marv before the Mahomedan invasion, not from any reason that they had to fear fire or sword, but only to avoid the loss of part of their goods. He testifies in the same letter that the conduct of the *Tayi*, as he calls the Mahomedans (whence, as M. Pauthier has somewhere pointed out, the *Ta shi* of the Chinese, v. *supra*, p. 48), was in general kindly towards the Christians. Assem. iii, Pt. i, pp. 130–1.

[2] *E.g.*, see in Assemani, p. 478.

[3] Indeed some of the Syrian authors ascribe all three metropolitan sees to much earlier dates. A writer quoted by Assemani says: "Heriæ et Samarkandæ et Sinæ Metropolitanos creavit Salibazacha Catholicos [714–728]. Aiunt vero quidam Achæum [411–415] et Silam [503–520] illos constituisse" (p. 522). The fact may be that Herat was constituted a *bishopric* in 411–415, and Samarkand in 503–520. We shall see that the existence of any bishopric in China before 635 is highly improbable.

to be metropolitan of China. In the middle of the ninth century we find the metropolitan of China mentioned along with those of India, Persia, Marv, Syria, Arabia, Herat, and Samarkand, as excused on account of the remoteness of their sees from attending the quadrennial synods of the church, but enjoined to send every six years a report of the state of their affairs, and not to neglect the collections for the support of the patriarchate[1]. There is thus good evidence from the ecclesiastical annals of Western Asia of the existence of the church in China during the eighth and ninth centuries; and the narrative of the Arab Abu Said, in consistence with this, speaks of Christians as forming one part of a very large foreign population at Khanfu in the year 878.

The institution of a *metropolitan* for China about the year 720 involves a presumption that Christianity had penetrated to that country some time before. Deguignes thought it had got thither *very much* earlier, but he seems to have been misled by a theory that some at least of the earlier notices of Buddhism in China alluded to Christianity[2].

67. For these extreme ideas there seems to be no evidence, unless we accept the loose statement of Arnobius about the Seres. Cosmas, in the sixth century, was not aware of the existence of any Christians further east than Taprobane, nor in Inner Asia does he speak of any beyond the Huns and the Bactrians, on the banks of the Indus and the Oxus. But that Christianity in China was nearly a century older than the date of its first metropolitan bishop is established by more than one Chinese record.

[1] Assem., p. 439.

[2] He refers, without the condemnation which it may be supposed to merit, to a medal representing the Virgin and Child united to a Chinese copper coin of A.D. 556, of which he says a cut is given in the *Lettres Édifiantes*, xvi. See Deguignes, i, 50.

The first of these, which would be obscure without the light reflected on it by the second and more important, is an edict issued in 745 by the Emperor Hiuan Tsung of the T'ang, wherein it is declared that the religion of the sacred books known as *Persian* had originally come from Ta Ts'in (the Roman Empire); propagated by preaching and tradition it had made its way to the Middle Kingdom, and had been for a long time practised therein. Temples of this worship had been erected from the first, and had got to be known popularly as Persian temples. But as this title was inaccurate it was by this edict enacted that throughout the empire the name of Persian temples should be thenceforward changed to TA TS'IN TEMPLES[1].

68. The second record is that celebrated monument of Si-ngan fu which has been the subject of so much discussion.

This monument was dug up in the year 1625 during a chance excavation in a suburb[2] of Si-ngan fu, preserving in its name of Ch'ang-ngan that of the city which was for so many ages the capital of successive dynasties. It was a stone slab [about 7½ feet high by 3 feet wide, and some 10 inches in thickness], with a cross carved at the top, [and beneath this are nine large characters in three columns, constituting the heading, which runs: "*Monument commemorating the introduction and propagation of the noble law of* Ta Ts'in *in the Middle Kingdom*"][3], and below that a continuous Chinese inscription of great length [consist-

[1] Pauth., *De l'Auth.*, pp. 79–80.

[2] [This slab *King-kiao-pei* was found in the sub-prefecture of Chau chi, a dependency of Si-ngan fu, among ancient ruins.—Havret, 2nd Pt., p. 71. Pelliot says that the slab was not found at Chau Chi, but in the western suburb of Si-ngan, at the very spot where it was to be seen some years ago, before it was transferred to the *Pei-lin*, in fact at the place where it was erected in the seventh century inside the monastery built by Olopun.—*Chrétiens d'Asie centrale*, *T'oung pao*, 1914.]

[3] *Marco Polo*, ii, p. 27 *n.*

ing of 1789 characters], besides lines of writing in an alphabetic character, which was soon after the discovery ascertained to be Syriac[1].

The contents of this inscription, attesting the ancient propagation of Christianity in China, speedily became known to the Jesuit missionaries; and a Chinese edition of it was published in the country [in 1641, by Father Emmanuel Diaz, *Yang Ma-no*, under the title *T'ang king kiao p'ai sung cheng ts'iuen*; it has been reprinted in 1878 at T'u se wei]. Long before the first date, however, copies or facsimiles had been sent to Europe, and the first attempt at a translation was published by Athanasius Kircher in 1636 [in his *Prodromus Coptus sive Ægyptiacus*, and again in his *China illustrata*].

[1] Extracts regarding the discovery of the monument will be found in Suppl. Note X. [M. Grenard, who reproduces (iii, p.152) a good facsimile of the inscription, gives to the slab the following dimensions: high 2 m. 36, wide cm. 86, thick cm. 25.—Father Havret has given a photolithographic reproduction of the inscription on the original scale, from a rubbing sent in 1894 from Si-ngan fu by Father Gabriel Maurice, in the first part of *La Stèle chrétienne de Si-ngan fou*, Shanghai, 1895. In 1891 a shed was built over the slab but soon disappeared. In 1907 a Danish gentleman, Mr. Frits V. Holm, took a photograph of the tablet as it stood outside the west gate of Si-ngan, south of the road to Kan Su; it was one of five slabs on the same spot; it was removed without the stone pedestal (a tortoise) into the City on the 2nd Oct. 1907, and it is now kept in the museum known as the *Pei-lin* (Forest of Tablets). Holm says it is ten feet high, the weight being two tons; he tried to purchase the original, and failing this he had an exact replica made by Chinese workmen; this replica was deposited in the Metropolitan Museum of Art in the City of New York, as a loan, on the 16th of June 1908. "The original Nestorian Tablet of A.D. 781, as well as my replica, made in 1907," Holm writes, "are both carved from the stone quarries of Fu Ping Hien; the material is a black, sub-granular limestone with small oolites scattered through it." (Frits V. Holm, *The Nestorian Monument*, Chicago, 1909.) In this pamphlet there is a photograph of the tablet as it stands in the Pei-lin.

Prof. Ed. Chavannes, who also visited Si-ngan in 1907, saw the Nestorian monument; in the album of his *Mission archéologique dans la Chine Septentrionale*, Paris, 1909, he has given (plate 445) photographs of the five tablets, the tablet itself, the western gate of the western suburb of Si-ngan, and the entrance of the temple *Kin Sheng Sze*.]

The inscription has since been several times translated[1], and has given rise to a large amount of controversy, sometimes of very acrimonious character. Many scholars have entirely refused to believe in its genuineness. Voltaire, as a matter of course, sneered at it. In our own day Renan (though apparently with some doubts) and Julien have denied its authenticity[2]; so has the German Neumann with singular rashness, roundly accusing the Jesuit Semedo of having forged it[3]. On the other hand, Abel Rémusat and Klaproth fully accepted and stoutly maintained its authenticity, which M. Pauthier seems, as far as I can judge, to have *demonstrated.* It is not easy to see why a Jesuit should have expended enormous labour in forging a testimonial to the ancient successes of a heretical sect; though perhaps one could not build entirely on this, as the mysteries of the hoaxing propensity in the human mind are great. But the utter *impossibility* of the forgery of such a monument at the time and place of its discovery is a more invulnerable argument, and to appreciate this the remarks of Rémusat and Pauthier must be read.

69. The monument exhibits, in addition to the Chinese text which forms its substance, a series of short inscriptions in Syriac, containing the date of erection, the names of the reigning patriarch of the Nestorian Church, of the Bishop of China (*Tzinisthán,* the form used by Cosmas), and of the chief clerical staff of the capital, which is here styled, as in the early Greek and Arabic sources already

[1] Cf. *Bibliotheca Sinica,* col. 772–781.

[2] [Renan in the fourth edition of his *Histoire des Langues sémitiques,* 1863, pp. 288–290, has fully recognized the authenticity of the inscription; so has Stanislas Julien.]

[3] See Pauthier, *De l'Auth.,* pp. 6 *seqq.*; 14 *seqq.*; 83 *seqq.*; and especially 91. [The fullest account of the inscription is to be found in *La Stèle chrétienne de Si-ngan-fou,* par le P. Henri Havret, Shanghai, 1895, 1897, 1902, being Nos. 7, 12, 20 of the Collection *Variétés sinologiques,* edited by the Jesuit Fathers at Zi-ka-wei.]

quoted, *Kúmdán*. To this are added in Syriac characters the names of sixty-seven persons, apparently Western Asiatics, the great majority of whom are characterised as priests (*Kashishá*), with those of sixty-one persons of the country in Chinese, all of whom are styled priests except two[1].

[1] The essential parts of the Syriac matter on the monument run as follows:

"*In the days of the Father of Fathers*, MAR HANAN ISHU'A *the Catholic Patriarch*:

[And] "ADAM *Priest and Bishop and Pope of* TZINISTHAN:

"*In the year one thousand and ninety-two of the Greeks* [A.D. 781] MAR IDBUZID, *Priest and Chorepiscopus of* KUMDAN, *the royal city, son of Milis of blessed memory, Priest of* BALKH, *a city of* THOKARESTHAN, *has erected this table of stone, on which are inscribed the Redemption by our Saviour, and the preachings of our Fathers to the King of* TZINIA:

"ADAM *the Deacon, son of Idbuzid, Chorepiscopus*:

"MAR SARGIS [Sergius], *Priest and Chorepiscopus*:

"SABAR ISHU'A, *Priest*:

"GABRIEL, *Priest, and Archdeacon and Church Ruler of the cities of* KUMDAN *and* SARAGH."

[This is the translation of Father Cheikho, S.J. (Havret, *l.c.*, iii, p. 6).

I. Adam prêtre chorévêque et pape de Chine [Sinestan].

II. Au temps du chef des évêques le seigneur Catholicos, le Patriarche Hananjesu.

III. En l'année 1092 des Grecs, le seigneur Jazedbouzid, prêtre et chorévêque de la capitale du royaume Koumdan, le fils du défunt Milis prêtre originaire de Balkh ville de Tahouristan, a élevé ce monument lapidaire où sont écrites la loi de notre Rédempteur et la prédication de nos Pères près des rois de Chine. [Then follow the names.]]

Anan Jesus II, according to Assemani (III, i, 155–7), was patriarch of the Nestorian Church from 774 to 778. It is justly pointed out by the same author that the fact of this patriarch's being represented as still reigning in 781 is a perfectly natural result of the long distance from the Patriarchal see. The anachronism is in fact, *quantum valeat*, evidence of the genuineness of the monument. *Saragh*, according to Pauthier, is Lo yang in Ho nan, one of the capitals of the T'ang, and occupied as such by the Imperial Government for a time, between the introduction of Christianity and the date of the monument.

[Assemani, iii, p. Dxlv, Ch. v, has "Mar Sergius Presbyter, and Chorepiscopus Sinarum." Prof. I. H. Hall (*Journ. Am. Orient. Soc.*, xiii, 1889, p. cxxvi) remarks that Assemani is taking Sinistân, *i.e.* China, for Shiangtsû, and he adds: "It is astonishing that he should make such a blunder, for the 'of Sinistân' occurs elsewhere in the inscription, on the face of the stone." With regard to the word *pope*, *papas* given to Adam, M. Pelliot remarks that the inscription has not *papas* but *papši* and that it is but a Buddhist title, *fa-shi* (*fap-ši*), "Master of the Law." As to Mar Sergius,

The chief contents of the long inscription in Chinese, which contains 1789 characters, may be thus summarised : —1st. An abstract of Christian doctrine, of a very vague and figurative kind. This vagueness is perhaps partly due to the character of the Chinese language, but that will scarcely account for the absence of all intelligible enunciation of the Crucifixion, or even of the death, of our Lord Jesus Christ, though his Ascension is declared. 2nd. An account of the arrival of the missionary, OLOPUN[1], from

chorepiscopus of Shiangtsû, according to the same authority Shiangtsû is not the name of a locality but also a Buddhist title *Shang tso*, sansk. *sthavīra*, *i.e.* the head of a monastery. Pelliot, *Deux titres bouddhistes*, *T'oung pao*, déc. 1911, pp. 664–670. Cf. F. Nau, *Journ. Asiat.*, Jan.—Fév. 1913, pp. 235–6.]

[1] This name according to Pauthier is Syriac; *Alo-pano* signifying the *Return of God*. If this, however, be an admissible Syriac name, it is singular that the original should have been missed by one so competent as Assemani, who can only suggest that the name was the common Syriac name *Jaballaha*, from which the Chinese had dropt the first syllable, adding a Chinese termination.

Might not *Olopăn* be merely a Chinese form of the Syriac *Rabban*, by which the Apostle had come to be generally known ?

[Dr F. Hirth (*China and the Roman Orient*, p. 323) writes : "O-LO-PÊN = Ruben = Rupen ?" He adds (*Journ. China Br. R. As. Soc.*, xxi, 1886, pp. 214–215) : "Initial *r* is also quite commonly represented by initial *l*. I am in doubt whether the two characters *o-lo* in the Chinese name for Russia (*O-lo-ssŭ*) stand for foreign *ru* or *ro* alone. This word would bear comparison with a Chinese transcription of the Sanskrit word for silver, *rūpya*, which in the *Pen-ts'ao-kang-mu* (ch. 8, p. 9) is given as *o-lu-pa*. If we can find further analogies, this may help us to read that mysterious word in the Nestorian stone inscription, being the name of the first Christian missionary who carried the cross to China, *O-lo-pên*, as 'Ruben.' This was indeed a common name among the Nestorians, for which reason I would give it the preference over Pauthier's Syriac 'Alopeno.' " But Father Havret (*Stèle chrétienne*, Leide, 1897, p. 26) objects to Dr. Hirth that the Chinese character *lo*, to which he gives the sound *ru*, is not to be found as a Sanskrit phonetic element in Chinese characters, but that this phonetic element *ru* is represented by the Chinese characters pronounced *lu*, and therefore he, Father Havret, adopts Sir Henry Yule's opinion as the only one which is fully satisfactory.]

It is fair, however, to observe that the name in the older versions used by Assemani is written *Olopuen*, which might have disguised from him the etymology proposed by Pauthier. The name of this personage does not appear in the Syriac part of the inscription.

Saragh, it may be added, is referred by Pauthier to the *Saraga*

the empire of Ta Ts'in in the year 635, bringing sacred books and images; of the *translation of the said books* (a notable circumstance); of the approval of his doctrine by the imperial authority, and the permission given to teach it publicly. There follows a decree of the emperor (T'ai Tsung) issued in 638 in favour of the new doctrine, and commanding the construction of a church in [the Square of Peace and Justice (*I-ning Fang*) at] the capital. The emperor's portrait was to be placed in the Church. After this comes a short description of Ta Ts'in (here, says Pauthier, especially meaning Syria) from Chinese geographical works; and then there are particulars given of the continued patronage of Olopun and his doctrine under the Emperor Kao Tsung (650–663)[1], and of the spread of Christianity in the empire. In the end of the century Buddhism establishes a preponderance, and succeeds for a time in depressing the new doctrines. Under Hiuan Tsung (713–755) the church recovers its prestige, and a new missionary called *Kiho* appears. Su Tsung (756–762), T'ai Tsung (763–779), and Te Tsung (780–783), continue to favour the Christians. Under this last reign the monument was erected, and this part of the inscription terminates with an elaborate eulogy of Issé[2], a sage and statesman, who, though apparently by profession a Budd-

of Ptolemy, a city placed by the geographer among the *Sinæ*, and according to his theory of course far to the south of the real position of Lo yang. But we have seen reason to believe that Ptolemy's view of the *Sinæ* and *Seres* is that of a person using his right and left eye separately. Binocular vision reduces the two objects to one, and corrects their displacement.

[1] Kao Tsung was also the devout patron of the Buddhist traveller Hiuen Tsang. Kúblái and Akbar are examples of like wavering among great kings.

[2] [Issé or Yi-se, according to Pelliot, is but the Chinese transcription of Idbuzid [Yazdbōzēd] who erected the tablet; he was not a monk but belonged to the Nestorian secular clergy; under the T'ang, one of the names given by the Chinese to Balkh was "the City of the Royal Residence." Pelliot, *Chrétiens d'Asie centrale*, *T'oung pao*, 1914.)]

hist, conferred many benefits upon the churches. 3rd. A recapitulation in octosyllabic stanzas of the purport of the inscription, but chiefly as regards the praises of the emperors who had favoured the progress of the church.

The record concludes with the date of erection, viz. the second year *Kienchung* of the Great T'ang [dynasty, the seventh day of T'ai Tsu, the feast of the great Yaosan. This corresponds, according to Gaubil, to 4th February 781[1]]; the name of the chief of the law, the Priest NING-CHU, charged with the instruction of the Christian population of the eastern countries (and, I presume, the same with the *Adam*, who appears as Metropolitan in the Syriac sentences); the name of a civil officer who wrote and engraved the Chinese inscription; and the official approval of the whole.

70. It is reasonably supposed that this remarkable monument, the idea of which was probably taken from a Buddhist custom[2], may have been buried about the year 845, when the Emperor Wu Tsung published an edict, still extant, denouncing the increase of Buddhist monks, nuns, and convents, and ordering the destruction of 4600 great monasteries, the 260,500 inmates of which were to return to civil life. 40,000 minor monasteries scattered about the country were also to be demolished, the lands attaching to them to be resumed by the state, and 150,000 slaves belonging to the bonzes to be admitted to civil privilege

[1] *Marco Polo*, ii, p. 28 *n*.

[2] Stone monuments and inscriptions highly analogous in character are very common in the precincts of pagodas and monasteries in Burma. Some account of a remarkable one on a marble slab, standing eight and a half feet high by six feet wide and eleven inches in thickness, is given at pp. 66, 351 of the *Mission to Ava in* 1855. This contains on each side eighty-six lines of inscription beautifully executed. It is not older than the seventeenth century, but imitates others of far greater antiquity. See the like in the old Cambodian temples described by Bastian. (*J. R. G. S.*, xxxv, p. 85.)

and duties. The edict also directs that foreign bonzes who had come to China to make known the law prevailing in their countries, whether that of TA TS'IN or of MUHUPA, amounting to some 3000, should also return to secular life, and cease to corrupt the institutions of the Central Flowery Kingdom[1].

[1] Pauthier (*De l'Auth.*, pp. 69–71) takes *Muhupa* for the Ma'bar of Southern India, and thinks that offshoots of the St. Thomas Christians are meant. But it may be questioned whether the name *Ma'bar* as applied to a country of Southern India occurs so early by some centuries. The opinion of Gaubil, quoted by Pauthier, that the *Mubids* or Guebers of Persia were meant, seems more probable. It will be recollected that Abu Zaid mentions among the foreigners slaughtered at Khanfu in 878 *Magians* as well as Mahomedans, Christians, and Jews (*supra*, p. 89).

["With regard to the temples of the Ta-ts'in and the Muh-hu, when Buddhism was exterminated, those heretical religions might thereupon not be left in existence; their adherents must be compelled to return in a body to the secular life, and settle down again in their original family circle, there to be enlisted as ground-rent-paying people; and the foreigners amongst them must be sent back to their native country, and there be taken under control by the authorities." And further on: "Of the 4600 and more convents that are to be pulled down within the empire, the 260,500 monks and nuns who must adopt secular life, shall be enlisted amongst the families who pay ground-tax twice a year. Of the 40,000 and more chao-t'i and lan-jok that are to be demolished, the fattest land of the best kind, measuring several thousand myriads of khing, shall be confiscated and the slaves of both sexes (employed in cultivating them?), to a number of 150,000, shall be enlisted among the families that pay ground-tax twice a year. And secular life shall be adopted by more than 3000 Ta-ts'in and Muh-hu-pat belonging to the class of the Buddhist monks and nuns, or to the Bureau for the Reception and Entertainment of Foreigners, who devote themselves to the explanation of foreign religious rescripts; with the customs of the Flowery Land of the Centre they shall no longer meddle." J. J. M. de Groot, *Sectarianism*, i, pp. 64, 66.

With regard to the relations between the Buddhists and the Nestorians we may quote this passage discovered by J. Takakusu in the *Cheng-yuen Sin-ting-Shih-kiâo-muh-luh*, The new catalogue of (the books of) the Teaching of Śâkya in the period of Chêng-yuen (A.D. 785–804), compiled by Yuen chao, a priest of Si-ngan fu regarding Adam, called King-tsing in Chinese, in the Si-ngan fu inscription: "Prajña, a Buddhist of Kapiśa, N. India, travelled through Central India, Ceylon, and the Islands of the Southern Sea (Sumatra, Java, etc.) and came to China, for he heard that Mañjuśrî was in China. He arrived at Canton and came to the upper province (North) in A.D. 782 [one year after the erection of the slab at Si-ngan]. He met a relation of his in A.D. 786, who

71. A century later, Christianity in China seems to have fallen to a very low ebb, though probably not quite to zero as the next information on the subject would imply. This is derived from a circumstance noted by an Arabian author, Mahomed, the son of Isaac, surnamed Abulfaraj, who says :—"In the year 377 (A.D. 987), behind the church in the Christian quarter (of Baghdad), I fell in with a certain monk of Najran, who seven years before had been sent to China by the Catholicos, with five other ecclesiastics, to bring the affairs of Christianity in that country into order. He was a man still young, and of a pleasant countenance, but of few words, opening his mouth only to answer questions. I asked him about his travels, and he told me that Christianity had become quite extinct in China. The Christians had perished in various ways; their Church had been destroyed; and but one Christian

came to China before him. He translated together with King-tsing (=Adam), a Persian priest of the monastery of Tâ-ts'in (Syria), the *Śaṭpâramitâ-sûtra* from a Hu text, and finished translating seven volumes. But because at that time Prajña was not familiar with the Hu language, nor understood the Chinese language, and as King-tsing (Adam) did not know the Brahma language (Sanskrit), nor was versed in the teaching of the Śâkya, so though they pretended to be translating the text, yet they could not, in reality, obtain a half of its gems (*i.e.* real meanings). They were seeking vainglory privately, and wrongly trying their luck. They presented a memorial (to the Emperor), expecting to get it propagated. The Emperor (Tê Tsung, A.D. 780–804), who was intelligent, wise and accomplished, who revered the canon of the Śâkya, examined what they had translated, and found that the principles contained in it were obscure and the wording was diffuse. Moreover, he said that, the Saṅghârâma of the Śâkya and the monastery of Tâ-ts'in (Syria) differing much in their customs, and their religious practices being entirely opposed to each other, King-tsing (Adam) ought to hand down the teaching of *Mi-shi-ho* (Messiah), and the Śakyaputriya-Śramanas should propagate the sûtras of the Buddha. It is, he said, to be wished that the boundaries of the doctrines may be made distinct, and the followers may not intermingle. Orthodoxy and heterodoxy are different things, just as the rivers King and Wei have a different course." *T'oung pao,* 1896, pp. 589–590.—King-tsing, *i.e.* Adam, who was a "master of the Law," *fapši*, was probably the translator of a great many Christian texts, and among others of a *Hymn to the Holy Trinity* found by Pelliot at Tun hwang. Pelliot, *l.c.*]

remained in the land. The monk, finding nobody whom he could aid with his ministry, had come back faster than he went[1]."

The capital of China at this time, according to the monk, was a city called *Taiúna* or *Thajúye*, in which Pauthier discovers a corruption of the name *Cháo* or *Chiao-fu*, by which Si-ngan fu was called under the Sung dynasty. In any case it was probably the same as that intended by the *Tájah*, which Edrisi and Abulfeda speak of as the capital of China. The form is more suggestive of *T'ai yuen fu* in the province of Shan si, the Taianfu of M. Polo, which had been for a time the capital of the T'ang in the eighth century[2].

72. To the early tide of Christianity in China which here reaches its ebb, probably belong those curious relics of the ancient ecclesiastical connexion which Layard found in the valley of Jelu in the mountains of Kurdistan. Here, in visiting a very old Nestorian church, he saw among many other motley curiosities, a number of China

[1] Reinaud's *Abulféda*, i, ccccii; also *N. Annales des Voyages* for 1846, iv, 90; and Pauth., *Auth.*, p. 95; also Mosheim, p. 13. The passage had previously been referred to by Golius, but it was not known whence he had derived it, till it was rediscovered by M. Reinaud in a work in the Bibl. Impériale.

[2] See Pauthier's *Polo*, p. 353. It must have been difficult to say what was the capital of China in the tenth century, when it was divided into five monarchies. That of the Sung, who acquired a predominance in 960, was first at Ch'ang-ngan or Si-ngan fu, and afterwards at K'ai fung fu. [During the period of the Five Dynasties (907–960), the capitals of China were very numerous: 1° *Leang* dynasty (907–923); in 907, the eastern capital was at K'ai-fung fu [Tung King], and the western capital [Si King] at Lo-yang.—2° *T'ang* dynasty (923–936); in 923, the eastern capital was at Ta-ming (Chi-li); the western capital at T'ai yuen (Shan-si), which in the same year became the northern capital [Pe King], while the western capital was transferred to Si-ngan fu; in 925, Ta-ming received the name of Ye-tu, and the eastern capital was transferred to Lo-yang; in 929, Ye-tu was suppressed.—3° *Tsin* dynasty (936–947); in 938, the eastern capital was at K'ai-fung fu; the western at Lo-yang; Ye-tu was restored.—4° *Han* dynasty (936–951); like the Tsin.—5° *Chau* dynasty (951–960); like the Tsin and the Han, except that Ye-tu was suppressed in 954.—I owe this information to Prof. Pelliot.]

bowls, black with the dust of ages, suspended from the roof. These, he was assured, had been brought from the distant empire of Cathay by those early missionaries of the Chaldean church, who bore the tidings of the Gospel to the shores of the Yellow Sea[1].

73. No more is known, so far as I am aware, of Christianity in China till the influx of European travellers in the days of Mongol supremacy. We then again find a considerable number of Nestorian Christians in the country. It is probable that a new wave of conversion had entered during the twelth and thirteenth centuries, consequent on the christianisation of large numbers among the Turkish and Mongolian tribes, of which we have many indications, and on the influence exercised by those tribes upon Northern China, both in the time of Chinghiz and his successors, and in the revolutions which preceded the rise of that dynasty. Already in the time of the patriarch Timothy (778–820) we hear of active and successful missions in the countries adjoining the Caspian, and of the consequent conversion of a Khakan of the Turks and of several minor princes[2]. The progress of Christianity among those nations then remains obscure till the con-

[1] *Nineveh and Babylon*, p. 433.

[2] There is a still older indication of the existence of Christians, however ignorant, among the Turks, in a curious story related by Theophylactus Simocatta and Theophanes. In the expedition sent by the Emperor Maurice to assist Chosroes II against Bahram near the end of the sixth century, the General Narses sent to Constantinople some Turks who had been taken prisoners. "And these bore marked on their foreheads the sign of the Lord (that which is called the *cross* by the followers of the Christian religion). The emperor therefore inquired what the meaning might be of this token being borne by the Barbarians. And they said their mothers had put it on them. For, once when a virulent pestilence prevailed among the Scythians in the east, certain of the Christians persuaded them to prick the foreheads of their children with this symbol. The Barbarians by no means despised this counsel, and the result was their preservation." (Theophyl., bk. v, ch. 10; see also *Theophanis Chronog.*, A.M. 6081. The latter says, "Some among them who were Christians.")

version of the Kerait Tartars at the beginning of the eleventh century[1], followed by those rumours of Christian potentates under the name of Prester John which continued to reach Europe during the following age[2]. Rubruquis, in the narrative of his journey to the court of Karakorum (1253–54), makes frequent mention of the Nestorians and their ecclesiastics, and speaks specifically of the Nestorians of Cathay as having a bishop in SEGIN or Si-ngan fu (p. 292)[3]. He gives an unfavourable account of the literature and morals of their clergy, which deserves more weight than such statements regarding those looked on as schismatics generally do; for the narrative of Rubruquis gives one the impression of being written by a thoroughly honest and intelligent person[4]. In the time

[1] See *infra*, II, p. 24.

[2] [The Chinese work *Neng kai chai man lu*, circa A.D. 1125, quotes a passage of the *Shu kiun ku shi* (second half of the eleventh century) in which mention is made of a "temple of Ta Ts'in" (Ta Ts'in sze), in all likelihood a Nestorian temple which had been "formerly" [no doubt under the T'ang] built at Ch'eng tu, in Sze-ch'wan by people from Central Asia (*Hou-jen*).—Note of Pelliot.]

[3] ["Living mixed among them, though of alien race (*tanquam advene*), are Nestorians and Saracens all the way to Cathay. In fifteen cities of Cathay there are Nestorians, and they have an episcopal see in a city called Segin, but for the rest they are purely idolaters." (Rockhill's *Rubruck*, p. 157.) Rockhill makes the following remarks regarding Segin: "*Segin* is usually supposed to be Si-ngan Fu, which was in the eighth and ninth centuries the centre of Nestorianism in China. This city in the thirteenth century did not bear the name of Si-ngan Fu, but was called by its older name, Ch'ang-ngan. However, in popular parlance it may have retained the other name. It is strange, however, that the two famous Uigur Nestorians, Mar Jabalaha and Rabban Cauma, when on their journey from Koshang in southern Shan-si to western Asia in about 1276, while they mention 'the city of Tangut,' or Ning hia on the Yellow River, as an important Nestorian centre, do not once refer to Si-ngan Fu or Ch'ang-ngan. Had Ch'ang-ngan been at the time the Nestorian episcopal see, one would think that these pilgrims would have visited it, or at least referred to it. (Chabot, *Mar Jabalaha*, 21.) *Segin* may represent the Chinese *Si King*, 'western capital,' a name frequently applied to Si-ngan Fu."]

[4] ["The Nestorians there know nothing. They say their offices, and have sacred books in Syrian, but they do not know the

of Marco Polo we find Nestorian Christians numerous not only at Samarkand but at Yarkand, whilst there are such also in Chichintalas (identified by Pauthier with the modern Urumtsi, north of the T'ien Shan)[1], in Su chau

language, so they chant like those monks among us who do not know grammar, and they are absolutely depraved. In the first place they are usurers and drunkards; some even among them who live with the Tartars have several wives like them. When they enter church, they wash their lower parts like Saracens; they eat meat on Friday, and have their feasts on that day in Saracen fashion. The bishop rarely visits these parts, hardly once in fifty years. When he does, they have all the male children, even those in the cradle, ordained priests, so nearly all the males among them are priests. Then they marry, which is clearly against the statutes of the fathers, and they are bigamists; for when the first wife dies these priests take another. They are all simoniacs, for they administer no sacrament gratis. They are solicitous for their wives and children, and are consequently more intent on the increase of their wealth than of the faith. And so those of them who educate some of the sons of the noble Moal, though they teach them the Gospel and the articles of the faith, through their evil lives and their cupidity estrange them from the Christian faith, for the lives that the Moal themselves and Tuins or idolaters lead are more innocent than theirs" (Rockhill's *Rubruck*, pp. 158–9).]

[1] It occurs to me as possible that the *Cyollos Kagan* (Kagan cyollos) of Marignolli (*infra*, II, p. 213) may be the same name as the *Chichintalas* of Polo. The position of the two corresponds in a general way, and both may be represented by the *Chagan Talas* ("White Plains") of some modern maps (see K. Johnston's *Royal Atlas*, Asia). [Regarding Chingintalas: "supposing that M. Polo mentions this place on his way from Sha-chow to Su-chow, it is natural to think that it is *Chi-kin-talas*, *i.e.* 'Chi-kin plain' or valley; Chi-kin was the name of a lake, called so even now, and of a defile, which received its name from the lake. The latter is on the way from Kia-yû kwan to Ansi chow." (Palladius, *Elucidations of Marco Polo's Travels*, 1876.) "*Chikin*, or more correctly *Chigin*, is a Mongol word meaning 'ear.'" (*Ibid.*) Palladius (p. 8) adds: "The Chinese accounts of Chi-kin are not in contradiction to the statements given by M. Polo regarding the same subject; but when the distances are taken into consideration, a serious difficulty arises; Chi-kin is two hundred and fifty or sixty *li* distant from Su-chow, whilst, according to M. Polo's statement, ten days are necessary to cross this distance. One of the three following explanations of this discrepancy must be admitted: either Chingintalas is not Chi-kin, or the traveller's memory failed, or, lastly, an error crept into the number of days' journey. The two last suppositions I consider the most probable; the more so that similar difficulties occur several times in Marco Polo's narrative." (*L.c.*, p. 8.)—Urumtsi has nothing to do with Chingintalas. At Chingintalas Marco Polo says (i, p. 212): "There are three different races of people in it—Idolaters, Saracens, and some Nestorian Christians."]

and Kan chau, and over all the kingdom of Tangut, in Tenduc[1] and the cities east of it, as well as in Manchuria and the countries bordering on Corea. Polo's contemporary Hayton also testifies to the number of great and noble Tartars in the Uighúr country who held firm to the faith of Christ[2]. As regards the spread of Nestorian Christianity in China Proper at this period we do not find in Polo so many definite statements, though various general allusions which he makes to Christians in the country testify to their existence. He also speaks of them specifically in the remote province of Yun nan, and at Chin kiang fu, where they had two churches, built in the traveller's own day [1278] by Mar Sergius, a Christian officer who was governor there[3]. Their number and influence in China at the end of the thirteenth century may also be gathered from the letter of John of Monte Corvino (II, pp. 46 *seqq.*) in this volume, and in the first part of the following century from the report of the Archbishop of Soltania, who describes them as more than thirty thousand in number, and passing rich

[1] See II, p. 244 *infra*.

[2] V. 2nd chapter of Hayton's *Hist.* "*De Regno Tarsiæ.*"

[3] ["You see, in the year just named [1278], the Great Kaan sent a Baron of his whose name was MAR SARGHIS, a Nestorian Christian, to be governor of this city for three years. And during the three years that he abode there he caused these two Christian churches to be built, and since then there they are. But before his time there was no church, neither were there any Christians." *Marco Polo*, ii, p. 177. A Christian monastery or temple is mentioned in the *Chi shun Chin-kiang chi* quoted by the Archimandrite Palladius: "The temple *Ta-hing-kuo-sze* stands in Chin-kiang fu, in the quarter called *Kia-t'ao h'eang*. It was built in the 18th year of *Chi-yuen* (A.D. 1281) by the *Sub*-darugachi, *Sie-li-ki-sze* (Sergius) *Liang Siang*, the teacher in the Confucian school, wrote a commemorative inscription for him." From this document we see that "*Sie-mi-sze-hien* (Samarcand) is distant from China 100,000 li (probably a mistake for 10,000) to the north-west. It is a country where the religion of the *Ye-li k'o wen* dominates...The founder of the religion was called *Ma-rh Ye-li-ya*. He lived and worked miracles a thousand five hundred years ago. *Ma Sie-li-ki-sze* (Mar Sergius) is a follower of him." (*Chinese Recorder*, vi, p. 108.)]

people. Probably there was a considerable increase in their numbers about this time, for Odoric, about 1324, found three Nestorian churches in the city of Yang chau, where Marco would probably have mentioned them had they existed in his time[1]. That Christians continued to rise in influence during the short remainder of the Mongol reign appears probable from the position which we find the Christian Alans to occupy in the empire at the time of the visit of John Marignolli.

[An instance of the important part played by the Nestorians from China is given in the history of two Uighúr Nestorians: Rabban Bar Çauma, born at Khan-baliq, was tonsured by Mar Guiwarguis (George), Metropolitan of Khan-baliq; Marcos son of Bainiel, born in 1245 at Ko shang, visited Çauma and was tonsured in his turn by the Metropolitan Mar Nestorios, probably the successor of Mar George. The two friends made up their mind to visit Jerusalem (1278) and travelled via Ko shang, Tangut, Khotan, Kashgar, Talas, Khorassan, Tús, Azerbaidjan, and on their way to Baghdad met at Maragha the catholicos Mar Denha who gave them letters for Palestine; the two travellers went on to Baghdad, Arbela, Mosul, Nisibis, Mardin, Gozart; they settled at the convent of Saint Mar Micael of Tar'el near Arbela, but were soon called for by Denha who entrusted them with a mission for the Mongol Sovereign of Persia, Abaka. Denha had been compelled to leave Baghdad in 1268, had retired to Arbela, then to Ushnej in Azerbaidjan; he wanted some favour from the king. In 1279 Denha had ordained as Metropolitan of China Bar Kaliq, bishop of Tûs in Khorassan; Bar Kaliq became arrogant and was thrown by Denha into a prison, where he died.

[1] [Speaking of the inhabitants of Yang chau, Marco Polo, ii, p. 154, says: "The people are Idolaters and use paper-money, and are subject to the Great Kaan."]

Denha chose to replace him Rabban Marcos who was elected Metropolitan of Cathay under the name of Jabalaha, in 1280, being thirty-five years of age; his friend Rabban Çauma being appointed Visiteur General. Denha died at Baghdad on the 24th February 1281 before Jabalaha had left. Jabalaha, on account of his knowledge of the Mongol language, was elected by his colleague patriarch in the place of Denha, and he was consecrated in November 1281, his nomination being approved of by Abaka. Jabalaha was the third of this name occupying the see of Seleucia and Ktesiphon with Baghdad as the place of residence. Ahmed, the successor of Abaka, who died on the 1st April 1282, was hostile to Jabalaha III, but he was murdered on the 10th of August 1284; the eldest son of Abaka, Arghún ascended the throne on the 11th August 1284, and granted great honours to the Metropolitan. Arghún, a clever and ambitious man, was desirous of conquering Palestine and Syria, and wishing to obtain the good-will of Christian Princes he sent as an ambassador to Europe Rabban Çauma, chosen for his knowledge of languages (1287). Çauma was received with honours at Constantinople by the *Basileus*, Andronicus II (1282–1328); he then went to Naples, and before he reached Rome he learnt the news of the death of the Pope Honorius IV on the 3rd April 1287; he was received at Rome by the College of Cardinals and questions were put to him by Cardinal Jerome of Ascoli, bishop of Palestrina and General of the Minor Friars, who was elected to replace Honorius IV as Pope on the 20th Feb. 1288. Çauma passed through Tuscany and Genoa, and arrived at Paris where he was well received by the King, Philip the Fair; from Paris he went to Gascony to visit the King of England, and returned to Rome where he had an audience of Nicholas IV. He went back to Arghún's court by the same route. Çauma died at Baghdad on the 10th of January 1294. Mar Jabalaha himself died at Maragha on the 13th of November 1317, being seventy-two years of age, in the reign of Abu Said, son of Oljaïtu. (†16 Dec. 1316[1].)]

74. That the Nestorians continued to exist in China or on its frontiers during the fifteenth century we shall see hereafter from the brief records of a mission which they appear to have sent to Rome in the time of Pope Eugenius IV. Even till near the end of that century a Metropolitan of China continued to be constituted, though we know not if he resided in the country. In the case of John, who was nominated Metropolitan of *Masin* (Maha-chin) in 1490, the charge seems to have been united with that of India, and therefore as regards China we may conjecture that the title had ceased to have more of practical meaning than the *Sodor* of the English bishop of Sodor and Man[2].

75. When China was re-occupied by the Jesuit Missions in the end of the sixteenth century the impression of the missionaries at first was that no Christianity had ever existed in China before their own day. Ricci must in any case have modified that opinion when he arrived at the conclusion that China was the Cathay of Marco Polo ; but he also met before his death with unexpected evidence of its having survived, in however degenerate a form, almost to his own time. Its professors he was informed had been numerous in the northern provinces, and had gained distinction both in arms and literature. But some sixty years before (*i.e.* about 1540) a persecution

[1] J.-B. Chabot, *Histoire de Mar Jabalaha III*. Paris, 1895, 8vo.

[2] See Assem., pp. 439, 523. [Mr. B. C. Patterson gives evidence of the existence of the old Nestorian Church in North Kiangsu in the *Journal of the North China Branch of the R. A. Soc.*, 1912, pp. 118, 119.]

against them had arisen which had driven all, or nearly all, to abandon or conceal their profession. At a later date a member of the Jesuit company visited the cities in which the descendants of these people were said to exist, furnished with the names of the families. But none of them would admit any knowledge of the subject on which he spoke[1].

Some years afterwards also the Jesuit Semedo chanced on faint traces of former Christianity in the neighbourhood of the chief city of Kiang si[2].

Some material relics also bearing like evidence came in the course of the seventeenth century into the hands of the Jesuit missionaries, such as a bell with a cross and Greek inscription, and at Chang chau in Fu kien sculptures of the Virgin, marble crosses, and the like. More than one mediæval MS. of the Scriptures was also met with, but as these were Latin they must have been relics of the Franciscan missions of John Montecorvino and his brethren rather than of the Nestorians[3].

[1] Trigault, *De Exped. Christianâ apud Sinas*, bk. i, ch. 11.

[2] Semedo, *Rel. della Cina*, 1643, p. 195. It does not seem necessary to do more than allude to the story told by Ferdinand Mendez Pinto of his coming on a Christian village on the canal between Nanking and Peking, the inhabitants of which were descended from converts made one hundred and forty-two years before (*i.e.*, about 1400) by one Matthew Escandel of Buda in Hungary, a hermit of Mount Sinai; all the history of which was shown to Ferdinand in a printed book (language not specified) by the people of the village! (ch. xcvi). [We have mentioned, II, p. 214, the discovery at Lin-ts'ing of two tombs of Franciscan missionaries of the fourteenth century; one of them being named Bernard and considered as a companion of Odoric; no Bernard is mentioned in any book with Odoric; this Bernard is probably Bernardino della Chiesa, a Friar Minor sent to China in 1680 with four brethren, who had been appointed before his departure bishop of Argolis, and who became subsequently coadjutor to the vicar apostolic of Yun nan and later bishop of Peking; he died on the 21st December 1721. See H. Cordier, *Imprimerie Sino-Européenne*, pp. 65–6.—M. Romanet du Caillaud has written a notice of Escandel, after Pinto, in the *Missions Catholiques*, 29 Jan. 1886, pp. 52–3.]

[3] Trigault, *u.s.*; Martini's *Atlas Sinensis*; Baldelli Boni, Introd. to *Il Milione*. One of these relics, a Latin Bible of the

76. It is a melancholy history. For ages after the rise of Mahomedanism, Christianity, in however defective a form, had a wide and even growing influence over extensive regions of the earth, across which now for centuries past a Christian has scarcely dared to steal. Leaving out China, where possibly the Church of Rome may number as many disciples now as the Syrian Church did in its most prosperous days, how many Christians are there in what were up to the thirteenth or fourteenth centuries the metropolitan sees of Tangut, Kashgar, Samarkand, Balkh, Herat, Sejistan, and Marv? Whilst at the other end of Asia, Socotra, once also the seat of a Christian Archbishop, and we may hope of some Christian culture, is sunk into the very depths of savagery[1].

eleventh century, which was obtained by the Jesuit Philip Couplet from a Chinese in the province of Nanking, is now in the Laurentian Library at Florence. [It is not mentioned in Bandini's Catalogue.] I tried to see it but could not. "How not to do it" is, or was till lately, the principle of administration in that institution, if I may judge from my own experience on two occasions, on the second with an introduction; in this a singular contrast to those other public libraries of Florence which are *not* under clerical management. [Father Martini wrote in the *Novus Atlas Sinensis*, p. 125, with regard to *Chang chau*: "locum hunc jam tum à plurimis navibus fuisse frequentatum, ac *M. Pauli Zartem* hic alicubi fuisse, accedit quod in hac urbe multa eaque luculenta reperta sint Christianorum vestigia, intraque ipsa moenia sculpti lapides non pauci, quibus salutiferae Crucis signum visitur impositum, atque etiam sanctissimae Virginis Dei genitricis Mariae, cum caelestibus geniis in terram prostratis imagines cum duabus pendulis lucernulis, imo & in praefecti cujusdam palatio reperta est pulcherrima crux marmorea, hanc obtenta ab eo facultate inde eduxere Christiani, ac in nostro urbis hujus templo summa cum pietate atque apparatu collocavêre. Vidi etiam unà cum sociis hic apud litteratum quendam volumen vetus, Gothicis characteribus diligentissime exaratum, adhibita fuit papyri loco tenuissima membrana; maxima Scripturae sacrae pars Latine erat conscripta; tentavi librum ut consequerer: at ejus dominus tametsi gentilis, nec prece nec pretio ullo adduci potuit, ut traderet, in sua familia per multas jam nepotum progenies tanquam rarissimum quoddam antiquitatis cimelium adservatum illud asserens."]

[1] There are one or two indications of the existence of Christians in the Indo-Chinese countries and islands which have perhaps been hitherto overlooked. One is found in Marignolli who speaks of there being a few Christians in *Saba*, which we shal see reason

VII. LITERARY INFORMATION REGARDING CHINA PREVIOUS TO THE MONGOL ERA.

77. Before speaking of that great opening of the Farther East to European travel, which took place under the reign of the Mongol dynasty in Asia, it will be well to take such a view as is practicable to me of the information regarding China which is to be found in literary works

to believe to be Java (*infr.* II, p. 220), and another in the Travels of Hier. Santo Stephano, who, when his comrade Hieronimo Adorno died in the city of Pegu in 1496, buried him "in a certain ruined church, frequented by none" (*India in the Fifteenth Century*, p. 6). If the *Sornau* of Varthema's Christian fellow-travellers be Siam, this affords a third indication of the same kind. [Pinto, ch. xcv, has "Kingdom of Sournau, vulgarly called Siam." Yule adds, in a note: "Mr. Badger in his notes on Varthema (p. 213) is not inclined to accept Mendez Pinto's authority, which he supposes to stand alone, for calling Siam *Sornau*. But I have recently found that the name *Sarnau* is used several times by Varthema's contemporary, Giovanni d'Empoli, in a connexion that points to Siam. In one passage he speaks of Pedir in Sumatra as being frequented by 'Junks, which are the ships of Bengala, Pecu (*Pegu*), Martamam (*Martaban*), SARNAU, and Tanazzar' (*Tanasserim*). In another passage he couples it again with Tenasserim as a place which supplied the finest Benzoin, Lac, etc. The Italian editor interprets the name as *Sirian*, but for this I see no ground (see Letters of G. d'Empoli in *Archivio Storico Italiano, Appendice*, tom. iii, pp. 54, 80; Firenze, 1845.)" Yule referred again to the same subject in *Hobson-Jobson, s.v.* SARNAU, SORNAU: "A name often given to Siam in the early part of the 16th century; from *Shahr-i-nao*, Pers. 'New-City'; the name by which Yuthia, or Ayodhya, the capital founded on the Menam about 1350, seems to have become known to the traders of the Persian Gulf. Mr. Braddell (*J. Ind. Arch.* v. 317) has suggested that the name (*Sheher-al-nawi*, as he calls it) refers to the distinction spoken of by La Loubère between the Thai-*Yai*, an older people of the race, and the Thai-*Noi*, the people known to us as Siamese. But this is less probable. We have still a city of Siam called *Lophaburī*, anciently a capital, and the name of which appears to be a Sanskrit or Pali form, *Nava-pura*, meaning the same as *Shahr-i-nao*; and this indeed may have first given rise to the latter name. The *Cernove* of Nicolo Conti (c. 1430) is generally supposed to refer to a city of Bengal, and one of the present writers has identified it with Lakhnāoti or Gaur, an official name of which in the 14th century was *Shahr-i-nao*. But it is just possible that Siam was the country spoken of." Valentijn, v. 319, has: "About 1340 reigned in the kingdom of Siam (then called *Sjahar-nouw* or *Sornau*) a very powerful Prince."]

of the middle ages antecedent to that era. These are all, with one slight exception, Arabic.

The earliest of them (at least as regards one half of it) is an Arab compilation of the middle of the ninth century and beginning of the tenth, which was first made known to Europe by the Abbé Eusebius Renaudot in 1718 under the title of *Anciennes Relations de l'Inde et de la Chine de deux Voyageurs Mahometans qui y allèrent dans le IXième siècle*[1]. The original from which Renaudot had translated was lost sight of, and some of his critics both in France and England went so far as to set his work down as a forgery. But the MS was discovered some fifty years later [1764] by Deguignes in the Bibliothèque Royale[2]; and in 1845 a new translation and commentary by M. Reinaud appeared, in company with an impression of the Arabic text, which had been lying since 1811 in the stores of the Government Printing Office at Paris[3].

78. The title given by Renaudot is acknowledged to be an incorrect description of the work. It is in two parts indeed, written at different times, and by different authors, but the author of the second part, Abu Zaid Hassan of Siraf on the Persian Gulf, certainly does not profess to have himself travelled in the east. He gives the date of his predecessor's work as A.H. 237 (A.D. 851), and his own is fixed by M. Reinaud from an apparent mention of him by

[1] An English version of Renaudot's translation appeared in 1733 (see Major's Introd. to *India in the Fifteenth Century*, p. xxiii), and has been reprinted or abstracted in Harris, i, 521, and Pinkerton, vii, p. 179.

[2] *Mém. de l'Acad. des Insc.*, xxxii, 366; *Not. et Extraits*, i, 136 *seqq*. Deguignes himself had fancied the work to be a compilation of Renaudot's own.

[3] [*Relation des Voyages faits par les Arabes et les Persans dans l'Inde et la Chine dans le IXe siècle de l'ère chrétienne*, texte arabe imprimé en 1811 par les soins de feu Langlès, publié avec des corrections et additions et accompagné d'une traduction française et d'éclaircissements par M. Reinaud....Paris, 1845, 2 vols. 12-mo.]

Mas'ūdī[1] to about 916. M. Reinaud says that the narrative which forms the basis of the first part of the work is derived from Suleiman a merchant, who had made voyages to India and China, but I have not been able to discover on what grounds this opinion is founded. The introductory passages of the work are missing, so that we are without explanation by the author as to his own identity or the sources of his information. The name of Suleiman is only once mentioned; nor is there any narrative, properly speaking, to be traced throughout the composition, though the first pages, amounting to about one third of the whole, contain a tolerably coherent account of the seas and islands between Oman and China, in the course of which twice, as well as once or twice again in subsequent pages of the book, passages occur in the first person. It may be observed, however, that none of these passages, if my examination may be trusted, refer to China. They relate to India, Ceylon, and the seas between those countries and Arabia. My conclusion would rather be that the book is a compilation of notes made by the author from his own experiences in a voyage to India, and from what he had collected from others who had visited China, Suleiman among them. The remainder of this first part of the book is in fact a medley of notes about India and China, including a detail of some of the chief kingdoms of the Indies of which the author had heard. It is clear from the vagueness of these accounts that the author's knowledge of India was slight and inaccurate, and that he had no distinct conception of its magnitude. An abstract of them will be found in the notes to this essay, with some remarks that it seems desirable to offer regarding this part of the subject, over which I venture to think that M. Reinaud, with all his great learning, has spread confusion rather than shed light[2].

[1] See *Prairies d'Or*, i, 322.

[2] See Note XI.

79. The names of seas and places described by this writer as encountered on the voyage to China have given rise to curious controversy. The views taken by M. Reinaud about many of them are very untenable, and the most consistent and probable interpretation yet published appears to be that of M. Alfred Maury[1].

According to this view, with trifling modifications, the seas and places passed are as follows:—The SEA OF PERSIA; the SEA OF LAR [Lārwī] (that which washes Gujarat and Malabar)[2]; the SEA OF HARKAND (the Indian Ocean from the DĪBAJĀT or Maldives, and SERENDIB or Ceylon[3] to AL RĀMNĪ or Sumatra)[4]; the LANJABALUS or LANKHABALUS (the Nicobar Islands)[5]; and the two (Andāmān) Islands in the SEA OF ANDĀMĀN; KALĀH-BĀR, a dependence of Zábaj (some port on the Malacca coast, perhaps Kadáh, commonly spelt Quedda; Zábaj[6] representing some great

[1] *Examen de la route que suivaient, au IXe siècle de notre ère, les Arabes et les Persans pour aller en Chine, d'après la relation arabe traduite successivement par* Renaudot et M. Reinaud. Published in the *Bulletin de la Société de Géographie*, 1846, pp. 203–238, and republished some years ago in a collection of essays by M. Maury.

[2] These first two are missing with the opening pages of the work, and are derived by Reinaud from a parallel passage in Mas'ūdī.

[3] Compare the *ab usque Divis et Serendivis* of Ammianus Marcellinus.

[4] See Odoric, *infra* II, p. 146, *note* 3.

[5] [Langabālūs] Probably we have in the second part of this name the Malay *Pulo* meaning *island*. I may observe that there is a considerable island belonging to Queddah, and surrounded by many smaller ones, at the northern entrance of the Straits of Malacca, which is called *Pulo Langkawi*.

[6] The Syrian bishops Thomas, Jabalaha, Jacob, and Denha, sent on a mission to India in 1503 by the Patriarch Elias, were ordained to go "to the land of the Indians and the islands of the Seas which are between *Dabag* and Sin and Masin." (Assemani, iii, Pt. i, 592.) This Dabag is probably a relic of the form *Zábaj* of the early narratives, used also by Al-Biruni. Ibn Khurdadhbah and Edrisi use *Jaba* for Zābaj. [Zābadj, ancient pronunciation *Zābag*, represents the initial form *Djāwaga* (Ferrand, p. 23).] Walckenær quoted by Mr. Major (*op. cit.*, p. xxvii) says: "The Puranas and Hindu books show that the title of Maharaja or Great

monarchy then existing on the Malay Islands, probably in Java, the king of which was known to the Arabs by the Hindu title of Maharaj); BATÚMA or TANÚMAH[1] (perhaps errors for Natúma, the Natuna Islands); KADRANJ[2] (Siam or some other region on the Gulf of Siam); SANF (Champa, but here used in a sense much more extensive than the modern Champa, and including Cambodia)[3]; SUNDAR FŪLĀT (the Sondur and Condur group of Marco Polo, the chief island of which is now called Pulo Condore)[4].

King was originally applied to the sovereign of a vast monarchy which in the second century comprised a great part of India, the Malay Peninsula, Sumatra, and the neighbouring islands. This dynasty continued till 628," etc. It is a pity that Baron Walckenær did not quote more definitely "the Puranas and Hindu books" which give this precise and interesting information, and in the absence of such quotation there must be some hesitation in accepting it. The truth appears to be that whilst the antiquities, literature, and traditions of Java and other islands show that communication with continental India in remote times must have been large and intimate, nothing distinct has yet been produced to show that any record of such communication or knowledge of those islands has been preserved on the Continent. Friedrich and Lassen certainly seem to have no knowledge of such records as Walckenær alludes to.

1 [*Batúma* transcribed by Reinaud *Betoumah* يتُومه for تيومة *Tiyūma*, island of Tiuman or Tioman on the south-eastern coast of the Malay Peninsula. Cf. Ferrand, p. 30.]

2 [*Kadranj* for *Kundrang* (ancient pronunciation) and *Kundrandj* (modern pronunciation), near the mouth of the Mekong River. Cf. Ferrand, p. 14.—The distance between Kundrang and Champa, and Champa and Chundur-fūlāt, is ten days. *Ibn al Fakīh*, translated by Ferrand, p. 58.]

3 [The Arabic ص gives صنو Chanf=Champa, not Sanf; cf. Ferrand, p. viii, 12.]

4 This is not in accordance with Maury, who places Sundar Fūlāt arbitrarily on the coast of Cochin China, perhaps from confining Sanf or Champa to the tract now retaining that name (for the names are identical, the Arabs, having no *ch* and no *p*, necessarily writing *Champa* as *Sanfa*). But Crawfurd states that the name Champa with the Malays really applies to the whole of Cambodia embracing the eastern coast of the Gulf of Siam (*Dict. Ind. Islands*, p. 80), whilst actual tradition in those regions ascribes to ancient Champa sovereignty over all the neighbouring kingdoms to the frontiers of Pegu and China (Mouhot's *Travels*, i, 223). Hence Pulo Condor would properly come between a port on this coast and China, as Sundar Fūlāt does in the Arab narrative. I do not know what is the proper Malay name of Pulo Condor, but it is probably connected with the Sanskrit

80. The port of China frequented by the Arab merchants was Khanfu[1], of which we have already spoken.

Sundara beautiful. And the *Fūlāt* is probably only an Arabic plural from the Malay *Pulo* or *Pulau* an island. All that is said of the place in the *Relations* is that Sundar Fūlāt is an island, ten days from Sanf and a month's voyage from China, where the ships find fresh water. [Mr. C. O. Blagden has some objection to Sundar Fūlāt being Pulo Condor: "In connexion with Sundar-Fūlāt, some difficulties seem to arise. If it represents Pulo Condor, why should navigators on their way to China call at it *after* visiting Champa, which lies beyond it? And if *fūlāt* represents a Persian plural of the Malay *Pulau*, 'island,' why does it not precede the proper name, as generic names do in Malay and in Indonesian and Southern Indo-Chinese languages generally? Further, if *sundur* represents a native form *čundur*, whence the hard *c* (= *k*) of our modern form of the word? I am not aware that Malay changes *č* to *k* in an initial position." *J. R. A. S.*, April 1914, p. 496.] According to Alex. Hamilton the Pulo Condor group consists of four or five islands, "producing nothing but wood, water, and fish for catching." There are two harbours or anchorages, but neither of them good. Mr. Allan Ketchpole established a factory for the East India Company on Pulo Condor in 1702, which speedily came to a disastrous end, [the Europeans being massacred by their Macassar garrison.] (*N. Acc. of the East Indies*, ed. 1744, ii, 205.) [The chief island is called by the Chinese *Kun lun*.] ["L'île de Sendi Foulat est très grande; il y a de l'eau douce, des champs cultivés, du riz et des cocotiers. Le roi s'appelle Resed. Les habitants portent la fouta soit en manteau, soit en ceinture.... L'île de Sendi Foulat est entourée, du côté de la Chine, de montagnes d'un difficile accès, et où soufflent des vents impétueux. Cette île est une des portes de la Chine. De là à la ville de Khancou, x journées." Edrisi, i, p. 90. In Malay Pulo Condor is called Pulau Kundur (Pumpkin Island) and in Cambodian, Koḥ Tralàch. See Pelliot, *Deux Itinéraires*, pp. 218–20.—Fūlāt = fūl (Malay *pulo*) + Persian plural suffix -āt. *Čundur fūlāt* means Pumpkin island. Ferrand, *Textes*, pp. ix, 2.]

[1] [De l'île "de Senfy à la ville de Loukiin, 3 journées. C'est la première *échelle* de la Chine.... On y fabrique diverses riches étoffes de soie de la Chine qui sont exportées au dehors, et notamment le ghazar-sini dont on fait commerce dans les pays voisins aussi bien qu'au loin. On y trouve du riz, des céréales, des noix de coco, des cannes à sucre. Les habitants portent la fouta; ils accueillent bien les étrangers; ils sont très magnifiques, et font un plus grand usage de parfums que les autres habitants de l'Inde.... De Loukin à Khancou, 4 journées de navigation, et 20 par terre. Cette dernière échelle est la plus considérable de la Chine." Edrisi, i, p. 84.]

[Khancou خانقو or Khanfou خانفو.]

["Ce pays est gouverné par un roi puissant et glorieux, qui a beaucoup de sujets, de troupes et d'armes. On s'y nourrit de riz, de noix de coco, de lait, de sucre et de mokl. La ville est située sur un golfe (ou à l'embouchure d'un fleuve) qu'on remonte durant deux mois de marche jusqu'à la ville de Badja, qui appar-

Here there was a Musulman Kazi and public worship. The houses were for the most part built of wood and bamboo matting, which led to frequent fires. When a foreign ship arrived, the officials took charge of the cargo and locked it up. When all the ships of the season had entered, a duty of 30 per cent. was exacted before placing the goods at the disposal of the owners. If the king wanted anything for himself, the highest price was paid for it in ready money.

Many particulars mentioned by this author regarding China are silly enough, but much also that is stated is perfectly correct. He notices the ancient Chinese customs of issuing food from public granaries in times of dearth, as well as of dispensing medicines to the poor; the support of schools by the government; the generally methodical and just character of the administration; the elaborate classification of official titles; the custom of doing all business by written documents, and the strict censure

tient au bagh bough, lequel est le roi de toute la Chine. Cette ville est le terme des voyages des Occidentaux; on y trouve toute espèce de fruits et de légumes, du blé, de l'orge et du riz." On ne trouve ni raisin ni figues dans la totalité de la Chine et des Indes, "mais bien le fruit d'un arbre qu'on nomme el-cheki et el-berki. Cet arbre croît particulièrement dans le pays du poivre. C'est un arbre dont les fruits sont durs, et dont les feuilles, d'un vert éclatant, ressemblent à celle du chou; il porte un fruit de la longueur de quatre palmes, rond, semblable à une conque marine, couvert d'une écorce rouge, et dans l'intérieur duquel est une graine ou un gland qui ressemble à celui du chêne; bouilli au feu, on le mange comme la châtaigne, dont il a exactement le goût. La pulpe de ce fruit forme un aliment très-doux et très-agréable, qui réunit au goût de la pomme celui de la poire, et quelque chose même de la saveur de la banane et du mokl. C'est un fruit appétissant, admirable, et le plus recherché de tous ceux qu'on mange dans l'Inde. On trouve également dans ce pays un arbre qu'on appelle el-i'nba; il est grand comme le noyer, ses feuilles ressemblent aux feuilles de cet arbre, et son fruit à celui du palmier doum. Lorsque ce fruit est noué, il est tendre; alors on le met dans du vinaigre, et son goût ressemble exactement à celui des olives. C'est chez les Indiens un hors d'œuvre destiné à exciter l'appétit."

"De la ville de Khancou à la ville de Djankou, on compte 3 journées." Edrisi, i, pp. 84–5.]

exercised on the style and tone of papers submitted to public departments[1]; the use of a copper currency instead of gold and silver; the custom of delaying the burial of the dead for years sometimes; the systematic protection afforded to travellers; the manufacture of porcelain; the use of rice-wine and of tea (*sákh* or *sáhh* for *chá*[2]). There is scarcely anything of Chinese Geography in this first part beyond the mention of Tibet and the Taghazghaz as the western neighbours of China, and of the Isles of SILA in the east, which appear to be Japan[3].

One custom he mentions with great apparent admiration. It is, that the governor of every city slept with a bell at his head communicating with a handle at the gate, which anyone claiming justice was at liberty to ring. And we learn from Abu Zaid that even the king had such a bell; only he who dared to use it must have a case justifying so strong an appeal from the ordinary course of justice, or he suffered for it[4].

[1] See III, p. 122 *infra* and note.

[2] See Reinaud, *Relation*, i, pp. 39, 46, 47, 43–4, 37, 33, 36, 42, 34, 40. None of the mediæval European travellers in China mention tea. The first notice of it so far as I know is in Ramusio's notes of Hajji Mahomed's information (see Note XVIII at the end of the essay). [Envoys from T'ien fang (Mecca) under the Ming dynasty in presenting tribute solicit silk, *tea-leaves*, and porcelain.—Bretschneider, *Med. Res.*, ii, p. 300.]

[3] Edrisi also speaks of the Isles of Silah, of which the chief city was ANKUAH, and where gold was so abundant that the people made dog-chains of it. The low value of gold in Japan up to the opening of the trade the other day is a familiar fact. M. Polo says of it: "*et je vous dy qu'ils ont tant d'or que c'est sans fin; car ils le treuvent en leurs isles.*" (Pauth., *Polo*, 538.) Possibly Ankúah may really represent *Miyako*. [Sila is not Japan but Corea. Ankúah has nothing to do with Miyako. Corea is sometimes called *Tung Kwo*, the Eastern Empire, in Chinese books, but I have not heard of *Ngan Kwo*, the equivalent of Ankúah.]

[4] Edrisi also speaks of this [i, p. 100]. It is a kind of story having a strong attraction for eastern people. Ibn Batuta heard that the same custom was adopted by Shamsuddin Altamsh, Sultan of Delhi (1211–1236). See Ibn Bat., iii, 158. The custom was a genuine Chinese one, but the summons seems to have been by a drum rather than by a bell. Thus in the Romance of "The Fortunate Union," the hero Teichungyu exclaims, "My lord,

The anonymous author was aware that the principles of the Chinese religion (here meaning Buddhism) came from India. Both countries, he says, accept the doctrine of metempsychosis, but with certain differences.

81. ABU ZAID, the author of the second part of the *Relation*, begins by remarking the great change that had taken place in the interval (some sixty years) since the first part of the book was composed. Events had happened which had entirely stopped the Arab trade with China, had thrown that country into anarchy, and had destroyed its power. He then proceeds to relate this revolution, which was due to a rebel whom he calls *Banshoa*, who, after sacking many cities of the empire, including Khanfu, which he took in A.H. 264 (A.D. 878), at length marched against the capital. The emperor fled to the frontiers of Tibet; but, after obtaining the aid of the King of the Taghazghaz (a great Turkish tribe), was enabled to renew the struggle and to regain his throne. His capital, however, was in ruins; his power and treasure had vanished; his generals had perished, and the best of his soldiers. The provinces had been seized by rapacious adventurers who scarcely made a pretence of allegiance. Foreign merchants and shipmasters were bullied, insulted, and plundered; the staple industries of the country were destroyed; trade could not go on; and thus the misfortunes and anarchy of China carried ruin to many families in distant Siraf and Oman.

Klaproth[1] has pointed out the correspondence of this

you are mistaken! The emperor himself suspends the drum at his palace gate, and admits all to state their hardships without reserve." (Davis's *Chinese Miscellanies*, p. 109.) This institution of the drum was adopted by a late king of Siam, according to Pallegoix, but the pages who had to answer it succeeded in extinguishing the practice. A curious Chinese drawing engraved in *Chine Ancienne* (*L'Univers Pittoresque*), pl. 3, represents this institution of the drum.

[1] *Tab. Historiques*, pp. 223–230.

statement with the account in the Chinese Annals of the rebellion of *Hwang-chao*, here called *Banshoa*, at the time mentioned by Abu Zaid; one of those tremendous insurrections which seem to recur in China almost periodically. The chief cities of the empire, including (880) Lo yang and Ch'ang ngan, the two imperial capitals, really fell into the hands of this chief, who declared himself emperor, but was eventually beaten from them by the aid of Turki auxiliaries. The Chinese account of the insubordination continuing to prevail in the provinces after the emperor's restoration, also corresponds almost in so many words with that of the Arab writer[1].

82. Abu Zaid adds to the notes of his predecessor many interesting particulars regarding India and the Islands, as well as regarding China. In reference to the latter country he gives a curious account of a visit which an acquaintance of his own, Ibn Wahab of Basra, paid to KHUMDAN, the capital of China (see *ante*, pp. 31, 108), and of the interview which he had there with the emperor, who must have been Hi Tsung of the T'ang, very shortly before the great rebellion broke out. The story of the interview is too long to extract; but there does not seem to be any sufficient reason to doubt its correctness, and we may gather from it further proof that the knowledge of the Chinese in the days of the T'ang was by no means confined to that circle of oblique-eyed humanity which we are accustomed to regard as the limit of Chinese ideas. Ibn Wahab describes Khumdan or Ch'ang ngan, which was two months' journey from Khanfu, as divided in two by a long and wide street. The city eastward of this was entirely devoted to the residences of the emperor and officers of Government. On the west side were the shops, places of business, and the miscellaneous population. The streets were

[1] Reinaud, i, 66–7; *Chine Ancienne*, p. 330.

traversed with channels of running water and bordered with trees.

Abu Zaid, like his predecessor, dwells upon the orderly and upright administration of China whilst in its normal state. This indeed seems to have made a strong impression at all times on the other nations of Asia, and we trace this impression in almost every account that has reached us from Theophylactus downwards[1], whilst it is also probably the kernel of those praises of the justice of the Seres which extend back some centuries further into antiquity.

He is acquainted with the general character of the overland communication between Sogdiana and China Proper. The frontier of the latter was a two months' journey distant, over a country which was almost a waterless desert, though the frontier of the *empire* was not far from Khorasan. The difficulty of passing this desert had alone prevented the Musulman warriors of Khorasan from attempting the invasion of China. A friend of the author told him, however, that he had seen at Khanfu a man with a bagful of musk on his back whom he found to have come on foot all the way from Samarkand[2].

He mentions that three of the chief officers of state were called the Master of the Right, the Master of the Left, and the Master of the Centre. I do not know if traces of these appellations still exist in the Chinese administration; but we find that under Kúblái Khan the two chief ministers of state bore the titles of "Minister of the Right, and Minister of the Left[3]."

[1] The Jesuit historian Du Jarric thinks that "if Plato were to rise from Hades he would declare that his imagined Republic was realised in China." (ii, 676.)

[2] i, p. 114.

[3] See Pauthier's *Polo*, p. 329, and Yule-Cordier's *M. Polo*, i, p. 432. In the case of Lord Amherst's Embassy the three members of the Legation were distinguished by the Chinese as *the Middle* or Principal, the *Left Hand* (which is the more honour-

83. We have some account of China from an Arab geographer who was contemporary with the earlier of the two compilers of the *Relation*, and wrote perhaps a few years later than the date assigned by Abu Zaid to the work of his predecessor. This was Abu'l-Kasim 'Ubaid-Allah called Ibn Khurdádhbah, born about 820–830, and who served under the Khalif Mutammid (869–885) as director of the posts in Jibal or the ancient Media. His work, "The Book of Routes and Provinces," in great part consists only of lists of stages and distances, but there are occasionally some descriptive details introduced. The following lines contain nearly all that he says of China[1]:

"From SANF (Champa) to AL-WAKÍN[2], which is the first port of China, is one hundred farsangs either by sea or by land. Here you find excellent Chinese iron, porcelain, and rice[3]. You can go from Al-Wakín, which is a great port, to KHANFU[4] in four days by sea, or in twenty days by land. Khanfu produces all sorts of fruits and vegetables,

able side), and the *Right Hand* Envoys. (Davis's *Chinese*, Supp. vol., p. 40.) In our Mission to Ava in 1855 the Envoy's secretary was termed by the Burmese "the Right Hand Officer." [In Corea there was a prime or middle minister, *seng-ei-tsieng*, a minister of the left, *tsoa-ei-tsieng*, and a minister of the right, *wu-ei-tsieng*. Also in Annam, the left is the place of honour. In the province of Nghê-an there were two sub-governors, the *Dao of the right*, Quan Hu'u Dao, and the *Dao of the left*, Quan Ta Dao.]

[1] From a translation by Barbier de Meynard in the *Journal Asiatique*, sér. vi, tom. v (see pp. 292–4).

[2] The *Lúkin* of Edrisi (v, § 85 and p. 129 *n.*, *supra*), who has derived several passages from Ibn Khurdádhbah. One would suppose it to be Canton, had not Ibn Batuta identified Canton with Sin-ul-Sin, which Edrisi describes quite distinctly from Lukin. Edrisi, however, had no distinct ideas about Eastern Asia, and this is not conclusive. This Lukin cannot of course be the *Lukinfu* of Rashid (III, p. 126 *infra*), but it may have something to do with the alternative name (apparently corrupt) of *Lumkali* applied in the same page to Canton.

[3] ["On trouve à Loukyn la pierre chinoise, la soie chinoise, de la porcelaine d'excellente qualité et du riz."—De Goeje.]

[4] ["On va de Loukyn à Khânfou, qui est l'échelle la plus considérable (de la Chine)."—De Goeje.] Khânfu is also pronounced Khâncu. De Goeje, p. 49, writes: "C'est le port de Canton (Hongkong)." Fancy Hongkong in the ninth century!

wheat, barley, rice, and sugar-cane. From Khanfu you arrive in eight days at JANFU[1], which has the same productions. Thence to KANTU, six days, also having the same productions[2]. In all the ports of China you find a great navigable river affected by the tide[3]. In that of Kantu there are geese, ducks, and other wild fowl. The greatest length of coast from AL MAÏD[4] to the other extremity of China is two months' voyage. China includes three hundred prosperous and famous cities[5]. It is bounded by the sea, by Tibet, and by the country of the Turk[6].

[1] Janfu is probably the Janku of others, and to be identified with Yang chau (*infra*, II, p. 209). *Kantu*, from the mountains of Sila or Japan opposite to it, as mentioned below, should be either Shang Haï or about the mouth of the Yellow River, if there was ever a port there. [The mouth of the Yellow River is out of the question; Shang Haï is possible, as it was the seat of one of the inspectors of foreign trade (*shi-po-shi*). Chau Ju-kwa held the office in Fu-kien. At the end of the eleventh century, "at the seaport of Hwa-ting, an officer was appointed to take account of the merchant-vessels, and to levy a toll on the goods; in this way was constituted the town of Shang Haï"; this is the first mention made of the name of Shang Haï in history; in 1156 the office of superintendent of the trading vessels at Shang Haï was abolished. (*Desc. of Shanghae, Chinese Miscel.*, iv, 1850.)—However, we may remark that it is impossible to see the mountains of Sila (Corea) from Shang Haï and indeed from any port of China proper; Prof. Pelliot writes to me that the organization of the commissaries of foreign trade (*shi po*) was due to the Sung and continued by the Mongols. It varied during the Yuen Dynasty, but according to the edict of 1293 there were seven commissaries: Ts'iuan chau, Shang haï, K'an p'u, Wen chau, Kwang Tung, Hang chau and K'in yuen. It will be noted that all these places are south of the Yangtze and that four out of the seven are situated in Che kiang.]

[2] [Khândjou, De Goeje, who identifies this place with Hang chau. "De là [Khândjou] à Kânçou, où l'on trouve aussi les mêmes productions, 20 journées."—De Goeje, who identifies Kânçou with Kian chau.]

[3] ["Chacune des échelles de la Chine est située à l'embouchure d'un grand fleuve navigable qui est soumis à l'influence de la marée."—De Goeje.]

[4] [Armâbyl.—De Goeje.]

[5] ["La Chine renferme 300 villes, toutes prospères, dont 90 célèbres."—De Goeje.]

[6] ["Ce pays est borné par la mer, le Tibet, le pays des Turcs, et, à l'occident, l'Inde."—De Goeje.

Mas'ūdī says also: "Au delà de la Chine il n'y a plus, du côté

Strangers from India are established in the eastern provinces.......

"What is beyond China is unknown. But in front of Kantu rise high mountains. These are in the country of SILA[1], which abounds in gold. Musulmans who visit this country are often induced to settle for good because of the advantages of the place. The products exported are *ghorraib* (a kind of plant), gum kino, aloes, camphor, sails, saddles, porcelain, satin, cinnamon, and galanga[2] [3]."

[Ibn Rosteh wrote his *Al-A'lāḳ al-Nafisa* about 903; he is not so well informed as Mas'ūdī; he says that there is but one sea from Basrah to China, and that the same water bathes the coasts of India and China: but that it was said that, properly speaking, there were seven seas having each its special characteristics, winds, taste, colour, fauna[4].]

83*. Mas'ūdī is our next writer; who in the *Meadows of Gold*[5] treats of all things in Nature and History, and of all at once rather than all in succession; of China among

de la mer, ni royaume connu, ni contrée qui ait été décrite, excepté le territoire d'es-Sila et les îles qui en dépendent." i, p. 346.]

[1] [Corea.]

[2] ["Quant à ce que la mer orientale fournit à l'exportation, on tire de la Chine la soie blanche (*haryr*), la soie de couleur (*firand*) et la soie damassée (*Kymkhâw*), le musc, le bois d'aloès, des selles, des fourrures de martre (*Sammour*), de la porcelaine, le *cylbandj*, la cinnamome et le galanga."—De Goeje.]

[3] [I have revised this abstract of Ibn Khurdâdhbah with the translation of the great Arabic scholar of Leyden, De Goeje, in the volume: Kitâb-al-Masâlik Wa'l-Mamâlik (*Liber Viarum et Regnorum*) auctore Abu'l-Kâsim Obaidallah ibn Abdallah Ibn Khordâdhbeh et excerpta e Kitâb al-Kharâdj auctore Kodâma ibn Dja'far quae cum versione gallica edidit, indicibus et glossario instruxit M. J. de Goeje.—Lugduni-Batavorum, E. J. Brill, 1889, 8vo.]

[4] [See Hartmann, p. 861, *Chine*, *Encycl. Islam.*]

[5] *Les Prairies d'Or*—translated by MM. Barbier de Meynard and Pavet de Courteille, Paris, 1861–77. [Published in nine octavo volumes in the *Collection d'Ouvrages Orientaux publiée par la Société Asiatique*. From Vol. iv, the name of Barbier de Meynard is the only one printed on the title-page.]

the rest. He travelled far and wide, and from a very early age, visiting Sind in 912 when quite a youth, and afterwards, according to his own account, Zanzibar and the Island of Kanbalu[1], Champa, China, and the country of Zabaj (*supra*, p. 127), besides travelling a long way into Turkestan. If he really visited China it must have been in a very cursory manner. I can find nothing of any interest respecting it that does not also appear in the *Relation*, chiefly in that part of it of which Abu Zaid is the professed author. M. Reinaud has treated of these coincidences, but has not I think quite satisfactorily accounted for them[2].

84. In the course of the tenth century we have another Arab traveller who professes to have visited China. This is Abū Dulaf Mis'ar Ibn Muhalhil who being, according to his own account, at the Court of Nasri Bin Ahmed Bin Ismail of the Samanidæ at Bokhara when ambassadors arrived from "the King of China Kalatin-bin-ul-Shakhir[3]," to negotiate a marriage between his own daughter and Noah the son of Nasri (who afterwards succeeded to the throne of Bokhara), took advantage of the opportunity of accompanying the ambassadors on their return, about the year 941. The whole narrative of this traveller is not extant, but much of it has been preserved in citations by Yākūt (A.H. 617, A.D. 1220), and Qazwini (A.H. 667, A.D. 1268–9), and a German editor has collected these passages

[1] The French translators take this for Madagascar. Ma'sūdī describes it as an island in the sea of Zanj, well cultivated and inhabited by Musulmans speaking the Zanj language. The Mahomedans got possession of it about the beginning of the Abasside dynasty, capturing the whole Zanj population (this never could be true of Madagascar). Sailors reckoned it roughly about five hundred farsangs to Oman. I should think it must be the Island of Zanzibar, or perhaps the Great *Comoro*, which has some resemblance in name, and is occupied by people of Arab descent.

[2] *Discours Préliminaire* to *Relation*, etc., pp. viii and xviii *seqq*.

[3] Or *Kalin bin-Shakhbar*. [*Qālin b. aš Sachīr*.—Marquart.]

into a tolerably continuous narrative, and translated them into Latin[1].

It is very difficult to say whether the narrative is genuine or not, or to guess how much it may have suffered from the manner in which it has been thus coopered out of loose fragments[2]. If the author really accompanied Chinese ambassadors from Bokhara back to their native country, it is not easy to understand why they should have made a grand tour of all the Turk and Tartar nations from the shores of the Black Sea to the banks of the Amur. The name which he attributes to the capital of China is SINDABIL, which is more like an Indian than a Chinese name, or rather like the Arabic perversion of an Indian name (compare *Kandábíl, Sandábúr*). The nearest Chinese name is that of CH'ENG TU FU[3], or as Marco Polo calls it SINDIFU, the chief city of the province of Sze ch'wan, and which was during parts of the tenth century the capital of the kingdom of SHU[4]. Neither would it be easy to discover

[1] *Abu Dolif Misaris Ben Mohalhel de Itinere Asiatico commentarius—Studio Kurd de Schloezer*, Berolini, 1845. [A better commentary has been given by J. Marquart, in his *Osteuropäische und ostasiatische Streifzüge*, Leipzig, 1903, 8vo. pp. 74–95: *Das Itinerar des Mi'sar b. al Muhalhil nach der chinesischen Hauptstadt.*—See also the French translation by G. Ferrand, pp. 208 *seq.* in *Relat. de Voyages...arabes, persans et turks*, i, Paris, 1913.]

[2] ["Jeder der es versuch, auf der Karte des Itinerar des Reisenden zu verfolgen, wird alsbald mit steigendem Kopfschütteln die sonderbaren Kreuz- und Querzüge betrachten, die uns bald nach Tibet und an die Grenze von China, bald wieder nach dem Irtischgebiet oder dem Tarimbecken führen." Marquart, p. 75.]

[3] [Marquart, *l.c.*, pp. 86–7, shows that it is impossible that Sindabil be Ch'eng tu; he identifies it with Kanchau. The great temple of Sindabil mentioned by Abū Dulaf is no doubt the idol temple of Kanchau, 500 cubits square, of Shah Rukh's ambassadors; the identity of Kanchau with Sindabil is confirmed by Qasvini. See *Marco Polo*, i, pp. 220–1.]

[4] [The first Shu Dynasty was the Minor Han Dynasty which lasted from A.D. 221 to A.D. 263; its capital was Ch'eng tu in modern Sze ch'wan; this Shu Dynasty was one of the Three Kingdoms (*San kwo chi*); the two others being Wei (A.D. 220–264) reigning at Lo Yang, and Wu (A.D. 222–277) reigning at Kien

in a list of Chinese sovereigns any name resembling Kalatin son of Shakhbar or Shakhir. In one of the notes appended to this paper will be given an abstract of the chief points of this journey, real or pretended[1].

84 *bis.* ["Now we should mention the relation of the land-route between Transoxiana and China to be found in a work of Abū Sa'īd 'Abd al-Haiy Ibn Duḥāk Gardēzi (Marquart, *Streifzüge*, writes Gūrdezī, but see Rieu, *Cat. Pers. Brit. Mus.*, 1071 a, and Raverty, *Tabaḳāt-i Nāṣiri*, p. 901) of whom Bartold had the insight to recognize the value and to edit a fragment from his important *Zain al-Akhbār* (written in 1050) (*Otčet o po'ezdkʲ e v Sredniuiu Aziiu*, 1893–4, Pet., 1897). Gardēzi describes China pp. 92^{17}–4^{5}. The most important passage is the itinerary Turfān-Khamdān 92^{9-16}: Činandjket (*i.e.* Turfān-Kara Khodjo) in the country of the Toghuzghuz to Kumul eight days; at Bagh Shūrā (one might see in *bagh* the Persian *bāgh* 'garden'; the word *shūrā* would answer to *čura* of Turkish names; thus one of the most considerable of the Volga Turks: Aḳčura Oghli) one must cross a river in a boat; then seven days in the steppe, with wells and pasturage, to Sha chau, with the remark that the town was called Dun chuan [Tun hwang] until the beginning of the seventh century; to-day the road passes through Ngan-si fu, to the N.W. of Sha chau: then three days' travelling to a stone desert (*senglākh*) then seven days to Sukhchau (*Sukh* reproduces an ancient pronunciation which Abulfeda renders by *sūkdjū*); then

Kang (Nan king). The second was the Ts'ien Shu Dynasty, founded in 907 by Wang Kien, governor of Sze chw'an since 891; it lasted till 925 when it submitted to the Hau T'ang; in 933 the Hau T'ang were compelled to grant the title of King of Shu (Hau Shu) to Mong Chi-siang, governor of Sze chw'an, who was succeeded by Mong Ch'ang, dethroned in 965; the capital was also Ch'eng tu under these two dynasties.] The names of the kings as given in Deguignes have no possibility of assimilation to those in the text (Deg., i, 124–9).

[1] See Note XII.

three days to Khamčau (= Khanchau); then eight days to Kuča (?); then in 15 days to a river called Kiyān (= Hwang ?), which is navigable. From Baghshūrā to Khamdān, the capital of China, the voyage lasts one month (which does not tally with the total of the days of the journey = 43). Relays are to be found on the road." Mr. Hartmann, from whom we borrow these particulars (*Encyclop. de l'Islam, s.v. Chine*), remarks that it was always the main route between China and the West.]

85. The account of China in the Geography of Edrisi, written under the patronage of King Roger II of Sicily, and completed in 1153–4, is, like the whole of his account of South-eastern Asia, including India, very meagre and confused. Professing to give the distances between places, he generally under-estimates these enormously, insomuch that in a map compiled from his distances Asia would, I apprehend, assume very contracted dimensions. Owing to his manner of dealing with the world in successive climates or zones of latitude the passages in his work treating of China are scattered over nearly all parts of the book; but the general result is something like the following:

China is a great and populous empire whose supreme king is called the *Baghbugh*[1]. This sovereign is just,

[1] This word in various forms, *Baghbúgh*, *Baghbúr*, *Faghfúr*, is applied as a generic title to the emperors of China by old Arabian and Persian writers, and appears in Marco Polo as applied to the dethroned Sung emperor in the form *Facfur* (ii, p. 148). [*Baghbūr* بغبور, *Faghfūr* فغفور, are the Arabic forms of the Persian *Baghpūr*, Son of God, translation of *T'ien tze*, in Chinese Son of Heaven. Cf. Ferrand, *Textes*, p. 2.] It is, according to Neumann, a translation of the Chinese title *T'ien tze* or "Son of Heaven" into old Persian, in which *Bak* is Divinity (Sansk. *Bhaga*, Hindi *Bhagwán*), and *Fur* is "Son" (Sansk. *putra*). The elements of the name are still to be found in the modern Persian dictionaries: "*Bagh*, The name of an Idol," and "*Púr*, A Son." So *Sháh Púr*, the Sapor of the Romans, is "King's Son" (see Bürck's *Polo*, p. 629; Pauthier's *Polo*, 453; F. Johnson's *Dict.*). ["The last of the Sung Emperors (1276) '*Facfur*' (*i.e.* the Arabic for *T'ien tze*) was freed by Kúblái from the (ancient Khotan) indignity of surrendering with a rope round his neck, leading a

powerful, sage, and provident, easy and gentle in his administration, generous in his gifts, attentive to what goes on in foreign countries, but much occupied with the interests of his own subjects, who are admitted to his presence readily, and without having to apply for the intervention of subordinates. In religion he follows an idolatrous faith differing but little from that of India; but he follows it devoutly, and is liberal to the poor.

The people are dark like those of Hind and Sind. They live upon rice, coco-nut, milk, sugar, and *mokl* (said to be the fruit of the dúm-palm of Upper Egypt). No arts are more valued among them than those of design and pottery.

Under the Baghbugh there are some three hundred flourishing cities and many fine seaports. The latter generally stand upon river-estuaries, up which ships ascend some distance from the sea. They are full of life and business, and the security of property in them is perfect. The greatest of the ports is KHANFU[1], which is the terminus of the western trade. It stands on (or near) the *Khumdan*, the great river of China, one of the greatest and most famous of all rivers; the Ganges itself is said to be an affluent of it[2]. Its banks are crowded with population, and many great cities stand upon them. Such are SUSAH[3], a very famous city whether for its buildings or its trade, or for the wealth of its citizens. Its commercial credit extends over the world. Here are made an unequalled

sheep, and he received the title of Duke: in 1288 he went to Tibet to study Buddhism, and in 1296 he and his mother, Ts'iuen T'aï How, became a bonze and a nun, and were allowed to hold 360 *k'ing* (say, 5000 acres) of land free of taxes under the then existing laws." (E. H. Parker, *China Review*, Feb., March 1901, p. 195.)]

[1] Jaubert has *Khanku*, but no doubt the right reading is Khanfu. It involves but the difference of a dot.

[2] So thought Fra Mauro, as his map shows.

[3] Qu. *Su chau* in Kiang nan, the celebrated rival of Hang chau?

kind of porcelain, the *Ghazár* of China, and silk-stuffs famous for their solidity and elegance. JANKU is also on the Khumdan about three days from Khanfu. This also is a city where there are manufactures of glass and silk stuffs. Two months' journey up the river is BAJAH[1], the capital of the Baghbugh, where is his palace with his guards, treasures, harem, and slaves. He is bound to keep always one hundred dowered wives and one thousand elephants. Another city is SÍNIA-UL-SÍN which Ibn Batuta enables us to identify with Canton (see *infra*, Vol. IV). And the first port of China coming from Sanfi or Champa is LUKIN (see *supra*, p. 135), where also are made rich silks, and among others a kind called *Ghazar-Sini*[2], which are exported far and near.

Many places besides these are named which it seems impossible to identify. Such are, on the borders of Indo-China, TARIGHURGHAN and KATIGHORA, the last a name which seems simply borrowed from the Cattigara of Ptolemy [see note on Kattigara, Note II], KHAIGHUN, ASFIRIA[3], BURA, KARNABUL, ASKHRA, SHARKHU or SADCHU, BASHIAR, TAUGHA (recalling the Taugas of Theophylactus), etc. KASGHARA, apparently Kashgar, is put only four days distant from Katighora upon the China Sea.

Exterior China, apparently corresponding in a general way to the Tangut of later days, is also mentioned by Edrisi. It is bounded by the Taghazghaz on the west, by Tibet on the south, and by the country of the Khizilji Turks on the north.

[1] The copies used by Jaubert read *Bájah* or *Nájah*. But probably the right reading is *Tájah*. Compare with Abulfeda quoted hereafter, and with the Taiuna or Thajuye at p. 114 *supra*.

[2] I do not find this word in the Arabic dictionaries. May it be the origin of our word *Gauze*, which has been referred to *Gaza* in Palestine ?

[3] It is very possible that this *Asfiria* also represents the Ptolemæan *Aspithra*, and perhaps some of the other names have a like origin, though too much corrupted to identify with the Greek.

86. To a date only a few years later than Edrisi belongs Benjamin of Tudela, who travelled between 1159 and 1173, and of whom some account has been given by Mr. Major in his Introduction to *India in the Fifteenth Century*, which need not be repeated. After speaking of the Island KHANDY, supposed to be Ceylon, this traveller says:—

"From hence the passage to CHINA is effected in forty days. This country lies eastward, and some say that the star Orion predominates in the sea which bounds it, and which is called the sea of Nikpha. Sometimes the sea is so stormy, that no mariner can conduct his vessel; and, whenever a storm throws a ship into this sea, it is impossible to govern it; the crew and the passengers consume their provisions and then die miserably, but people have learned how to save themselves from this fate by the following contrivance"; and so he proceeds to tell how the sailors sew themselves in bulls' hides, and being found floating in the sea are carried ashore by great eagles, and so forth. This stuff (literally a cock and a bull story) is all that Benjamin relates in connexion with China[1].

It is remarked by the English editor of Benjamin that this author is the first European who mentions China by that name. But Edrisi at least precedes him, and a Sicilian Arab writing of *Sin* in Arabic at Palermo, has at least as good a title to be considered a European author writing of China, as a Spanish Jew writing of *Tsin* in Hebrew at Tudela. Benjamin appears to have heard these tales of the voyage to China at the island of Kísh, which would seem to have been the limit of his travels[2]; what he relates

[1] Bohn's ed. (in *Early Travellers in Palestine*), pp. 116–117.

[2] *Kais* or *Kish* was the real terminus of Indian trade for several ages, and the seat of a principality, *Quisci* of Polo. Marco, I sec, shows the true approximate position of Quisci as two hundred miles further up the Gulf than Hormuz. Kish, in the map before me (*Stieler's Hand-Atlas*), is termed *Guase* or *Kena*. [The island and city of Kish or Kais is about 200 miles from the mouth of

of India likewise being to all appearance mere hearsay. Indeed the eleventh and twelfth centuries are more bare of notices of communication between China and western nations than almost any others since the beginning of our era.

87. ABULFEDA (1273–1331) belongs to a date subsequent to the rise of the Mongol power, which we have fixed as a dividing mark in the treatment of this subject; but it will be more convenient to dispose of his notices of China now, in connexion with those of the other Arab writers who have been already cited. Notwithstanding the facilities which his age afforded for obtaining correct information about China, he does not seem to have been in the way of profiting greatly by them. His knowledge of those regions is, as he himself complains, very much restricted, and his accounts are chiefly derived from books long antecedent to his own time and to that of the Mongol sovereigns, though they are not altogether devoid of recent information. Some extracts of the essential part of his information on China will be found in the supplementary notes, and will show this curious mixture of the obsolete statements of the geographers of the tenth or eleventh centuries with items of modern knowledge[1]; affording an analogy to the maps of the sixteenth and seventeenth centuries, which in remoter Asia sometimes present a strange jumble of Ptolemy, Marco Polo, and recent discoveries.

the Gulf, and for a long time was one of the chief ports of trade with India and the East. The island, the *Cataea* of Arrian, now called Ghes or Kenn, is singular among the islands of the Gulf as being wooded and well supplied with fresh water. The ruins of a city [called Harira, according to Lord Curzon] exist on the north side. See Yule-Cordier's *Marco Polo*, I, p. 64 *n.*—See p. 85 and *n.* I, *supra.*]

[1] See Note XIII.

VIII. CHINA UNDER THE MONGOL DYNASTY, KNOWN AS CATHAY.

88. We now arrive at the epoch of the Mongols, during whose predominance the communication of China with the western nations was less impeded by artificial obstacles than it has been at any other period of history. For even now, though our war-steamers have ascended the Kiang to Han kau, and a post runs from Peking to Petersburg, every land frontier excepting that towards Russia remains as impervious as in the darkest age of the past[1].

It was in the days of the Mongols also that China first became really known to Europe, and that by a name which, though especially applied to the northern provinces, also came to bear a more general application, CATHAY[2].

89. This name, KHITAI [or K'ITAI], is that by which China is styled to this day by all, or nearly all, the nations which know it from an inland point of view, including the Russians Китай, [the Greeks, *Κιτάϊα*] the Persians, and the nations of Turkestan [Khitaï]; and yet it originally belonged to a people who were not Chinese at all. The K'ITANS were a people of Manchu race who inhabited for centuries a country to the north-east of China, lying east of the Khingan mountains and north of the river Sira, and whose allegiance was rendered alternately to the Khakans of the Turks and the Emperors of China. In the beginning of the tenth

[1] [It must be borne in mind that these last lines were written nearly half a century ago.]

[2] Several names strongly resembling *Cathay* appear in ancient geographers; but, of course, none of them have any connexion with the name as applied to China. The Χαῖται Scythians of Ptolemy probably represent *Khotan* (vi, 15). The Καθέα of Strabo is in the Punjab, apparently, from what he says, including the Salt Range (Bk. xv). The *Kataia* of Arrian is the island of Kish in the Persian Gulf. [The Northern Chinese of Cathay were called by the Southern Chinese, *Pe tai*, the fools of the North; in retaliation the Cathayans named the Southerners *Man tze*, Barbarians: hence the *Manzi* or *Mangi* of mediaeval travellers.]

century the chief of one of their tribes made himself supreme first over his own entire race, and then successively over the adjoining nations of Asia from the sea of Corea to the Altai. The son of this conqueror having assisted to place on the throne Kao Tsu of the brief dynasty of the later Tsin, this prince in return not only transferred to the Tartar a large tract of Northern China, but agreed to pay him yearly tribute, and to acknowledge his supremacy. The next Chinese sovereign kicking against these degradations, the K'itan overran all the provinces north of the Yellow River, and established his own empire within them, under the name of *Leao* or the Iron Dynasty. This K'itan empire subsisted for two centuries, in Northern China[1] and the adjoining regions of Tartary. The same curious process then took place which seems always to have followed the intrusion of Tartar conquerors into China, and singularly analogous to that which followed the establishment of the Roman emperors in Byzantium. The intruders themselves adopted Chinese manners, ceremonies, literature, and civilisation, and gradually lost their energy and warlike character. It must have been during this period, ending with the overthrow of the dynasty in 1125, and whilst this northern monarchy was the face which the Celestial

[1] [The Eastern Tartars, K' itans of Tungusic origin, founded an empire in Northern China; nine sovereigns belonged to their dynasty:

1. Ye-liu A-pao-ki = T'ai tsu, 907
2. Ye-liu Te Kwang = T'ai tsung, 927
3. Ye-liu Yuen = Shi tsung, 947
4. Ye-liu King = Mo tsung, 951
5. Ye-liu H'ien = King tsung, 968
6. Ye-liu Lung-siu = Sheng tsung, 983
7. Ye-liu Tsung-chin = Hing tsung, 1031
8. Ye-liu H'ung-ki = Tao tsung, 1055
9. Ye-liu Yen-hi = T'ien tso, 1101–1125.

In 937 Te Kwang, T'ai tsung, took the *nien hao* of Hwei T'ung and gave to his dynasty the name of *Leao*. The capital of the Leao was Leao yang in Leao tung, and was transferred by A-pao-ki to Yen king (Peking). They were replaced by the Niu che (Kin).]

Empire turned to Inner Asia, that the name of Khitan, Khitat, or Khitaï, became indissolubly associated with China[1].

90. In the year just named the last prince of the dynasty was captured by the leader of the revolted *Churchés*, who had proclaimed himself emperor, and founder of a dynasty under the name of the *Golden*, the *Kin* of the Chinese.

This dynasty, like its predecessor, adopted the Chinese civilisation, and for a brief period prospered. Their empire, the chief capital of which was established at the city which they called Chung tu, the modern Peking, embraced in China itself the provinces of Pe Che-li, Shan si, Shan tung, Ho nan, and the south of Shen si, whilst beyond the wall all Tartary acknowledged their influence. Their power, however, soon passed its climax, and their influence over Mongolia had already declined before the middle of the twelfth century[2].

91. Temuchin, afterwards known as Chinghiz, was born of a Mongol tribe on the banks of the Onon in 1162.

[1] [When the Leao were expelled by the Kin, they retired westward into Kashgaria, took the place of the Kara-Khanids (Ileks, or Al-i-Afrasyab), and founded the new dynasty of Kara K'itaï, Si Leao or Western Leao; five sovereigns belong to this dynasty:

1. Te tsung, 1125 = Ye-liu Ta Shi.
2. Kan T'ien Hau, 1136 = Ta Pu-yen, Princess Regent, Hien Tsing.
3. Jin tsung, 1142 = Ye-liu I-lie.
4. Cheng t'ien, 1154 = Ye-liu Shi (Princess Regent).
5. Mo Chu, 1168 = Ye-liu Che-lu-ku.

Che-lu-ku, second son of Jin tsung, was dethroned by his son-in-law Kuchluk, chief of the Naïmans, a Turkish tribe, subjugated later by the Mongols of Chinghiz Khan; see *Notice of the Kara Khitai or Si Liao* in *Mediaeval Researches from Eastern Asiatic Sources*, by E. Bretschneider, i.]

[2] [The *Niu che* or *Niu chen* Tartars, another Tungusic tribe, expelled the Leao in 1125 and lasted until the Mongol conquest (1234). At first tributary of Corea, Hien-phu became independent; however the first real chief was Ukunaï, his sixth successor (1021); Aguda (O-ko-ta), fifth successor of Ukunaï, is the founder of the *Kin* dynasty (1113) with the *miao hao* (temple name) of T'ai Tsu.]

It is not needful to follow the details of his rise and of his successes against the nations of Tartary which led to his being saluted in 1206 by the diet of his nation as Chinghiz Khan[1].

The conquest of China was commenced by Chinghiz,

[1] Chinghiz, according to Quatremère, did not use the higher appellation of *Káan* (or rather Qáan), which was adopted by his son Okkodai and his successors as their distinctive title, identical with *Kháqán*, the Χαγάνος of the Byzantine historians. Properly a distinction should therefore be preserved between *Khan*, the ordinary title of Tartar chiefs, and which has since spread to Persian gentlemen and come to be a common affix to the name of Hindustanis of all classes, and *Qáan*, as the peculiar title of the Supreme Chief of the Mongols. The Mongol princes of the subordinate empires of Chagatai, Persia, and Kipchak, were entitled only to the former affix, though the other is sometimes applied to them in adulation, whilst the successors of Chinghiz, viz., Okkodai, Kuyuk, Mangu, Kúblái, and those who followed him on the throne of Khanbaliq, the *Magni Canes* of our ecclesiastical travellers, should properly be designated as *Qáan*. But I have not ventured on such a refinement. (See Quatremère on Rashid, pp. 10 *et seqq.*) [See note in Yule-Cordier's *Marco Polo*, i, p. 10.]

[Mr. Rockhill, *Rubruck*, p. 108 *n.* writes: "The title *Khan*, Rubruck's *Cham*, though of very great antiquity, was only used by the Turks after A.D. 560, at which time the use of the word *Khatun* came in use for the wives of the Khan, who himself was termed *Ilkhan*. The older title of *Shan-yü* did not, however, completely disappear among them, for Albiruni says that in his time the chief of the Ghuz Turks, or Turkomans, still bore the title of *Jenuyeh*, which Sir Henry Rawlinson (*Proc. Roy. Geog. Soc.*, v, 15) takes to be the same word as that transcribed *Shan-yü* by the Chinese (see *Ch'ien Han shu*, bk. 94, and *Chou shu*, bk. 50, 2). Although the word *Khakhan* occurs in Menander's account of the embassy of Zemarchus, the earliest mention I have found of it in a western writer is in the *Chronicon* of Albericus Trium Fontium, where (571), under the year 1239, he uses it in the form *Cacanus*." Albericus has: "cepit unum Regem eorum nomine Cacanum (Cutanum)." (*Chronicon*, 1698, p. 571.)—Terrien de Lacouperie (*Khan, Khakan, and other Tartar Titles*, *Bab. and Orient. Record*, Nov. 1888) says, p. 272, that the "Kha Kan or Khagan خاقان, the supreme title of authority among the Tartars, makes its first appearance in history in 402 A.D. It was assumed by Tulun, the Khan of the Jöujen, after he had established his supremacy all over Tartary. He disdained the old title of Shen-yu, which hitherto had been always assumed by the supreme rulers of these regions, and he struck out for himself and his successors in power the new title of *Khakan*....stated to be the same as Hwang Ti, *i.e.* Supreme Ruler...the ruler of the Karákhitai started the title of *Gurkhan*." With regard to Temujin, Terrien adds, p. 274, that he received in 1206 the title of Chinghiz Khan or the "Very Mighty Khan" because he had conquered so many Gurkhans: he could not adopt that humbled title.]

although it was not completed for several generations. Already in 1205 he had invaded TANGUT, a kingdom occupying the extreme north-west of China, and extending beyond Chinese limits in the same direction, held by a dynasty of Tibetan race, which was or had been vassal to the Kin. This invasion was repeated in succeeding years; and in 1211 his attacks extended to the empire of the Kin itself. In 1214 he ravaged their provinces to the Yellow River, and in the following year took Chung tu or Peking. In 1219 he turned his arms against Western Asia, and conquered all the countries between the Bolor and the Caspian and southward to the Indus, whilst his generals penetrated to Russia, Armenia, and Georgia; but a lieutenant whom he had left behind him in the East continued to prosecute the subjection of Northern China. Chinghiz himself on his return from his western conquests renewed his attack on Tangut, and died on that enterprise 18th August, 1227.

92. Okkodai, the son and successor of Chinghiz, followed up the subjugation of China, extinguished the Kin finally in 1234, and consolidated with his empire all the provinces north of the Great Kiang. The southern provinces remained for the present subject to the Chinese dynasty of the Sung, reigning now at King sze or Hang chau. This kingdom was known to the Tartars as NANGKIASS, and also by the quasi-Chinese title of MANGI or MANZI, made so famous by Marco Polo and the travellers of the following age, a title which the Western Mahomedans not unnaturally confounded and identified with MACHÍN, a term of another origin and properly of a larger application[1].

[1] *Máchin* is merely a contraction of Mahachina, "Great China," the name by which the Hindus anciently styled the Great Empire (see *supra*, p. 68), and in this application I have heard it still vernacularly used by them. In this sense, also, it would appear

93. After establishing his power over so much of China as we have said, Okkodai raised a vast army and set it in motion towards the west. One portion was directed against Armenia, Georgia, and Asia Minor, whilst another

to have been understood in old times by the more intelligent Mahomedans, as when Al Biruni, speaking of the Himalayas, says that beyond those mountains is *Mahachin*. That geographer's contemporary, Firdusi, also uses the name (see *Journ. As.*, sér. iv, tom. iv, 259; Klaproth, *Mém.*, iii. 257, *seqq.*). But the majority, not knowing the meaning of the expression, seem to have used it pleonastically coupled with *Chin* to denote the same thing, "*Chin* and *Machin*"; a phrase having some analogy to the way *Sind* and *Hind* was used to express all India, but a stronger one to *Gog* and *Magog*, as applied to the northern nations of Asia; for Sind and Hind are capable of divorce. And eventually Chin was discovered to be the eldest son of Japhet, and Machin his grandson, which is much the same as saying that Britain was the eldest son of Brut the Trojan, and Great Britain his grandson. In the Mongol days, when Chinese affairs were for a time more distinctly known in Western Asia, and the name of *Mánzí* as the southern portion of the Empire was current in men's mouths, it would appear that this name was confounded with *Máchín*, and the latter word thus acquired a specific application, though an erroneous one. For though accident thus gave a specific meaning to *Machin*, I cannot find that *Chin* ever had a similar specific meaning given to it. One author of the sixteenth century, indeed, quoted by Klaproth, distinguishes North and South China as the Chin and Machin of the Hindus (*Journ. As.*, sér. ii, tom. i, 115). But there is no proof that the Hindus ever made this distinction, nor has anyone that I know of quoted an instance of *Chin* being applied peculiarly to Northern China. Ibn Batuta, on the contrary, sometimes distinguishes *Sín* as South China from *Khitai* as North China.

In times after the Mongol *régime*, when intercourse with China had ceased, the double name seems to have recovered its old vagueness as a rotund way of saying *China*. Thus Barbaro speaks of *Cini* and *Macini*, Nikitin of *Chin* and *Machin*, the commission of Syrian bishops to India (*supra*, p. 127) of *Sin* and *Masin*, all apparently with no more plurality of sense than there is in Thurn and Taxis. And yet, at the same time, there are indications of a new application of *Máchin* to the Indo-Chinese countries. Thus Conti applies it to Ava or Siam, in which Fra Mauro follows him, and the *Ayin Akbari*, if I remember rightly, applies it to Pegu.

The use of a double assonant name, sometimes to express a dual idea but often a single one, is a favourite Oriental practice. As far back as Herodotus we have Crophi and Mophi, Thyni and Bithyni; the Arabs have converted Cain and Abel into Kabil and Habil, Saul and Goliah into Talut and Jalut, Pharaoh's magicians into Risam and Rejam, of whom the Jewish traditions had made Jannes and Jambres; whilst Christian legends gave the names of Dismas and Jesmas to the penitent and impenitent thieves in the Gospel. Jarga and Nargah was the name given to the great circle

great host under Batu, the nephew of the Great Khan, conquered the countries north of Caucasus, overran Russia making it tributary, and still continued to carry fire and slaughter westward. One great detachment under a lieutenant of Batu's entered Poland, burned Cracow, found Breslau in ashes and abandoned by its people, and defeated with great slaughter at Wahlstatt near Liegnitz (April 9th, 1241) the troops of Poland, Moravia, and Silesia, who had gathered under Duke Henry II of the latter province to make head against this astounding flood of heathen. Batu himself with the main body of his army was ravaging Hungary. The king had been very slack in his preparations, and when eventually he made a stand against the enemy his army was defeated with great loss, and he escaped with difficulty. Pesth was now taken and burnt, and all its people put to the sword.

The rumours of the Tartars and their frightful devastations had scattered fear through Europe, which the defeat at Liegnitz raised to a climax. Indeed weak and disunited Christendom seemed to lie at the foot of the barbarians. The Pope to be sure proclaimed a crusade, and wrote circular letters, but the enmity between him and the Emperor Frederic II was allowed to prevent any co-operation, and

of beaters in the Mongol hunting matches. In geography we have numerous instances of the same thing, *e.g.*, Zabulistan and Kabulistan, Koli Akoli, Longa Solanga, Ibir Sibir, Kessair and Owair, Kuria Muria, Ghuz and Maghuz, Mastra and Castra (*Edrisi*), Artag and Kartag (*Abulghazi*), Khanzi and Manzi (*Rashid*), Iran and Turan, Crit and Mecrit (*Rubruquis*), Sondor and Condor (*Marco Polo*), etc. (See Quatremère's *Rashid*, pp. 243–6; D'Avezac, p. 534; *Prairies d'Or*, i, p. 399.)

The name of *Achin* in Sumatra appears to have been twisted in this spirit by the Mahomedan mariners as a rhyme to *Machin*; the real name is *Atcheh*.

In India, such rhyming doublets are not confined to proper names; to a certain extent they may be made colloquially at will upon a variety of substantives. The *chauki-auki* means "chairs" simply (*chauki*), or, at most, "chairs and tables"; *lakri-akri*, "sticks and stakes." In some such sense probably grew up the use of *Chin Machin*, China and all its appurtenances.

neither of them responded by anything better than words to the earnest calls for help which came from the King of Hungary. No human aid merited thanks when Europe was relieved by hearing that the Tartar host had suddenly retreated eastward. The Great Khan Okkodai was dead in the depths of Asia, and a courier had come to recall the army from Europe.

94. In 1255 a new wave of conquest rolled westward from Mongolia, this time directed against the Ismaelians or "Assassins[1]" on the south of the Caspian, and then successively against the Khalif of Baghdad[2] and Syria. The conclusion of this expedition under Húlakú may be considered to mark the climax of the Mongol power. Mangu Khan, the emperor then reigning, and who died on a campaign in [Sze-ċh'wan] China in 1259, was the last who exercised a sovereignty so nearly universal. His successor Kúblái extended indeed largely the frontiers of the Mongol power in China, which he brought entirely under the yoke, besides gaining conquests rather nominal than real on its southern and south-eastern borders, but he ruled effectively only in the eastern regions of the great empire, which had now broken up into four, (1) The immediate Empire of the Great Khan, seated eventually at Khanbaliq or Peking, embraced China, Corea, Mongolia, and Manchuria, Tibet, and claims at least over Tong King and countries on the Ava frontier; (2), the Chagatai Khanate, or Middle Empire of the Tartars, with its

[1] [The Assassins were defeated at the end of 1256 by Húlakú, and the eighth Prince of Alamut, Rocn uddin Khurshah, was put to death. Cf. *Marco Polo*, i, pp. 145 *seqq.*; and the French edition of *Odoric*, pp. 473–483.]

[2] [Mostas'im Billah was the last of the Abbasid Khalifs; cf. *Marco Polo*, i, pp. 63–4, 67 *n.*—Rashiduddín says: "The evening of Wednesday, the 14th of Safar, 656 (20th February, 1258), the Khalif was put to death in the village of Wakf, with his eldest son and five eunuchs who had never quitted him."]

capital at Almaliq, included the modern Dzungaria, part of Chinese Turkestan, Transoxiana, and Afghanistan; (3), the Empire of Kipchak, or the Northern Tartars, founded on the conquests of Batu, and with its chief seat at Sarai on the Volga, covered a large part of Russia, the country north of Caucasus, Khwarizm, and a part of the modern Siberia; (4), Persia, with its capital eventually at Tabriz, embraced Georgia, Armenia, Azerbaijan and part of Asia Minor, all Persia, Arabian Irak, and Khorasan.

95. Though the Tartar host had retired spontaneously when Europe seemed to lie at its mercy, the fears of renewed invasion hung over the west for years. Pope Innocent IV, who had succeeded Gregory IX, summoned a council at Lyons in 1245, the chief alleged object of which was to devise measures for the protection of Christendom against this enemy. But even before the meeting of the Council the Pope had taken one of the steps which was to stand instead of a hearty union to resist the common foe, by sending missions to the Tartar chiefs which should call upon them to shed no more Christian blood, but to adopt the Christian faith. There seems indeed, even when the early panic caused by the vast scale of the Tartar atrocities had scarcely passed away, (and the feeling for many years grew rather than diminished), an undercurrent of anticipation to have run through Europe that these barbarians were in some way ripe for conversion; and this sentiment is traceable, more or less, in most of the missions that from this time forth were sent to them by Christian Pontiffs and Princes. At its maximum, as we have seen, the power of the Grand Khan extended from the Gulf of Tong King almost to the Baltic. None, or next to none, of the Mongol princes were at this time Mahomedans, and the power of Islam over the length of Asia was for a time prostrated.

The heavy blows thus dealt at the Mahomedan enemy; then the old stories of Prester John with whom early rumour had confounded Chinghiz; the vagueness of religious profession in the Khans and their captains, facilitating the ascription to them of that Christianity which was no doubt really professed by some of the tribal chiefs under them; the tolerance and patronage in some cases extended to Christians in the conquered countries; all these circumstances perhaps contributed to create or to augment in Europe the impression of which we have spoken.

And the accomplishment of the missions to which allusion has been made was facilitated by the very extent of the Tartar flood which had thus washed down all artificial barriers from the Yellow River to the Danube. Nor only to those missionaries and ambassadors, or to the crowned kings who bore their own homage to the footstool of the Great Khan, was the way thus thrown open; the circulation of the tide extended far lower, and the accidents of war, commerce, and opportunity carried a great variety of persons in various classes of European life to remote regions of Asia.

96. "'Tis worthy of the grateful remembrance of all Christian people," says Ricold of Montecroce, "that just at the time when God sent forth into the eastern parts of the world the Tartars to slay and to be slain, He also sent forth in the west his faithful and blessed servants Dominic and Francis, to enlighten, instruct, and build up in the Faith." Whatever we may think on the whole of the world's obligations to Dominic, it is to the friars, but more especially indeed to the Franciscans, that we owe much interesting information about the Tartars and Cathay. Thus, besides the many wanderers dumb to posterity who found their way to the Great Khan's camp in the depths

of Mongolia, there went also John of Plano Carpini, and William [of Rubruck or] Ruysbroek or Rubruquis, both Franciscan monks of superior intelligence, who have left behind them narratives of what they saw and learned. And these were the first, so far as I know, to bring to Western Europe the revived knowledge of a great and civilised nation lying in the extreme east upon the shores of the ocean. To this kingdom they give the name, now first heard in Europe, of CATHAY.

JOHN OF PLANO CARPINI, deriving his name from a place in the territory of Perugia[1], and an immediate disciple of the founder of his order, was the head of one of the missions dispatched by Pope Innocent to call the chief and people of the Tartars to a better mind. He set out from Lyons on the 16th of April 1245, accompanied by Friar Stephen, a Bohemian, who speedily broke down and had to be left behind, was joined at Breslau by Friar Benedict, the Pole, who was intended to act as interpreter, and in February 1246 reached the head-quarters of Batu on the Volga. After some stay here, they were sent on to the camp of the Great Khan near Karakorum, (a fatiguing journey of three months and a half, which must have sorely tried an elderly and corpulent man like Friar John), arriving on the 22nd July. We shall not go into any further details on the mission or narrative of Plano Carpini which has been so ably reviewed and edited by M. D'Avezac[2],

[1] ["The editors of the *Analecta Franciscana* (iii, 266) remark that it would be more correct to write his Latin names *Plano Carpinis* or *de Carpine*, Planum Carpinis or Planum Carpi being the Latin form of the Italian Pian di Carpina, the modern Pian la Magione or Magione, about fourteen miles from Perugia." Rockhill, p. xxii, *n.*]

[2] See that able and admirable essay "Notice sur les Anciens Voyageurs en Tartarie en général, et sur celui de Jean du Plan de Carpin en particulier," *Recueil de Voyages et de Mémoires*, iv, 399.
[The best editions are: *The Journey of William of Rubruck to the Eastern Parts of the World*, 1253–5, *as narrated by himself, with two accounts of the earlier journey of John of Pian de Carpine.*

but be content to say that he obtained his dismissal from Kuyuk Khan on the 13th November, with a brief and haughty reply to the Pope's address, and returned safely, reporting his mission to the Pope apparently some time in the autumn of 1247[1].

97. After mentioning the wars of Chinghiz against the Cathayans (*Kitai*), he goes on to speak of that people as follows:

"But one part of the country of the Cathayans which lies upon the sea-shore has not been conquered by the Tartars to this day. Now these Cathayans of whom we have been speaking are heathen men, and have a written character of their own. Moreover 'tis said they have an Old and New Testament, and Lives of the Fathers, and religious recluses, and buildings which are used for churches as it were, in which they pray at their own times: and they say that they have also some saints of their own. They worship the one God, honour the Lord Jesus Christ, and believe in eternal life, but are entirely without baptism. They pay honour and reverence to our Scriptures, are well disposed towards Christians, and do many alms deeds. They seem indeed to be kindly and polished folks enough. They have no beard, and in character of countenance have a considerable resemblance to the Mongols, but are not so broad in the face. They have a language of their own. Their betters as craftsmen in every art practised by man are not to be found in the whole world. Their country is

Translated from the Latin, and Edited, with an Introductory Notice, by William Woodville Rockhill...London, Hakluyt Society, M.DCCCC.—*The Texts and Versions of John de Plano Carpini and William de Rubruquis as printed for the first time by Hakluyt in* 1598 *together with some shorter pieces. Edited by* C. Raymond Beazley, London, Hakluyt Society, 1903. See also: G. Pullé.—*Historia Mongalorum. Viaggio di F. Giovanni da Pian del Carpine ai Tartari nel* 1245–7. Firenze, 1913, 8vo.]

1 The last date is that of his arrival at Kiev a fortnight before St. John Baptist's day (*i.e.*, 9th June 1247).

very rich in corn, in wine, gold, silver, silk, and in every kind of produce that tends to the support of mankind."

98. William of RUBRUQUIS, a Fleming [from Ruysbroek, in French Flanders], was sent by St. Lewis on a mission to the Tartar chiefs, the object of which is not to be very clearly gathered. It was suggested, however, by the report that Sartach, the son of Batu, who was in command near the Don, was a Christian, and probably partook of the character of a religious as well as a political reconnaissance. The friar, though carrying letters from the king, was evidently under orders to deny all pretension to the character of an envoy, and to put forward his duty as a preacher of the Gospel as the motive of his journey. His narrative is a remarkably interesting one, showing that the author had a great deal of sagacity and observation; and his remarks, in reference to language in particular, show much acumen. There are difficulties in connexion with the indications of his route across Tartary, which it would be interesting to discuss, but scarcely appropriate here[1]. Suffice it, therefore, to say, that he entered the Black Sea on the 7th May, 1253, and after visiting successively Sartach, Batu, and the court of the Great Khan Mangu near Kara Korum, got back to Antioch about the end of June 1255.

99. After describing several of the nations of Further Asia, he says: "Further on is Great Cathay which I take to be the country which was anciently called the Land of the Seres. For the best silk stuffs are still got from them, and the people themselves call such stuffs *Seric*[2]; the

[1] Some remarks on the subject will, however, be found at the end of Supp. Note XVII.

[See RUBRUQUIS, by Sir H. Yule, *Encycl. Britannica*, xxi, pp. 46–7.—*Über Rubruk's Reise von* 1253–5...*von* Franz Max Schmidt, Berlin, 1885. (*Zeit. Ges. Erdk.*, xx.)]

[2] This is probably a reference to the Mongol word *Sirkek* (*supra*, p. 20), and Rubruquis thus anticipated Klaproth in tracing an

nation getting the name of Seres from a certain town of theirs. I was really given to understand that there is a town in that country which has silver walls and golden battlements[1]. The land in question is divided into many provinces, several of which have not yet been subdued by the Mongols, and the sea lies between it and India. Those Cathayans are little fellows, speaking much through the nose, and as is general with all those eastern people their eyes are very narrow. They are first-rate artists in every kind of craft, and their physicians have a thorough knowledge of the virtues of herbs, and an admirable skill in diagnosis by the pulse[2]. But they don't examine the urine or know anything on that subject; this I know from my own observation. There are a great many of these people at Karakorum; and it has always been their custom that all the sons must follow their father's craft whatever it be. Hence it is that they are obliged to pay so heavy a tribute; for they pay the Mongols daily 1500 *iascot* or *cosmi*[3]; the *iascot* is a piece of silver weighing ten marks, so that the daily sum amounts to 15,000 marks without counting the silk stuffs and food in kind which is taken from them, and the other services which they are obliged

eastern etymology of the term SERICA. I do not know what town he can allude to, but see the *Siurhia* of Moses the Armenian, and the *Saragh* of the Si-ngan fu inscription (*supra*, pp. 93, 108, 110).

[1] Martini alludes to a popular Chinese saying about the golden walls of Si-ngan fu (*Atlas Sinensis*). And these passages are remarkable with reference to the remark of Ptolemy about the metropolis *Thinæ*, that there was no truth in the stories of its brazen walls.

[2] Martini speaks of the great skill of the physicians in diagnosis by the pulse, and Duhalde is very prolix on that matter.

[A number of Chinese treatises has been written on the Art of feeling the Pulse.—See H. Cordier's *Bib. Sinica*, col. 1470–3.]

[3] I do not know what the word *iascot* is; but *cosmi* is possibly intended for the same word as the *sommi* of Pegolotti (*infra*, III, p. 148), though the value here assigned would be about ten times that of the *sommo*, taking the mark as ⅔ of a pound. [See Rockhill's *Rubruck*, pp. 156–7 *n*.]

to render[1]....And in answer to my inquiries of the priests who came from Cathay I was told that from the place where I found Mangu-Chan to Cathay was twenty days' journey going south-east....One day there sat with me a certain priest from Cathay clothed in a crimson stuff of a splendid colour[2], so I asked him whence that colour was got. In reply he told me that in the eastern parts of Cathay there are lofty rocks inhabited by certain creatures which have the human form in every respect except that they can't bend their knees, but get along by some kind of a jumping motion. They are only a cubit high, and are hairy all over, and dwell in inaccessible holes in the rock. So the huntsmen bring beer with them, which they know how to brew very strong, and make holes in the rocks like cups which they fill with beer. (For they have no wine in Cathay, but make their drink of rice, though now they are beginning to plant vines[3].) So the huntsmen hide themselves, and then the creatures come out of their holes and taste the drink that has been set for them and call out 'Chin chin!' and from this call they get their name: for they are called *Chinchin*. Then they gather in great numbers and drink up the beer and get tipsy and fall asleep. So the huntsmen come and catch them sleeping and bind them hand and foot, and open a vein in the neck of the creatures, and after taking three or four drops of blood let them go. And 'tis that blood, he told me, that

[1] Pp. 291–2.

[2] [Rockhill remarks, *l.c.*, p. 199 *n.*: "This priest must have been a Tibetan lama who had visited China. Chinese priests (whether Buddhist or Taoist) have never worn red gowns, and Friar William has told us that all the *Tuin* among the Mongols dressed in yellow."]

[3] [Rockhill remarks, *l.c.*, p. 199 *n.*: "Though the Chinese have never made wine from the grape, the vine has been cultivated in China since the second century B.C., when it was brought there from Turkestan by the great traveller, Chang-k'ien."]

gives this most precious purple dye[1]. And they also used to tell as a fact, though I don't believe a word of it, that there is a certain province on the other side of Cathay, and whatever a man's age be when he enters that province he never gets any older. Cathay lies on the Ocean....The common money of Cathay consists of pieces of cotton paper about a palm in length and breadth, upon which certain lines are printed resembling the seal of Mangu Chan. They do their writing with a brush such as painters paint with, and a single character of theirs comprehends several letters so as to form a whole word[2]."

100. Another traveller, of whose journey some account has come down to us, visited the Court of Mangu Khan immediately after Rubruquis. This was Hethum or HAYTON I, King of Little Armenia, [residing in the city of Sis, in Cilicia] who at an early date saw the irresistible power of the Tartars and made terms with them; *i.e.*, acknowledged himself the Khan's vassal. On the accession of Kuyuk Khan (1246) the king sent his brother Sempad or Sinibald, Constable of Armenia, to secure the continuance

[1] This is a genuine Chinese story.

["The story here told is found in a Chinese work, entitled, *Chu ch'uan* or *Records of Notes* by Wang-kang of T'ai-yuan, in Chu, but I have been unable to ascertain the date at which it was written....The other details of Friar William's story are supplied by another Chinese work, entitled *Hua-yang kuo chih*, or 'Topographical description of the state of Hua-yang.' Hua-yang included part of the present province of Ssŭ-ch'uan. This work says: 'The *hsing-hsing* is found in the Shan (*Ai-lao*) country, in the province of Yung-chan. It can speak. A red dye can be made with its blood.' The above quotations are taken from Ma Tuan-lin, bk. 329,8." (Rockhill, *l.c.*, p. 200 *n.*) Yule, *Hobson-Jobson*, p. 154, with regard to the story of Rubruck, writes: "And it is equally remarkable to find the same story related with singular closeness of correspondence out of 'the Chinese books of geography' by Francesco Carletti, 350 years later (in 1600). He calls the creatures *Zinzin* (*Ragionamenti di F. C.*, pp. 138–9)."]

[2] Pp. 327–329. Neither Marco Polo, nor, I believe, any other traveller previous to the sixteenth century, had the acumen to discern the great characteristic of the Chinese writing as Rubruquis has done here.

of good understanding. This prince was four years absent, and we possess a letter from him written on the journey in which some allusions are made to Tangut and Cathay, with reference to the general delusion as to the Christianity of those countries[1].

[1] The letter is addressed to the King and Queen of Cyprus and others at their court, and was written apparently from Samarkand (printed *Saurequant*, probably for *Samrequant*). Here is an extract: "We understand it to be the fact that it is five years past since the death of the present Chan's father [Okkodai]; but the Tartar barons and soldiers had been so scattered over the face of the earth that it was scarcely possible in the five years to get them together in one place to enthrone the Chan aforesaid. For some of them were in India, and others in the land of CHATA, and others in the land of CASCHAR and of TANCHAT. This last is the land from which came the Three Kings to Bethlem to worship the Lord Jesus which was born. And know that the power of Christ has been, and is, so great, that the people of that land are Christians; and the whole land of Chata believes in those Three Kings. I have myself been in their churches and have seen pictures of Jesus Christ and the Three Kings, one offering gold, the second frankincense, and the third myrrh. And it is through those Three Kings that they believe in Christ, and that the Chan and his people have now become Christians. And they have their churches before his gates where they ring their bells and beat upon pieces of timber. ......And I tell you that we have found many Christians scattered all over the East, and many fine churches, lofty, ancient, and of good architecture, which have been spoiled by the Turks. Hence the Christians of the land came before the present Khan's grandfather; and he received them most honourably, and granted them liberty of worship, and issued orders to forbid their having any just cause of complaint by word or deed. And so the Saracens who used to treat them with contumely have now like treatment in double measure.......And let me tell you that those who set up for preachers (among these Christians), in my opinion, deserve to be well chastised. Let me tell you, moreover, that in the land of India, which St. Thomas the Apostle converted, there is a certain Christian king who stood in sore tribulation among the other kings who were Saracens. They used to harass him on every side, until the Tartars reached that country, and he became their liegeman. Then, with his own army and that of the Tartars, he attacked the Saracens; and he made such booty in India that the whole East is full of Indian slaves; I have seen more than 50,000 whom this king took and sent for sale" (Mosheim, App., p. 49).

[I have given in the Supplementary Notes the full text of this letter from the old French translation in the *Vie de Saint Louis par Guillaume de Nangis*, pp. 361–3 of vol. xx of the *Recueil des Historiens des Gaules et de la France*, 1840.]

The motive in the letter is perhaps the justification of his brother Hayton for having, like this questionable Indian king, become the Tartar's liegeman. The writer [died aged 68, at Sis, in 1276, from a wound to his foot received during his pursuit of

Hayton himself went to the court of Mangu Khan soon after the latter's accession, to assure his position with that potentate, and to obtain certain advantages for himself and his states. He set out apparently in the beginning of 1254, first visiting Bachu Noian, the general of the Tartar army at Kars, and then passing through Armenia Proper and by the Pass of Derbend to the Volga, where he saw Batu and his son Sartach, whom this narrative alleges to have been a Christian, in opposition to Rubruquis, who says such stories were all nonsense[1]. The chiefs received Hayton well, and sent him on to Kara Korum by a route far to the north of that followed by Plano Carpini and Rubruquis. Leaving the court of Batu on the 13th May, the party arrived at the royal camp before the 13th September; they saw the Great Khan in state on the 14th and offered their gifts. King Hayton was treated with honour and hospitality, and on the 1st November set out on his homeward journey, passing by Bishbaliq, [Almaliq, Ili baliq] and through the modern Dzungaria to Otrar, Samarkand, and Bokhara; thence through Khorasan and Mazanderan to Tabriz, and so to his own territories [where he arrived at the end of July 1255].

King Hayton related many wonderful things that he had seen and heard of the nations of barbarians, and among others of the *Ghotaians* or Cathayans. In their country there were many idolaters who worshipped a clay image called *Shakemonia*. This personage had been

the Turkmen who had invaded Cilicia near Marasch. See *Historiens des Croisades,—Documents Arméniens*, i, 1869, p. 606.]

[1] See III, p. 19. When Friar William was leaving the camp of Sartach, one of the Tartar officers said to him: "Don't you be saying that our master is a Christian; he is no Christian, but a Mongol!" (p. 107). Just as Sir Walter Scott tells somewhere of a belated southron traveller in the old days, who, seeking vainly for shelter in some town on the border, exclaimed in despair: "Would no good Christian take him in?" To which an old woman who heard him, made answer: "Christian? Na, na! we're a' Jardines and Johnstones here."

Deity for the last 3040 years, and had still to rule the World for 35 tumans or 350,000 years, when he was to be deprived of his divinity. They had also another god (who should then reign ?) called *Madri*, of whom they had made a clay image of incredible size. In these statements we have a rough indication of Buddhism with its last Buddha or deified sage, SAKYA-MUNI, and its coming Buddha, Maitreya or MAIDARI, awaiting his time in the development of the ages. The king heard, too, of a people beyond Cathay whose women had the use of reason *like men*, whilst the males were great hairy dogs, a story which Plano Carpini had also heard, and which Klaproth has found in the Chinese books of the period[1]. The information regarding Cathay and other countries of the far East, contained in the history written half a century later by the king's namesake and relative, Hayton the Younger, was also probably derived in part from the former and his companions.

101. We do not mean here to enter into any details regarding that illustrious Venetian family whose travels occupy a large space in the interval between the journeys of Rubruquis and King Hayton and the end of the thir-

[1] See *Pl. Carpini*, pp. 12, 36. King Hayton, in his later years, abdicated and became a monk; as did at a later date his son Hayton II, and again, their kinsman, Hayton the historian.

[The account of Hethum's journey was originally written in Armenian by Kirakos Gandsaketsi who belonged to the suite of the King. It has been translated into Russian by Argutinsky and from Russian by Klaproth. (*Nouv. Journ. Asiatique*, 2 Sér., xii, pp. 273 *seq.*) In 1870, it was again translated into French by Brosset (*Mém. Acad. des Sciences St. Pétersb.*, July 1870) and into Russian by K. P. Patkanov in 1874. See H. Cordier's *Bib. Sinica*, col. 1998–9.—An English translation was given in 1876 by E. Bretschneider. (*Journ. North China B. R. As. Soc.*, x, 1876, pp. 297 *seq.*; reprint. in *Mediaeval Researches*, i, 1883, pp. 164 *seq.*) It is interesting to note that "it seems to be the only instance that any mediaeval author mentions a city of this name [Ili baliq]. The city was evidently situated on the Ili river, perhaps near the place where now the post-road from Kuldja to Tashkend crosses the river. There is on the left the borough *Iliskoye*." (Bretschneider, *Med. Res.*, II, p. 44.)]

teenth century, those travels which more than all other narratives together familiarised Europe with the name and wonders of Cathay. Indeed, all other travellers to that region are but stars of a low magnitude beside the full orb of MARCO POLO. There was a time when he fell into discredit[1]; but that is long past, and his veracity and justness of observation still shine brighter under every recovery of lost or forgotten knowledge. Nearly fifty years ago a Quarterly Reviewer received with disparaging anticipations the announcement of a new Italian edition of Polo[2], as if deeming that little could be added in illustration of the Traveller to what Marsden had effected. Much as Marsden really did in his splendid edition, it would be no exaggeration to say that the light thrown on Marco's narrative has since that day been more than doubled from the stores of Chinese, Mongol, and Persian history which have been rendered accessible to European readers, or brought directly to bear on the elucidation of the Traveller, by Klaproth, Rémusat, Quatremère, and many other scholars, chiefly Frenchmen. And within the last year Paris has sent out an edition of the Traveller, by M. Pauthier, which leaves far behind everything previously attempted, concentrating in the notes not only many of the best suggestions of previous commentators, but a vast mass of entirely new matter from the editor's own Chinese studies[3].

[1] The editors of the *Histoire Générale des Voyages* (I am afraid this is a translation from the English) express doubts whether Polo ever was really in China or Tartary, because he says nothing of the great Wall, of tea, of the compressed feet of the ladies, etc. (Baldelli Boni, *Il Milione*, p. lxxv). [See *Marco Polo*, i, p. 292 *n.*]

[2] Baldelli Boni's: see that work, i, p. civ. Perhaps, however, the terms quoted may refer only to the improbability of fresh light from Italian archives.

[3] [We need not remind the reader that Yule's *Book of Ser Marco Polo* had not yet been published; the first edition appeared in 1871, the second in 1875, and the third, revised by the present writer, in 1903.]

102. During a period including the last thirty years of the thirteenth century and the first few years of the fourteenth many diplomatic communications took place between the Mongol Khans of Persia and the sovereigns of Christendom; and in these we find a tone on the part of the Tartar princes very different from the curt insolence of the previous age. They no longer held the same domineering supremacy, and their great object now was to obtain Christian alliances against their bitter rivals, the Sultans of Egypt. These communications do not, however, bear upon our subject, except in one curious incidental aspect. The Khans of Persia, as liegemen of the Great Khan, still received from him their seals of state, and two of their letters preserved in the French archives exhibit the impressions of these seals bearing inscriptions in ancient Chinese characters, in the case of the earlier letter perhaps the first specimens of such characters that reached Europe[1].

[1] See Rémusat's Memoir in *Mém. de l'Acad. des Inscript.*, vii, 367, 391, etc. The earlier letter is from Arghún Khan, and is dated 1289. It is written in Uighûr characters in the Mongol language on a roll of cotton paper six feet and a half long by ten inches wide. The seal is thrice impressed on the face of the letter in red. It is five inches and a half square, containing six characters; "Seal of the Minister of State, Pacificator of Nations." The second letter is from Khodabandah, otherwise called Oljaitu, and written in May, 1305. The seal in this case contains the words, "By a supreme decree the Seal of the Descendant of the Emperor charged to reduce to obedience the 10,000 barbarous nations." A duplicate of this perhaps went to Edward II, as his reply, dated Northampton, 16th October, 1307, is in Rymer's *Fœdera* (Rémusat, *u.s.*).

[These two documents addressed to the King of France, Philip the Fair, are kept in the National Archives in Paris; a facsimile has been given of both in Pl. xiv of *Documents de l'époque mongole*, edited by Prince Roland Bonaparte.]

[It is quite possible that a first embassy was sent to Honorius IV by Arghún in the first year of his reign (1285), according to a letter sent by this prince to the Pope in the month of May of the first year of his reign. (See *Annales Ecclesiat.*, 1285, p. 619. Chabot, *Mar Jabalaha*, pp. 188 *seq.*) Then the second embassy would be Bar Cauma's (1287–8, see *supra*, p. 120). The answer of Nicholas IV to Jabalaha is printed by Chabot, *l.c.*, pp. 195 *seq.*,

This peculiar relation, which the Mongol conquests produced between China and Western Asia, not only introduced strangers from the remote West to China and its borders, but also carried Chinese to vast distances from the Middle Kingdom. Not only were corps of Alans and Kipchaks seen fighting in Tong King, but Chinese engineers were employed on the banks of the Tigris, and Chinese astronomers, physicians, and theologians could be consulted at Tabriz[1]. The missions of Kúblái himself extended to Madagascar.

103. There must have been other Frank travellers to Cathay contemporary with the Polos, such as the German engineer, whom Marco mentions as employed under his father, his uncle, and himself, in the construction of mechanical artillery to aid Kúblái Khán in his attack on the city of Saianfu or Siang yang fu in Hu kwang, but no other narrative from the time of their sojourn in China has come down to us[2].

as well as his letters to Arghún, pp. 200 *seq*. A third embassy was sent by Arghún (1289–90) with the Genoese Christian Buscarel at its head; the original letter which he took to Philip the Fair, king of France, is in the Archives Nationales in Paris; it is written in Uighúr character, and a facsimile of it has been given in the *Documents mongols* edited by Prince Roland Bonaparte; he also visited Edward I, King of England; he arrived in London on the 5th January, 1290; see *Unpublished Notices of the times of Edward I, especially of his relations with the Moghul Sovereigns of Persia*, by T. Hudson Turner. (*Archæological Journal*, viii, 1851, pp. 45–51.) A fourth embassy was sent to Rome by Arghún (1290–1) with Chagan or Zagan as its chief. (See Chabot, pp. 235 *seq*.)]

[1] See *Polo*, iii, 35; D'Ohsson, ii, 611; iii, 265; Quatremère's *Rashid*, pp. 195, 417, and Rashid's own grandiloquence, p. 39. Marco Polo's will bequeaths liberty and a legacy to a Tartar servant, thirty years after his return home.

["Also I release PETER the Tartar, my servant, from all bondage, as completely as I pray God to release mine own soul from all sin and guilt. And I also remit him whatever he may have gained by work at his own house; and over and above I bequeath him 100 *lire* of Venice denari." (*Marco Polo*, i, p. 72.)]

[2] [Cf. *Marco Polo*, ii, pp. 158–169.]

[*Marco Polo*, ii, p. 159, says: "The Khan bade them with all his heart have such mangonels made as speedily as possible.

An interesting chapter on Cathay is found in the geographical part of the work of Hayton, Prince of Gorigos, already alluded to. This prince, after long experience of eastern war and politics, [was exiled from Little Armenia in 1305, went to Cyprus and became, at the abbey of Lapaïs, in Cyprus, a monk of the Order of Praemonstrants. He arrived in France probably at the end of 1306, and by order of Clement V he dictated his history in French in August 1307 in the city of Poitiers to Nicholas Faulcon of Toul, who translated it afterwards into Latin[1]]. It contains in sixty chapters a geography of Asia, the history of the Mongol Khans, and notices of the Holy Land and the Eastern Christians.

The first fifteen chapters contain short successive accounts of the chief kingdoms of Asia, and form altogether probably the best geographical summary of that continent which had yet been compiled. In the Supplementary

Now Messer Nicolo and his brother and his son immediately caused timber to be brought, as much as they desired, and fit for the work in hand. And they had two men among their followers, a German and a Nestorian Christian, who were masters of that business, and these they directed to construct two or three mangonels capable of casting stones of 300 lbs. weight." Yule says rightly, *l.c.*, p. 167, "this chapter is one of the most perplexing in the whole book, owing to the chronological difficulties involved." The siege of Siang yang was undertaken in the latter part of 1268, and it fell with Fan ch'eng only in March of 1273. Marco Polo had not yet arrived in China. Cf. *Marco Polo*, ii, pp. 167–9.]

[1] [The history ends thus, in French: "Lequel livre je, Nicole Falcon de Toul, escris primierement en françois, si come le dit freire Hayton me disoit de sa bouche, sanz note ne exemplaire, e de romanz le translatei en latin. Et celui livre ont nostre signor le Pape, en l'an Nostre Seignor MCCCVII, en mois d'aost. *Deo gracias. Amen.*"]

[In Latin: Explicit liber Hystoriarum parcium Orientis, a religioso viro fratre Haytono, ordinis Beati Augustini, domino Churchi, consanguineo regis Armenie, compilatus, ex mandato summi pontificis domini Clementis pape quinti, in civitate Pictavensi, regni Franchie, quem ego, Nicolaus Falconi, primo scripsi in galico ydiomate, sicut idem frater H. michi ore suo ditabat, absque nota sive aliquo exemplari, et de galico transtuli in latinum, anno Domini M° IIIc septimo, mense augusti. Deo dicamus gratias."]

Notes to this Essay will be found the chapter on Cathay [with the French and Latin texts[1]].

[Hayton arrived at Cyprus on the 6th May, 1308, with a letter of the Pope to the Prince of Tyre concerning the Templars. He then returned to his native land, was appointed constable, and died probably after 1314 in Armenia, not at Poitiers.]

104. Just as the three Poli were reaching their native city, the forerunner of a new band of travellers was entering Southern China. This was JOHN OF MONTE CORVINO, a Franciscan monk, who, already nearly fifty years of age, was plunging alone into that great ocean of Paganism, and of what he deemed little better, Nestorianism, to preach the Gospel. After years of uphill work and solitary labour others joined him; the Papal See woke up to what was going on; it made him Archbishop in Khanbaliq or Peking, with patriarchal authority, and sent him spasmodically batches of suffragan bishops and friars of his order; the Roman Church spread; churches and Minorite Houses were established at Khanbaliq; at Zaytún or Chin chau, at Yang chau and elsewhere; and the missions flourished under the immediate patronage of the Great Khan himself. Among the friars whose duty carried them to Cathay during the interval between the beginning of the century and the year 1328, when Archbishop John was followed to the grave by mourning multitudes, Pagan as well as Christian, several have left letters or more extended accounts of their experiences in Cathay. Among these may be mentioned ANDREW OF PERUGIA, Bishop of Zaytún; JOHN DE CORA, Archbishop of Sultania (though it is not quite certain that his account was derived from personal knowledge), and above all FRIAR ODORIC OF PORDENONE. A short though interesting notice of China belonging to

[1] See Note XIV.

this period, but derived from the information of others, is also contained in the *Mirabilia* of FRIAR JORDANUS[1].

The only ecclesiastical narrative subsequent to the time of Archbishop John is that contained in the reminiscences of JOHN MARIGNOLLI, who spent four years at the court of Peking (1342–6) as Legate from the Pope.

105. But the Exchange had its emissaries at this time as well as the Church. The record is a very fragmentary and imperfect one, but many circumstances and incidental notices show how frequently the far East was reached by European traders in the first half of the fourteenth century; a state of things which it is very difficult to realise, when we see how all those regions, when reopened only two centuries later, seemed almost as absolutely new discoveries as the empires which about the same time Cortes and Pizarro were annexing in the West.

This frequency of commercial intercourse, at least with China, probably did not commence till some years after the beginning of the fourteenth century. For Montecorvino, writing in 1305, says it was then twelve years since he had heard any news of the Court of Rome or European politics, the only western stranger who had arrived in that time being a certain Lombard chirurgeon who had spread awful blasphemies about the Pope. Yet, even on his first entrance into Cathay, Friar John had been accompanied [from Tabriz] by one Master Peter of Lucalongo, whom he describes as a faithful Christian man and a great merchant [at whose expense ground was purchased at Khanbaliq to build a Christian Church]. The letter of Andrew, Bishop of Zaytún, lately referred to, quotes

[1] The journey of Ricold of Montecroce, one of the most learned of the monk travellers of the age (d. 1309), did not apparently extend beyond Baghdad. He mentions Cathay only once in noticing the conquests of Chinghiz. (*Pereg. Quat.*, 120.)

the opinion of the Genoese merchants of his acquaintance at that great seaport touching a question of exchanges. Marino Sanuto, the Venetian, writing about 1306 to propound a great scheme for the subversion of the Mahomedan power, alludes to the many merchants who had already gone to India to make their purchases and come back safely. About 1322 Friar Jordanus, the Dominican, when in sore trouble at Tana near Bombay, where four of his brethren had been murdered by the Mahomedans, falls in with a young Genoese who gives him aid; and in one of his letters from Gujarat, he speaks of information received from "Latin merchants." In the stories connected with the same martyred friars, we find mention of a merchant of Pisa owning a ship in the Indian seas. Mandeville, too, speaks of the merchants of Venice and Genoa coming habitually to Hormuz to buy goods[1]. Odoric, dictating his travels in 1330, refers for confirmation of the wonders related of the great city of Cansay or Hang chau, to the many persons whom he had met at Venice since his return, who had themselves been witnesses of all that he asserted. A few years later (1339) we find William of Modena, a merchant, dying for the Faith with certain friars at Almaliq on the banks of the Ili. John Marignolli mentions that when he was in Malabar about 1347–8, his interpreter was a youth who had been rescued from pirates in the Indian seas by a merchant of Genoa. And from the same authority we find that there was a *fondaco* or factory, and warehouse for the use of the Christian merchants, attached to one of the Franciscan convents at Zaytún.

106. But the most distinct and notable evidence of the importance and frequency of the European trade from

[1] [We need only refer the reader to our note, pp. 598–605 of *The Book of Ser Marco Polo*, Vol. ii, with regard to the value or rather lack of value of the Travels written by the so-called Mandeville.]

Cathay, of which silk and silk goods were the staple, is to be found in the work of F. BALDUCCI PEGOLOTTI, of which an account and extracts are given in the present collection. That the ventures on this trade were not insignificant is plain from the example taken by the author to illustrate the question of expenses on the journey to Cathay, which is that of a merchant carrying goods to the amount of some £12,000[1].

107. To the same period of the Mongol domination and active commerce with the west, belongs the voyage, about 1347, of the Moor, IBN BATUTA, to China, which forms a part of this work.

But, as regards Christian intercourse, missions and merchants alike disappear from the field soon after the middle of the fourteenth century, as the Mongol dynasty totters and comes down. We hear, indeed, once and again of friars and bishops despatched from Avignon; but they go forth into the darkness and are heard of no more. For the new rulers of China revert to the old indigenous policy and hold foreigners at arm's length; whilst Islam has recovered its ground and extended its grasp over Middle Asia, and the Nestorian Christianity which once prevailed there is rapidly vanishing and leaving its traces only in some strange parodies of church ritual which are found twined into the worship of the Tibetan Lamas, like the cabin gildings and mirrors of a wrecked vessel adorning the hut of a Polynesian chief. A dark mist has descended upon the farther east, covering MANGI and CATHAY with those cities of which the old travellers told such wonders, CAMBALEC and CANSAY and ZAYTÚN and CHINKALAN.

[1] [The following work has come to hand since Vol. III of *Cathay* was printed: *Der Mittelalterliche Welthandel von Florenz in seiner Geographischen Ausdehnung* (*nach der* Pratica della Mercatura *des* Balducci Pegolotti) *von* Dr. Eduard Friedmann. (*Abh. K. K. Geog. Ges. in Wien*, X Bd., 1912.)]

And when the veil rises before the Portuguese and Spanish explorers a century and a half later, those names are heard of no more. In their stead we have CHINA and PEKING, HANG CHAU and CHIN CHAU and CANTON. Not only are the old names forgotten, but the fact that those places had been known before, is utterly forgotten also. Gradually Jesuit missionaries went forth again from Rome. New converts were made and new vicariats constituted; but the old Franciscan churches and the Nestorianism with which they had battled had been alike swallowed up in the ocean of Paganism. In time, as we have seen, slight traces of the former existence of Christian churches came to the surface, and when Marco Polo was recalled to mind, one and another began to suspect that China and Cathay were one.

IX. CATHAY PASSING INTO CHINA.—CONCLUSION.

108. But we have been going too fast over the ground, and we must return to that dark interval of which we have spoken, between the fall of the Yuen dynasty and the first appearance of the Portuguese in the Bocca Tigris. The *name* of Cathay was not forgotten; the poets and romancers kept it in memory[1], and the geographers gave it a prominent place on their maps. But this was not all; some flickering gleams of light came now and then from behind the veil that now hung over Eastern Asia. Such are the cursory notices of Cathay which reached Ruy Gonzalez de Clavijo on his embassy to the court of

[1] E.g., the story of Mitridanes and Nathan in Boccaccio is laid in Cathay. And in the *Orlando Innamorato* the father of Angelica is King Galafron:

> "Il qual nell' India estrema signoreggia
> Una gran terra ch' ha nome il CATTAJO." x, 18.

Timur at Samarkand (A.D. 1403–5)[1], and John Schiltberger the Bavarian who served for many years in the armies of Bajazet and Timur, and returned to his native land in 1427[2].

109. More detail is found in the narrative of Nicolo Conti, as taken down in Latin by Poggio Bracciolini about 1440, of which a version has been given in *India in the*

[1] Clavijo speaks of an ambassador whom the Lord of Cathay had sent to Timur Beg, to demand the yearly tribute which was formerly paid. When Timur saw the Spaniards seated below this Cathayan ambassador, he sent orders that they should sit above him; those who came from the King of Spain, his son and friend, were not to sit below the envoy of a thief and scoundrel who was Timur's enemy. Timur was at this time meditating the expedition against China, in entering on which he died at Otrar (17th Feb. 1405).

The Emperor of Cathay, Clavijo tells us, was called *Chuyscan*, which means "Nine Empires." But the Zagatays (Timur's people) called him Tangus, which means *Pig Emperor* (*supra*, p. 33). The best of all merchandise coming to Samarkand was from China (it is not quite clear whether Clavijo understands Cathay and China to be the same); especially silk, satins, musk, rubies, diamonds, pearls, and rhubarb. The Chinese were said to be the most skilful workmen in the world. They said themselves that they had two eyes, the Franks one, and the Moors (Mahomedans) none (an expression which we find repeatedly quoted by different authors). Cambalu, the chief city of Cathay, was six months from Samarkand, two of which were over steppes. In the year of the embassy 800 laden camels came from Cambalu to Samarkand. The people with them related that the city was near the sea and twenty times as big as Tabriz. Now Tabriz is a good league in length, so Cambalu must be twenty leagues in length (bad geometry Don Ruy !). The emperor used to be a Pagan but was converted to Christianity. (Markham's *Trans.*, pp. 133 *seq.*, 171, 173 *seq.*)

[2] Schiltberger seems to have been at Samarkand at the same time with Clavijo. All that he says of China is with reference to the embassy spoken of by the latter, and Timur's scheme of invasion: "Now at this time had the Great Chan, the King of CHETEY, sent an envoy to Thämerlin with four hundred horses, and demanded tribute of him, seeing that he had neglected to pay it and kept it back for five years past. So Thämerlin took the envoy with him to his capital aforesaid. Then sent he the envoy away and bid him tell his master he would be no tributary nor vassal of his, nay he trusted to make the emperor *his* tributary and vassal. And he would come to him in person. And then he sent off despatches throughout his dominions to make ready, for he would march against Cetey. And so when he had gathered 1,800,000 men he marched for a whole month," etc. (*Reisen des Johannes Schiltberger*, etc., München, 1859, p. 81).

Fifteenth Century. The narrative does not distinctly assert that Nicolo himself had been in Cathay[1]; but I think there is internal evidence that he must have been. He briefly notices Cambalec (CAMBALESCHIA) and another city of great size which had been established by the emperor, to which he gives the name of NEMPTAI, and which was the most populous of all[2]. He speaks of the great wealth of the country and of the politeness and civilisation of the people, as quite on a par with those of Italy. Their merchants were immensely wealthy, and had great ships much larger than those of Europe, with triple sides and divided into water-tight compartments for security. "Us," he says, "they call Franks, and say that whilst other nations are blind, we see with one eye, whilst they are the only people who see with both." Alone of all eastern nations they use tables at dinner, and silver

[1] [I do not believe that Conti actually visited China. Had he done so, he would not have used the obsolete geographical words of Marco Polo's nomenclature, *i.e.* words used by foreigners, but the real Chinese names of places, as the Portuguese did when they arrived in China in the first half of the XVIth century.]

[2] I suppose this to be Nan King. The "ab imperatore condita" appears to imply recent construction or reconstruction, which would justly apply to Nan King, established as the capital of the Ming dynasty at the time the Mongols were expelled (1367–8). Indeed Ramusio's Italian version of Conti has "*la quale da poco tempo in qua è stata fatta di novo di questo rè.*" Thirty miles, the circuit ascribed by Conti to Nemptai, though above the truth, is less than more recent travellers have named (see p. 205 *infra*). I am not able to explain the name, though I have little doubt that it was a Mongol appellation of Nan King, perhaps connected with *Ingtien*, a name given to that city by the Ming when they made it their capital (*Martini*), and that it is the same which occurs in Sharifuddín's life of Timur, where it is mentioned that from *Tetcaul* (qu. Karaúl of Shah Rukh's ambassadors? *infra*), the fortified gate of the Great Wall on the Shen si frontier, it was fifty-one days' journey to KENJANFU (i.e., Si-ngan fu, *vide infra*, p. 246), and from that city forty days alike to Canbalec and NEMNAI. The reading should probably be *Nemtai* as in Conti. One dot missing makes the difference (Pétis de la Croix, iii, 218). [The city meant is possibly Nan King, not Hang chau, as suggested in a note of Poggio's ed. and of Winter Jones' translation; but Nemptai or Nemtaï is a transcription of Nam tai, the island in the Min River, on which the foreign settlement of Fu chau was built after the treaty of 1842.]

dishes. The women paint their faces. Their tombs are caves dug in the side of a hill, arched over, and revetted on the exterior with a handsome wall. All these particulars are perfectly accurate, and can scarcely have been acquired except from personal knowledge[1].

110. The information brought home by Nicolo was eagerly caught at by the cosmographers of the period, and much of it is embodied both in the *Cosmographia* in the Palatine Library at Florence[2], and in the more important map of FRA MAURO, now in the Ducal Palace at Venice. The latter map indeed embraces so much more than is noticed in Poggio's narrative, especially in the valleys of the Ganges and the Irawadi, that there can be little doubt that Conti, when at Venice, was subjected to

[1] See *India in the XVth cent.*, pp. 14, 21, 23, 27. The passage about the tombs is, indeed, in the printed edition given as of *Anterior India*; but I have no doubt that this is a mistake for *Interior India*, a term which Conti uses for China, as where he quotes the proverb about the one eye of the Franks, etc., as used by the *Interiores Indi*. This is inexactly translated by Mr. Winter Jones as "The natives of *Central* India"; but the word is used for *remoter*, as by Cosmas, when he says that Ceylon receives silk "from the parts further in (ἀπὸ τῶν ἐνδοτέρων), I speak of Chinista and the other marts in that quarter," and again of China, "ἧς ἐνδοτέρω ('further *ben*,' as they say in Scotland), there is no other country." Ptolemy uses a like expression for *remoter* (see ext. *infra*). The description of the tombs applies accurately to those of the Chinese and of no other people.

Poggio has evidently not followed Conti's Geography with any insight, and thus has mixed up features belonging to very different eastern nations. Thus the passage which is given as applicable to all the nations of India, of writing *vertically*, was probably meant only to apply to the Chinese.

[2] This map is described by Zurla (*Dissert.*, ii, 397) as of 1417, and, if I am not mistaken, it is so entered in the Palatine Catalogue. But the coincidences with Conti, *e.g.*, his Java Major and Minor, his islands of Sandai and Bandan, his lake in Ceylon, etc., are too many and too minute to admit question of their origin. The third figure of the date is half obliterated, and can just as well be read 4 as 1. The date is certainly 1447 at the earliest.

I had noted these remarks from examination of the original before I became aware, from a passage in Professor Kunstmann's *Die Kenntniss Indiens im 15ten Jahrhunderte* (p. 33), that Neigebauer, an author whom I do not know, had already made the correction.

a more effectual cross-examination by the cosmographic friar[1].

III. Poggio helps us to another very ill-focussed glimpse of Cathay in the notices which he adds at the end of Conti's narrative. Here he states that whilst he was preparing that story for publication a person had arrived "from Upper India towards the north," who had been deputed to visit the Pope and to collect information about Western Christians, by the Patriarch of his own country, which was a Nestorian kingdom, twenty days' journey from Cathay. The imperfections of interpretation made it difficult to acquire information of interest from this personage. He spoke, however, of the Great Khan, and of his having dominion over nine potent kings[2]. This seems to be the same envoy who is spoken of by the Italian philosopher and mathematician, Paolo del Pozzo Toscanelli,

[1] Thus in Burmah we have not only, as in the narrative by Poggio, AVA and PAIGU (Pegu, transmuted by Poggio into *Pancovia*, and printed *Panconia* in Winter Jones' ed.), but also CHESMI (Cosmin, the port representing the modern Bassein till the beginning of last century, but the exact site of which seems lost), MARTABAN; and up the river PERHÉ (Prome, in the true Burmese form *Pré*), POCHANG (Pagán, the ancient capital), CAPELANG (the Ruby country north of Ava, a name preserved to a much later date, but not now traceable), MOQUAN (Mogoung). And near the head of the Irawadi, *i.e.*, at Bhamó, is the rubric, "Here goods are transferred from river to river, and so go on into Cathay." In Bengal, again, we have ORIÇA, BENGALLA (see Ibn Batuta, *infra*), SONARGAUAM (*ibid.*), SATGAUAM (Satganw, or perhaps Chittagong), and in the interior SCIERNO (*Cernoue* in Poggio; *i.e.*, Gaur under the name of *Shahr-i-nau*, see *ibid.*), ZUANAPUR (Jaunpur), CHANDAR (Chunar ?). But there are enormous fundamental confusions in Fra Mauro's ideas of the rivers of India. Thus, the Indus takes in a great measure the place of the Ganges, whilst the Ganges is confounded with the Kiang. And some of the towns of Bengal named are placed on the Indus and some are transported eastward.

[2] See the extract from Clavijo above. This notion may be taken from some traditional title bearing reference to the oldest division of China under Yu (B.C. 2286) into *Nine* Provinces (*Chine Moderne*, p. 37); also in the division of the empire under the Mongols into 12 sings (*infra*, III, p. 128): three of these, Solangka, Corea, and Yun nan, were considered exterior, the other *nine to constitute China Proper* (D'OHSSON, ii, 478). *Nine Provinces* was anciently a name applied to China Proper. (*Chine Moderne*, 211; and *Vie de Hiouen Thsang*, p. 298.)

in a letter addressed in 1474 to his friend Fernando Martinez, canon of Lisbon, of which the writer afterwards sent a copy to Columbus, when replying to a communication from the latter on the great object of his life. The statement of Poggio that the envoy came from a Christian ecclesiastic seems much more probable than that he came, as Toscanelli thought, from the Great Khan himself. But it remains a difficult problem to say whence he did really come. It would seem as if some tribe of the Kerait or the Uighúrs had maintained their Christianity till near the middle of the fifteenth century[1].

112. To this period also belong the notices of Cathay which were collected by JOSAFAT BARBARO, and are recounted in the history of his Embassy to Persia. Whilst he was on this mission, the Lord Assambei (*i.e.*, Uzun Hassan, a Turcoman chief, who, in the civil strifes that accompanied the decay of Timur's dynasty, acquired the whole of Western Persia), being one day greatly pleased with the acumen shown by Barbaro in judging of a Balass ruby, called out "O, Cathayers, Cathayers! (said you not well that) three years have been allowed mankind, and you have got two of them, and the Franks the third!" Barbaro understood what he meant, for he had already heard the proverb (as we have now three times before[2]) from a certain ambassador in the service of the Khan of

[1] See the letter in Note XV. The curious statements in Varthema about Christians of *Sarnau* [Siam], a country towards Cathay, with whom he travelled in the Archipelago, are here brought to mind. I think Mr. Badger has referred to this passage of Poggio; but I cannot turn to his edition now. The letter of Toscanelli is extracted from "*Del Vecchio e Nuovo Gnomone Fiorentino, etc., di Lionardo Ximenes della Comp. di Gesù, Geografo di sua Maestà Imp.* Firenze, 1757," pp. lxxxi–xcviii.

Another traveller, who returned from the Indies in 1424 after wandering there for twenty-four years, by name Bartolomeo Fiorentino, related what he had seen to Pope Eugenius at Venice; but, unfortunately, nothing of this narrative seems to have been preserved. (See Humboldt, *Examen Critique*, etc., i. 260.)

[2] From Hayton (in Note XIV), Clavijo, and Conti.

the Tartars of the Volga, who had come from Cathay in 1436, and whom Barbaro had entertained in his house at Tana (or Azov) "hoping to get some jewel out of him." From this ambassador he gathered a good deal of detail about Cathay, which he gives in a later part of his work[1].

113. Somewhat earlier in the century occurred the mission sent by Shah Rukh, the son of Timur, to the court of Ch'eng Tsu, the third Emperor of the Ming dynasty. Of this embassy a narrative written by Khwája Ghaiassuddín, surnamed Nakkásh or the Painter, a member of the mission, has been preserved in Abdur Razzak's History of Shah Rukh, and has been translated by M. Quatremère[2]. The embassy took place in A.H. 823–5 (A.D. 1420–2), and was one out of several such interchanged between the courts, of which mention is made in the same history[3]. It is amusing to find the Emperor of China, in a letter carried by one of his embassies, speaking of the steadfastness with which his correspondent's father, Timur, had maintained his loyalty to the Court of China[4]. An abstract of the narrative, with notes, will be found in the sequel[5].

114. Except the brief and fabulous stories of Chin and Machin, which ATHANASIUS NIKITIN picked up in the ports of Western India (1468–74) I am not aware of any other European notices of China previous to the voyages of Columbus and De Gama. The former, it is scarcely

[1] Ramusio, ii, ff. 106 *v.* and 107. See the extracts in Note XVI.

[2] *Notices et Extraits*, xiv, pt. i, pp. 387 *seqq.* There is a slightly abridged translation in *Astley's Voyages.* Quatremère is mistaken in supposing that the narrative of the Embassy is translated in *Chambers's Asiatic Miscellany.* There is only an extract containing some account of the preceding intercourse between the courts.

[3] See *op. cit.*, pp. 213 *seqq.*, 216 *seqq.*, 304–6. There seems to be some variation as to the correct date. It is not worth going into here, but a comparison of the passage where Abdur Razzak speaks of the embassy in the ordinary course of his history (p. 306) with that where he introduces the special narrative (p. 387) will show the inconsistency.

[4] P. 214.

[5] See Note XVII.

needful to say, in his great enterprise was seeking no new continent but a shorter route to the Cathay and Cipangu of Marco Polo, and died believing that the countries which he had discovered were the eastern skirts of Asia, a belief which was not extinct for some twenty years and more after his death[1].

115. The Portuguese first visited a port of China in 1514, and the adventurers on this occasion sold their goods to great profit though they were not allowed to land. In 1517 took place the trading expedition to Canton under Andrade, carrying the unfortunate ambassador Pirez, who died in fetters in China[2].

116. With this event, perhaps, our sketch ought to conclude. But it was a good many years longer before China was familiarly known from the seaward access, and with the revived interest in discovery and in the perusal

[1] In a letter, *De Orbis Situ ac Descriptione*, from a certain Franciscan Friar Francis, addressed to the Archbishop of Palermo, which is attached to some copies of the *Peregrinatio Joannis Hesei* (Antwerp. 1565), the city of "Themistetan" or Mexico is identified with the Quinsai of Marco Polo, Hispaniola with Cipangu, and so forth.

[2] This last is generally stated as the first Portuguese expedition to China. But the former one is noticed by Andrew Corsalis in his letter to Duke Lorenzo de' Medici, dated 6th January, 1515 (Ramusio, i, ff., 180, 181): "The merchants of the land of China also make voyages to Malacca across the Great Gulf to get cargoes of spices, and bring from their own country musk, rhubarb, pearls, tin, porcelain, and silk and wrought stuffs of all kinds, such as damasks, satins, and brocades of extraordinary richness. For they are people of great skill, and on a par with ourselves (*di nostra qualità*), but of uglier aspect, with little bits of eyes. They dress very much after our fashion, and wear shoes and stockings (? *scarpe e calciamenti*) like ourselves. I believe them to be pagans, though many allege that they hold our faith or some part of it. During this last year some of our Portuguese made a voyage to China. They were not permitted to land; for they say 'tis against their custom to let foreigners enter their dwellings. But they sold their goods at a great gain, and they say there is as great profit in taking spices to China as in taking them to Portugal; for 'tis a cold country and they make great use of them. It will be five hundred leagues from Malacca to China, sailing north." [See *L'Arrivée des Portugais en Chine*, par Henri Cordier; ext. from the *T'oung pao*, xii, 1911.]

of the old travellers, attention became again directed to CATHAY, as a region distinct from these new found Indies, so that it might be considered yet to hold an independent place in geographical history. Cathay had been the aim of the first voyage to the north-west of the Cabots in 1496, and it continued to be the object of many adventurous English voyages to the north-west and the north-east till far on in the succeeding century, though in the later of these expeditions China no doubt had assumed its place. At least one memorable land journey too was made by Englishmen, of which the investigation of the trade with Cathay was a chief object; I mean of course that in which Anthony Jenkinson and the two Johnsons reached Bokhara from Russia in 1558–9. The country regarding which they gathered information at that city is still known to them only as Cathay, and its great capital is still as in the days of Polo Cambalu and not Peking[1].

117. Other narratives of Asiatic journeys to Cathay are preserved by RAMUSIO, and by AUGER GISLEN DE BUSBECK. The first was taken down by the Venetian geographer from the lips of HAJJI MAHOMED, an intelligent Persian merchant whom he fell in with at Venice[2]; the second was noted by Busbeck, when ambassador from the Emperor Charles V to the Porte (1555–62), from the narrative of a wandering Turkish dervish[3]. Large extracts from these last words about Cathay will be found in the notes to this essay[4].

118. We arrive now at the term of our subject in the journey of BENEDICT GOËS, undertaken in 1603 with the

[1] Such is the case also in the narrative of the Russian Embassy of Feodor Isakovich Baikov in 1653 (*Voyages au Nord*, iv, 150).

[2] Preface to the 2nd vol. of the *Navigationi*.

[3] *Busbequii Epistolæ*, Amsterd., 1660, pp. 326–330. The letter containing this narrative was written at Frankfort, 16th December, 1562, after the ambassador's return.

[4] See Notes XVIII and XIX.

specific object of determining whether the Cathay of old European travellers and modern Mahomedans was or was not a distinct region from that China of which parallel marvels had now for years been recited. Benedict, "seeking Cathay found Heaven," as one of his brethren has pronounced his epitaph; but not before he had ascertained that China and Cathay were one. His journey we have chosen as a fitting close to our collection. After the publication of that narrative inexcusable ignorance alone could continue to distinguish between Cathay and China, and though such ignorance lingered for many years longer, here we may fairly consider our task at an end[1].

[1] Ricci and his companions, as we have seen, were before the journey of Goës satisfied of the identity of Cathay and China. So appears to have been, at an earlier date, the Italian Geographer Magini. Purchas perceived the same, and the Jesuit Martini, in his *Atlas Sinensis*, expounded the identity in detail. Yet the Geographical Lexicon of Baudrand, in a revised edition of 1677, distinguishes between them, remarking that "some confound Cathay with China." I have not had access to Müller's *Disquisitio de Chataja*, which probably contains interesting matter on the subject.

[The full title of Müller's book published at Berlin in 1670 is: AndreaeMülleri, Greiffenhagii, Disquisitio Geographica & Historica, De Chataja, In Quâ 1. Praecipuè Geographorum nobilis illa Controversia: Quaenam *Chataja* sit, & an sit idem ille terrarum tractus, quem *Sinas*, & vulgò *Chinam* vocant, aut pars ejus aliqua? latissimè tractatur; 2. Eâdem verò operâ pleraque rerum, quae unquam de *Chataja*, dèque Sinis *memorabilia* fuerunt, atque etiam nunc sunt, compendiosè narrantur. The opinion of all the authors is given, but I do not see that it has much interest now.]

A faint attempt to repeat the journey of Goës, but apparently in ignorance of that enterprise, was made a good many years later by the Jesuit Aimé Chesaud starting from Ispahan. He does not seem to have got further than Balkh, if so far. He still speaks of "getting to Chatao and *thence* to China." There is no date given. (See his letter in Kircher's *China Illustrata*, 1667, p. 86.)

SUPPLEMENTARY NOTES TO PRELIMINARY ESSAY

NOTE I.

EXTRACT FROM THE PERIPLUS OF THE ERYTHRÆAN SEA.

(Circa A.D. 80–9.)[1]

"BEHIND this country[2] the sea comes to a termination somewhere in THIN; and in the interior of that country, quite to the north, there is a very great city called THINÆ, from which raw silk and silk thread and silk stuffs are brought overland through Bactria to Barygaza[3], as they are on the other hand by the Ganges River to Limyrice[4]. It is not easy, however, to get to this Thin, and few and far between are those who come from it. The place lies quite under the Little Bear; and it is said that its territories adjoin the remoter frontiers of Pontus and the Caspian Sea, beside which you find the Lagoon Mæotis which has a communication with the ocean.

"Every year there come to the frontier of Thin certain people of dwarfish stature and very broad in the face, scarcely superior to wild creatures, but harmless, who are said to be called SESADÆ[5].

[1] This is Müller's view; see his *Prolegomena* to *Geog. Græci Minores*, i, xcvi–vii.

[2] *Viz. Chryse*, "The Golden Land," apparently Pegu and thereabouts, the *Suvarna Bhumi* or Golden Land of the old Indian Buddhists. *Sonaparanta*, a term of like meaning, is still the sacred or classical term for the central territories of Ava. [On the Golden Island, see p. 201, abstracts from Dionysius Periergetes, Rufus Festus Avienus and Priscianus.]

[3] ["Ex qua lana (*lanugo arboris laniferae*) et filum et othonium Sericum Barygaza per Bactriam terrestri itinere." C. Müller, i, p. 303.]

[4] The meaning is probably the same as that of Ptolemy's statement, extracted in the next note, that there was not only one road from the Sinæ or Seres to Bactriana by the Stone Tower, but also another direct to Palibothra on the Ganges.

[5] In the work styled *Palladius on the Brahmans*, embodied in the Pseudo-Callisthenes published by Müller (*Script. de Alex. Magno*, pp. 103–4) there is an account apparently of the same people under the name of *Bisades*, the gatherers of pepper. They are described as "a dwarfish and imbecile race who dwell in rocky caves, and from the nature of their country are expert at climbing cliffs, and thus able to gather the pepper from the thickets.... These Bisades are pygmies, with big

They come accompanied by their wives and children, and bring with them great loads in creels[1] that look as if they were made of green vines. These people halt at some place on the frontier between their own country and Thin, and hold a feast for several days, during which they strew [the materials of] their baskets about on the ground, and then they depart to their own homes in the interior. When the other people are aware of their departure they come to the spot and gather those withes[2] that had been strewn about. To these they give the name of *Petri*[3]. Getting rid of the [stalks and] fibrous parts they take the leaves and double them up into little balls which they stitch through with the fibres of the withes. And these they divide into three classes, forming from the largest leaves what is called *Big-ball* Malabathrum, from the next size *Middle-ball*, and from the smallest leaves *Little-ball*. And thus originate the three qualities of Malabathrum, which the people who have prepared them carry to India for sale[4].

heads and long straight unclipt hair." Sir J. E. Tennent applies this to the Veddahs of Ceylon. But there is nothing, I think, in the passage to fix it to Ceylon. It is given on the authority of a certain Scholasticus of Thebes, who finding an Indian vessel in a port of the Axum country took the opportunity it offered of visiting distant parts. The story is probably not genuine. For as Müller points out, the *Besidæ* are mentioned by Ptolemy (vii, 1) as a people, otherwise called Tiladæ, who live north of Mæandrus (a mountain chain on the east of Bengal), "dwarfish and stumpy and platter-faced, but white in complexion." Lassen locates them as a Bhotiya race in the Himalaya near Darjiling; his map (by Kiepert) in the Garo and Kasia Hills north of Silhet.

[1] The word is ταρπόνας, the meaning of which is doubtful. ["Magnas portantes sarcinas et sirpeas viridis vitis foliis comparandas." Müller, p. 304.]

[2] The word is καλάμοι, and would usually mean reeds or canes. But it seems absurd so to term what had been described as like green vine-twigs.

[3] Not the withes but the *leaves*, as Lassen (iii, 38) has pointed out, must have been called thus; Sanskt. *Patra*, a leaf; mod. Hindust. *Patti*.

[4] The same terms (*hadrospherum, mesospherum, microspherum*) are applied by Pliny to varieties of *Nard*; perhaps a mistake of his, as Dioscorides observes that some people made the mistake of regarding *malabathrum* as the leaf of Indian Nard.

Some of the early writers after the Portuguese discoveries took the *pān* or betel leaf for the *malabathrum* of the ancients, but the physician Garcia Da Horta, in his work on the aromatics of India (first published at Goa in 1563) pointed out that malabathrum was the *Tamālapattra*, the leaf of a species of cassia, still valued in India though in a greatly inferior degree (see ch. xix; I quote an Ital. transl., Venice, 1589). Curiously enough Ramusio gives as a representation of the "Betelle" a cut which really represents with fair accuracy the Tamālapattra, commonly called (at least in Bengal) *Tejpāt*. Linschoten describes it accurately, noticing its pleasant clove-like smell, and says it was in great repute among the Hindus as a diuretic, etc., and to preserve clothes from moths, two of the uses expressly assigned to malabathrum by Dioscorides and Pliny. He also observes that the natives considered it to rival spikenard in all its qualities. Linschoten's commentator Paludanus says much was imported to Venice in his time; and that it

"But as for the regions beyond those places that we have mentioned, whether it be that the wintry climate and excessive cold renders it hard to penetrate them, or whether it be the result of some supernatural influence from the gods, it is the fact that they never have been explored." From Müller's *Geogr. Gr. Minores*, i, pp. 303–5.

NOTE I BIS.

EXTRACTS FROM THE LATIN POETS.

(A.D. First Century.)

Publius VIRGILIUS MARO.

Georg., lib. II, v. 120–1:

> Quid nemora Æthiopum, molli canentia lana?
> Velleraque ut foliis depectant tenuia Seres?

was called by the Arabs *Cadegi Indi* (Read *çadegi*). I see that in F. Johnson's *Persian Dictionary, Sádaj* is defined "Indian spikenard," and *Sádhaji Hindi*, "Indian leaf," which seems to show the persistence of the confusion between the two articles. This leaf was abundant in the forests of the Kasia Hills, where I passed a part of my earliest service in India, and so was a cassia producing a coarse cinnamon, of which there was a considerable export to the plains. The trees were distinct, if I be not mistaken, though evidently of the same genus. The *Tejpāt* was narrow, like that of the Portugal laurel, that of the other tree much broader, both noticeable for their partition by *three* main longitudinal nerves, like the lines of longitude on a map of the hemisphere. The Kasias in features would answer well to the *Besadæ* or *Sesadæ*, but they are no dwarfs, whilst some of the Tibetan tribes of the Himalaya are very short. Domestically among Anglo-Indians this once prized malabathrum, some qualities of which the Romans purchased at three hundred denarii per pound, is, as far as I know, used only to flavour tarts, custards, and curries. But (besides what Linschoten says) Rheede mentions that, in his time in Malabar, oils in high medical estimation were made from both the root and the leaves of the *Karua* or wild cinnamon of that coast, a plant no doubt closely allied. And from the former a *camphor* was extracted, having several of the properties of real camphor and more fragrant.

Mr. Crawfurd has suggested that the finer malabathrum was *benzoin*, but I believe all the authorities on the subject speak of it as derived from a *leaf;* indeed Dioscorides, like our author here, speaks of the *stitching* up of the leaves. Some part of what Dioscorides says seems indeed to apply to a solid extract, but it may have been of the nature of Rheede's camphor. (See Pliny, xii, 25, 26, 59; xiii, 2; xxxiii, 48; Dioscorides, *loc. cit.*; Linschoten, Latin version, Hague, 1599, p. 84; Rheede, *Hortus Malabaricus*, i, 107; Crawf. *Dict. Indian Islands*, p. 50; on Malabathrum, see also Lassen, i, 283; iii, 37, 154 *seq.*) [Yule in *Hobson-Jobson*, s.v. *Malabathrum*: "There can be little doubt that this classical export from India was the dried leaf of various species of *Cinnamomum*, which leaf was known in Sanskrit as *tamāla-pattra*." Garcia writes, ff. 95ᵛ, 96: "the *folium indu* is called by the Indians *Tamalapatra*, which the Greeks and Latins corrupted into *malabathrum*," etc.]

Quintus Horatius Flaccus.

Lib. I. *Carmen* XII: *Ad Caesarem Augustum.*

Ille, seu Parthos Latio imminentes
Egerit justo domitos triumpho,
Sive subjectos Orientis orae
 Seras et Indos,
Te minor latum reget aequus orbem.

Lib. I. *Carmen* XXIX: *Ad Iccium.*

 Puer quis ex aula capillis
 Ad cyathum statuetur unctis,
Doctus sagittas tendere Sericas
Arcu paterno?...

Lib. III. *Carmen* XXIX: *Ad Maecenatem.*

Tu, civitatem quis deceat status,
Curas, Urbi sollicitus times,
 Quid Seres, et regnata Cyro
 Bactra parent, Tanaisque discors.

Lib. IV. *Carmen* XV: *Caesaris Augusti laudes.*

Non, qui profundum Danubium bibunt,
Edicta rumpent Julia, non Getae,
 Non Seres, infidive Persae,
 Non Tanaïn prope flumen orti.

Epod. VIII:

Quid? quod libelli Stoici inter Sericos
 Jacere pulvillos amant.

Sextus Aurelius Propertius.

Elegiae, lib. I. XIV, 22:

Quid relevant variis serica textilibus?

Lib. IV. VIII:

Serica nam taceo vulsi carpenta nepotis.

Publius Ovidius Naso.

Amores, Lib. I. XIV, 5–6:

Quid, quod erant tenues, et quos ornare timeres,
 Vela colorati qualia Seres habent.

Silius Italicus.

Punicorum Lib. VI, 1–4:

Iam, Tartessiaco quos solverat aequore, Titan,
In noctem diffusus, equos iungebat Eois
Litoribus, primique novo Phaethonte retecti
Seres lanigeris repetebant vellera lucis.

Lib. XV, 79–81:

...Quid cui, post Seras et Indos
Captivo Liber cum signa referret ab Euro,
Caucaseae currum duxere per oppida tigres?

Lib. XVII, 595–6:

Videre Eoi, monstrum admirabile, Seres
Lanigeros cinere Ausonio canescere lucos.

A complete list of quotations will be found in the valuable book of G. Coedès, *Textes d'auteurs grecs et latins relatifs à l'Extrême Orient*, Paris, 1910, 8vo.

NOTE II.

EXTRACTS FROM THE GEOGRAPHY OF PTOLEMY.

(Circa A.D. 150.)

"The inhabited part of our earth is bounded on the east by the Unknown Land which lies along the region occupied by the easternmost nations of Asia Major, the SINÆ and the nations of SERICE; and on the south likewise by the Unknown Land which shuts round the Indian Sea, and encompasses that Ethiopia to the south of Libya which is called the land of Agisymba; to the west by the Unknown Land which embraces the Ethiopic Gulf of Libya, and then by the Western Ocean which lies along the most westerly parts of Libya and of Europe; and on the north by that continuation of the same ocean which encircles the Britannic Isles and the most northerly parts of Europe, and which goes by the names of Duecalydonian and Sarmatic, and by an Unknown Land which stretches along the most northerly parts of Asia Major, viz., Sarmatia, Scythia, and Serice....

"The Hyrcanian Sea, called also Caspian, is everywhere shut in by the land, so as to be just the converse of an island encompassed by the water. Such also is the case with that sea which embraces the Indian Sea with its gulfs, the Arabian Gulf, the Persian Gulf, the Gangetic Gulf, and the one which is called distinctively the Great Gulf, this sea being encompassed on all sides by the land. So we see that of the three Continents Asia is joined to Libya both by that Arabian Isthmus which separates Our Sea from the Arabian Gulf, and by the Unknown Land which encompasses the Indian Sea....

"The eastern extremity of the known earth is limited by the meridian drawn through the metropolis of the Sinæ, at a distance from Alexandria of 119½°, reckoned upon the equator, or about eight equinoctial hours...." (Book vii, ch. 5.)

In his first book Ptolemy speaks of Marinus as the latest Greek writer who had devoted himself to geography. Editions of his revision of the geographical tables had been very numerous. But his statements required much correction, and he forms too great an estimate of the extent of the inhabited world both in length and breadth. As regards latitude Ptolemy illustrates this by criticising the position which Marinus had assigned, on the basis of certain journeys and voyages, to the extreme southern region of Ethiopia called Agisymba. The calculation of distance in the rough from those routes would have placed this region 24,680 stadia south of the equator, or as Ptolemy says almost among the antarctic frosts[1]. Marinus had summarily cut this down to 12,000

[1] Bk. i, ch. 8.

stadia, bringing it nearly to the southern tropic, and Ptolemy again on general reasoning as to the nature of the animals met with, etc., reduces the distance to 8,000 stadia. So also, he says, Marinus had exaggerated the longitude, giving an interval of 15 hours between the Fortunate Islands in the west and the most easterly regions of Sera, of the Sinæ, and of Cattigara in the east, which should not be more than 12 hours. In determining the position of Sera, etc., Marinus had made use of the route of certain mercantile agents who had travelled thither, and this Ptolemy proceeds to criticise. He assents to the longitude assigned by Marinus between the Fortunate Isles and the Euphrates Ferry at Hierapolis[1], and then proceeds (Bk i, ch. 11) :

"But as regards the distance between the said Euphrates Ferry and the Stone Tower, which he deduces to be 876 *schœni*, or 26,280 stadia, and the distance from the Stone Tower to Sera, the capital of the Seres[2], a journey of seven months, which he calculates at 36,200 stadia running on one parallel (*i.e.* due east) we shall apply a correction in reduction of each of these. For in neither section has he made any diminution on account of the exaggeration caused by deviations from a straight course, whilst in the second portion of the route he has fallen into the same errors as in regard to the itinerary from the country of the Garamantes to that of Agisymba. In that case it was found necessary to cut down more than the half on the distance as calculated from a journey of four months and fourteen days, for it was not to be supposed that travelling should have gone on without intermission all that time. And as regards this seven months' journey the same consideration will apply even more forcibly than on the route from the Garamantes. For in the latter case the business was carried out by the king of the country, and as we may suppose with more than ordinary forethought, and they had fine weather all along. But on the journey from the Stone Tower to Sera bad weather was to be looked for, seeing that it ran (according to Marinus's own hypothesis) in the latitudes of Hellespont and Byzantium. And on this account there must have been many halts on the journey. Moreover it must be remembered that it was on a trading expedition that the information about this road was acquired.

"For he tells us that the distances were taken down by one Maës called also Titianus, a Macedonian, and a merchant like his father before him ; not that he made the journey himself, but he had sent agents to the Seres. Now Marinus himself (on other occasions) has shown little faith in traders' stories, as (for example)

[1] N.E. of Aleppo.

[2] Most editions I believe read "capital of the *Sinæ*," which, however, with Ptolemy's views, as clearly enough shown in these extracts, *cannot* be the genuine reading.

when he refuses to believe the statement of Philemon (founded on the talk of some traders), that the island of Iuvernia was 20 days' journey in length from east to west. For such people, he observes, don't take any trouble to search into the truth of things, being constantly taken up with their business and often exaggerating distances through a spirit of brag. Just so, as there seems to have been nothing else that they thought worth remembering or telling about this seven months' journey, they made a wonder about the length of time it had occupied.

CHAPTER XII.

"For these reasons, and because the journey was not really upon one parallel (the Stone Tower being in the latitude of Byzantium, whilst Sera is further south than Hellespont) it might have seemed advisable to reduce the distance of 36,200 stadia ascribed to this seven months' journey by more, rather than by less, than a half. But let us keep the reduction *within* the half, so as to calculate the distance on a round estimate at 22,625 stadia or 45¼°...And the first distance (I speak of that from Euphrates to the Stone Tower) should be reduced from 876 schœni to 800 only, *i.e.* 24,000 stadia, on account of deviations from the straight line....For the road from the ferry of the Euphrates at Hierapolis through Mesopotamia to the Tigris, and thence through the territory of the Garamæans of Assyria[1], and Media, to Ecbatana and the Caspian Gates[2], and through Parthia to Hecatompylos[3], is

[1] In the country S.E. of Mosul; see the *Beth-Garma* of the list at III, p. 22.

[2] Pass in the Elburz, east of Demawend.

[3] Somewhere near Damghan. ["We are indebted to Quintus Curtius and Diodorus for indicating Hecatompylus as the place where Alexander made this prolonged halt. The name is not mentioned by Arrian. The site of the city, though undoubtedly one of considerable importance, has unfortunately not been determined; it was clearly situated south of the mountain chain which forms the prolongation of Mt. Elburz, on the line of road leading from the Caspian Gates towards Meshed and Herat." (Bunbury, *Ancient Geog.*, i, p. 479.)

"Urbs erat ea tempestate clara Hecatompylos, condita a Graecis: ibi stativa rex habuit commeatibus undique advectis." (Curtius, vi, 2.)

Τὴν μὲν γὰρ ἀπὸ τῆς κατὰ Ἱεράπολιν τοῦ Εὐφράτου διαβάσεως διὰ τῆς Μεσοποταμίας ἐπὶ τὸν Τίγριν ὁδὸν καὶ τὴν ἐντεῦθεν διὰ Γαραμαίων τῆς Ἀσσυρίας καὶ Μηδίας εἰς Ἐκβάτανα καὶ Κασπίας Πύλας καὶ τῆς Παρθίας εἰς Ἑκατόμπυλον ἐνδέχεται περὶ τὸν διὰ τῆς Ῥοδίας πίπτειν παράλληλον, οὗτος γὰρ καὶ κατ' αὐτὸν γράφεται διὰ τῶν εἰρημένων χωρῶν. (Ptolem., i, c. 12.)

εἰσὶ δ' ἀπὸ Κασπίων πυλῶν...εἰς δ' Ἑκατόμπυλον, τὸ τῶν Παρθυαίων βασίλειον, χίλιοι διακόσιοι ἑξήκοντα." (Strabo, xi, c. 9.)

"Damghan is too near the Pylae Caspiae: on the whole, it is probable that any remains of Hecatompylos ought to be sought in the neighbourhood of a place now called Jah Jirm." (W. Smith, *Dict. Greek and Roman Geog.*)

"What I wish to establish is that the position of Hecatompylos cannot be reasonably assigned to any other spot than the one now occupied by

assumed to lie in the parallel of Rhodes, for Marinus himself draws that parallel through all those places. But the road from Hecatompylos to Hyrcania[1] must decline to the north, for the city of Hyrcania lies somewhere between the latitudes of Smyrna and of the Hellespont....Then the route runs on through Aria[2] to Margiana Antiochia[3], first declining to the south (for Aria lies in the same latitude as the Caspian Gates), and then to the north, Antiochia being somewhere near the parallel of the Hellespont. Thence the road proceeds eastward to Bactra[4], and from that northward up the ascent of the hill country of the Comedi, and then inclining somewhat south through the hill country itself as far as the gorge in which the plains terminate. For the *western* end of the hill country is more to the *north* also, being (as Marinus puts it) under the latitude of Byzantium, the *eastern* end more to the *south*, being under the latitude of Hellespont. Hence [the hills running thus from south of east to north of west] the road runs as he describes in the opposite direction, *i.e.* towards the east with an inclination south; and then a distance of 50 schœni extending to the Stone Tower would seem to tend northward. This Stone Tower stands in the way of those who ascend the gorge, and from it the mountains extend eastward to join the chain of Imaus which runs north to this from (the territory of) Palimbothra.[5]"...

Shah-rood and Bostam, as being one of the extremities of the capital of the ancient Parthians." (Ferrier, *Caravan Journeys*, p. 70.)

Curzon is in favour of Damghan and writes: "Ferrier, I think erroneously, endeavours to combat this theory by the argument that the City of Hundred Gates must mean a city in which many roads met, whereas at Damghan there are only two. He, therefore, prefers the Shahrud-Bostam site for that Hekatompylos. Apart, however, from the fact that more roads meet at Damghan than two, it is by no means certain that the Greeks, when they used this descriptive epithet, referred to city gates at all. The title was equally applied by them to Egyptian Thebes, where it has been conjectured to refer to the *pylons*, or gateways, of the many splendid temples by which the capital of the Rameses was adorned; and it may have had some similar application in the case of the Parthian city." (*Persia*, i, p. 287.) One may well hesitate between Damghan and Shah-rud, but I think Ferrier is right.]

[1] Jorján, N.W. of Astrabad.

[2] The territory of Harah, Heri or HERAT.

[3] Supposed to be MARV.

[4] BALKH.

[5] I have not perhaps succeeded in rendering this description very intelligible. The old Latin versions and the Abbé Halma's French translation seem simply to shirk the difficulties of the passage. I have not access to any others or to Humboldt's *Asie Centrale*, which I believe contains a dissertation on this route.

The account would perhaps be easier to understand if we knew more of the geography of the country towards Karategin, in which I suppose the hill country of the Comedi must lie. [In a note in *Ancient Khotan*, p. 54, Stein writes: "The discussion of the Ptolemy passage in *Cathay*, i, p. cxlix, is still of value, as showing how Sir H. Yule, by a chain of sound critical reasoning, had been led to Karategin as the probable

And so on, bringing out the whole distance from the Fortunate Isles to the city of Sera to be 177¼°. In chapters 13 and 14 he tries to estimate the longitude run by sea from Cape Cory in Southern India to Cattigara the port of the Sinæ, determining the latter to lie in 177°; and as all were agreed that the metropolis

position of the Komedi, even before information became available as to the survival of the local name into Mohammedan times."] The chief difficulties arise in connexion with the expression "as far as the gorge in which the plains terminate" (μέχρι τῆς ἐκδεχομένης τὰ πεδία φάραγγος), and the statement that fifty schœni (one hundred and fifty miles ?) before reaching the Stone Tower the route lay northward. The former expression is intelligible if with Ritter we understand the passage of Imaus to have been that running from Kokand up the Jaxartes Valley to Andijan and across the Terek Dawan to Kashgar, but in that case how could the route approaching the Stone Tower which he places at USH (where there are said to be ancient remains of importance) by any possibility run northward? (see Ritter, vii, 483, 563; viii, 693.) In the time of the Sui dynasty, or beginning of the seventh century, the Chinese knew three roads from Eastern into Western Turkestan, among which we naturally seek that of Maës Titianus. Of these three the first or north road seems from the description to have run north of the T'ien Shan, and is out of the question; a second or middle road passed from Kashgar to Farghânah, and is no doubt that of the Terek Dawan; the third or south road passed through Khotan, and then through *Chukiupo* (said to be Yangihissar) [cf. Yule's *Notes on Hwen Thsang's Account of Tokhdristán*, pp. 119 and 120], and *Kopantho* (said to be Selekur or Sarikul; see *N. Ann. des Voy.*, 1846, iii, 47). Ritter takes the second for the route of Titianus, supposing the third route to be that by the Sirikul [General Cunningham has identified Sirikol with the kingdom of *Khia pwan to, Khavanda* (Hiuan Tsang). Tash Kurghan is reputed the old capital. Cf. Yule, *Notes on Hwen Thsang's Account of Tokhdristán*, p. 119] into Badakhshan, which is certainly inconsistent with Ptolemy's data. But it is certain that there was no route in former use *intermediate* between the pass to Farghânah and that to Badakhshan, *e.g.* passing from Tashbaliq towards Karategin? *Kiumi*, which is probably the country of Ptolemy's Comedi, is mentioned in Rémusat's list of states tributary to China under the T'ang. He says indeed it lay "among the mountains of Tokharestan south of the Oxus, towards Balkh and Termedh," but *north of the Oxus* would be more consistent with the data, and it is north of the Oxus that the kingdom of *Keumitho* mentioned by Hiuan-Tsang appears to lie, which is doubtless the same (see *Mém. de l'Acad. R. des Inscr.*, viii, 92–3; *Vie de Hiouen Thsang*, p. 464; and Chino-Japanese ancient Map, in Klaproth's *Mémoires*, tom. ii). I see that Kiepert in his map of Asia (1864) inserts *Kumid* above Karategin with a query (?). It seems possible, however, that we have the name of the Comedi in *Kawadián* or *Kabadiân*, which Edrisi applies to the country between Termedh and Hissar, and which still survives as the name of a town or village. [Yule, in his *Notes on Hwen Thsang's Account of the Principalities of Tokhdristán* (*Jour. Roy. As. Soc.*, N.S., vi, 1873, pp. 97–8), has the following on the Comedi: "*Kiu-mi-tho*, Kumidha. This kingdom was some 20 days' journey (2000 *li*) from east to west, and two days from north to south, lying among the Thsungling mountains. On the S.W. it adjoined the Oxus; on the south it was in contact with the kingdom of *Shikhini* or Shighnán. The state of Kiumi is also mentioned along with *Shikhini* and *Humi* in the historical extracts of Abel Rémusat [*Extension de l'Empire chinois du côté de l'Occident; Mém. Acad. Insc.*, viii, p. 93], as sending tribute to China in the seventh

of the Sinæ lay still further to the east, he puts that in 180°. The whole calculation is based on the loosest possible data, and made to bring out a foregone conclusion. The following is a specimen of the data:

"Marinus does not exhibit the mileage from the Golden

century. Major General Cunningham, though not giving any specific modern identification of this State, most happily connects it with the Comedae of Ptolemy, who inhabited the hill country east of Bactriana, and up whose valley lay the route of the caravans from Bactra, bound for Serica across Imaus or the Thsungling. The proportions of length and breadth ascribed to the territory of *Kiumitho*, 20 by 2, show that a valley is in question. The passage in Ptolemy just alluded to is one of the most notable in regard to the geography of Inner Asia of all that have come down to us from classic times. There can be little doubt that Gen. Cunningham's identification of *Kiumitho* with the Comedae is well founded, and we could scarcely desire a more precise definition of their position than Hwen Thsang has here given us. 'They lay to the eastward of Khotl, among the roots of Pamir, to the northward of Shighnán, and had the Oxus on their south-west.'" Stein, *Ancient Khotan*, p. 54, writes: "It is the joint merit of Sir H. Yule and Sir H. Rawlinson to have demonstrated beyond all doubt the identity of the mountain tract of the Komedi with the Chü-mi-t'o of Hsüan-tsang on the one hand and the 'land of the Kumēdh' of early Mohammedan writers on the other. It thus became possible to locate with certainty 'the valley of the Komedi' in the mountains which divide the Wakhshāb river and the adjacent alpine tracts of Karategin from the course of the Oxus. From Karategin a direct and comparatively easy line of communication leads along the Wakhshāb up to the rich grazing grounds of the wide Alai plateau. Ascending the latter to its eastern end, it then crosses the watershed range between the Oxus and the Tārīm at its lowest point, the Taun-murun Pass; and a short distance below, near the headwaters of the Kāshgar river, it joins the great route which connects Kashgar with Farghânah over the Terek Dawān."]

Beyond the Stone Tower, and in Imaus itself, there was a ὁρμητήριον or station for the traders to the Seres (bk. vi, ch. 13). This may have been about Tashbaliq. Smith's *Dict. of Gr. and Roman Geography*, article *Serica*, states as a fact that in the ancient conduct of the silk trade the Serés deposited their bales of silk in the Stone Tower with the prices marked, and then retired, whilst the western merchants came forward to inspect. Where is the authority? And if it were so, why did Maës send his agents seven months' journey further? Or did the writer of the article find the dumb trade in Pliny and the Stone Tower in Ptolemy, and like a celebrated character of Dickens's "combine the information"? ["An exact location of the famous 'Stone Tower' (λίθινος πύργος) is not possible at present, and can be hoped for only from antiquarian investigations effected on the spot. In regard, however, to the traders' station which Maës' account mentions to the east of the Stone Tower and on the road starting for Sera, I think that unchanging geographical conditions afford us some guidance. Baron Richthofen has justly pointed out that this station must be looked for close to the watershed crossed by the above route, since Ptolemy places it in the line of the Imaus, which undoubtedly corresponds to the range buttressing the Pamir region on the east, and dividing the drainage areas of the Oxus and the Tarīm. He has also rightly observed that the point where the much-frequented route coming from Farghânah over the Terek Dawān is joined by the route from the Wakhshāb valley was the most likely position for such a station." Stein, *Ancient Khotan*, pp. 54–5. Ptolemy's Stone Tower must not be confounded with Tāsh Kurghān.]

Chersonese to Cattigara. But he says that Alexander has described the land beyond (that Chersonese) to lie facing the south, and that after sailing by this for 20 days you reach the city of Zaba[1], and still sailing on for some days southward but rather to the left you reach Cattigara[2]. He exaggerates the distance, for the expression is *some days* not *many days*. He says indeed that no numerical statement of the days was made because they were so many: but this I take to be ridiculous," etc., etc.

In chapter 17, speaking of persons who had made the voyage to India and spent much time in those parts, he proceeds:

"From these persons also we have got more exact information about India and its kingdoms, as well as about the remoter[3] parts of the region extending to the Golden Chersonèse and thence to Cattigara. For example they all agree in stating that in going thither your course is to the east, and in coming back again it is to the west, and they agree also in saying that no determinate time can be named for the accomplishment of the voyage, which varies with circumstances. They also agree that the land of the Seres with their metropolis lies to the north of the land of the Sinæ, and that all that is further east than these is a Terra Incognita full of marshy lagoons in which great canes grow, and that so densely that people are able to cross the marshes by means of them. They tell also that there is not only a road from those

[1] ["The locality of the ancient port of Zabai [Ζάβα or Ζάβαι] or Champa is probably to be sought on the west coast of Kamboja, near the Campot, or the Kang Kao, of our maps." Yule, *Notes on the Oldest Records of the Sea-Route to China*, *Proc. R. Geog. Soc.*, 1882, p. 657.]

[2] ["To myself, the arguments adduced by my friend Baron F. von Richthofen in favour of the location of Kattigara in the Gulf of Tongking, are absolutely convincing. This position seems to satisfy every condition. For:

1. Tongking was for some centuries at that period (B.C. 111 to A.D. 263), and that period only, actually *incorporated* as part of the Chinese Empire.

2. The only port mentioned in the Chinese annals as at that period open to foreign traffic was Kiau-chi, substantially identical with the modern capital of Tongking, Kesho, or Hanoi. Whilst there are no notices of foreign arrivals by any other approach, there are repeated notices of such arrivals by this province, including that famous embassy from Antun, King of Ta-ts'in, *i.e.* M. Aurelius Anton-inus (A.D. 161–180), in A.D. 166.

3. The province in question was then known as Ji-nan (or Zhi-nan, French *J*); whence possibly the name *Sinae*, which has travelled so far and spread over such libraries of literature. The Chinese annalist, who mentions the Roman embassy, adds: 'The people of that kingdom (*Ta-ts'in*, or the Roman Empire) come in numbers for trading purposes to *Fu-nan*, *Ji-nan*, and Kiau-chi.' Fu-nan, we have seen, was Champa or Zabai. In Ji-nan, with its chief port Kiau-chi, we may recognise with assurance '*Kattigara, portus Sinarum*.'" Yule, *Notes on the Oldest Records of the Sea-Route to China*, *Proc. R. Geog. Soc.*, 1882, pp. 658–9.]

[3] *Lit.* "Interior."

countries to Bactriana by the Stone Tower, but also a road to India which goes through Palimbothra. And the road from the metropolis of the Sinæ to the port of Cattigara runs towards the south-west; so the former city would appear not to fall on the meridian of Sera and Cattigaras, as Marinus will have it, but to lie further east."

SERICE.

"SERICE is bounded on the west by Scythia beyond Imaus, according to the line already defined (*i.e.*, a line whose northern extremity is in *long.* 150°, *N. lat.* 63° and its southern extremity in *long.* 160°, *N. lat.* 35°); on the north, by the Terra Incognita, in the latitude of the Island of Thule; on the east, by the Eastern Terra Incognita in the meridian of 180° from lat. 63° down to 3°o: on the south, by the remaining part of India beyond the Ganges along the parallel of 35° to the termination of that country in *long.* 173°, and then by the Sinæ along the same line till you reach the frontier of the Terra Incognita, as it has just been defined[1].

"Serice is girdled round by the mountains named Anniba[2], by the easternmost part of the Auxacian Mountains, by the mountains called Asmiræan, the easternmost part of the Kasian Mountains, by Mount Thagurus, by the most easterly part of the ranges called Hemodus and Sericus, and by the chain of Ottorocorrhas. Two rivers of especial note flow through the greater part of Serice; the river Œchordas is one of these, one source of which is that set forth as flowing from the Auxacian range, and the other from the Asmiræan range.... And the other is the river called Bautes, which has one source in the Kasian Mountains and another in the mountains of Ottorocorrhas[3].

"The most northern parts or Serice are inhabited by tribes

[1] One might be reading the legislative definitions of the boundaries of an American state or an Australian colony. We see here how Ptolemy's Asiatic Geography was compiled. It is evident that he first drew his maps embodying all the information that he had procured, however vague and rough it might be. From these maps he then educed his tables of latitudes and longitudes and his systematic topography. The result is that everything assumes an appearance of exact definition; and indications on the map which meant no more than "somewhere hereabouts is said to be such a country," become translated into a precision fit for an Act of Parliament.

[2] I omit the latitudes and longitudes of the mountains, rivers, and cities named in this chapter.

[3] There is, I suppose, no question that the Serice described here is mainly the basin of Chinese Turkestan, encompassed on three sides by lofty mountains. In *Auxacia* we probably trace the name of Aqsu (Deguignes and D'Anville), in Kasia perhaps Kashgar (D'Anv.). The *Oikhardai*, on the river of that name, which is probably the Tarim, may represent the *Uighúrs*. [This is no doubt an error; the Uighúrs did not exist then.]

of cannibals[1]. Below these the nation of the Annibi dwells to the north of the mountains bearing the same name. Between these last and the Auxacian Mountains is the nation of the Sizyges[2]; next to them the Damnæ; and then the Piaddæ, extending to the river Œchardus. Adjoining it are a people bearing the same name, the Œchardæ.

"And again, east of the Annibi are the Garenæi and the Nabannæ[3]. There is the Asmiræan country lying north of the mountains of the same name, and south of this extending to the Kasian Mountains the great nation Issedones; and beyond them to the east the Throani. Below them come the Ethaguri to the east of the mountains of the same name, and south of the Issedones the Aspacaræ, and then the Batæ, and furthest to the south, near the mountain chains Hemodus and Sericus, are the Ottorocorrhæ[4]."

The names of the following cities of Serice are given: "Damna, Piada, Asmiræa, Tharrhana, Issedon Serica, Aspacara, Drosache, Paliana, Abragana, Thogara, Daxata, Orosana, Ottorocorrha, Solana, Sera Metropolis" (book vi, ch. 16).

The Land of the SINÆ.

"The Sinæ are bounded on the north by part of Serice, as has been defined already; on the east and the south, by the Terra Incognita; on the west, by India beyond the Ganges, according to the boundary already defined extending to the Great Gulf, and then by the Great Gulf itself, and those gulfs that follow it in succession, by the gulf called *Theriodes*, and by part of the gulf of the Sinæ, on which dwell the fish-eating Ethiopians[5], according to the detail which follows."

He then gives the longitude and latitude of various points on the coast; viz., River Aspithra, city of Bramma, River Ambastes, Rhabana, R. Senus, Cape Notion, Satyr's Cape, R. Cottiaris, and Cattigara, to the Port of the Sinæ. Of inland cities are named

[1] As late as the middle of the thirteenth century King Hethum of Armenia in the deserts near Bishbaliq speaks of wild men with no covering but the hair of their heads; "They are real brutes," it is added. I do not know any other reference to tribes in Tartary in so low a state. (*Journ. Asiat.*, sér. ii, tom. xii, pp. 273 *seqq.*)

[2] The name *Sizyges* in its probable etymology appears to refer to the chariot- or waggon-driving habits of the people. A tribe of the Uighúrs hereabouts were called by the Chinese *Chhessé* or "The Car Drivers." (Rémusat in *Acad.*, viii, 112.)

[3] Possibly the *Naiman* horde so notable in the Mongol history.

[4] *Utara Kuru* of the Hindus, see Lassen, i, 846.

[5] Marcianus of Heraclea in the corresponding passage has the "Ichthyophagi *Sinae*," which is, perhaps, an indication that *his* Ptolemy did not contain the perplexing appellation *Æthiopes*. As this appellation (Ichthyophagi Æthiopes) occurs more appropriately (Bk. iv, chap. 9) as that of a tribe on the remote west coast of Africa, it is not improbable that its introduction here is due to officious, or perhaps unconscious, interpolation by a transcriber.

Akadra, Aspithra, Cocco- or Coccora-Nagara, Saraga, and Thinæ the Metropolis.

"But this last, they say, hath in reality neither brazen walls nor anything else worth mentioning[1] " (book vii, ch. 3).

NOTE III.

FROM POMPONIUS MELA *DE SITU ORBIS.*

(Supposed about A.D. 50.)

"In the furthest east of Asia are the Indians, Seres, and Scythians. The Indians and Scythians occupy the two extremities, the Seres are in the middle " (i, 2)[2].

In another passage, after speaking of certain islands in the Caspian, and on the Scythian coast, he proceeds :

"From these the course (of the shore) makes a bend and trends to the coast line which faces the east. That part which adjoins the Scythian promontory is first all impassable from snow ; then an uncultivated tract occupied by savages. These tribes are the Cannibal Scythians and the Sagæ, severed from one another by a region where none can dwell because of the number of wild animals. Another vast wilderness follows, occupied also by wild beasts, reaching to a mountain called Thabis which overhangs the sea. A long way from that the ridge of Taurus rises. The Seres come between the two; a race eminent for integrity, and well known for the trade which they allow to be transacted behind their backs, leaving their wares in a desert spot " (iii, 7)[3].

NOTE IV.

EXTRACTS FROM PLINY'S NATURAL HISTORY.

(Born A.D. 23, Died A.D. 79.)

"From the Caspian Sea and the Scythian Ocean the course (of the coast) makes a bend till the shore faces the east. The first part of that tract of country, beginning from the Scythian Pro-

[1] See note at p. 159.

[2] ["In ea primos hominum ab oriente accipimus Indos, et Seres et Scythas. Seres media ferme coæ partis incolunt, Indi et Scythæ ultima : ambo late patentes, neque in hoc tantum pelagus effusi." Pomponius Mela, Lib. I, c. 2.]

[3] ["Ab iis in Eoum mare cursus inflectitur, inque oram terræ spectantis orientem. Pertinet hæc a Scythico promontorio ad Colida : primumque omnis est invia ; deinde ob immanitatem habitantium inculta. Scythæ sunt androphagi et Sacæ, distincti regione, quia feris scatet, inhabitabili. Vasta deinde iterum loca belluæ infestant, usque ad montem mari imminentem, nomine Tabim. Longe ab eo Taurus attollitur. Seres intersunt; genus plenum justitiæ, et commercio, quod rebus in solitudine relictis absens peragit, notissimum." Pomponius Mela, Lib. III, c. 7.]

montory, is uninhabitable from eternal winter; the next portion is uncultivated and occupied by savage tribes, among whom are the Cannibal Scythians who feed on human flesh; and alongside of these are vast wildernesses tenanted by multitudes of wild beasts hemming in those human creatures almost as brutal as themselves. Then, we again find tribes of Scythians, and again desert tracts occupied only by wild animals, till we come to that mountain chain overhanging the sea, which is called Tabis. Not till nearly half the length of the coast which looks north-east has been passed, do you find inhabited country[1].

"The first race then encountered are the SERES, so famous for the fleecy product of their forests. This pale floss, which they find growing on the leaves, they wet with water, and then comb out, furnishing thus a double task to our womenkind in first dressing the threads, and then again of weaving them into silk fabrics. So has toil to be multiplied; so have the ends of the earth to be traversed: and all that a Roman dame may exhibit her charms in transparent gauze[2].

[1] It is evident from a comparison of this with the passage of Mela quoted in the preceding note, that both authors are drawing from some common source.

[2] Seneca is still stronger in expressions to like purport: "Video sericas vestes, si vestes vocandæ sunt, in quibus nihil est quo defendi aut corpus, aut denique pudor possit; quibus sumptis, mulier parum liquido, nudam se non esse jurabit. Hæc ingenti summâ, ab ignotis etiam ad commercium gentibus, arcerssuntur, ut matronæ nostræ, ne adulteris quidem, plus sui in cubiculo, quam in publico ostendant." *De Beneficiis*, vii, 9. [Cf. Hirth, *China and the Roman Orient*, p. 259.]

From these passages it would appear that the silk textures in such esteem among the Romans of those days were not what we should call *rich* silks, like the satins and damasks which were imported from China in later days, but *gauzes*, the value of which lay in their excessive delicacy. And that this continued to be the character of the China silks in most general estimation for several centuries later may be gathered from Abu Zaid, who tells us that the chief Chinese officers wore "silks of the first quality, such as were never imported into Arabia," and illustrates this by the story of an Arab merchant whose curiosity was attracted by a mark upon the chest of an officer of the imperial household, which was plainly visible through several folds of the silk dress which he wore; and it proved that the officer had on five robes of this texture, one over the other (*Relation*, i, p. 76). Like stories are told in India of the Dacca muslins. One tells, I think, of Akbar that he rebuked one of his ladies for the indecent transparency of her dress, and in defence she showed that she had on *nine*, of the kind which was called *Bád-baft*, or "Woven Wind."

The passage of Pliny here translated, coupled with another to be noticed presently, has led to a statement made in many respectable books, but which I apprehend to be totally unfounded, that the Greeks and Romans picked to pieces the rich China silks and wove light gauzes out of the material. This is asserted, for example, in the treatise on Silk Manufacture in Lardner's *Cyclopædia* (pp. 5, 6), and in the *Encyclopædia Britannica* (7th ed., article *Silk*). Smith's *Dictionary of Greek and Roman Geography* also (article *Serica*) says: "Pliny records that a Greek woman of Cos, named Pamphila, first invented the expedient of

"The Seres are inoffensive in their manners indeed; but, like the beasts of the forest, they eschew the contact of mankind; and, though ready to engage in trade, wait for it to come to them instead of seeking it" (vi, 20).

Further on, when speaking of Taprobane, he says:

"So far we have from the ancients. But we had an opportunity of more correct information in the reign of Claudius, when

splitting these substantial silk stuffs, and of manufacturing those very fine and web-like dresses which became so celebrated under the name of *Coæ Vestes.*"

The whole passage of Pliny here alluded to is as follows (xi, 25): "Among these there is a fourth kind of *Bombyx* produced in Assyria and greater than those of which we have been speaking. These make nests of clay, having the appearance of salt, fastening them upon stone; and these nests are so hard that they can scarcely be pierced with a pointed tool. They secrete wax in these nests more copiously than bees do, and the grub too is of proportionately larger size.

"26. There is one with another mode of development produced from a yet larger grub which has two peculiar horns as it were. From this it becomes first a caterpillar; then what is called *bombylius*; next *necydalus*; and then in six months a *bombyx*. These spin webs like spiders, which are turned to the account of female dress and extravagance under the name of *Bombycina*. The process of dressing these webs and again of weaving them into fabrics was first invented in Ceos by a woman called Pamphila, the daughter of Latous. Let us not cheat her of her glory in having devised a method by which women shall be dressed and yet naked!

"27. They say that *Bombyces* are also produced in the island of Cos by the genial action of the earth on the flowers of cypress, turpentine-tree, ash, or oak, when shaken down by rain. The first form of the creature produced is that of a butterfly, little and naked; then as the cold affects it, it develops a rough coat, and against the winter prepares for itself a thick envelope by scraping off the down of leaves with its feet, which are adapted to this purpose. Carding, as it were, and spinning out this substance to a fine thread with its claws, it stretches it from branch to branch, and then lays hold of it and winds it round its body till entirely wrapped in the nest so formed. The people then gather the creatures and put them in earthen pots with warm bran, the effect of which is to develop on them a new plumage, clothed with which they are let go to the other functions reserved for them. The woolly web that they had spun is moistened so as to disengage more easily, and wound off on a reel of reed. The stuffs made from this are worn without shame even by men as light summer clothing. So far have we degenerated from the days when cuirasses of mail were worn that even a coat is too great a burden for us! The produce of the Assyrian Bombyx however we as yet leave to the ladies."

On these passages we may remark:

1. That the account of the Bombyx in § 25 appears to be substantially taken from Aristotle, *De Animal. Hist.*, v, 24, and to refer to some kind of mason bee. The "*in Assyria proveniens*" of Pliny, which the reference to "*Bombyx Assyria*" again at the end of the extract seems to connect with the produce of some kind of texture, does not appear in Aristotle at all. And yet Pliny gives no explanation as to what the produce of the Assyrian Bombyx was.

2. In § 26 Pamphila's invention and some kind of web-weaving bombyx are referred to *Ceos;* in § 27 another kind of weaving bombyx (with its anomalous history) is referred to *Cos;* whilst Aristotle, as we

ambassadors came from the island. A freedman of Annius Plocamus, who had farmed the customs of the Red Sea from the Imperial Exchequer, after sailing round Arabia, was driven by storms past Carmania, and on the fifteenth day made the port of Hippuri[1]. Here he was entertained by the king with kindness and hospitality for six months; and, when he had learned to speak the language, in answer to the king's questions, told him all about Cæsar and the Romans. Nothing that the king heard made such a wonderful impression on him as the opinion of the exactness of our dealings which he formed from seeing in some Roman money that had been taken that the coins were all of the same weight, though the heads upon them showed that they had been struck by different princes. And the stranger having particularly urged him to cultivate the friendship of the Romans, he sent these four ambassadors, the chief of whom was named

shall see, refers Pamphila to Cos. Has not Pliny here been merely emptying out of his note-book two separate accounts of the same matter?

3. In § 26 Pliny's words *redordiri rursusque texere* are verbatim the same that he uses in the passage about the Seres translated in the text, and seem to be merely affected expressions, indicating nothing more than the carding and reeling the *sericum* and the *bombycinum* respectively out of the entanglement of their natural web (as Pliny imagines it) and then re-entangling them again (as it were) in the loom. This is put beyond doubt by the fact that § 26 is merely a paraphrase from Aristotle (*De An. Hist.*, v, 19), who, speaking of various insect transformations, says: "From a certain great grub, which has as it were horns, and differs from the others, is produced, first by transformation of the grub, a caterpillar, and then *bombylius*, and then *necydalus*. In six months it goes through all these changes of form. And from this creature some women disengage and reel off the *bombycina* and then weave them. And the first who is said to have woven this material was Pamphile, daughter of Plates in Cos." Whatever material this *bombycina* may have really been, there is evidently here no question of picking foreign stuffs to pieces, a figment which seems entirely based on Pliny's rhetoric. [" It must be admitted that as long as we had no clear idea as to what kind of texture was meant by Pliny's 'telae araneorum modo textae,' we were free to assume that the stuff 'slipt and re-woven' was either the cocoon itself, or raw silk pressed into skeins. Yet, it seems to me that the passage in the *Wei-lio* and Ma Tuan-lin's extension of it, fully confirm the matter of fact as represented by Pliny. It looks very much, as if the texture called *hu-ling* in the two passages referred to was identical with the thin gauzes of which Seneca [speaks]" (see *supra*). Hirth, *l.c.*, p. 259.] Cuvier considered the description in § 27, however erroneous, clearly to indicate some species of silkworm, which had been superseded by the introduction of that from China (see Didot's edition of Pliny with Cuvier's notes *in loco*). And, indeed, as regards the *Assyrian* Bombyx, we learn from Consul Taylor that its wild silk is still gathered and used for dresses by the women about Jazirah on the Tigris (see *J. R. G. S.*, xxxv, p. 51).

[1] Tennent says this is the modern Kudra-mali on the north-west of Ceylon, near the pearl banks of Manaar (i, 532). [See the "Taprobane" of Pliny and Ptolemy. By Donald Ferguson. (*Jour. R. As. Soc.*, July, 1904, pp. 539–541.)]

Rachias[1]....These men also related that the side of their island which was opposite India, extended ten thousand stadia towards the south-east. The Seres, too, who dwell beyond the mountains of Emodus, and who are known to us by the commerce which is carried on with them, had been seen by these people ; the father of Rachias had visited their country ; and they themselves, on their travels, had met with people of the Seres. They described these as surpassing the ordinary stature of mankind, as having red hair, blue eyes, hoarse voices, and no common language to communicate by. The rest of what they told was just as we have it from our own traders. The goods carried thither are deposited on the further side of a certain river beside what the Seres have for sale, and the latter, if content with the bargain, carry them off ; acting, in fact, as if in contempt of the luxury to which they ministered, and just as if they saw in the mind's eye the object and destination and result of this traffic[2] " (vi, 24).

In a later passage, after speaking of the simplicity of primitive habits, he goes on :

" Hence, one wonders more and more, how from beginnings so different, we have come now to see whole mountains cut down into marble slabs, journeys made to the Seres to get stuffs for clothing, the abysses of the Red Sea explored for pearls, and the depths of the earth in search of emeralds ! Nay, more, they have taken up the notion also of piercing the ears, as if it were too small a matter to wear these gems in necklaces and tiaras, unless holes also were made in the body to insert them in ! " (xii, 1).

And again :

" But the sea of Arabia is still more fortunate ; for 'tis thence it sends us pearls. And at the lowest computation, India and the Seres and that Peninsula put together drain our empire of one hundred million of sesterces every year. That is the price that our luxuries and our womankind cost us ! " (xii, 41).

[1] On the possible interpretations of this name see Tennent's *Ceylon*, i, 532–3.

[2] I cannot attempt to solve the difficulties of this passage, on which I have seen nothing satisfactory. Putting aside the red hair and blue eyes, it is difficult to conceive that the Chinese ever practised this dumb trade, which in all other known cases I believe has been found only where one party to it was in a very low state of civilisation. A certain kind of dumb trade indeed prevails more or less in most Asiatic countries, including Mongolia (Huc and Gabet, 112) and *possibly* China, I mean that by which bargains are driven and concluded by the two parties fingering each other's knuckles under a shawl without a word spoken. Could the stories of the Seric trade have risen out of this practice ?

NOTE IV BIS.

FROM DIONYSIUS PERIERGETES[1].

(A.D. 2nd Century.)

Verum ubi Scythici oceani gurgitem profundum
navis secueris, ulteriusque ad mare orientale deflexeris,
iter tibi Auream insulam adducit, ubi
solis ipsius ortus conspicitur purus. (587–590.)

Post hunc propter Jaxartis cursus Sacæ habitant
sagittiferi, quos haud facile alius refutaverit
sagittarius, quippe quibus non sit fas irrita jaculari,
et Tochari Phrunique et barbaræ Serum nationes,
qui boves pinguesque oves detrectant,
sed versicolores vastæ regionis flores intexunt
ac vestes multa arte conficiunt pretiosas,
quæ colore pratensis herbæ honorem referant,
ut ne opus quidem aranearum cum illis certet. (749–757.)

FROM RUFUS FESTUS AVIENUS[2].

(4th Century.)

Descriptio Orbis Terræ.

...Tum cyaneis erepit ab undis
insula, quæ prisci signatur nominis usu
Aurea, quod fulvo sol hic magis orbe rubescat. (769–771.)

...Inde cruenti
sunt Tochari, Phrunique truces, et inhospita Seres
arva habitant. Gregibus permixti oviumque boumque
vellera per silvas Seres nemoralia carpunt. (933–936.)

FROM PRISCIANUS[3].

(Beginning 4th Century.)

Periegesis.

At navem pelago flectenti aquilonis ab oris
ad solem calido referentem lumen ab ortu
Aurea spectetur tibi pinguibus insula glebis. (592–594.)

Inde Sacæ nimium certis gens mira sagittis,
flumen Iaxartem juxta quibus arva coluntur;
et Tochari Phrurique et plurima millia Serum:
illis nulla boum, pecoris nec pascua curæ,
vestibus utuntur, texunt quas floribus ipsi,
quos tenuant lectos desertis finibus ipsi. (725–730.)

[1] *Geographi Græci Minores,*...ill. C. Müllerus, ii, 1861, pp. 141 151–2.

[2] *Geographi Græci Minores,*...ill. C. Müllerus, ii, 1861, pp. 184, 185.

[3] *Geographi Græci Minores,*...ill. C. Müllerus, ii, 1861, pp. 195, 196.

NOTE V.

FROM THE ITINERARY OF GREECE OF PAUSANIAS.

(Circa A.D. 174.)

"Now, the Land of Elis is not merely fruitful in other products, but also, and it is not the least of them, in *Byssus*[1]. Hemp and flax and byssus are sown by such as have soils appropriate to the cultivation of each. But the filaments from which the Seres make their stuffs are the growth of no plant, but are produced in quite another manner; and thus it is. There exists in their country a certain insect which the Greeks call *Sēr;* but by the Seres it is not called Sēr, but something quite different. In size 'tis twice as big as the biggest of beetles: but, in other respects, it resembles the spiders that spin under trees; and, moreover, it has eight legs as spiders have. The Seres keep these creatures, and make houses for their shelter adapted to summer and winter respectively. And the substance wrought by these insects is found in the shape of a slender filament entangled about their legs. The people feed them for about four years upon millet, and in the fifth year (for they know that the creatures will not live longer than that) they give them a kind of green reed to eat. This is the food that the insect likes best of all; and it crams itself with it to such an extent that it bursts from repletion. And when it is thus dead, they find the bulk of what it has spun in its inside[2].

"Now, SERIA is known to be an island in a recess of the Erythræan Sea. But I have been told that it is not the Erythræan Sea which makes it an island, but a river which they call SĒR, just as the Delta of Egypt is isolated by the Nile and not by a sea compassing it all round. And these Seres are of the Ethiopic race; and they hold also the adjoining islands, ABASA and SAKAIA. Yet others say that they are not Ethiopians at all, but a cross between the Scythians and the Indians. This is what they tell of these matters" (vi, 26).

[1] Cotton?

[2] Erroneous as this account is, it looks as if it had come originally from real information, though afterwards misunderstood and perverted. The "shelter adapted to winter and summer" seems to point to the care taken by the Chinese in regulating the heat of the silk-houses; the "five years" may have been a misunderstanding of the five *ages* of the silkworm's life marked by its four moultings; the reed given it to eat when the spinning season has come may refer to the strip of rush with which the Chinese form receptacles for the worms to spin in (see Lardner's *Cyc. Silk Manufacture*, p. 126).

NOTE VI.

FROM THE HISTORY OF AMMIANUS MARCELLINUS.

(Circa A.D. 380.)

"Beyond these regions of the two Scythias, towards the east, a circling and continuous barrier of lofty mountains fences round the Seres, who dwell thus secure in their rich and spacious plains. On the west they come in contact with the Scythians; on the north and east they are bounded by solitary regions of snow: on the south, they reach as far as India and the Ganges. The mountains of which we have spoken are called Anniva and Nazavicium and Asmira and Emodon and Opurocarra[1]. And these plains, thus compassed on all sides by precipitous steeps, are traversed by two famous rivers, Œchardes and Bautis, winding with gentle current through the spacious level; whilst the Seres themselves pass through life still more tranquilly, ever keeping clear of arms and war. And being of that sedate and peaceful temper whose greatest delight is a quiet life, they give trouble to none of their neighbours. They have a charming climate, and air of healthy temper; the face of their sky is unclouded; their breezes blow with serviceable moderation; their forests are spacious, and shut out the glare of day.

"The trees of these forests furnish a product of a fleecy kind, so to speak, which they ply with frequent waterings, and then card out in fine and slender threads, half woolly fibre, half viscid filament. Spinning these fibres they manufacture *silk*, the use of which once confined to our nobility has now spread to all classes without distinction, even to the lowest. Those Seres are frugal in their habits beyond other men, and study to pass their lives in peace, shunning association with the rest of mankind. So when foreigners pass the river on their frontier to buy their silk or other wares, the bargain is settled by the eyes alone with no exchange of words. And so free are they from wants that, though ready to dispose of their own products, they purchase none from abroad" (xxiii, 6).

NOTE VII.

THE INTRODUCTION OF THE SILK-WORM INTO THE ROMAN EMPIRE, FROM PROCOPIUS, *DE BELLO GOTHICO.*

(A.D. 500–565.)

"About the same time certain monks arrived from the (country of the) Indians, and learning that the Emperor Justinian had it

[1] Read "Anniba, Auxacius, Asmiraeus, Emodon, and Ottorocorrhas." See extract from Ptolemy, *supra*, p. 195.

much at heart that the Romans should no longer buy silk from the Persians, they came to the king and promised that they would so manage about silk that the Romans should not have to purchase the article either from the Persians or from any other nation; for they had lived, they said, a long time in a country where there were many nations of the Indians, and which goes by the name of SERINDA. And when there they had made themselves thoroughly acquainted with the way in which silk might be produced in the Roman territory. And when the emperor questioned them very closely, and asked how they could guarantee success in the business, the monks told him that the agents in the production of silk were certain caterpillars, working under the teaching of nature, which continually urged them to their task. To bring live caterpillars indeed from that country would be impracticable, but arrangements might be made for hatching them easily and expeditiously. For the eggs produced at a birth by one of those worms were innumerable; and it was possible to hatch these eggs long after they had been laid, by covering them with dung, which produced sufficient heat for the purpose. When they had given these explanations, the emperor made them large promises of reward if they would only verify their assertions by carrying the thing into execution. And so they went back again to India and brought a supply of the eggs to Byzantium. And having treated them just as they had said, they succeeded in developing the caterpillars, which they fed upon mulberry leaves. And from this beginning originated the establishment of silk-culture in the Roman territory" (iv, 17).

Zonaras (*Annals*, xiv, vol. ii, p. 69 of Paris ed. 1687), in relating this story after Procopius, says that till this occurred the Romans did not know how silk was produced, nor even that it was spun by worms.

The same as told by THEOPHANES of Byzantium.

(End of sixth century.)

"Now in the reign of Justinian a certain Persian exhibited in Byzantium the mode in which (silk) worms were hatched, a thing which the Romans had never known before. This Persian on coming away from the country of the Seres had taken with him the eggs of these worms (concealed) in a walking-stick, and succeeded in bringing them safely to Byzantium. In the beginning of spring he put out the eggs upon the mulberry leaves which form their food; and the worms feeding upon those leaves developed into winged insects and performed their other operations. Afterwards when the Emperor Justinian showed the Turks the manner in which the worms were hatched, and the silk which they produced, he astonished them greatly. For at that time the Turks were in possession of the marts and ports frequented by the Seres, which had been formerly in the possession of the Persians. For when Ephthalanus King of the Ephthalites (from whom indeed the race derived that name) conquered Perozes and the Persians, these latter were deprived of their places, and the Ephthalites became possessed of them[1]. But somewhat later the Turks again conquered the Ephthalites and took the places from them in turn." In Müller's *Fragmenta Histor. Græc.*, iv, 270.

NOTE VIII.

EXTRACTS REGARDING INTERCOURSE BETWEEN THE TURKISH KHANS AND THE BYZANTINE EMPERORS.

From the Fragments of MENANDER PROTECTOR.

(End of sixth century.)

"In the beginning of the fourth year of the Emperor Justin [568] an embassy from the Turks arrived at Byzantium; and it came about thus. The power of the Turks had now grown to a great pitch, and the people of Sogdia who had formerly been subject to the Ephthalites[2] but were now under the Turks, besought the king to send an embassy to the Persians, in order to obtain permission for them to carry silk for sale into Persia. Dizabulus[3] consented to send an embassy of Sogdians, and

[1] Perozes (Firoz) reigned 458–484. The circumstances as gathered from other Greek writers are set forth in Lassen, ii, 773.

The mention here of the "*ports* frequented by the Seres" is remarkable, and I believe the only indication of the Seres (under that name) as a sea-faring people. *If the expression can be depended on*, the ports in question must have been in Sind. We have seen that a record of the Chinese trade to Sind at a date somewhat later exists (*supra*, p. 87). This passage then becomes a final link of identification between Seres and Chinese.

[2] [The Hephthalites or Ephthalites, known as the White Huns, derive their name from their chief *Ye-tai-i-li-t'o*, who sent an embassy to China in 516. The Chinese Historians say that the *Ye ta* (Ephthalites) were of the race of the Ta Yue-chi, came from Kin shan (Altaï), and settled west of Yu t'ien (Khotan). It is very doubtful whether they were a branch of the Ta Yue-chi. They were at first a small people called *Hoa*, subject to the Juan Juan; they grew in importance during the fifth century and became the neighbours of the Persians; Talikhan, west of Balkh, being the frontier town between the two nations in 500. The capital of the Ephthalites was Bāmyin (Badhaghis) (Pai-ti-yen), near Herat. We saw that the Ephthalites were destroyed by the Western Turks between 563 and 567. [See *supra*, p. 59.]—Specht, *Études sur l'Asie centrale*, *J. As.*, 1883. Chavannes, *Tou-Kiue*.]

[3] The Great Khan of the Turks at this time, according to the Chinese histories, was *Mokan*. There was also a great chief called by these authorities *Titeupuli*, who is mentioned as joining Mokan Khan in an expedition to China a few years before this time. It is difficult not to identify this name with that of *Dizabulus*, but the latter is so distinctly represented as the supreme chief that Deguignes hesitates whether to

Maniach was put at the head of the mission. So they presented themselves before the Persian king, and solicited permission to carry on their silk trade without obstruction. The King of the Persians, however, was not at all pleased at the notion that the Turks should have free access from that side into the Persian territories, and so he put them off till the morrow, and when the morrow came again deferred reply. After he had thus staved off the matter for a length of time on one pretext or other, the solicitations of the Sogdian people became very importunate, and at last Khosroes called a council where the matter was brought up for consideration. And then that same Ephthalite Katulphus, who, in revenge for the king's ravishing his wife, had betrayed his nation to the Turks, and who had on that account abandoned his country and taken up with the Medes, exhorted the Persian king on no account to let the silk have free passage, but to have a price put upon it, buy it up, and have it burnt in the presence of the ambassadors. It would thus be seen that though he would do no injustice, he would have nothing to do with the silk of the Turks. So the silk was put into the fire and the ambassadors turned homeward, anything but pleased with the result of their journey, and related to Dizabulus what had taken place. He was, however, exceedingly desirous to obtain the good will of the Persians for his government, so he immediately despatched a second embassy. When this second Turkish embassy arrived at the Persian court, the king, with the Persian ministers and Katulphus, came to the conclusion that it would be highly inexpedient for the Persians to enter into friendly relations with the Turks, for the whole race of the Scythians was one not to be trusted. So he ordered some of the ambassadors to be taken off by a deadly poison, in order to prevent any more such missions from coming. Most of the Turkish envoys accordingly, in fact all but three or four, were put an end to by a deadly poison which was mixt with their food, whilst the king caused it to be whispered about among the Persians that the Turkish ambassadors had died of the suffocating dry heat of the Persian climate ; for their own

identify him with Mokan or Titeupuli (ii, 380–5). [Prof. Chavannes, *Tou-Kiue*, pp. 227–8, has a paragraph on the name Silzibul (Dizabul) which he derives from the proper name *Sin* and the title *jabgu* (*Sin jabgu*) ; Marquart, *Êranšahr*, p. 216, in Silzibul sees *Syr-jabgu*, the people of the *Syr* Country.]

Another of the fragments of Menander contains an account of the embassy of Valentine who was sent some twelve years later by the Emperor Tiberius II. In this occur the names of *Tardu* and *Bochanos*, two Turkish chiefs who appear in the Chinese Annals as Ta t'eu Khan and Apo Khan (see Deguignes i, 226, 227 ; ii, 395, 463). [The Western Turks (see above, p. 58) had for ancestor T'u wu, grandson of Na-tu-lu ; his two sons were T'u men and She-tie-mi : Ta t'eu kagan (Tardu) was the son of She-tie mi (Dizabul). Mu han or Se kin who died *c.* 572 after reigning twenty years was a son of T'u men ; Mu han's son was Ta lo pien or Apo Kagan. See Chavannes, *Tou-Kiue*, pp. 47 *seq.*]

country was subject to frequent falls of snow, and they could not exist except in a cold climate. Dizabulus, however, a sharp and astute person, was not ignorant of the real state of the case. And so this was the origin of ill-will between the Turks and the Persians. Maniach, who was chief of the people of Sogdia, took the opportunity of suggesting to Dizabulus that it would be more for the interest of the Turks to cultivate the friendship of the Romans, and to transfer the sale of silk to them, seeing also that they consumed it more largely than any other people. And Maniach added that he was quite ready to accompany a party of Turkish ambassadors, in order to promote the establishment of friendly relations between the Turks and the Romans. Dizabulus approved of the suggestion, and despatched Maniach with some others as ambassadors carrying complimentary salutations, with a present of silk to no small value, and letters to the Roman Emperor. So Maniach . . . at last arrived at Byzantium, and presenting himself at the court, conducted himself before the Emperor in accordance with the obligations of friendship, and when he had made over the letter and presents to the proper officers, prayed that all the toils of his long journey might not have been wasted. The Emperor when he had by aid of the interpreters read the letter, which was written in Scythian, gave a gracious reception to the embassy, and then put questions to them about the government and country of the Turks. They told him that there were four chiefs, but that the supreme authority over the whole nation rested with Dizabulus. They also related how he had subdued the Ephthalites and even made them pay tribute. Then said the Emperor, 'Has then the whole power of the Ephthalites been overthrown?' 'Altogether,' answered the envoys. Again the Emperor: 'Did the Ephthalites live in cities or villages or how?' *The Envoys*: 'They are a people who live in cities, O king.' 'Is it not of course then,' said the Emperor, 'that you are become masters of all their cities?' . . . The ambassadors having counted up to the Emperor all the nations who were subject to the Turks, begged him to give his sanction to the establishment of amity and alliance between the two nations, and said that on their part they would always be ready to attack the enemies of the Roman power wherever they might show themselves in their part of the world. And as he said this Maniach and his companions raised their hands and swore a great oath that they were speaking with their whole hearts, and invoked curses on themselves and on Dizabulus, and on all the nation, if their promises were not true and such as they would carry out. And thus it was that the nation of the Turks became friends with the Romans." * * * * * * * * *

(*Another Fragment.*)

"Now Justin, when the Turks, who were anciently called

Sacæ, had sent to arrange a treaty with him, resolved to send them an embassy also. So he ordered Zemarchus the Cilician, who was then Præfect of the cities of the East, to prepare for this. And when he had got everything ready that he required for so long a journey, which was towards the end of the fourth year of the reign of Justin, in the month which the Latins call August, Zemarchus started from Byzantium with Maniach himself and his company." * * * * *

(*Another.*)

"After accomplishing a journey of many days, Zemarchus and his party arrived in the territories of the Sogdians. And as they dismounted from their horses certain Turks, sent as it seemed for that purpose, presented some iron which they offered for sale; this being, I fancy, in order to show that they had mines of iron in their country. For the manufacture of iron is reckoned among them to be by no means an easy art; and we may guess that this was a kind of brag by which they intended to indicate that theirs was a country in which iron was produced[1]. Some others of the tribe also showed off their performances (in a different line). These, announcing themselves as the conjurors away of evil omens, came up to Zemarchus and taking all the baggage of the party set it down in the middle. They then began ringing a bell and beating a kind of drum over the baggage, whilst some ran round it carrying leaves of burning incense flaming and crackling, and raged about like maniacs, gesticulating as if repelling evil spirits. Carrying on this exorcism of evil as they considered it, they made Zemarchus himself also pass through the fire, and in the same manner they appeared to perform an act of purification for themselves[2]. After

[1] It may have had a different import. For according to the Chinese authority followed by Deguignes, the tribe which founded the Turkish power shortly before this time had long inhabited the Altai, where they worked as smiths for the service of the Khan of the Geu-gen or Juan-Juan; and the Khans of the Turks instituted in memory of their origin the ceremony of annually forging a piece of iron. The presentation of iron to the Byzantine envoys may have had some kindred signification (Deguignes, ii, 350, 373). [The Juan-Juan who became very powerful during the fifth century were defeated by the Turks in 552; they took refuge, part of them at the court of the Wei Sovereigns in China; the others at Byzantium. They are known in Western History as the Avars. See Chavannes, *Tou-Kiue*, p. 230.]

[2] When Plano Carpini and his companions came to the camp of Batu they were told that they must pass between two fires, because this would neutralise any mischievous intentions they might entertain, or poison that they might be carrying. And in another place the traveller says: "To be brief, they believe that by fire all things are purified. Hence when envoys come to them, or chiefs, or any other persons whatever, they and the presents they bring must pass between two fires, to prevent their working any witchcraft or bringing any poison or evil thing with them" (p. 744 and p. 627). In the French note which Buscarel, the ambassador in 1289 of Arghún Khan of Persia, presented with his

these performances the party proceeded with those who had been sent to receive them to the place where the Khagan was, in a certain mountain called ECTAG, or as a Greek would say 'the Golden Mountain.' And when they got there they found the camp of Dizabulus in a certain hollow encompassed by the Golden Mountain[1]. The party of Zemarchus on their arrival were immediately summoned to an interview with Dizabulus. They found him in his tent, seated on a golden chair with two wheels, which could be drawn by one horse when required. Then they addressed the Barbarian in accordance with the fashion of those people, and laid the presents before him, which were taken charge of by those whose office it was. Zemarchus then made a polite speech [which may be omitted], and Dizabulus replied in like manner. Next they were called to a feast, and passed the whole day in conviviality in the tent. Now this tent was furnished with silken hangings of various colours artfully wrought. They were supplied with wine, not pressed from the grape like ours, for their country does not produce the vine, nor is it customary among them to use grape wine; but what they got to drink was some other kind of barbarian liquor[2]. And at last they departed to the place assigned for their quarters. Next day again they assembled in another pavilion, adorned in like manner with rich hangings of silk, in which figures of different kinds were wrought. Dizabulus was seated on a couch that was all of gold[3], and in the middle of the pavilion were drinking vessels and flagons and great jars, all of gold[4]. So they engaged in another drinking match, talking and listening to such purpose as people do in their drink, and then separated[5]. The following day there was another bout in a

master's letter to the King of France (both of which are preserved in the French archives) it is said: "priant vous que se vous li envoiez yceuls ou autres messages, que vous vouliez souffrir et commander leur que il li facent tele reverence et honneur comme coustume et usage est en sa court *sanz passer feu*." (Rémusat, in *Mém. de l'Acad. Insc.*, vii, 432.)

[1] *Ek-tag* or *Ak-tagh* would be "White Mountain." The Altai or Golden Mountain of the Mongols, which was the original seat of these Turks, may be meant, but it is very remote. [See Chavannes, *Tou-Kiue*, p. 236.] All that can be deduced from the narrative is that it was beyond *Talas*, for the party pass that place on their march towards Persia (*infra*). Simocatta also says it was an established law among the Turks that the Golden Mountain should be in the hands of the most powerful Khagan (vii, 8). [See p. 201.]

[2] No doubt *Darassun*; see Shah Rukh's embassy in Note XVII *infra*.

[3] So Rubruquis describes Batu as seated "on a long broad throne like a bed, gilt all over" (p. 268).

[4] "At the entrance of the tent there was a bench with Cosmos (*Kumis* or fermented mare's milk), and great goblets of gold and silver set with precious stones" (*Ibid.*). See also Shâh Rukh's Embassy *infra*.

[5] This constant drinking corresponds exactly to the account of the habits of the Mongol court in Plano Carpini and Rubruquis. Thus the former, on the occasion of Kuyuk Khan's formal inthroning, says that

pavilion supported by wooden posts covered with gold, and in which there was a gilded throne resting on four golden peacocks[1]. In front of the place of meeting there was a great array of waggons, in which there was a huge quantity of silver articles consisting of plates and dishes, besides numerous figures of animals in silver, in no respect inferior to our own. To such a pitch has attained the luxury of the Turkish Sovereign!

"And whilst Zemarchus and his party continued there, Dizabulus thought proper that Zemarchus with twenty of his servants and followers should accompany him on a campaign against the Persians, sending the rest of the Romans back to the land of the CHOLIATÆ[2] to await the return of Zemarchus. These last Dizabulus dismissed with presents and friendly treatment; and at the same time he honoured Zemarchus with the gift of a handmaiden, one of those called *Kherkhis*, who was the captive of his spear[3]. And so Zemarchus went with Dizabulus to fight the Persians. Whilst they were on this expedition, as they were pitched at a place called TALAS, an ambassador from the Persians came to meet Dizabulus, who invited him to dinner as well as the ambassador of the Romans[4]. When the party had met, Dizabulus accorded to the Roman much the more honourable treatment, and made him occupy the more honourable place at table. Moreover he heaped great reproaches on the Persians, telling the

after the homage had been done "they began to drink, and as their way is, continued drinking till hour of vespers." (p. 758.) Rubruquis's account of his residence at the Court of Mangu Khan is quite redolent of drink. One sees how Sultan Baber came by his propensity to strong drink.

[1] Probably the lineal predecessor of the Peacock Throne of Delhi.

[2] Or *Chliatæ*. The *Kallats* are mentioned with the Kanklis, Kipchaks, and Kharliks as four Turkish tribes descended from the Patriarch Oguz Khan. (Deguignes, ii, 9.)

Were these the four divisions of the Turks of whom Maniach spoke to the Emperor?

Deguignes, however, identifies the Chliatæ with the *Kangli* who lay north of the country between the Caspian and Aral (ii, 388). And St. Martin in his notes on Lebeau's *History* says that in the tenth and eleventh centuries the Russians called the Turk and Fin nations near the Caspian *Khwalis*, and knew that sea as the *Sea of Khwalis*. (*Hist. du Bas Empire*, 1828, x, 61.)

[3] This girl might be either Kirghiz or Circassian. St. Martin thinks the latter. (*Ib.*)

[4] Near Talas about sixty years later the Chinese pilgrim, Hiuen Tsang, on his way to India fell in with the Great Khan of the Turks, a successor of Dizabulus, whom the Chinese traveller calls *Shehu*. His account is very like that of Zemarchus. The Khan "occupied a great tent adorned with gold flowers of dazzling richness. The officers of the court sat in two long rows on mats before the Khan, brilliantly attired in embroidered silk; the Khan's guard standing behind them. Although here was but a barbarian prince under a tent of felt, one could not look on him without respect and admiration." (*H. de la Vie de H. T.*, pp. 55–6.)

injuries he had received at their hands, and how he was coming on that account to attack them[1]. So as the abuse of Dizabulus waxed more and more violent, the Persian envoy, casting off all regard for that etiquette of theirs which imposes silence at feasts, began to speak with heat, and in the most spirited manner to refute the charges of Dizabulus; insomuch that all the company wondered at the way in which he gave rein to his wrath. For, contrary to all rule, he used all sorts of intemperate expressions.

"And in this state of things the party broke up and Dizabulus prosecuted his preparations against the Persians. And then he summoned Zemarchus and his party, and when they had presented themselves he renewed his declarations of friendship for the Romans and gave them their dismissal homewards, sending also with them another embassy. Now Maniach the leader of the former embassy was dead, and the name of the one next in rank was Tagma, with the dignity of *Tarchan*[2]. So this personage was sent by Dizabulus as ambassador to the Romans, and along with him the son of the deceased, I mean of Maniach. This was quite a young fellow, but he had succeeded to his father's honours, and obtained the next place in rank to Tagma Tarchan. * * * *

"Now when the rumour spread through Turkey[3] and among the neighbouring nations how ambassadors from the Romans were among them, and were going back to Byzantium accompanied by a Turkish embassy, the chief of the tribes in that quarter sent a request to Dizabulus that he might be allowed also to send some of his own people to see the Roman state. And Dizabulus granted permission. Then other chiefs of the tribes made the same petition, but he would grant leave to none except the chief of the Choliatæ. So the Romans taking the latter with them across the River OECH, after a long journey came to that huge wide lagoon[4]. Here Zemarchus halted for three days and sent off George, whose business it was to carry expresses, to announce to the Emperor the return of the party from the Turks. So George with a dozen Turks set out for Byzantium by a route which was without water, and altogether desert, but was the shortest way. Zemarchus then travelled for twelve days along the sandy shores of the Lagoon, and having to cross some very difficult places,

[1] A curious parallel to the scene at Samarkand, related by Clavijo (*supra*, p. 174), where Timur takes the place of Dizabulus, the Castilian envoy that of Zemarchus, and the Chinese ambassador that of the Persian.

[2] See III, pp. 146–7 *n. infra*. [Cf. Chavannes, *Tou-Kiue*, p. 239.]

[3] "Κατὰ τὴν Τουρκίαν."

[4] If this was the Aral we may suppose the Oech to be the Sir or Jaxartes. But this is scarcely consistent with the position assigned to the Chliatæ.

came to the streams of the River ICH[1], and then to the DAICH[2], and then by other swampy tracts to the ATTILA[3], and then again to the land of the UGURS[4]. And these sent to say that four thousand Persians were stationed in ambuscade in the bush about the River KOPHEN[5] to lay hands on the party as it passed," etc., etc.

Zemarchus escapes the Persians, and after visiting the chief of the ALANS gets to the Phasis, and so to Trebizond, whence he rode post to Byzantium. (From Müller's *Fragmenta Histor. Græc.*, iv, p. 235.)

NOTE IX.

EXTRACTS FROM THE *TOPOGRAPHIA CHRISTIANA* OF COSMAS THE MONK.

(Circa 545.)

1. "But, as is said by those who are without[6], in discoursing of this matter (and here they speak truth), there are on this earth four gulfs which enter the land from the ocean; to wit, this one of ours which penetrates the land from the west side, and extends from Gades[7] right through Romania[8]; then the Arabian Gulf called also Erythræan[9] and the Persian Gulf, both which are offshoots from that of Zinj, and penetrate the southern and eastern side of the earth over against the region called Barbary, which forms the extremity of the land of Ethiopia[10]. And those who

[1] Probably the *Emba*. It appears to be called *Tic* by Sharifuddín (*Pétis de la Croix*, ii, 95, 129).

[2] The Ural or *Iaik*, called by Constantine Porphyrogenitus Γεήχ. (*De Administ. Imper.*, cap. xxxvii.)

[3] The *Athil* or Volga.

[4] On these Ugurs, see Vivien St. Martin in *N. Annales des Voyages* for 1848, iv.

[5] *Kuban* I presume.

[6] Οἱ ἔξωθεν, meaning those who are not Christians.

It should be noted that the book is illustrated with sketches and diagrams, the originals of which would appear to have been drawn by Cosmas himself.

[7] Gadeira (McCrindle).

[8] [Romania = Rome, J. W. McCrindle, who quotes, p. 38, the following note of Montfaucon (ii, p. 132 *n.*): "'Ρωμανία, *Romania*, hic intelligitur terra illa omnis, quæ ad Romanam ditionem pertinebat. Quo item usu Athanasius, p. 364 & Epiphanius, p. 728, 'Ρωμανίαν memorant." The numbers refer to the pages in his own editions of these two authors.]

[9] ["The Erythræan, in its wider sense, includes both the Arabian and Persian Gulfs, beside the ocean between Africa and India." (McCrindle, p. 38 *n.*)]

[10] ["Cosmas is here in agreement with the author of the *Periplus* who makes the Aromatic Cape (Guardafui) the end of Barbaria:

navigate the Indian Sea are aware that Zinj[1], as it is called, lies beyond the country where the incense grows, which is called Barbary, and which is compassed round by the ocean as it passes on into those two gulfs. And the fourth gulf enters from the north side of the earth, further to the east, and is called the Caspian or Hircanian Sea[2]. Now navigation is confined to these gulfs only. The ocean it is impossible to navigate, on account of the multitude of currents and the fogs that rise and obstruct the rays of the sun, and because of its vast extent. These things, then, I have made known as I received them from the Man of God (as has been mentioned); or indeed, I might rather say in this case, from my own experience. For I myself, for purposes of trade, have sailed on three out of those four gulfs; to wit, the Roman, the Arabian, and the Persian; and I have got accurate information about the different places on them from the natives as well as from seafaring men.

"Once upon a time, when we were sailing to Further India[3], we had crossed over within a little way of Barbary, beyond which is Zinj (for so they call the mouth of the Ocean), and there I saw to the right of our course a great flight of the birds called *suspha*[4]. These are birds twice as big as kites and somewhat more. And

τελευτοῖον τῆς βαρβαρικῆς ἠπείρου. Ptolemy, however, makes it begin here, and extends it to Rhaptum in the Gulf of Zanguebar." (McCrindle, pp. 38–9 *n.*)]

[1] [On Zinj see *Reports of Miss. Friars*, p. 183 note, and Marignolli, p. 324, *Int.*—Montfaucon has the following note (*l.c.*, p. 132): "Zingium ex ævi sui usu vocat Cosmas, non modo fretum Arabici sinus, sed etiam oram maritimam Africanam ultra fretum; itemque mare adjacens; quod nomen hodieque perseverat littus, quippe Zanguebaricum, a freto Arabici sinus, pene ad usque promontorium Bonæ Spei, quotidianis Europæorum navigationibus frequentatum, ab incolis Zangui vocatur. Zanguebar enim significat, mare Zangui."]

[2] ["Cosmas shared the error prevalent in ancient times, that the Caspian was not a land-locked sea but was a gulf of the great ocean. Herodotus, however, is not chargeable with having been under this delusion." (McCrindle, p. 39 *n.*)]

[3] Literally "Inner India." ["This generally means that part of India which lies on the further side of Cape Comorin or of the Straits between Ceylon and the mainland. But as the name of India was sometimes applied to Southern Arabia, and even to Eastern Africa, India as lying beyond these countries may be here meant. John Malela, or Malala, the Byzantine historian, who wrote not long after the time of Cosmas, calls both of them *India*: 'At this time it happened that the *Indians* warred against each other, those called Auxumites with those called Homerites....The Roman traders go through the Homerites into Auxumê, and to the interior kingdoms of the Indians, for there are seven kingdoms of the Indians and Ethiopians.' Friar Jornandes calls Eastern Africa *India Tertia*." (J. W. McCrindle, p. 39 *n.*) See III, p. 27 note, *Introductory Notices, Reports of Missionary Friars*.]

[4] ["The size of these birds, and the fact afterwards mentioned that they kept flying aloft, might indicate them to be albatrosses." (McCrindle, p. 40 *n.*)]

I observed that in that quarter there were signs of very unsettled weather. So all the men of experience on board, whether mariners or passengers, began to say that we were getting near the Ocean, and so they called out to the steersman, 'steer the ship to port, and bear up into the gulf, or the currents will sweep us into the Ocean, and we shall be lost.' For the Ocean driving up into the gulf was creating a very heavy sea, and the currents from the gulf again were drifting the ship towards the Ocean; a terrible thing indeed for us who saw what was happening, and in great fear were we. And all this time flocks of those birds called *suspha* followed us flying high over our heads, which was a sign that the Ocean was nigh[1]." (Book ii, p. 132.—Book ii, pp. 37–40, in McCrindle's ed.)

2. "For if Paradise were really on the surface of this world, is there not many a man among those who are so keen to learn and search out everything, that would not let himself be deterred from reaching it? When we see that there are men who will not be deterred from penetrating to the ends of the earth in search of silk[2], and all for the sake of filthy lucre, how can we believe that they would be deterred from going to get a sight of Paradise? The country of silk, I may mention, is in the remotest of all the Indies, lying towards the left when you enter the Indian Sea, but a vast distance farther off than the Persian Gulf or that island which the Indians call SELEDIBA[3] and the Greeks TAPROBANE. TZINITZA is the name of the country, and the Ocean compasses it round to the left, just as the same Ocean compasses Barbary round to the right. And the Indian philosophers, called Brachmans, tell you that if you were to stretch a straight cord from Tzinitza through Persia to the Roman territory, you would just divide the world in halves. And mayhap they are right[4].

[1] With reference to the terrors of the Southern Ocean see *infra*, II, p. 160 *note*. Edrisi says: "The Ocean Sea, which is called the Dark Sea, because it *is* dark, and is almost always in commotion with violent winds, and covered by thick fogs." (i, 87.)

[2] [*μετάξιον* = silk. "Sometimes written *ματάξιον*—a foreign word, and only found in later Greek. In classical Greek the name for silk is *βόμβυξ*, and also *σηρικόν*, from which our word *silk* is derived by the change, which is not uncommon, of *r* into *l*." (McCrindle, p. 47 *n*.)]

[3] [Montfaucon's note (*l.c.*, p. 137 *n*.): "*Σελεδίβα*, inferius legitur, *Σιελεδίβα*. Estque insula Ceylan, nomine tantis per immutato. Nam *δίβα*, aut *diua*, insulam sibi vult; hinc *Maldive*, ita ut Sielediva, insulam Siele significet. Mox *Τζινίτζα*, inferius in Vaticano Codice legitur *Τζινη*, Tsina, sive Sina; nempe Sinarum regio: quæ, ipso teste Cosma, Oceano ab oriente terminatur."]

[4] [Beazley (*Dawn of Modern Geography*, i, p. 193 *n*.) thinks that Tzinista "is probably only a dim notion of Malaya or Cochin-China; the northern bend he describes is probably that of the Gulf of Siam; and this shadowy account does not at all anticipate the real discovery of these regions, for Europe, by Marco Polo or, for the Caliphate, by the Arabs."]

"For the country in question lies very much to the left, insomuch that loads of silk passing through the hands of different nations in succession *by land* reach Persia in a comparatively short time, whilst the distance from Persia *by sea* is vastly greater. For, in the first place, just as great a distance as the Persian Gulf runs up into Persia has the voyager to Tzinitza to run up from [the latitude of] Taprobane and the regions beyond it to reach his destination. And, in the second place, there is no small distance to be traversed in crossing the whole width of the Indian Sea from the Persian Gulf to Taprobane, and from Taprobane to the regions beyond [where you turn up to the left to reach Tzinitza][1]. Hence it is clear that one who comes by the overland route from Tzinitza to Persia makes a very short cut. And this accounts for the fact that such quantities of silk are always to be found in Persia.

"Further than Tzinitza there is neither navigation nor inhabited country.

"And here I may observe, that if anyone should actually measure the earth's longitude with a straight line running from Tzinitza westward, he would find it to be four hundred marches more or less[2], taking the marches at thirty miles each. And the measurement will run thus: From Tzinitza to the frontier of PERSIA, including all UNNIA[3] and INDIA, and the Land of the Bactrians, will be about a hundred and fifty marches, if not more, certainly not less. The whole of Persia will be eighty marches.

[1] I believe this is the meaning, but the passage is very elliptical. [McCrindle (p. 49) translates this passage: "For just as great a distance as the Persian Gulf runs up into Persia, so great a distance and even a greater has one to run, who, being bound for Tzinitza, sails eastward from Taprobanê; while besides, the distances from the mouth of the Persian Gulf to Taprobanê and the parts beyond through the whole width of the India sea are very considerable." He remarks in a note that "the Persian Gulf has a length of 650 English miles, while the distance from Ceylon to the Malacca peninsula only is nearly twice that distance."]

[M. Robert Gauthiot remarks that in one of the Sogdian letters of the beginning of our era brought back from Central Asia by Sir Aurel Stein, he reads the word *čynstn* with the sense of China. *Čynstn* is evidently *čīnastān*, "country of the Čina"; in Sogdian the *a* of *°stan* is not noted; in the Syriac part of the Si-ngan fu inscription there is a similar orthography, without notation of *a*, if not in the name of China, at least in this of Tokharestan. Prof. Pelliot adds that it clearly appears that Čin was the name of China just before our era, and that it is very probably the name of the kingdom and of the princes of Ts'in. *T'oung pao*, 1913, p. 428.]

[2] ["Si quis ergo a Sina usque ad occidentem, recta longitudinem terræ funiculo dimetiatur, inveniet mansiones circiter 400 triginta milliarium singulas." (Montfaucon, p. 138.)]

[3] [Unnia.—Montfaucon, Ιουνία, Juvia.—McCrindle, Iouvia, "this would mean the country of the Huns." p. 49.]

From Nisibis[1] to Seleucia[2] thirteen marches. From Seleucia by ROME and the GAULS and IBERIA (the country of those who are nowadays called Spaniards), to Outer GADES on the Ocean a hundred and fifty marches and more. So the total of the distances will be four hundred marches, more or less.

"Now, as regards the earth's latitude. From the far north to Byzantium will not be more than fifty marches[3] (for we may form a good guess at the extent of those northern regions, both inhabited and uninhabited, from the position of the Caspian Sea which is a gulf of the ocean)[4]. From Byzantium again to Alexandria is fifty marches. From Alexandria to the Cataracts thirty marches[5]. From the Cataracts to Axum[6] thirty marches. From Axum to the

[1] [On the site of Nisibis was built the present Nisibin, Nissibin, chief town of the caza of Nisibin, in the sandjak of Mardin, vilayet of Diarbekir, on the banks of the Jaghjagha (Mygdonius) at the foot of Mount Massius. Under the Seleucids Nisibis was called Antiocheia of Mygdonia; the Greeks named it also Anthumusia on account of the fragrant scent of its flowery plain. It belonged to the Kings of Armenia and was the capital of Tigranes, was taken by Lucullus, passed into the hands of the Parthians and was annexed by Trajan to the Roman Empire; it was ceded by the emperor Jovian to the Sassanid King Sapor II. After the defeat of Ismael Shah by Sultan Selim I at Chaldiran (1514) it formed part of the Ottoman Empire.]

[2] [Seleucia or Seleuceia was built near the right bank of the Tigris by Seleucus Nicator with materials brought mainly from Babylon, just as Ctesiphon was constructed with the ruins of Seleucia destroyed during the Parthian Wars.]

[3] ["Latitudo vero terræ ab Hyperboreis partibus ad usque Byzantium, mansiones non plures quinquaginta sunt." (Montfaucon, p. 138.)]

[4] I suppose there is here to be understood a comparison of the Caspian, regarded as a gulf, with the Red Sea or Persian Gulf, and a deduction that the Ocean cannot lie further north from the innermost point of the Caspian than it lies south of the innermost point of one of those gulfs.

[5] [McCrindle makes the following remark, p. 50: "Gr. *μοναὶ λ'*. Here the numeral λ' = 30 must be an error for κ' = 20, because the distance from Alexandria to Syênê, in the neighbourhood of the Great Cataract, is about 600 Roman miles; and because, moreover, in the summing-up of the figures as in the text there is an excess of ten over the given total. Montfaucon has not noticed this discrepancy."]

[6] ["La première mention des Axoumites et de leur capitale est dans le Périple de la mer Erythrée, ouvrage qui doit avoir été rédigé à Alexandrie vers l'année 80 de Jésus-Christ. La conséquence que l'on est fondé à tirer de ces rapprochements, c'est que les établissements commerciaux des Grecs d'Egypte sur les parties méridionales de la côté éthiopienne, et les rapports habituels qui en furent la suite, amenèrent de grands changements dans l'état social et politique de quelques parties de l'intérieur, et qu'un royaume dont Axoum fut la capitale se forma alors dans le haut pays... Plusieurs faits bien connus, prouvent d'ailleurs l'action directe de l'hellénisme égyptien sur le développement de la civilisation axoumite. Ainsi l'auteur du Périple rapporte que le roi d'Axoum, qu'il nomme *Zoskalès*, était familiarisé avec les lettres grecques; et ce qui montre que cette influence eut une longue durée, c'est que deux siècles et demi plus tard on voit la langue grecque employée à Axoum dans les inscriptions concurremment avec la langue

projecting part of Ethiopia, the country where the incense grows, and which is called Barbary[1], lying along the Ocean, and including the territory of SAS which is the remotest part of Ethiopia, and is anything but a narrow tract of country, indeed quite the reverse, fifty marches, more or less. So that we may take the whole breadth at two hundred marches, more or less. And thus we see that the Holy Scripture speaks the truth when it puts the length of the earth at double its breadth : '*For thou shalt make the Table* (which is, as it were, a pattern of the Earth) *in length two cubits, and in breadth one cubit*[2].'

"Now, the country where the incense grows lies in the projecting parts of Ethiopia, being itself indeed an inland region, but having the ocean on the other side of it. Hence the people of Barbary, being in the vicinity, are able to visit the interior for trading purposes, and bring back with them many kinds of aromatics, such as incense, cassia, calamus[3], and a great variety

éthiopienne. Ce qui existe encore de l'ancienne Axoum, particulièrement ses obélisques, est d'un style grec, bien qu'on y sente une réminiscence égyptienne. Enfin, la religion des Grecs d'Égypte avait pénétré dans le royaume d'Axoum, en même temps que leur langue et leurs artistes, car dans les inscriptions le roi éthiopien se dit 'fils de l'invincible Arès.'" (Vivien de Saint-Martin, *Inscription d'Adulis*, *Jour. Asiat.*, Oct. 1863, pp. 332–4.)

"E regione igitur Orinæ insulæ in continente viginti a mari stadiis sita est Abduli, pagus mediocris, a quo ad Coloen, urbem mediterraneam primumque eboris emporium, via est tridui. Hinc ad ipsam metropolim Auxumitarum iter est aliorum dierum quinque; in hanc omne ebur e regione trans Nilum sita per Cyeneum quem vocant tractum deportatur, hinc vero Adulin. Cuncta scilicet quæ cæditur elephantorum et rhinozerotum multitudo in superioribus degit locis, non nunquam tamen, raro licet, in maritima etiam regione circa ipsam Adulin conspiciuntur." (*Periplus Maris Erythraei*, *Geographi Græci Minores*...illust. Carolus Müllerus, i, Parisiis, 1855, § 4, pp. 260–1.)

"At this time there is no settled City in all Ethiopia; formerly the Town of Aczum was very famous among the Abyssinians, and still preserves somewhat of its Renown; and this place seems to have been a City, at least they look upon it as most certain, that the Queen of Sheba kept her Court there, and that it was the Residence of the Emperors for many Ages after, and that they are Crown'd there to this Day... ; at present it is only a Village of about 100 Houses." (*The Travels of the Jesuits in Ethiopia*, by F. Balthazar Tellez, 1710, p. 59.)

Axum "was distant from its sea-port, Adulê, which was situated near Annesley Bay, about 120 miles, or an eight days' caravan journey. It was the chief centre of the trade with the interior of Africa."... "Christianity was introduced into Axum in the fourth century by Œdisius and Frumentius, the latter of whom was afterwards appointed its first bishop. Sasu, which is next mentioned, is near the coast, and only 5° to the north of the equator." (McCrindle, pp. 50–1 *n.*)—The ruins of Axum are to the west of the Adua, present capital of Tigré.]

[1] The modern Somali country. The name of Barbary is still retained in that of Berberah on the coast over against Aden. See also Ptolemy, i, 17.

[2] [*Exodus* xxxvii. 10.]

[3] ["The sweet calamus mentioned in *Exodus* xxx. 23." McCrindle, p. 51.]

of others, and these again they carry by sea to Adule[1] and Homerite, and to Further India and to Persia. And this is just as you will find it written in the Book of Kings, where the Queen of Saba, *i.e.*, of Homerite (and whom again in the Gospels the Lord terms the Queen of the South), brings to Solomon aromatics from this very Barbary (she residing hard by on the coast just opposite), and brings him also staves of ebony, and monkeys, and gold from Ethiopia, the whole of Ethiopia being in fact quite in her vicinity, and just across the Arabian Gulf. Again, let us look at some of Our Lord's words, as when he calls those places *the Ends of the Earth*, saying, '*The Queen of the South shall rise up in judgment with this generation and shall condemn it, for she came from the* Ends of the Earth *to hear the wisdom of Solomon.*' The fact is, Homerite is at no distance from Barbary, for the sea between them has only a width of some two days' sail. And beyond that is the Ocean, which thereabouts is called the Sea of Zinj[2]. And just as the Incense Country has the Ocean near it, so also has the Land of Sas where the gold mines are. Now, year by year the King of the Axumites, through the ruler of Agau[3], sends men of his own to Sas for the purchase of gold. And many others bound on the same speculation accompany them on this expedition, so there shall be more than five hundred in the party. They take with them beeves, and pieces of salt, and iron. And when they get near the country they make a halt at a certain place, and take a quantity of thorns with which they make a great hedge, within which they establish themselves, and there they slaughter the oxen and cut them up, and put the meat, and the pieces of salt, and the iron on the top of the hedge. So the natives then approach with gold in nuggets, like peas, which they call *Tancharan*[4], and each of them deposits one or two of these upon the joints of meat, or the salt, or the iron as he pleases, and then stands aloof. Then the owner of the beef etc., comes up, and if he is satisfied he takes the gold, whilst the other party comes and removes the flesh, or piece of salt or iron. But if the trader is not satisfied he leaves the gold where it is, and when the native comes up and sees that his

[1] ["'Αδούλη, Adule, ex qua mare adjacens, sinus Adulitanus appellabatur, vide Ptolemæum." (Montfaucon, p. 140 *n.*)]

[2] ["The ocean which is there called Zingion." McCrindle, p. 52.]

[3] Alvarez in Ramusio speaks of certain lordships of Abyssinia "the people of which are called *Agaos*," and who are a mixture of Gentiles and Christians. The Agaus appear to be scattered widely over Abyssinia. Salt speaks of them along the Takazzé to the east of Gondar, and one of Petermann's maps shows Agau also to the south-west of Tzana Lake, which again lies south-west of Gondar. A country including both of these positions would lie south and a little west of Axum. (Ramusio, i, f. 250; Salt's *Second Travels, French transl.*, 1816, ii, 21 *seq.*; *Petermann's Mitteilungen*, 1857, pl. 23.)

[4] [*Tancharan*, Montfaucon, p. 139.—*Tancharas*, McCrindle, p. 53.]

gold has not been taken, he either adds to the quantity or takes up his gold and goes away. This is the mode of barter among the people in that quarter; for they are of different language and have no supply of interpreters[1]. The time of their stay to do business in that country extends to five days, more or less, according to the rate at which customers present themselves until they have sold off all their goods. And on the return journey they all form themselves into an armed body; for there are certain people in the tract they pass through who hang about them and endeavour to plunder the gold. The whole business carried on in this way takes some six months; the journey thither being accomplished more slowly than the return, chiefly because of the cattle that accompany them, and also because they make great haste on the way back that the winter rains catch them not on the journey. For the head of the Nile is somewhere thereabouts, and the rivers that feed it cross the route, and in winter become greatly swollen by the rains. Now, the winter there is in the time of our summer, extending from the month called by the Egyptians *Epiphi*[2], till that called *Thoth*: and all these three months it rains with great violence, so as to give rise to a multitude of rivers, all of which discharge themselves into the Nile[3]" (book ii, pp. 138–140, McCrindle, pp. 47–54).

Cosmas then proceeds to give an account of an ancient marble throne which he had seen at Adule (then the port of Abyssinia, a little south of Massawah), with Greek inscriptions on it, of which he gives a professed transcript; but I shall not attempt to enter

[1] [" Est hodieque his in partibus, in regno scilicet Habessinorum Æthiopum regio Agau nomine, ubi celebres illæ Nili scaturigines, ut inferius narratur. Quod vero narrat hic Cosmas de singulari illa mercaturam exercendi consuetudine: qua nempe Æthiopes & Barbari illi lingua discrepantes, admotis rebus commutandis; tum negotiationem perficerent, cum is qui venumdabat, adpositum pretium acciperet; hodiéque in plerisque Africæ partibus usu venit, ut videas in itinerariis & descriptionibus Africæ." (Montfaucon, p. 139 *n.*)]

[2] *Epiphi* (June 25th—July 25th) was the eleventh month of the Egyptian year, and *Thoth* (August 29th—September 28th) the first month; represented by the modern Coptic months *Ebib* and *Tút* (see Nicolas, *Chron. of Hist.*, pp. 13, 15).

[3] Alvise Cadamosto gives nearly the same account of the dumb barter of salt for gold as carried on by negro traders from Timbuktu and Melli with a certain people in the remote interior.

The *Sasus* of Cosmas must also have lain towards the centre of the continent and south-west from Abyssinia. This is shown by the relative position of Agau to Axum (see preceding note); by the fact that the route crossed numerous Nile feeders, apparently those which show so thickly in the map between 7° and 10° N. lat.; and again because the Adule inscription mentioned in the next paragraph of the text speaks of conquests extending *east* to the Thuriferous country, and *west* to Sasus. Cosmas indeed speaks of Sasus as not far from the Ocean. But then he supposes the Ocean to cut across Africa somewhere about the equator. [See note, *supra*, p. 217.]

upon this subject, which has been treated by competent commentators[1]. (pp. 140–3.)

3. In a later passage, speaking of the Gospel's being preached throughout the world, he says:

"So that I can speak with confidence of the truth of what I say, relating what I have myself seen and heard in many places that I have visited.

"Even in the Island of TAPROBANE in Further[2] India where the Indian Sea is, there is a church of Christians with clergy and a congregation of believers, though I know not if there be any Christians further on in that direction. And such also is the case in the land called MALÈ, where the pepper grows[3]. And in the place called KALLIANA[4] there is a bishop appointed from Persia, as well as in the island which they call the Isle of Dioscoris[5] in the same Indian Sea. The inhabitants of that island speak Greek, having been originally settled there by the Ptolemies who ruled after Alexander of Macedon. There are clergy there also, ordained and sent from Persia to minister among the people of the island, and a multitude of Christians[6]. We sailed past the island, but did not land. I met, however, with people from it who were on their way to Ethiopia, and they spoke Greek. And so likewise among the Bactrians and Huns and Persians and the rest of the Indians, and among the Persarmenians and Greeks and Elamites, and throughout the whole land of Persia, there is an infinite number of churches with bishops, and a vast multitude of Christian people, and they have many martyrs and recluses leading a monastic life. So also in Ethiopia, and in Axum, and in all the country round about, among the Happy Arabians, who are nowadays called Homeritæ, and all through Arabia and Palestine, Phœnicia, and all Syria, and Antioch and Mesopotamia; also among the Nubians and the Garamantes[7], in Egypt, Libya,

[1] See Salt's *Travels*, and De Sacy in *Annales des Voyages*, xii, 350.

[2] "*Inner*."

[3] Malabar. Compare the *Kaulam-Malé* of the Arab *Relation*.

[4] Probably the *Kalliena* of the Periplus, which Lassen identifies with the still existing *Kalyáni* on the mainland near Bombay. Father Paolino indeed will have it to be a place still called *Kalŷanapúri* on the banks of a river two miles north of Mangalore, but unreasonably. (*Viag. alle Indie Orientali*, p. 100.)

[5] [Dioscoris or Dioscorides = Socotra, see Yule-Cordier, *Marco Polo*, II, p. 408.]

[6] See *On the Christianity of Socotra*, III, p. 7 *infra*, where this passage of Cosmas should have been referred to. Some further particulars on the subject, apparently taken from the letters of Francis Xavier, are given in du Jarric (*Thesaurus Rerum Indicarum*, i, pp. 108–9). On the use of the Greek language in Abyssinia and Nubia, see Letronne in *Mém. de l'Acad.* (New), ix, 170 *seqq*.

[7] [" The Garamantes were the inhabitants of the great oasis in the Libyan desert called Phazania, and now Fezzan, but the name was often

and Pentapolis[1], and so through Africa and Mauritania as far as Southern Gades[2], in a very great number of places are found churches of Christians with bishops, martyrs, monks, and recluses, wherever in fact the Gospel of Christ hath been proclaimed. So likewise again in Cilicia, Asia, Cappadocia, Lazice, and Pontus, and in the Northern Regions of the Scythians, Hyrcanians, Heruli, Bulgarians, Greeks, and Illyrians, Dalmatians, Goths, Spaniards, Romans, Franks, and other nations till you get to Ocean Gades." (Book iii, p. 178.—McCrindle, pp. 118–121.)

4. He says the place in the Red Sea where the Egyptians perished is "in Klysma[3], as they call it, to the right of people travelling to the Mount (Sinai); and there also are to be seen the tracks of chariot-wheels over a long tract extending to the sea. These have been preserved to this day, as a sign, not for believers, but for unbelievers." (Book v, p. 194.—McCrindle, p. 142.)

5. "— Elim, now called *Raithu*, where there were twelve springs, which are still preserved[4]... Raphidin, now called *Pharan*, whence Moses went with the elders to Mount Choreb, *i.e.* in Sinai, which is about six miles from Pharan." (*Ib.*, pp. 195, 196.—McCrindle, p. 144.)

6. "And when they (the Israelites) had received the written Law from God, they then and there first learned letters. For God made use of the wilderness in its quiet as a kind of school for them, and allowed them there to practise their letters for forty years. And you may see in that desert of Sinai, at every place

used in a wider sense to denote the people of northern Africa who lived to the south of the Syrtis." (McCrindle, p. 120.)]

[1] ["Pentapolis, the name of any association of five cities, denotes here the five chief cities of the province of Cyrenaïca in north Africa. These were Cyrênê, Berenicê, Arsinoê, Ptolemaïs, and Apollonia, the port of Cyrênê." (McCrindle, p. 120.)]

[2] "ἕως Γαδείρων, τὰ πρὸς νότον," an odd construction, which, however, seems intended to be distinctive from "Γαδείρων τοῦ Ὠκεανοῦ" mentioned a few lines further on, and to indicate some place in Africa, perhaps Tingis, or Cape Spartel, called by Strabo Κώτεις. I do not know if this Southern Gades is mentioned by any other author, but something analogous will be found in the passage quoted from Mandeville at III, p. 219 *infra*, where Gades is used for the World's End, eastern as well as western.

[3] At or near Suez, whence the *Kolzum* of the Arabs, and the name *Bahr-Kolzum* given to the Red Sea. ["The Heroöpolitan, or Western Gulf at the northern extremity of the Red Sea, is called by Eusebius *Clysma*. As it was said to have been so designated from a town at the northern extremity of the gulf, Clysma was probably situated at, or somewhere near, Suez. Orosius mentions the wheel tracts here spoken of by Cosmas, as does also Philostorgius in the abstract of his *Ecclesiastical History* made by Photius (Book III, c. 6). Athanasius, however, and others thought Clysma was in Arabia, near the mountain to which Philo, an Egyptian bishop, was banished by Constantius." McCrindle, p. 142 *n.*)]

[4] *Raithu* was the seat of a monastery, as is mentioned by Cosmas himself (at p. 141).

where you halt, that all the stones which have rolled down from the mountains are written over with Hebrew characters. And to this I can myself bear witness, having travelled that ground on foot. And these inscriptions were explained to us by certain Jews who could read them, and they were to this effect: 'The departure of So-and-so of such a tribe, in such a year and such a month;' just such things in fact as you often find scribbled on the walls of inns by people among ourselves. But the Israelites, as is the way of people who have but recently learned to write, were always making use of their new accomplishment, and were constantly writing, so that all those places are quite covered with Hebrew characters. And these have been preserved to this day,—for the sake of unbelievers as I think. And anyone who likes may go there and see for himself, or may ask from those who have been there, and learn that I am saying what is true." (Pp. 205–6.—M^c^Crindle, pp. 159–160.)

Nearly the whole of Book xi is worth translating. It contains "*Details regarding Indian Animals, and the Islands of Taprobane.*"

"*Rhinoceros.*

"This animal is called Rhinoceros because he has horns over his nostrils; when he walks his horns jog about, but when he is enraged with what he is looking at he erects his horns, and they become so rigid that he is able to uproot trees with them, especially if they are straight before him[1]. His eyes are placed low down near his jaws. He is altogether a fearful beast, and he is somehow especially hostile to the elephant. His feet and his skin are, however, very like those of the elephant. His skin when dried is four fingers thick, and some people have used it instead of iron to put in the plough, and have ploughed the ground with it! The Ethiopians in their own dialect call him *Arue Harisi*, using in the second word an aspirated *a* with *rhisi* added. The word *Arue* expresses the beast as such, but *Harisi* expresses *ploughing*, a nickname that they give him from his form about the nose, and also from the use to which his skin is turned[2]. I saw this creature

[1] ? τὰ ἐν αὐτοῖς μάλιστα τὸ ἔμπροσθεν. The fact about the animals carrying the horn loose when not irritated is confirmed by Salt. (2d *Travels, French Trans.*, 1816, ii, 191.)

[2] Ludolf mentions *Arweharis* as a great and fierce beast, of which his friend Abba Gregory often used to speak. He quotes Arab. *Hharash, Hharshan*, "Unicorn," but I do not find these in the dictionaries. Salt again says: "The name by which the rhinoceros (two horned) is designated to this day all over Abyssinia is absolutely the same as that given by Cosmas. In the *Gheez* it is written *Arué Hâris*, pronounced with a strong aspiration of the *Ha*... *Arué*, signifying always *fera* or *bestia* in genere; a coincidence so extraordinary as to convince me that the language spoken at the court of Axum was the *Gheez*" (Ludolf, i, 10, 78; Salt as above).

Hhars means 'ploughing" in Arabic, which may illustrate the etymology of Cosmas.

alive once in Ethiopia, but I kept a good distance from him. And I have seen one dead, skinned and stuffed with straw, standing in the king's palace, so that I have been able to draw him accurately.

" *Taurelaphus.*

" This creature, the Taurelaphus (or Bull-stag), is found both in India and Ethiopia. Those in India are tame, and they make them carry loads of pepper and other such articles in sacks; they also milk them and make butter from their milk. We also eat their flesh, Christians cutting their throats and Greeks felling them. Those of Ethiopia again are wild beasts, and have not been domesticated[1].

" *Cameleopard.*

" The Cameleopard is found only in Ethiopia. These also are wild beasts, and have not been domesticated. But in the palace[2] [at Axum] they have one or two which they have tamed by the king's command by catching them when young, in order to keep them for a show. When milk or water to drink is given to these creatures in a dish, as is done in the king's presence, they cannot reach the vessel on the ground so as to drink, except by straddling with their fore-legs, owing to the great length of their legs and height of the chest and neck above the ground. It stands to reason therefore that they must widen out their fore-legs in order to drink. This also I have drawn (or described) from personal knowledge.

" *The Wild Ox.*

" This Wild Ox is a great beast of India, and from it is got the thing called *Tupha*, with which officers in the field adorn their horses and pennons. They tell of this beast that if his tail catches in a tree he will not budge, but stands stock-still, being horribly vexed at losing a single hair of his tail; so the natives come and cut his tail off, and then when he has lost it altogether he makes his escape! Such is the nature of the animal[3].

[1] This appears to be the buffalo. Everything applies accurately except the name, which does not seem a very appropriate one. The picture is that of a lanky ox with long *tusks*.

[2] Cosmas here uses the Latin word: παλατίῳ (McCrindle).

[3] This is evidently the *Yak* [*Bos grunniens*], which Cosmas could only have known by distant hearsay. *Tupha* is probably *Túgh* or *Tau*, which according to Rémusat is the Turkish name of the horse-tail standard, applied also by the Chinese to the *Yak-tail*, which respectively with those nations mark the supreme military command (*Rech. sur les langues Tartares*, 303; also D'Ohsson, i, 40).

"The Musk Animal.

"This little animal is the Musk. The natives call it in their own tongue *Kasturi*[1]. When they hunt it they shoot it with arrows, and after tying up the blood collected in the navel, cut it off. For this is the fragrant part of the beast, or what we call the *musk*. The rest of the body they throw away.

"The Unicorn.

"This creature is called a Unicorn. I can't say I ever saw him, but I have seen bronze figures of him in the four-towered palace of the King of Ethiopia, and so I have been able to make this drawing of him. They say he is a terrible beast, and quite invincible, and that all his strength lies in his horn. And when he is encompassed by many hunters so that he is hard put to it, he makes a leap over some high precipice, and as he falls he turns over, so that his horn bears the whole force of the fall, and he escapes unhurt[2]. So also the Scripture discourses of him, saying: '*Save me from the mouths of lions and my humility from the horns of the Unicorns*[3];' and again in the blessings wherewith Balaam blessed Israel, he saith twice over: 'Thus hath God led him out of Egypt like the glory of the unicorn[4];' in all these passages testifying to the strength and audacity and glory of the creature[5].

"The Hog-stag and Hippopotamus.

"The Chœrelaphus (or Hog-stag) I have both seen and eaten. The hippopotamus I have not seen indeed, but I had some great teeth of his that weighed thirteen pounds which I sold here [in Alexandria]. And I have seen many such teeth in Ethiopia and in Egypt[6].

[1] *Kastúri* is a real Sanskrit name for the perfume *musk* (see Lassen, i, 316; and iii, 45). This author says that in the Himalaya *Kastúri* is also applied to the animal. He observes that "Cosmas is the first to mention the musk animal and musk as products of India, but he is wrong in representing the animal as living in Taprobane." Cosmas does nothing of the kind.

[2] From this story some kind of Ibex or Oryx would seem to be meant. The practice is asserted of animals of that class in parts of the world so remote from each other that it can scarcely be other than true.

[3] "Save me from the lion's mouth: for thou hast heard me from the horns of the unicorns." (*Ps.* xxii, 21.)

[4] "God brought him out of Egypt: He hath as it were the strength of a unicorn." (*Numbers* xxiii, 22; xxiv, 8.)

[5] [Unicorn Monoceros, see Ctesias of Cnides. Yule-Cordier's *Polo* ii, 291.]

[6] The *Chœrelaphus* is represented in the drawing as a long-legged hog with very long tusks. It has certainly nothing to do with the so-called hog-deer of India, which has no resemblance to a hog. It looks a good deal like the *Babirussa*, but that is I believe peculiar to the Archipelago. Yet this description by Pliny of a kind of swine in India comes very near that animal: "In Indiâ cubitales dentium flexus gemini ex rostro, totidem a fronte ceu vituli cornua, exeunt" (viii, 78).

"*Pepper.*

"This is the pepper-tree. Every plant of it is twined round some lofty forest tree, for it is weak and slim like the slender stems of the vine. And every bunch of fruit has a double leaf as a shield[1]; and it is very green like the green of rue.

"*Argellion* (the Coco-nut).

"Another tree is that which bears the *Argell*[2], *i.e.* the great Indian Nut. In nothing does it differ from the date-palm, excepting that it surpasses it in height and thickness, and in the size of its fronds. All the fruit it produces is from two or three stalks bearing three Argells each[3]. The taste is sweet and very pleasant, like that of fresh nuts. The Argell at first is full of a very sweet water, which the Indians drink from the nut, using it instead of wine. This drink is called *Rhoncosura*[4], and is exceedingly pleasant. But if the Argell be pluckt and kept, the water congeals gradually on the inside of the shell; a small quantity remaining in the middle, till in course of time that also gets quite dried up. If, however, it be kept too long the coagulated pulp goes bad and cannot be eaten.

"*Phoca, Dolphin, and Turtle.*

"The Phoca, Dolphin, and Turtle we eat at sea if we chance to catch them. To eat the dolphin or turtle we cut their throats; the phoca's throat we don't cut, but strike it over the head as is done with large fishes. The flesh of the turtle is like mutton, but blackish; that of the dolphin is like pork, but blackish and rank; that of the phoca is also like pork, but white and free from smell.

"*Concerning the Island of Taprobane.*

"This is the great island in the ocean, lying in the Indian Sea. By the Indians it is called SIELEDIBA [Σιελεδίβα][5], but by the

[1] I do not find any confirmation of this in modern accounts. But Ibn Khurdádhbah (see *ante*, p. 135) says: "The mariners say every bunch of pepper has over it a leaf that shelters it from the rain. When the rain ceases the leaf turns aside; if rain recommences the leaf again covers the fruit" (in *Journ. As.*, sér. vi, tom. v, p. 284). [See Chau Ju-kua, pp. 222–3.]

[2] Pers. *Nárgil.*

[3] This is obscure in the original: *οὐ βάλλει δὲ καρπὸν εἰ μὴ δύο ἢ τρία σπάθια ἀπὸ τριῶν ἀργελλίων.* But his drawing explains, showing two stalks with three nuts to each. He must have seen but poor specimens.

[4] Possibly Cosmas has confounded the coco-nut milk with the coco-palm toddy. For *Sura* is the name applied on the Malabar coast to the latter. *Roncho* may represent *Lanha*, the name applied there to the nut when ripe but still soft, in fact in the state in which it gives the milk (see Garcia dall' Orto, Venice, 1589, p. 114; Rheede, vol. i).

[5] This represents fairly the Pali name SIHALADIPA. Síhala or (Sansk.) *Sinhala*, the "Dwelling of the *Lions*," or as otherwise explained "The Lion-Slayers." Taprobane, from (Pali) TAMBAPANNI (Sansk.)

Greeks TAPROBANE. In it is found the hyacinth stone[1]. It lies on the other side of the Pepper Country[2]. And round about it there are a number of small islands, in all of which you find fresh water and coco-nuts. And these are almost all set close to one another[3]. The great island, according to what the natives say, has a length of three hundred *gaudia*, and a breadth of the same number, *i.e.* nine hundred miles[4]. There are two kings on the island, and they are at enmity with one another[5]. The one possesses the hyacinth[6], and the other has the other part in which is the great place of commerce and the chief harbour. It is a great mart for the people of those parts. The island hath also a church of Persian Christians who have settled there, and a Presbyter who is appointed from Persia, and a Deacon, and all the apparatus of public worship. But the natives and their kings are quite another kind of people[7]. They have many temples on the island,

TAMRAPARNI, the name of a city founded near Putlam by Wijaya (son of Sihabahu) the first human king and colonist. These names are explained in the Mahawanso thus:

"At the spot where the seven hundred men, with the king at their head, exhausted by (sea) sickness, and faint from weakness, had landed out of the vessel, supporting themselves on the palms of their hands pressed on the ground, they set themselves down. Hence to them the name of *Tambapanniyo* ('copper-palmed,' from the colour of the soil). From this circumstance that wilderness obtained the name of TAMBAPANNI. From the same cause also this renowned land became celebrated (under that name).

"By whatever means the monarch Sihabahu slew the *Siho* (Lion), from that feat his sons and descendants are called *Sihala* (Lion-Slayers). This Lanka having been conquered by a Sihalo, from the circumstance also of its having been colonized by a Sihalo, it obtained the name of SIHALA" (in Turner's *Epitome*, p. 55). The more approved etymologies of the names will be found in Lassen, i, 200 *seq.*; Tennent's *Ceylon*, i, 525; *Hobson-Jobson.*

[1] [Some think this is not our jacinth, but rather the sapphire; others take it to be the amethyst. (McCrindle, p. 364.)]

[2] Malabar, so called by the Arabs (*Balad-ul-Falfal*); see Ibn Batuta, *infra*, Vol. IV.

[3] ἀσσοβαθαὶ, perhaps a mistake for ἀσσόται. He here seems to speak of the Maldives. [The Laccadives. The name means, *islands by the hundred thousand*. (McCrindle, p. 364.)]

[4] "This singular word *gaou*, in which Cosmas gives the dimensions of the island, is in use to the present day in Ceylon, and means the distance which a man can walk in an hour" (Tennent, i, 543).

[5] Tennent translates: "at opposite ends of the island."

[6] This has been thought by some to mean the part of the island containing the ruby mines; but Tennent considers it to refer to *the* Ruby mentioned below (see *Ceylon*, i, 543). The expression, however, "the Hyacinth" for the "district producing hyacinths" seems quite in the vein of Cosmas. Thus below he uses τὸ καρυόφυλλον for the Clove Country. Tennent considers the Port to be Galle, but I have noticed this elsewhere (Note XII).

[7] ἀλλόφυλλοι, *i.e.* as I understand it, *Gentiles*; at any rate not Persian Christians. But Sir E. Tennent renders it: "The natives and their kings are of different races."

and on one of these temples which stands in an elevated position there is a hyacinth, they say, of great size and brilliant ruddy colour, as big as a great pine-cone, and when it is seen flashing from a distance, especially when the sun's rays strike on it, 'tis a glorious and incomparable spectacle[1].

"From all India and Persia and Ethiopia many ships come to this island, and it likewise sends out many of its own, occupying as it does a kind of central position. And from the remoter regions, I speak of Tzinista and other places of export, the imports to Taprobane are silk, aloes-wood, cloves[2], sandal-wood[3], and so forth, according to the products of each place. These again are passed on from Sielediba to the marts on this side, such as Malê, where the pepper is grown, and Kalliana, whence are exported brass, and sisam logs[4], and other wares, such as cloths (for that also is a great place of business); also to SINDU, where you get the musk or castorin, and androstachyn[5]; also to Persia, Homerite, and Adule. And the island receives imports again from all those marts that I have been mentioning, and passes them on to the remoter ports, whilst at the same time it exports its own produce in both directions.

"SINDU is where India begins. Now, the Indus, *i.e.*, Phison, the mouths of which discharge into the Persian Gulf, is the boundary between Persia and India. And the most notable places of trade are these: SINDU, ORRHOTHA, KALLIANA, SIBOR[6], and then

[1] This is spoken of by Hiuen Tsang as on the Buddha-Tooth Temple near Anurajapura. "Its magical brilliance illumines the whole heaven. In the calm of a clear and cloudless night it can be seen by all, even at a distance of 10,000 *li*" (*Vie de H. T.*, p. 199; also 371–2).

[2] Here Tennent, following Thévenot's edition, has "clove-wood," but it is not in Montfaucon. As regards clove-wood see Vol. III, 168, and Ibn Batuta, *infra*.

[3] Τζάνδανη, representing the Sanscrit *Chandana*.

[4] The Periplus mentions among exports from Barygaza (*Baroch*) *brass*, sandal-wood, beams, horns, and *planks of sasam* and ebony. I suppose the suggestion has been made before, though I cannot find it, that these sisam logs or sasam planks were the wood of the *sissu* or *shisham*, one of the most valuable Indian timbers. I believe the black-wood of Western India, much used for carved furniture, is a species of sissu. The *brass* was probably manufactured into pots and vessels; still so prominent a business in Indian towns.

[5] Sindu, doubtless a port at the mouth of the Sinthus or Indus, probably Diul or Daibul, which we have seen to be a port known to the Chinese soon after this (*supra*, p. 57, *Hobson-Jobson*, p. 247). *Androstachyn* is probably, as Lassen suggests, an error for *Nardostachys* or spikenard, the chief sources of which seem to have been the countries on the tributaries of the Upper Indus (see Lassen, iii, 41, 42; also i, 288–9).

[6] *Sibor*, probably the Supera of Jordanus and Suppara of Ptolemy (*infra*, III, p. 76). [Sibor, Ptolemy's Symulla or Timulla, Saimur and Jaimur of the Arab travellers, probably Chaul (Cheul), on the coast, 30 miles south of Bombay.] Orrhatha is supposed by Lassen to be

the five marts of Malê, from which pepper is exported, to wit, PARTI, MANGARUTH, SALOPATANA, NALOPATANA, PUDOPATANA[1]. Then there is SIELEDIBA ; *i.e.*, Taprobane, which lies hitherward about five days and nights' sail from the Continent ; and then again on the Continent, and further back is MARALLO, which exports conch shells[2] ; KABER, which exports alabandinum[3] ; and then again further off is the Clove Country ; and then TZINISTA, which produces the silk. Beyond this there is no other country, for the ocean encompasses it on the east.

" This same Sielediba then, set, as it were, in the central point of the Indies, and possessing the Hyacinth, receiving imports from all the seats of commerce, and exporting to them in return, is itself a great seat of commerce. Here let me relate what there befel one of the merchants accustomed to trade thither. His name was Sopatrus, and he has been dead, to my knowledge, these thirty-five years past. Well, he had gone to the island of Taprobane on a trading adventure, and a ship from Persia happened to put in there at the same time. So when the Adule people, with whom Sopatrus was, went ashore, the people from Persia went ashore likewise, and with them they had a certain venerable personage of their nation[4]. And then, as their way is, the chief men of the place and the officers of the custom-house received the party, and conducted them before the king. The king having granted them an audience, after receiving their salutations, desired them to be seated, and then asked, ' In what state are your countries ? and how go your own affairs ? ' They answered, ' Well.' And so as the conversation proceeded, the king put the question, ' Which of you has the greatest and most powerful king ? ' The Persian elder snatching the word, answered, ' Our king is the greatest and the most powerful and the wealthiest, and indeed is the king of kings ; and whatever he desires, that he

Ptolemy's *Soratha* on the Peninsula of Gujarat, identified with the Surata of Hiuen Tsang, not to be confounded with modern *Surat.* (Reinaud, *Mém. sur l'Inde* in *Acad.*, p. 155.)

[1] Of these five ports of Malabar, Mangaruth is no doubt Mangalore, Pudopatana the port which bore the same name till a recent century (see *infra*, Ibn Batuta); the others I cannot identify.

[2] In position and perhaps in name identical with Marava or Marawar opposite Ceylon. The fishing of *chank* shells hereabouts was till recently I believe a government monopoly like the pearl-fishery. Walckenær says Marallo is " Morilloum, opposite Ceylon." Is there such a place ?

[3] *Kaber*, from the name and position, may be the Chabēris of Ptolemy (*Kâvêrîpattam*) [a little north of Tranquebar]—[Kâvêra is the Sanskrit word for *saffron.* M'Crindle], but I can get no light on the *alabandinum.* Pliny speaks of alabandic carbuncles and of an alabandic black marble, both called from a city of Caria. The French apply the name almandine or albandine to a species of ruby. (Pliny, xxxvii, 25 ; xxxvi, 13 ; *Dict. de Trévoux.*) If rubies be meant it is just possible that Pegu may be in question.

[4] "πρεσβύτης." A *Shaikh?* Montfaucon's Latin has *orator.*

is able to accomplish.' But Sopatrus held his peace. Then, quoth the king, 'Well, Roman! hast thou not a word to say?' Said Sopatrus, 'Why, what is there for me to say, after this man hath spoken as he hath done? But if thou wouldst know the real truth of the matter thou hast both the kings here; examine both, and thou shalt see thyself which is the more magnificent and potent.' When the prince heard that, he was amazed at the words, and said, 'How make you out that I have both the kings here?' The other replied, 'Well, thou hast the coins of both—of the one the *nomisma*, and of the other the *dirhem* (*i.e.*, the *miliaresion*). Look at the effigy on each, and you will see the truth.' The king approved of the suggestion, nodding assent, and ordered both coins to be produced. Now, the nomisma was a coin of right good ring and fine ruddy gold, bright in metal and elegant in execution, for such coins are picked on purpose to take thither, whilst the miliaresion, to say it in one word, was of silver, and of course bore no comparison with the gold coin. So the king, after he had turned them this way and that, and had studied both with attention, highly extolled the *nomisma*[1], saying that in truth the Romans were a splendid, powerful, and sagacious people. So he ordered great honour to be paid to Sopatrus, causing him to be set on an elephant, and conducted round the city with drums beating in great state. These circumstances were told me by Sopatrus and the others who had accompanied him from Adule to that island. And, as they told the story, the Persian was very much ashamed of what had happened" (p. 338).

"But in the direction of those most notable places of trade that I have mentioned, there are many others (of minor importance) both on the coast and inland, and a country of great extent. And in India further up the country, *i.e.*, further north, are the White Huns[2]. That one who is called Gollâs, 'tis said, goes forth

[1] *Nomisma* was usually applied to the gold solidus, as here. [This would be an *aureus*. Constantine the Great coined *aurei* of seventy-two to the pound of gold, and at this standard the coin remained to the end of the empire. McCrindle, p. 369.] The *miliarésion* or *miliarense* was a silver coin, the twelfth part of the solidus (Ducange, *de Inf. Aevi Numism.*). The latter coin continued to be well known in the Mediterranean probably to the end of the Byzantine Empire. *Migliaresi* are frequently mentioned by Pegolotti *circa* 1340. [*Miliarésion*, a silver drachma of which twenty made a *daric*, which was equivalent to an Attic *Stater*. (McCrindle.)] [Probably in 312, Constantine issued the *aureus* of seventy-two to the pound or 4 gr. 55, and gave the name of *solidus aureus* or simply *solidus* to the new gold standard. (Babelon, *Traité des Monnaies grecques et romaines*, i, 1901, pp. 532–3.)] [The *miliarense* was 1/14 of the *solidus aureus* of 4 gr. 55. When Constantine coined his gold solidus he coined also a new silver coin of 72 to the pound which weighs, consequently, like the gold coin, 4 gr. 55; this coin is the *miliarense*. (Babelon, *l.c.*, p. 570.)]

[2] On the Yue chi, Ye tas or White Huns, called also Ephthalites, see Lassen, ii, 771 *seqq.*, and iii, 584 *seqq.* [Vivien de Saint-Martin has written a special dissertation on *Les Huns Blancs ou Ephthalites des Historiens byzantins*. (Paris, Thunot, 1849, 8vo.) See p. 205 *n.*, *supra*.]

to war with not less than a thousand elephants, besides a great force of cavalry. This ruler tyrannises over India and exacts tribute from the people. Once upon a time, as they tell, he would lay siege to a certain inland city of India; but the city was protected all round by inundation. So he sat him down before it for many days, and in course of time what with his elephants and his horses and the people of his camp the whole of the water was drunk dry, so that at last he was able to cross over dry-shod, and took the city.

"These people have a great fondness for the emerald stone, and it is worn by their king in his crown[1]. The Ethiopians who obtain this stone from the Blemmyes in Ethiopia, import it into India and with the price they get are able to invest in wares of the greatest value.

"Now, all these matters I have been able thus to describe and explain, partly from personal experience, and partly from accurate inquiries which I made when in the vicinity of the different places." (p. 339.)

"There are other kings (I may observe) of different places in India who keep elephants, such as the King of Orrhotha, and the King of the Kalliana people, and the Kings of Sindu, of Sibor, and of Malê. One will have six hundred elephants, another five hundred, and so on, some more, or less. And the King of Sielediba [gives a good price for][2] both the elephants that he has, and the horses. The elephants he buys by cubit measurement; for their height is measured from the ground, and so the price is fixed according to the measurement, ranging from fifty to a hundred nomismata or more[3]. Horses they bring to him from Persia, and these he buys, and grants special immunities to those who import them.

"The kings on the mainland cause wild elephants to be tamed,

[1] [Yule in his additional notes writes: "So Mas'ūdī says one species of emerald from the country of the Bejah (Blemmyes ?) was called *Bahri*, because so much prized by the Kings of Transmarine countries, such as Hind, Sind, Zinj, and Sin, who sought it diligently "*to set in their diadems*,' etc. (*Prairies d'Or*, iii, 44.)

"The Blemmyes were fierce predatory nomads of the Nubian wilds and the regions adjacent. Emeralds were found in the mines of Upper Egypt, and were no doubt shipped from Adulê for the Indian markets by the Ethiopian traders who bought them from the Blemmyes. If taken to Barygaza (Bharoch), they could be transported thence by a frequented trade-route to Ujjain, thence to Kabul, and thence over the Hindu Kush to the regions of the Oxus." McCrindle, p. 371.]

[2] This is conjectural, as some words are evidently wanting. Montfaucon's Latin supplies *pretio emit*.

[3] From £32 to £65. The price of elephants in Bengal now may run from twice to thrice these amounts. Height is always one of the elements in estimating the price of an elephant. Edrisi says: "The Kings of India and China make a great work about the height of their elephants; they pay very dear in proportion as this attribute increases." (i, 97.)

and make use of them in war. And it is a common practice to get up elephant fights as a spectacle for the king. For this purpose they set up between the two elephants a pair of upright timbers with a great crossbeam fastened to them which reaches as it might be to the chests of the elephants. A number of men are also stationed on this side and on that to prevent the animals coming to close quarters, but at the same time to stir them up to engage one another. And so the beasts thrash each other with their trunks till at length one of them gives in.

"The Indian elephants are not furnished with great tusks[1]. And even when they have them naturally the people saw them off, in order that their weight may not be an incumbrance in war. The Ethiopians do not understand the art of taming elephants; but if their king should want one or two for a show they catch them young and bring them up in captivity. For in their country there are great numbers of elephants, and they are of the kind that have great tusks. And these tusks are exported by sea from Ethiopia into Persia and Homerite and the Roman territory, and even to India. These particulars are derived from what I have heard." (p. 339.—McCrindle, pp. 358–373.)

BIBLIOGRAPHY.

— Collectio nova Patrum et Scriptorum Græcorum, Eusebii Cæsariensis, Athanasii, & Cosmæ Ægyptii. Hæc nunc primum ex Manuscriptis Codicibus Græcis Italicis Gallicanisque eruit, Latine vertit, Notis & Præfationibus illustravit D. Bernardus de Montfaucon, Presbyter & Monachus Ordinis Sancti Benedicti, e Congregatione S. Mauri. Tomus secundus, fol. [Parisiis, C. Rigaud, MDCCVI].

Cosmas, pp. xxiv+pp. numbered 113–345.

Cosmæ Monachi Ægyptii Topographia Christiana. *Fasciculus rerum græcarum ecclesiasticarum...omnia græce nunc primum prodeunt ex Medicea Bibliotheca cura et studio* Ang. Mar. Bandini...Florentiæ Typis Cæsareis Anno CIↃ. D. CCLXIII, 8vo, pp. 21–35.)

— Bibliotheca Veterum Patrum Antiquorumque Scriptorum Ecclesiasticorum, postrema Lugdunensi multo locupletior atque accuratior.—Cura & studio Andreæ Gallandii Presbyteri Congregationis Oratorii.—Tomus XI.—Venetiis CIↃ. D.CCLXXVI, large fol.

Cosmæ Ægyptii Monachi Christiana Topographia, sive Christianorum Opinio de Mundo, pp. 399–578, 4 plates.

[1] It is well known that a large proportion of male elephants in India have only very small tusks like the females. Such in Bengal are called *makhna*.

— Description des Animavx et des Plantes des Indes. Avec vne relation de l'isle Taprobane, tirée de la Topographie Chrestienne de Cosmas le Solitaire. [Greek Text and Translation.] (*Relation de divers voyages curieux...par...feu* M. Melchisedec Thevenot...Nouvelle édition, Augmentée de plusieurs Relations curieuses. T. I. Contenant la I. et II. Partie. A Paris, Chez Thomas Moette,...M.DC.XCVI, fol.)

— Cosmas Indicopleustes, Voyageur égyptien [Sixième siècle après Jésus-Christ]. (Edouard Charton, *Voyageurs Anciens et Modernes*, II, Paris, 1861, pp. 1–30.)

With a Bibliography, p. 30.

— ΚΟΣΜΑ ΑΙΓΥΠΤΙΟΥ ΜΟΝΑΧΟΥ ΧΡΙΣΤΙΑΝΙΚΗ ΤΟΠΟΓΡΑΦΙΑ.— The Christian Topography of Cosmas, an Egyptian Monk. Translated from the Greek, and Edited, with Notes and Introduction by J. W. McCrindle...London, Printed for the Hakluyt Society. M.DCCC.XCVII, 8vo, pp. xxvii.—398.

Vol. 98 of the Works issued by the Hakluyt Society, in 1897. The English text only.

— Zizi. Ein Beitrag zur Erklärung einer Stelle bei Cosmas. Von Jos. Teige. (*Forschungen zur Deutschen Geschichte*, Bd. XXIV, Hft. 1.—Göttingen, Dieterich, 1883, pp. 203–4.)

— *The Dawn of Modern Geography. A History of Exploration and Geographical Science*...by C. Raymond Beazley. London; John Murray, 1897, 8vo. pp. xvi–538.

Cosmas, pp. 273–303; also pp. 190–6.

NOTE IX BIS.

EXTRACTS FROM *THEOPHYLACTUS SIMOCATTA*[1].

Lib. VII, Caput VII. "Ergo deuictis a Chagano Abaris (sursum enim redeo) alii eorum ad Taugastenses confugerunt (est autem Taugast Turcarum nobilis colonia, stadiis mille quingentis ab India distans, cuius indigenæ, & strenuissimi, & frequentissimi, & præstantia quouis populo in orbe terrarum superiores) alii propter amissam libertatem humiliorem sortiti conditionem, ad Mucritas qui dicuntur, Taugastensibus vicinissimos se contulerunt, ad prælia ineunda tum propter quotidiana belli exercitia, tum propter tolerantiam in periculis eximio animorum robore præditos." (P. 174.)

Lib. VII, Caput IX: "Chaganvs igitur ciuili bello finito, rem felicibus auspiciis administrat, & cum Taugastensibus foedus

[1] Theophylacti Simocattæ expræfecti et observatoris coactorvm Historiarvm libri VIII. Interprete Iacobo Pontano Societatis Iesv. Editio priore castigatior, & Glossario Græco-barbaro auctior. Studio & opera Caroli Annibalis Fabroti IC. Parisiis, E Typographia regia.— M.DC.XLVII, fol.

Greek text and Latin translation in *Corpus Byzantinae Historiae*.

percutit, vt tranquillitatem & pacem supremam vndique nactus, principatum sibi omnis seditionis expertem efficeret. Princeps autem in Taugast Taisan audit, quæ vox græca lingua filium Dei sonat. Hoc regnum nullis intestinis discordiis agitatur, propterea quod Princeps illic a successione generis creatur. Statuas venerantur: iustis reguntur legibus, frugalitatem in omni vita excolunt. Consuetudo est apud eos, vim legis obtinens, vt mares ornatu aureo in perpetuum abstineant: quanquam auro argentoque propter magnorum mercimoniorum commoditatem abundant. Hanc vrbem fluuius discriminat, qui olim duos frequentissimos populos dissidentes diuidebat, quorum alter nigra, alter cocco tincta veste vtebatur. Nostris itaque temporibus, Mauricio Imperatore, nigram gestantes, transmisso fluuio rubram indutis bellum intulerunt, victoresque toto illo imperio potiti sunt. Vrbem Taugast barbari memorant Alexandrum condidisse, quando Bactrianos, & Sogdianam, centum viginti barbarorum millibus igne consumptis subiugauit. Vxores regiae auro & lapillis pretiosissimis conspicuæ, curribus vehuntur aureis, quorum singuli a singulis iuuencis, frænis auro, & gemmis sumptuose exornatis trahuntur. Princeps cum feminis septingentis noctem exigit. Nobilium coniugibus pilenta sunt argentea. Fama est, Alexandrum aliam quoque vrbem, non multis millibus distantem, quam barbari Chubdan nominant, ædificasse. Eius principem demortuum, ipsius vxores rasis capitibus, & pullatæ continenter lugent: neque per legem eius sepulcrum deserere vnquam possunt. Chubdan duo latissimi amnes disterminant, quorum ripis cupressi (vt ita loquar) annuunt. Multos habent elephantos, & cum Indis negotiantur.

Hos autem Indos in plaga Boreali habitantes, albis corporibus esse prædicant. Bombycum, vnde fila serica, magna & diuersicolor apud eos copia: in quibus curandis barbari magnum, & artificiosum studium præstare solent. Verum ne historiam a meta proposita abducamus, hactenus de Scythis ad Bactrianam, Sogdianam, & nigrum fluuium a nobis dictum esto." (Pages 176–7.)

NOTE IX TER.

EXTRACTS FROM CHAU JU-KWA[1].

Ta Ts'in.

"The country of Ta-ts'in," *also called Li-kién*, "is the general mart of the natives of the Western Heaven, the place where the foreign merchants of the Ta-shï assemble."

[1] Chau Ju-kua: His Work on the Chinese and Arab Trade in the twelfth and thirteenth Centuries, entitled *Chu-fan-chi*, Translated from the Chinese and Annotated by Friedrich Hirth and W. W. Rockhill.—St Petersburg, 1912, large 8vo, pp. 102–4.

"Their King is styled Ma-lo-fu"; *he rules in the city of An-tu.* "He wears a turban of silk with gold embroidered characters, and the throne he sits upon is covered with a silken rug."

"They have walled cities" *and markets with wards and streets.* "In the King's residence" *they use crystal in making pillars, and* "plaster in guise of tiles. Wall-hangings abound. The circuit (of the wall) is pierced with seven gates, each guarded by thirty men.

"Tribute bearers from other countries pay homage below the platform of the (palace) steps, whence they withdraw after having offered their congratulations."

The inhabitants are tall and of a fine bright complexion, somewhat like the Chinese, which is the reason for their being called Ta-ts'in.

They have Keepers of official records, and in writing they use Hu characters. They trim their hair and wear embroidered gowns. They also have small carts with white tops, flags, etc. (*Along the roads*) *there is a shed every ten li, and every thirty* li *there is a beacon-tower. There are many lions in this country that interfere with travellers and are likely to devour them unless they go in caravans of an hundred well-armed men.*

"Underneath the palace they have dug a tunnel through the ground communicating with the hall of worship at a distance of over a *li*. The king rarely goes out except to chant the liturgy and worship. On every seventh day he goes by way of the tunnel to the hall of worship for divine service, being attended by a suite of over fifty men. But few amongst the people know the king's face. If he goes out he rides horseback, shaded by an umbrella; the head of his horse is ornamented with gold, jade, pearls and other jewels.

"There is among the Kings of the Ta-shï country he who is styled *Su-tan*; every year he deputes men to send in tribute, and, if trouble is apprehended in the country, he orders the Ta-shï to use their military force to keep order.

"The food consists principally of cooked dishes, bread and meat. They do not drink wine; they make use of vessels of gold and silver, helping themselves to the contents with ladles. After meals they wash their hands in golden bowls full of water.

"The native products comprise opaque glass, coral, native gold (or gold bullion), brocades (or Kincobs), sarsenets, red cornelian and pearls"; also (the precious stone called) *hié-ki-si* or *túng-t'ién-si.*

In the beginning of the yen-hi *period of the Han* (A.D. 158–176) *the ruler of this country sent an embassy which, from outside the frontier of Ji-nan, came to offer rhinoceros* (horns), *elephants'* (tusks), *and tortoise-shell;—this being the first direct communication with China. As the presents comprised no other rarities, it may be suspected that the envoys kept them back.*

During the t'ai k'ang *period of the Tsin* (A.D. 280–9) *tribute was again brought from there.*

There is a saying that in the west of this country is the Jo-shui and the Liu-sha, near the place where the Si-wang-mu resides and almost where the sun goes down.

Tu Huan in the King-hing-ki says: "The country of Fu-lin is in the west of the Chan country; it is also called Ta-ts'in. The inhabitants have red and white faces. The men wear plain clothes, but the women brocades set with pearls. They like to drink wine and eat dry cakes. They have many skilled artisans and are clever weavers of silk.

"The size of the country is a thousand li. *The active army consists of over ten thousand men. It has to ward off the Ta-shi.*

"In the Western Sea there is a market where a (silent) *agreement exists between buyer and seller that if one comes the other goes. The seller first spreads out his goods; afterwards the* (would-be) *purchaser spreads out the equivalent* (he offers), *which must lie by the side of the articles for sale till taken by the seller, when the objects purchased may be carried off. This is called the 'Devil* (or *Spirit*) *market.'"*

NOTE X.

THE DISCOVERY OF THE SYRO-CHINESE CHRISTIAN MONUMENT AT SI-NGAN FU.

From the RELAZIONE DELLA CINA *of* P. ALVAREZ SEMEDO, *Rome*, 1643.

"In the year 1625, whilst the foundations of a house were a-digging in the neighbourhood of the city of Si-ngan fu, the capital of the province of Shen si, the workmen hit upon a stone slab more than nine palms long, by four in width, and more than a palm in thickness. The head of this slab, *i.e.* one of the ends in its longer dimension, is finished off in the form of a pyramid more than two palms high with a base of more than one palm, and on the surface of this pyramid is a well-formed cross with floreated points, resembling those which are described to be sculptured on the tomb of St. Thomas at Meliapur, and such as were also at one time in use in Europe, as we may see by some examples that have been preserved to the present day.

"There are some cloudy marks round about the cross, and (immediately) below it three transverse lines, each composed of three large characters clearly carved, all of the kind employed in China. The whole (of the rest) of the surface of the stone is seen to be sculptured over with characters of the same kind, and so also is the thickness of the slab, but in the last the characters are different from the others, for some of them are outlandish, and their nature was not known at the time of the discovery.

"No sooner had the Chinese cleaned this notable piece of antiquity and seen what it was, than, with the vivid curiosity which is natural to them, they ran to tell the Governor. He came in all haste to see it, and straightway caused it to be set up on a handsome pedestal under an arch which was closed at the sides and open in front, so that it might at once be protected from the weather, and accessible to eyes capable of enjoying and appreciating an antique of such a venerable kind. The place which he selected for it was also within the enclosure of a Bonze Temple, not far from where the discovery occurred.

"Great numbers of people flocked to see this stone, attracted in part by its antiquity and in part by the novelty of the strange characters that were visible on it. And as the knowledge of our religion has now spread far and wide in China, a certain Pagan who happened to be present, and who was on very friendly terms with a worthy Christian mandarin called Leo, when he discerned the bearing of this mysterious writing, thought he could not do his friend a greater pleasure than by sending him a copy of it. And this he did, although the Mandarin was a six weeks' journey off, residing in the city of Hang chau, whither most of our fathers had retired on account of the persecution that had occurred, of which we shall speak in its place. He received the transcript with pious joy, and visible demonstrations of delight, seeing the irrefragable testimony of the ancient Christianity of China which it contained (a thing such as had been much desired and sought for), as we shall explain.

"Three years later, in 1628, some of the fathers had an opportunity of visiting the province in question in company with a Christian mandarin called Philip, who had to go thither. A church and a house (of the Society) were erected in that metropolis; for the Blessed God who had willed the discovery of so fine a monument of the ancient occupation of this country by His Divine Law, was also pleased to facilitate its restitution in the same locality. It was my fortune to be one of the first to go thither, and I thought myself happy in having that post, on account of the opportunity it gave me of seeing the stone; and on my arrival I could attend to nothing else until I had seen it and read it. And I went back to read it again, and examined it in a leisurely and deliberate manner. Considering its antiquity, I could not but admire that it was so perfect, and exhibited letters sculptured with such clearness and precision.

"Looked at edge-wise there are on it many Chinese characters which contain a number of names of priests and bishops of that age. There are also many other characters which were not then known, for they are neither Hebrew nor Greek, but which, as far as I understand, contain the same names, in order that if by chance some one from abroad should come who could not read the writing of the country, he might, perhaps, be able to understand these foreign characters.

"Passing afterwards through Cochin on my way to Cranganor, the residence of the Archbishop of the Coast, I consulted on the subject of those letters Father Antonio Fernandez of our Society, who was very learned in the literature of those St. Thomas Christians, and he told me that the letters were Syriac, and the same as were in use by that body." (P. 197 *seq.*)

The following account is given in a Chinese work entitled "LAICHAI's *Brief examination of Inscriptions on Stone and Metal.*"

"At present this inscription exists in the enclosure of the monastery Kinching ('Golden Victory') to the west of the city of Si-ngan. In the years Tsung ching of the Ming (1628–43) the Prefect of Si-ngan, Doctor Tseu Tsing chang, a native of Tsin-ling, had a young child called Hoaseng who was endowed from his birth with a very rare degree of intelligence and penetration. Almost as soon as he could speak he would already join his hands to adore Fo. When he had reached his twelfth year, the child, without knowing where was the seat of his ailment, pined away; his eyes insensibly closed; he opened them for an instant with a smile, and died. Chang, seeing that his son was gone, cast lots, and these indicated for the place of his burial a spot to the south of the monastery *T'sung jin* ('Sublime Humanity') in Chang-ngan. After digging here to a depth of several feet, they hit upon a stone which was no other than that bearing the inscription," etc. (From Pauthier, *L'Inscription Chrétienne de Singanfou*, pp. 70–1.)

NOTE X BIS.

FROM THE *ISTORIA* OF P. D. BARTOLI.

P. Daniello Bartoli in his *Istoria della Compagnia di Gesù* has given in the third part of Asia devoted to China (Torino, 1825, Lib. 4°, pp. 4 *seq.*) a history of the discovery of the Si-ngan fu inscription which is more complete in its particulars than the account of Semedo. I have thought it might prove of good service and I insert it here:

Descrizion d'una lapida
trovata nella Provincia di Scensì in memoria
della Fede già fiorita nella Cina.

La Provincia di Scensì, fra tutte le quindici della Cina, è in venerazione come di madre; perciochè si ha fino ab immemorabili, che i primi padri e fondatori della Nazion cinese quivi abitassero, e quinci, multiplicando, diffondessero i lor nipoti e discendenti, a popolar tutte le quattordici altre Provincie. E par vero; perochè chi vien da verso l' India per la via di terra a quel Regno, la Provincia di Scensì è la prima a farsi loro incontro a riceverli, sì come quella, che più di niun' altra si stende in quel verso, fino a Sifàn, cioè a' Regni di Tibèt e Cascàr: e le carovane de' Mori, che ad ogni tanti anni si portano alla Cina, le lontanissime dalla Persia e dal Mogòr, e l' altre da più vicino, tutte vengono a metter capo a Scensì nel suo lato a Settentrione, dove ha la gran muraglia che la divide da' Tartari. Quivi anco ebbero per più secoli il lor seggio i primi Re della Cina, e la Corte in Sigàn metropoli della Provincia; per ciò tutta sontuosissimi edificj, e per almen dodici miglia nostrali, quante (oltre a' gran borghi) ne volge il suo circuito, intorniata d' un muro di pietra viva, la sì bella fabrica a vedersi, e sì forte a difendere la città, ch' ella giustamente ne va con nome di Muraglia d' oro. Or' in questa Provincia di Scensì, e in questa sua maestosa metropoli Sigàn, si apparecchiavano i Padri a portar la luce dell' Evangelio; quando, pochi mesi innanzi al lor giungervi (e non, pochi anni prima del lor' entrar nella Cina, come altri ha scritto: ed è fallo d' almen quarantacinque anni), aprendosi dove gittare i fondamenti di non so qual nuovo edificio presso a Ceuce, città non delle grandi, un qualche trenta miglia lungi dalla metropoli in ver Levante, i cavatori s' avvennero in certe rovine di fabrica, e fra esse, nello scassinarle, diedero in una gran piastra di marmo, che tratta fuori, e rinetta con diligenza, si vide tutta esser messa a caratteri, altri cinesi, altri di stranissima formazione, niuno sapea di che lingua: ma gli uni e gli altri, quanto all' intaglio, opera di mano eccellente. Così dell' invenzione di questa memorabile anticaglia si è scritto fin' ora da chi ne fa menzione, attribuendola a fortuito avvenimento de' cavatori, che, senza nulla cercarne, si abbatterono in lei. Ma io, nelle memorie inviateci dalla Provincia di Scensì l' anno 1639, truovo la testimonianza d' un vecchio, il quale, accoltosi cortesemente il P. Stefano Fabri, gran ministro dell' Evangelio in quel Regno, ad albergo una notte nel suo povero casolare, posto colà fra le più erme pendici di quella montagnosa Provincia, gli contò per indubitabil saputa, i paesani della contrada, colà onde si trasse la pietra, avere osservato, che coprendosi sin dal primo far del verno di foltissime nevi tutto intorno il paese, solo un pochissimo di terreno ne rimaneva al tutto libero e scoperto: e ciò per più anni seguentemente: dunque, forza essere, che ivi sotto si nascondesse o un tesoro (come desideravano), o, che che altro si fosse, cosa degna di sapersi che fosse: e da ciò essersi indotti a cercarne, e cavare, e avervi trovato in verità il tesoro della pietra che dicevamo. Tanto ne riferiva il vecchio. Curiosissimi sono i Cinesi di ciò che sa dell' antico: nè più caro dono può farsi ad uomo di profession Letterato, che un che che sia, tanto più prezioso, quanto più antico, massimamente memorie di secoli andati, che colà sono reliquie del tempo sacrosante, e ne arricchiscono que' loro sontuosi

Musei, ch' essi chiamano Case di studio. Perciò v' ebbe gara a chi portasse il primo l' annunzio della pietra al Governatore di Ceuce; il quale accorsovi, e lettone quel che v' era in sua lingua, altro non ne comprese, se non ch' ella era cosa di gran mistero, e antichissima, sì come fin dal tempo della real famiglia Tam, e di Chienciùn, un de' successori d' essa regnante. Era la pietra meglio di quattro palmi in largo, lunga oltre a nove, e grossa un sommesso. D' in su'l lato superiore, spiccavasi un' altro minor quadrato; la cui sommità levandosi un poco alta, e stringendosi, finiva in acuto; e quivi entro all' angolo superiore una Croce ben disegnata, su l' andar di quella de' Cavalieri di Malta, con a' capi alcune giunterelle da renderla di bel garbo. Sotto essa, nove sì gran caratteri, ch' essi soli empiono tutto il quadrato superiore, disposti in tre righe a tre per ciascuna. Ma nel pian del quadrato maggiore, elle eran da trenta righe, non coricate come le nostre, ma ritte in piè, e da leggersi calando dalla cima al fondo: chè tale ho detto altrove essere il proprio scrivere de' Cinesi: e in esse contavansi mille diciotto caratteri; i quali, tra perchè ciascun di loro è una voce intera, e per la mirabil forza che hanno nell' esprimere e significare i concetti dell' animo, a volerli ridurre a scrittura in lettere uguali d' ogni altra lingua d' Europa, empierebbono tre e quattro volte più spazio. Oltre a questi cinesi, correvanle per su il lembo attorno altri caratteri, di soriano all' antica, ma quivi non conosciuti, nè pur di che lingua si fossero.

Letta da' Gentili la pietra, e non intesa:
se ne manda copia al Dottor Lione, e si stampa.

Il Governator dunque, adorato quel marmo, venerabilissimo per l' antichità di presso ottocencinquanta anni (come indubitato appariva dal tempo in che vissero i Re quivi expressi), e contenente, nella sua natia favella, misteri da lui poco intesi, e nulla quel che dicea la straniera, il mandò trasportar di colà in un tempio di Taosi, un miglio presso a Sigàn, e quivi alzarlo su un piedestallo, sotto un bel capannuccio portato da quattro colonne: e al par di lui, un' altra piastra di marmo, con incisavi dentro una ben composta memoria del ritrovamento di quella antichità presso a Ceuce, colà dov' egli era Governatore. Tutta Sigàn vi trasse, con gara eziandio fra' più dotti a comprenderne o indovinarne il significato, difficilissimo a rinvenire, non tanto perchè il dettato della scrittura era in istile sollevatissimo, quanto per le figurate maniere dell' accennarvisi i misteri della Fede nostra, quivi non ancora divulgati. E già lo stesso era avvenuto a que' di Ceuce, senza trovarsi chi di loro si apponesse al vero, fuor che, come a Dio piacque, un solo del secondo ordine de' Letterati, che colà chiamano Chiugin. Questi, eran de gli anni presso a diciotto, che stretta in Pechìn amicizia col P. Matteo Ricci, ne aveva udito della Legge cristiana quanto ora tornandolsi alla memoria, e riscontrandolo con quel che leggea nella pietra, il rendè certo, quivi di lei trattarsi: e senza più, sovraposto alla medesima pietra uno o due di que' loro fran fogli, coll' arte dello stampare in pietra che colà è in uso, ne ricavò fedelmente la scrittura a carattere bianco in campo nero, e per messaggio a posta l' inviò sino ad Hanceu al Dottor Lione suo vecchio amico, e, come egli ben sapeva, Cristiano. Così appunto andò il fatto: ed hollo per narrazione fattane dallo stesso Dottor Lione: il quale tutto per ciò festeggiante venne a darne avviso a' Padri. Indi egli, e poscia anche il Dottor Paolo, ridottala a carattere di minor forma, e stampatene in gran numero copie, le publicarono a tutto il Regno, aggiuntivi lor proemj, e interpretazion letterali delle metafore, e postille, e chiose necessariamente richieste all' intelligenza del testo. E qui altresì a me farà bisogno frametterne almen quelle, senza il cui lume si andrebbe mezzo alla cieca, per la troppa scurità del semplice testo; massimamente trasportato, per più fedeltà, a verbo a verbo, quanto il diversissimo scriver cinese si comporta col nostro: il non così necessario, per meno interrompere, avrà suo luogo nel margine. E ne ho di colà, in tre diverse lingue, otto interpretazioni di valent' uomini, che tutte nel sustanziale sono quasi una medesima: benchè, a dir vero, in non poche particolarità fra sè differenti, per lo sì vario sentimento che posson probabilmente ricevere que' caratteri della scrittura cinese, la quale ha un non so che del simile a' geroglifici de gli antichi Egiziani. In tutte poi si dà in passi tanto difficili e scuri, che si può dir ben da vero, che l' interpretazione stessa ha bisogno d' interprete. Ma il suo peggio, e per cui appena sarà che leggendosi non annoi, è il riuscir l' interpretazione un cadavero dell' originale, mancandole, senza potersene altramente, quello spirito e quell' ingegno, che ha la maniera dell' esprimer cinese, a forza del mistero ch' è ne' caratteri e semplici e accozzati. Pure, qual che sia per riuscir questa, che non sarà niuna delle otto, e ne avrà parte di tutte, m' è paruta da stendersi qui tutta intera. E vuolsene sapere avanti, che dovunque in essa si nomina il paese di Tacin, ella è la Giudea: e gl' Illustri, o la Legge o dottrina illustre, sono in vece di nome proprio, a significar Cristiano, e Legge cristiana. I nomi poi de' Re Cinesi, che qui per ordine di successione si contano (e tutti furono della stessa famiglia Tam), come altresì de' Mandarini di Lettere e d' Armi, tutti si accordano fedelmente colle istorie cinesi, che ne fan memoria co' medesimi nomi e col medesimo ordine: e da esse abbiamo, che il presente entrar della Fede in quel Regno cadde ne gli anni di Cristo 636, e'l rizzar che si fece di questa lapida fu nel 782. Se già non paresse in ciò aver maggior peso l' autorità del Dottor Lione cinese, che di cinque anni anticipa l' un conto e l' altro. Or le nove gran lettere, ch' erano in testa alla pietra, e riempievano tutto il quadrato superiore, così dicono: Pietra, in memoria dell' essersi propagata per lo regno della Cina la Legge illustre del Tacin (cioè, la Legge cristiana, venutavi di Giudea). Poi nel quadrato maggiore incomincia la narrazione sotto questo brieve preambolo : Chincin, Sacerdote di Tacin, così propone, e dice : [the translation follows].

NOTE XI.

THE KINGDOMS OF INDIA IN THE NINTH CENTURY, SPOKEN OF BY THE ARAB WRITERS IN THE *RELATIONS* TRANSLATED BY REINAUD.

The first king named is the BALHARA, who is said to have been regarded as the most exalted of Indian princes, and whom the Indians and Chinese classed with the Khalif, the Emperor of China, and the King of the Romans, as the four great kings of the world. There is, however, scarcely anything definite stated about him except that his empire began at the country of *Komkam* (the Konkan) on the sea coast.

The name of *Balhara* Lassen considers to be a corruption of *Ballabhiráa* or *raja*, the title of a great dynasty which reigned at Ballabhipura in the Peninsula of Gujarat[1], but which had fallen long before this time. Nor indeed does there appear to have been any *very* powerful dynasty in this region in the ninth century[2]. Al Birúni, who in Indian matters knew what he was talking about a great deal better than other old Arabic writers, says nothing of the Balhara[3]. He mentions a kingdom of Konkan with its capital at *Tálah* [read *Tánah*][4].

Among the other kings with whom the Balhara was often at war was one named the JURZ, who was noted for his cavalry, and had great riches, and camels and horses in great numbers. His states are said to form a tongue of land, *i.e.*, I presume, to be on the sea coast. Yet Abu-Zaid says that Kanauj formed his empire, and to this M. Reinaud holds. But Mas'ūdī, who gives the same account of the Jurz (or *Juzr* as it is in his book as printed), makes him entirely distinct from the King of Kanauj, whom he calls the

[1] Called by Mas'ūdī *Manekir*, and identified by Lassen with the *Minnagara* of Ptolemy.

[2] See Lassen, iii, 533 *seqq.*, and iv, 917 *seqq.* It is a curious illustration of the expanse of the Mahomedan power and consequent circulation of its agents that the name of this Indian prince, the *Balhara*, was applied to a village in the neighbourhood of Palermo, now the well-known Monreale, and from it again to a market in the city, *Súk-Balhara*, now called *Piazza Ballarò*. Similar illustrations are found in the names of *Mansil-Sindi*, near Corleone ; *Jibal-Sindi*, near Girgenti ; and *'Ain-Sindi*, in the suburbs of Palermo : all preserved by mediæval documents, and the last still surviving under the corrupted name of Fonte *Dennisinni* (Amari, *St. dei Musulm. di Sicilia*, i, 84 ; ii, 33, 34, 300).

[3] Reinaud, *Mém. sur l'Inde* in *Mém. de l'Acad.*

[4] Reinaud in *J. As.*, sér. iv, tom. iv, p. 251.

Bawurah[1]. Lassen and the editors of Mas'ūdī[2] make this kingdom Gujarat, apparently from the slight resemblance of name. But it seems much more likely that it is the King *Jor* of Al Birúni, whom that writer places on the eastern coast of the Peninsula, either in the Tanjore country or in Telinga, or extending over both. And from Hiuen Tsang also we hear of a kingdom called *Juri* or *Jurya*, which lay some three hundred miles north of Dravida (the capital of which last was the present Konjeveram), and this may have been the same[3].

There is then the kingdom of THÁFAK, or THÁFAN as Mas'ūdī has it, which was noted for its women, who were the *whitest* and most beautiful in India. The author of the *Relations* calls it *beside* the Jurz, but no great weight can be attached to this where his knowledge was evidently so dim. Because of Ibn Batuta's praise of the Mahratta women, M. Reinaud will have Tháfan to be in the Dekkan, nay he localises it "in the present province of Aurungabad," and Lassen following up this lead with equal precision will prefer to put it in *Baglana*, which was then the Mahratta country[4]. But Ibn Batuta certainly does not say that the Mahratta women were *white*, the very last attribute I suppose that they could claim, and we find that Mas'ūdī couples Tháfan with Kashmir and Kandahar (*i.e. Gandhára*, the country about Peshawar and Attok) as one of the countries in which the Indus had its sources[5]. The traveller Ibn Muhalhil speaks of *Thábán* as a chief city of Kabul, but whether that be meant for the same place or no, this Tháfan is certainly to be sought on the N.W. frontier of India, and the fair women are very probably those of the race now called *Kafirs*, whose beauty and fair complexion are still so much extolled[6].

[1] Or *Baurawa*. Gildemeister says on this: "*Paurav* [in Nagari letters] esse puto, nam eo nomine Reges Kanyakubgenses gloriati sunt"; but gives no authority (p. 160). Mas'ūdī also speaks of a *city* Bawurah on one of the Panjab rivers, which is perhaps the *Parvata* of Hiuen Tsang. (*Pr. d'Or*, i, 371; *Vie de H. T.*, p. 210.)

[2] Lassen, iv, 921; *Prairies d'Or*, i, 383, 384. In the last passage the French translator puts simply *le Guzerat* to represent *Al-Jurz* or *Juzr*, which is scarcely fair translating of so doubtful a point.

[3] See *Vie de H. T.*, pp. 189, 190, 453; also Lassen, iii, 205, *note*. The *Jurz* of the *Relations* is evidently the *Malik-al-Jizr* of Edrisi, who puts him on what he calls the Island of Madai on the way to China, but Edrisi's information about the South Eastern Indies, is a hopeless chaos (see i, 86, 98).

[4] Lassen, iv, 921.

[5] *Prairies d'Or*, i, 207.

[6] See the notices of the Kafir women quoted Vol. IV, Goës, *infra*. Kazwini mentions a very strong fortress of India called *Thaifand*, on the summit of a mountain almost inaccessible, but which had water, cultivation, and everything needful for the maintenance of its garrison. It was taken, he says, by Mahmud Sabaktagin in the year 414 (A.D. 1023), and five hundred elephants were found in it. This is like the

Contiguous to these, according to the Arab writer, was the Kingdom of Ruhmi, Rahma, or RAHMAN[1], who was at war with the Jurz and the Balhara. He was not of great consideration, though he had the greatest army, and was accompanied by some fifty thousand elephants and fifteen thousand washermen! Muslins that could pass through a ring were made in his country. Gold, silver, aloes-wood, and chowries were also found in it. Cowries were the money used; and in the forests was the rhinoceros, of which a particular description is given under the name of *Karkadan*[2]. The Kingdom of Rahma, adds Mas'ūdī, extends both inland and on the sea.

Of this Reinaud says: "This seems to me to answer to the ancient Kingdom of Visiapur"; and Lassen will have it that it fits none but the Kingdom of the Chalukyas of Kalliani (in the Dekkan). Why, it would be hard to say; the washermen doubtless exist in those regions, and to a certain extent the elephants, but none of the other alleged products. Gold, silver, aloes-wood, chowries, rhinoceroses, and the fabulous stud of elephants all point to Transgangetic India, perhaps including Assam, whilst the muslins that pass through a ring are the produce of Eastern Bengal (Dacca muslins). Pegu is known in Burma, Buddhisto-classically, as *Rahmaniya*[3], and I have little doubt that this is the name involved, though I should be sorry to define more particularly the limits of the region intended by the Arab writer[4].

Then come an inland people of white complexion with pierced ears, and remarkable for their beauty, called KASHIBÍN, or, as Mas'ūdī has it, *Káman*. M. Reinaud says Mysore, but only because he had last said Visiapur. He cannot suppose that the people of Mysore are white in any sense. All that can be said is

account given of a stronghold on the west of the Indus, at *Mahaban*, which had been admirably identified by Col. James Abbott with Aornos. The name may have to do with our Tháfan (see Gildem., p. 208).

[1] Some copies of Mas'ūdī have *Wahman*, which seems to point to Rahman as the proper name (see Reinaud, *Relations*, i, cii). *Edrisi* (in Jaubert, i, 173) has *Dumi*.

[2] This is probably the word which Aelian intends in his description of the Indian unicorn, which he calls καρταζῶνον. (*De Nat. Animalium*, xvi, 20.)

[3] The great Burmese inscription at Kaungmúdhau Pagoda, near Ava, thus defines: "All within the great districts of Hanzawadi (*i.e.*, the city of Pegu), Digun (Rangoon), Dala (opposite Rangoon), Kothian, Youngmyo, and Mauttama (Martaban) is the great kingdom of RAMANIYA" (*Mission to Ava*, p. 351). *Arramaniya* is also used in the Ceylonese annals to designate some country of the Transgangetic Peninsula (see Turnour's *Epitome*, p. 41). The sounding titles of many of the Indo-Chinese princes refer to their possession of vast numbers of elephants.

[4] The kings of India, as given by Ibn Khurdádhbah (*supra*, p. 135), are the Balhara, the kings of Jábah, Táfan, Juzr, *Ghanah* or *'Anah*, Rahma, and Kámrún. Ghanah seems to have no parallel in other lists, nor can I conjecture what is meant.

that this and all the other kingdoms mentioned afterwards appear to be in Farther India. These are KAIRANJ, said to be on the sea, probably the sea called *Kadranj*, in the list of seas between Oman and China[1]; then MUJAH, where there is much good musk and very long ranges of snowy mountains; and MABAD or MAYAD, the people of both of which resemble the Chinese, whilst the latter touch the Chinese frontier. These are to be sought in the vicinity of Yun nan, which has much musk and very long ranges of snowy mountains.

NOTE XII.

ABSTRACT OF THE TRAVELS OF IBN MUHALHIL.

Quitting Khorāsān and the Mahomedan cities of Mávara-un-Nahr, with the ambassadors of China, as mentioned in the text, the party came first to the territory of HARKAH (or Harkat)[2]. It took a month[3] to pass through this region, and then they came to that of THATHÁH[4], through which they travelled for twenty days[5]. The people of this country are in alliance with those of Harkat to repel the inroads of the Pagans, and they are subject to the orders of the Emperor of China. They pay tribute also to Harkat, as the latter lies between them and the Musulman countries with which they desire to have commerce. Next they reached NAJA[6], tributary to Thatháh. Here they have wine, figs, and black meddlars, and a kind of wood which fire will not burn. The Christians carry this wood away, believing that Christ was crucified upon it[7]. Next they came to the BAJNAK[8], a people

[1] A passage quoted by Dulaurier, in relation to camphor, from an Arabic author, Ishak Bin Amram, says that the best camphor comes from "*Herenj*, which is Little China." This seems to point either to Borneo or to Cochin China. (*Jour. Asiat.*, sér. iv, tom. viii, p. 218.)

[2] [Chargāh, Marquart.—Kharkāh, Ferrand.]

[3] ["During which we lived on wheat and barley." Ferrand, p. 210.]

[4] [Tachṭāch, Marquart.—Takhṭākh, Ferrand.]

[5] ["In peace and security." Ferrand.]

[6] Or *Baja*. [Bağā, Marquart.—Badja, Ferrand.]

[7] ["Das Land ist reich an Feigen, Trauben und schwarzem Mispel, und es gibt daselbst eine Holzart, die das Feuer nicht verzehrt. Aus diesem Holze machen sie Götzenbilder. Durchreisende Christen pflegen dies Holz fort zu nehmen, und behaupten, dass es von dem Balken stamme, an welchem Jesus gekreuzigt wurde." Marquart, p. 76. This wood is probably teakwood.]

[8] On the three preceding peoples or countries, *Harkah* [Harkah Yarkand], *Thathdh*, and *Naja*, I can throw no light. The *Bajnak* [*Bağnāk*, Marquart] are the Pechinegs, or Πατζινακῖται of the Greeks [of Turkish race, of Huns stock], much discoursed of by Constantine Porphyrogenitus, who evidently stood in great fear of them, in his book *De Administrando Imperio*. In his time they were on the

with beards and mustachios, and went twenty-two days[1] through their territory which extended north to the confines of the SCLAVES[2]. Next to the JIKIL[3], a people who keep no cattle; they marry their daughters and sisters without regard to unlawful affinities, and are subject to the Turks[4]. They have a herb called *Kalkan*

Dnieper and Dniester, but he tells us that fifty years before they had been driven from their original seats on the *Atil* and *Geech* (Volga and Iaic) by the *Uz* (or *Ghuz*) and Khazars. Their original settlement is described by an Arab writer as having on the north Kipchak, to the south the Khazars, to the east the Ghuz, to the west the Slavs. (Const. Porph. in Banduri, *Imper. Orientale*, vol. i; Defrémery, *Fragments de Géographes*, etc., in *Jour. As.*, sér. iv, tom. xiii, 466; Mas'ūdī, *Prairies d'Or*, i, 262.) [They were exterminated by John Comnen in 1123.]

[Klaproth, *Mémoire sur les Khazars* (*Journal Asiatique*, iii, 1823, pp. 153–160):

"Les écrivains Byzantins font pour la première fois mention des *Khazars* en l'an 626. Ils les appellent aussi *Turcs* ou *Turcs orientaux*." p. 155.

From Ibn Hhauqual: "La langue des *véritables Khazars*," he says, "diffère de celle des Turcs et des Persans," p. 158.—"La langue des *Bulgares* est aussi celle des *Khazars*. Les *Berthas* ont une autre langue, et celle des *Russes* diffère entièrement des idiômes des *Khazars* et des *Berthas*," p. 158.

From Constantine Porphyrogenitus: "Près du Danube inférieur, vis-à-vis de *Dristra*, commence le pays des Petchenèghes, et leur domination s'étend jusqu'à Sarkel, forteresse des *Khazars*, dans laquelle il y a une garnison qu'on change de tems en tems. Chez eux *Sarkel* signifie *habitation blanche*," p. 159.

Klaproth comes to the conclusion that the Wogouls of western Siberia, the Khazars and the Bulgares belong to the race of the eastern Finns...this fact shows that "Schloezter et Thunmann ne se sont pas trompés en supposant que les *Hongrois blancs* cités dans la Chronique russe de Nestor, n'étaient autres que les *Khazars* des *Byzantins*," p. 160.

Physically the greater part of the Bulgarians are Finno-Ugrians, but mixed with Slavs; their language and customs have suffered the Slav influence and they make use of the Cyrillic alphabet.]

1 [Twelve days, Ferrand.]

2 ["Hierauf kamen wir zu einem Stamme, namens Bağnāk (Pečenegen), mit langen Bärten und Schnurrbärten, rohen Barbaren, die einander gegenseitig überfallen. Sie essen nur Hirse. Ihre Frauen begatten sie auf offener Strasse. Wir reisten durch ihr Gebiet 12 Tage lang, und es wurde uns erzählt, dass ihr Land nach Norden und den Slawenländern zu ungeheuer sei. Sie zahlen niemanden Tribut." Marquart, p. 75.]

3 [Čikil, Marquart.—Ferrand.]

4 ["Les indigènes se nourrissent exclusivement d'orge, de pois chiches et de viande de mouton. Ils n'égorgent pas les chameaux; ils n'élèvent pas de vaches; il n'y en a pas dans leur pays. Leurs vêtements sont en laine et en fourrure; ils n'en ont pas d'autres que ces deux sortes-là. Il y a chez eux quelques chrétiens [manichéens]. Ils sont beaux de visage. Les hommes, chez eux, épousent leurs filles, leurs sœurs et toutes les femmes interdites [par l'Islam]. Ils ne sont pas Mages, et cependant telle est leur doctrine en ce qui concerne le mariage. Ils adorent Canope [*Suhayl*, α du Navire], Saturne, les Gémeaux, Banāt Na's [the tails of the Little and of the Great Bear], le Chevreau; ils appellent Sirius, le Seigneur des Seigneurs. Chez eux la tranquillité règne; ils ne font rien de mal; toutes les tribus turques qui les entourent cherchent à les attaquer et à les dépouiller." Ferrand, p. 211.]

which they boil with their meat[1]. Bezoars are found here, and malignant serpents haunt the country in the beginning of winter. Their houses are of wood and clay[2]. Then to the BAGHRAJ, whose king is descended from 'Ali, and who are very skilful in the manufacture of arms[3]. Next to TOBBAT, and travelled forty days therein. There was a great city there built of reeds and a temple made of ox leather covered with varnish. There is also an idol made of the horns of musk oxen[4]. Next they came to KIMAK[5], where the houses are of the skins of beasts, and there are vines with grapes which are half black and half white. There is also a stone here with which they produce rain as often as they will[6]. Gold is found on the surface, and diamonds are disclosed by the rivers. They have no king nor temple. They venerate greatly

[1] *Kalank* in *Pers.* is the kitchen herb *purslain*. The *Ashkal, Szekely* or *Siculi*, no doubt the same as these Jikil, are mentioned in the extracts by Defrémery just quoted (p. 473), as being to the south of the Majgars or Majars, who again were south of the Bajnaks. [Read *kīlkan*, the leek; it grows at Rey and in Khorāsān. *Notices et Ext.*, xxvi, 1883, p. 162.—Ferrand, p. 211.]

[2] [Bone ? Ferrand, p. 212.—" Ils n'ont pas de rois. Nous avons traversé leur pays en quarante jours, en paix, quiétude et tranquillité." Ferrand, p. 212.]

[3] Qu. Georgians ? (whose kings were *Bagratidæ*); or Bulgarians ? (of the Volga). [" La particularité merveilleuse de ceux qu'ils choisissent pour roi parmi les descendants de Zayd, c'est que ceux-ci ont de la barbe, le nez droit et de grand yeux. Les indigènes se nourrissent de millet et de viande de mouton mâle. Il n'y a dans leurs pays ni vaches ni chèvres. Leurs vêtements sont en feutre ; ils n'en revêtent pas d'autres. Nous voyageâmes chez eux pendant un mois dans la peur et la crainte; nous dûmes leur donner le dixième de tout ce que nous avions avec nous." Ferrand, p. 212. Sir Henry H. Howorth, in his paper *The Northern Frontagers of China* (*Journ. Roy. Asiat. Soc.*, 1893, pp. 467–502), has devoted some pages to Boghra Khan. The Bagrač were perhaps the subjects of the Boghra Khan.]

[4] Some regions of Siberia ? [Tobbat: *Tŭbăt* تُبَّت and not *Tubbat* تُبَّت...... " Dans cette ville se trouvent des musulmans, des juifs, des chrétiens, des Mages et des Indiens; [les habitants] payent l'impôt à l'Alide [roi de la tribu] des Baghrač. Les [Tŭbăt] tirent leur roi au sort. Ils ont une prison pour les criminels et [infligent] des amendes. Ils prient en se mettant dans la direction de la *Kibla* de la Mekke." Ferrand, p. 213.]

[5] [Kaimāk, Marquart.—Kaymāk, Ferrand.]

[6] On the *rain-stone* used by the Turk and Tartar tribes to conjure rain, and still known among the Kalmaks, see one of Quatremère's long but interesting notes on *Rashiduddin*, pp. 428 *seqq.*; also Hammer's *Golden Horde*, pp. 42 and 436. This stone was called by the Turks *Jadah* (Pers. *Yadah*). Is this the origin of our Jade-stone ? and is it connected with the (*Pers.*) word *Jádú*, conjuring, in common use in India ? [" Der Regenstein (Nephrit) ' wird bekanntlich seit Alters südlich von Khuttan aus anstehendem Felsgestein gebrochen (H. v. Schlagintweit, *Hochasien*, iv, 161 f.) und die Flüsse von Khuttan, Yarqand, Kiria und Čarčan führen Nephrit im Gerölle.' " Marquart, p. 79.]

those who attain eighty years without being ill. The travellers were thirty-five days among them[1]. Then they came to the GHUZ, whose city is of stone, timber, and reeds. They have a temple but no images. Their king is very powerful and trades with India and China. Their clothes are of linen and camel's hair. They have no wool. They have a white stone which is good for colic, and a red[2] stone which by touching a sword prevents it from cutting. The route lay securely for one month through this country[3]. Then came the TAGHAZGHAZ[4] who eat flesh, both raw and cooked, and wear wool and cotton. They have no temples; they hold horses in high esteem. They have a stone that stops bleeding at the nose. They celebrate a feast when they see a rainbow. In prayer they turn to the west. The king is very powerful, and at the top of his castle is a round structure of gold which holds a hundred men, and is seen for five parasangs. Their standards are black. The travellers went twenty days through this country in great fear[5]. Next they came

[1] ["Ils ont des caractères pour écrire." Ferrand, p. 213.] The *Kimaks* are represented by Edrisi as the greatest of the Turk (or Tartar) nations. They had the Taghazghaz to the south, the Khiziljis (*Kharlikhs ?*) to the south-west, the Khilkhis to the west, on the east the Dark Sea. They had numerous cities, all on a great river flowing eastward. El-Wardi calls them a race of Eastern Turks, bordering on Northern China. In the Chinese Annals we find embassies repeatedly from the *Kumuki*, coupled with the K'itans, to the court of the Wei dynasty in the fifth century (Edrisi, i, 25; ii, 217–223, etc.; Ibn Khurdádhbah in *Jour. As.*, sér. vi, tom. v, 268; D'Herbelot in v.; Deguignes, i, 183, 184). The river was perhaps the *Irtish*, as Mas'ūdī speaks of the "Black and White *Irshat* (the French transl., however, prints *Avasht*) on the banks of which is the kingdom of the *Keimak-Baigur*, a Turkish tribe originating in the country beyond the Jihun." (*Prairies d'Or*, i, 230; also 288.)

[2] [Green, Ferrand, p. 214.]

[3] The *Ghuz* or *Uzes* had their seats about the Aral and to the east of it. In the reign of Constantine Ducas they penetrated into Macedonia, and got large sums from the emperor to make peace. On their return they were cut to pieces by the Pechinegs. The Ghuz are identified with the *Turkomans* (Edrisi, i, 7; ii, 339 *seqq.*; Deguignes, ii, 522; Mas'ūdī, *Prairies d'Or*, i, 212). ["Ils se nourrissent exclusivement de froment; il n'y a pas chez eux de légumes. Ils mangent la chair des moutons et des chèvres, mâles et femelles." Ferrand, p. 214.]

[4] [Toγuzγuz (Uiguren), Marquart, p. 80.—Toguzoguz, Ferrand, p. 214.]

[5] The Taghazghaz (printed in Edrisi, *Bagharghar*) were one of the greatest tribes of the Turks, according to the early Arab geographers. Their country seems to have been that afterwards known as the Uighúr country, whether they were the same people or not (see Edrisi, i, 490 *seq.*; Ibn Khurdádhbah, *u.s.*, 268). Mas'ūdī says they occupied the city of Kushan between Khorāsān and China, supposed to be the *Kao ch'ang* of the Chinese, the modern Turfan. He says they were in his day the most valiant, powerful, and best governed of the Turks. (*Prairies d'Or*, i, 288.) The round structure of gold was probably a

to the KHIRKHIZ[1], a people who have temples for worship and a written character, and are a very intelligent people. They never put a light out[2]. They have a little musk. They keep three feasts in the year. Their standards are green, and in prayer they turn to the south. They adore the planets Saturn and Venus, and predict the future by Mars. They have a stone that shines by night and is used for a lamp. No man under forty sits down

gilt Dagoba. ["Reinaud, in the preface to his Abulfeda, pp. 360 *seq.*, affords evidence that the Turkish race called *Tagazgaz* by the Arabian geographers of the ninth and tenth centuries is identical with the Uigurs. Mas'ūdī states that in his days (he died 956) the Tagazgaz were the most valiant, numerous and best governed among the Turk tribes. Their empire extended from Khorassan to Sin (China). Their principal city was called *Kushan*; their king had the title *irkhan*. Mas'ūdī adds that the Tagazgaz were the only Turk tribe who professed the Manichean doctrine. Reinaud thinks that *Kushan* is *Kucha* in Eastern Turkestan; Barbier de Meynard identifies this name with *Kao ch'ang* of the Chinese Annals. As to the doctrine of Mani (or Manes), I may observe that Wang Yengte, in his narrative, notices in Kao ch'ang a temple (devoted to) Mani (*Ma-ni sz'*), and served by monks from Persia, who have their particular rules, and who declare the books of the Buddhists to be heretical." Bretschneider, *Mediaeval Researches*, i, p. 252.]

["Les Tagazgaz, qui occupent la ville de Kouchan (Kao-tchang), située entre le Khoraçan et la Chine, et qui sont aujourd'hui, en 332, de toutes les races et tribus turques, la plus valeureuse, la plus puissante et la mieux gouvernée. Leurs rois portent le titre d'Irkhan, et seuls entre tous ces peuples ils professent la doctrine de Manès." (Mas'ūdī, i, p. 288.).... "Leur royaume [des Chinois] est contigu à celui des Tagazgaz, qui, comme nous l'avons dit plus haut, sont manichéens et proclament l'existence simultanée des deux principes de la lumière et des ténèbres." (*l.c.*, pp. 299–300.)]

[Mas'ūdī (i, 288, 299) says that among the Turks, the Taghazghaz were the only ones following the religion of Manes. According to Edrisi, they were mazdeans. The Taghazghaz were certainly the Uighúrs who are called in Orkhon Inscriptions Toquz Oguz = Nine Oguz. Cf. Vilh. Thomsen, *Insc. de l'Orkhon*, 1896, pp. 112, 147, Monument I.—Chavannes, *Journ. As.*, i, 1897, p. 80.]

["Ensuite il faut compter celui des rois turcs qui possède la ville de Kouchan et qui commande aux Tagazgaz. On lui donne le titre de roi des bêtes féroces et de roi des chevaux, parce qu'aucun prince de la terre n'a sous ses ordres des guerriers plus valeureux et plus disposés à répandre le sang, et qu'aucun d'eux ne possède un plus grand nombre de chevaux. Son royaume est isolé entre la Chine et les déserts du Khoraçan; quant à lui, il porte le titre de *irkhan*, et bien qu'il y ait chez les Turcs plusieurs princes et beaucoup de peuples qui ne sont pas soumis à un roi, aucun n'a la prétention de rivaliser avec lui." Mas'ūdī, i, p. 358.]

[1] [Kirgiz, Ferrand, p. 214; in Chinese, *Kie Ku* and *Kien Wen*.]

[2] Wood mentions this prejudice, against *blowing* out a light, not indeed among the Kirghiz, but among the immediate neighbours of the Kirghiz of Pamir, the people of Wakhan and Badakhshan; "A Wakhani considers it bad luck to blow out a light by the breath, and will rather wave his hand for several minutes under the flame of his pine-slip than resort to the sure but to him disagreeable alternative." (*Oxus*, p. 333; see also p. 274.)

in the king's presence[1]. Next to the HAZLAKH[2], who are great gamblers, and stake wife, mother, or daughter on their play. When a caravan of travellers comes into their country the wife or sister or daughter of some chief comes and washes them. And if any of these ladies takes a fancy for one of the strangers she carries him home and entertains him with all kindness, and makes her husband or son or brother provide for him in every way; nor as long as the guest is keeping company with her does the husband come near them unless for necessary business[3]. Next they

[1] ["Nous voyageâmes chez [les Kirgiz] pendant un mois, en toute tranquillité et sécurité." Ferrand, p. 215.]

[2] ["Nous arrivâmes ensuite dans la tribu des Kharlok. Ils se nourrissent de pois chiches et de lentilles. Ils fabriquent une boisson avec du millet. Ils ne mangent que de la viande salée. Ils s'habillent de vêtements de laine. Il y a chez eux une maison de prière sur les murs de laquelle on voit l'image de leurs anciens rois. La maison est en bois incombustible. Il y a beaucoup de ce bois dans leur pays. La violence et la rébellion règnent parmi eux; ils sont ennemis les uns des autres. Le libertinage y est courant et licite." Ferrand, p. 215.]

I suspect it should be *Kharlikh* (it is a question of points only), [الخرلخ, *al-Kharlokh*] the name of one of the greatest Turkish tribes, and sometimes written *Carligh*, whose country seems to have been north of Farghānah. They are probably the *Khizilji* of the French Edrisi, and the *Khuzluj* of Mas'ūdī, "remarkable for their beauty, stature, and perfect features. Formerly they ruled over all the other tribes. From their race descended the Khakan of the Khakans who united under his empire all the kingdoms of the Turks, and commanded all their kings" (p. 288).

[3] This discreditable custom is related by Marco Polo of the people of Qamul; he says of it ["And it is the truth that if a foreigner comes to the house of one of these people [at Camul] to lodge, the host is delighted, and desires his wife to put herself entirely at the guest's disposal, whilst he himself gets out of the way, and comes back no more until the stranger shall have taken his departure. The guest may stay and enjoy the wife's society as long as he lists, whilst the husband has no shame in the matter, but indeed considers it an honour. And all the men of this province are made wittols of by their wives in this way. The women themselves are fair and wanton." Yule-Cordier's *Marco Polo*, i, p. 210, and note 3, p. 212.—We find the same custom at Caindu, *l.c.*, ii, pp. 53–4. "I must tell you of a custom that they have in this country regarding their women. No man considers himself wronged if a foreigner, or any other man, dishonour his wife, or daughter, or sister, or any woman of his family, but on the contrary he deems such intercourse a piece of good fortune. And they say that it brings the favour of their gods and idols, and great increase of temporal prosperity. For this reason, they bestow their wives on foreigners and other people as I will tell you.

"When they fall in with any stranger in want of a lodging they are all eager to take him in. And as soon as he has taken up his quarters the master of the house goes forth, telling him to consider everything at his disposal, and after saying so he proceeds to his vineyards or his fields, and comes back no more till the stranger has departed. The latter abides in the caitiff's house, be it three days or be it four, enjoying himself with the fellow's wife or daughter or sister, or whatsoever woman of the family it best likes him; and as long as he abides there

reached the KHATHLAKH[1], the bravest of all the Turks. These admit marriage with sisters. Women are allowed to marry but once, and there is no divorce except for breach of marriage vows; in which case both the offending parties are burnt. The wife is endowed with all the man's worldly goods, and he must serve her father for a year. They have the custom of exacting blood-money; and the king is not allowed to marry on pain of death. Next they came to the KHATIYAN[2]. These do not eat meat unless

he leaves his hat or some other token hanging at the door, to let the master of the house know that he is still there. As long as the wretched fellow sees that token, he must not go in. And such is the custom over all that province."]

It is a notorious allegation against the Hazaras of the Hindu Kush that they exercise the same practice (Wood, p. 201, and Burnes). But what shall we say to its being ascribed also by a Byzantine historian of the fifteenth century to a certain insular kingdom of Western Europe (the capital of which was *Λούνδρας*), at least if we trust to the Latin version of Conrad Clauser. The Greek runs: "*νομίζεται δὲ τούτοις τά τ' ἀμφὶ τὰς γυναῖκάς τε καὶ τοὺς παῖδας ἁπλοϊκωτέρα ὥστε ἀνὰ πᾶσαν τὴν νῆσον ἐπειδάν τις ἐς τὴν τοῦ ἐπιτηδείου αὐτῷ οἰκίαν ἐσῄει καλούμενος, κύσαντα τὴν γυναῖκα, οὕτω ξενίζεσθαι αὐτὸν, καὶ ἐν ταῖς ὁδοῖς δὲ ἁπανταχῇ περιέχονται τὰς ἑαυτῶν γυναῖκας ἐν τοῖς ἐπιτηδείοις....καὶ οὐδὲ αἰσχύνην τοῦτο φέρει ἑαυτοῖς κύεσθαι τάς τε γυναῖκας αὐτῶν καὶ τὰς θυγατέρας*" (Laonicus Chalcondylas, in ed. Paris, 1650, pp. 48–9). The translation of Clauser gives substantially the same meaning as Ibn Muhalhil's account of the Kharlikh practice, except that it is much more grossly expressed. We need not defend our ancestors and ancestresses against the Byzantine; but was he really such a *gobe-mouches* as his translator makes him? I must needs speak very diffidently, but do the words mean more than this? "They take things very easily in regard to their wives and children. For over all the island, when anyone goes to visit a friend, he kisses the good wife on entering the house. And if friends meet on the highway 'tis the universal custom that they embrace each other's wives....Nor do they think shame that their wives and daughters should be kissed."

["Les [Kharlok] ont une fête où ils revêtent des vêtements de soie à ramages; ceux qui ne peuvent pas le faire, mettent un morceau de soie à ramages à leurs vêtements [habituels]. Il y a chez eux une mine d'argent mélangé à du mercure. Ils ont un arbre qui a l'aspect du myrobolan et est de la grosseur de la jambe. Quand on oint de son suc les tumeurs chaudes, elles sont guéries instantanément. Ils ont une grande pierre qu'ils vénèrent et devant laquelle ils viennent plaider leurs affaires; ils lui égorgent des victimes. Cette pierre est de couleur vert-poireau. Nous voyageâmes chez les Kharlok pendant vingt-cinq jours, en toute paix et tranquillité." Ferrand, p. 216.]

[1] [Khuṭlukh, Ferrand, p. 216.]

[2] I have elsewhere (Benedict Goës, *infra*) intimated a suspicion that this is Khotan. The civilised character of the people; their temples; and their having musk, are favourable to this supposition, as well as the juxtaposition of *Bai*. [" H. Yule will dagegen in den الختيان die Einwohner von *Chotan* erkennen, so dass zu lesen wäre الخُتَنان *Chutanān*, also einfach der persische Plural, wie z. B. in خُتّلان *Chutalān* neben خُتّل *Çhutal*. Dies würde in der That viel besser in den Zusammenhang des folgenden Itinerars passen. Allein es ist schwer einzusehen, warum Abū Dulaf dann nicht die gewöhnliche Form dieses bei den Arabern so bekannten Namens gebraucht hätte. Man müsste geradezu annehmen,

cooked; they have civilised laws of marriage and wise institutions; they have no king; they use no cruelties towards foreigners. They have no dyed clothes; they possess musk, and a stone which heals poisoned bites[1], etc., also the bezoar. Then they came to BAHI. This is a great city and territory, with palm trees, vines, etc. In the city are Mahomedans, Jews, Christians, Magians, and idolaters. They have a green stone which is good for the eyes, and a red stone which is good for the spleen; also excellent indigo[2]. They travelled forty days in this territory[3]. Then they came to KALIB[4], in which there is a colony of the Arabs of Yemen, who were left behind by the army of Tobba, after he had invaded the Chinese. They use the ancient Arabic language and the Himyaritic character. They worship idols, and make a drink from dates. The king pays tribute to the King of China[5]. After travelling for one month through their territory they came to the *Makám ul Báb* (House or Halting-place of the Gate), in a sandy region. Here is stationed an officer of the King of China, and anyone desiring to enter China from the Turkish countries or elsewhere must ask leave here. He is entertained three days at the king's expense and is then allowed to set out. In the first parasang of the journey the travellers met with beasts loaded with necessaries for them, and then they arrived at the *Wadi ul-Makâm* (Valley of the Station or Halting-place), where they had to ask leave to enter, and after abiding three days at the king's expense in that valley, which is one of the pleasantest and fairest regions

dass er absichtlich durch die Wahl dieser ungewöhnlichen Form es seinen Lesern unmöglich machen wollte, in diesem Orte das bekannte Chotan wiederzuerkennen. Auch wäre es immerhin sehr auffällig, dass dieser Name von den Abschreibern so sehr entstellt werden konnte." Marquart, p. 83.]

[1] [" Une pierre qui arrête la fièvre; il n'en existe pas hors de leur pays." Ferrand, p. 217.]

[2] ["Ils ont un excellent indigo rouge (*sic*), léger sur l'eau, qui, si on le met dans l'eau, ne va pas au fond." Ferrand, p. 218.]

[3] [" Pima," Ferrand, p. 217.] This is probably the *province of Pein*, which in Marco Polo follows Khotan, and is now represented by the town and district of *Bai* between Aqsu and Kucha (see Benedict Goës, *infra*). [Pein has nothing to do with Bai. Sir M. A. Stein appears to have exactly identified Pein with Uzun-Tati, on the road from Khotan to Nia, leaving Kiria to the south. See *Marco Polo*, i, p. 192; ii, p. 595.]

[4] [Ḳulaybu, Ferrand, p. 218.]

[5] The name of this country seems to be corrupt. *Tibet* is probably meant, of which Mas'ūdī says: "the population is in great part composed of Himyarites mixed with some descendants of Tobba," etc. (*Prairies d'Or*, i, p. 350.) He also in his account of the Kings of Yemen speaks of one of them, Malkíkarib, son of Tobba al Akrán, who "overran various countries of the East, such as Khorāsān, Tibet, China, and Sejistan" (iii, 154). *Tobba* was the hereditary title of the ancient Kings of Yemen. They seem to have been as useful to the Arabian antiquaries as the Phœnicians to ours. Samarkand was said to have been built by them, and a Himyarite inscription on one of the gates to testify thereunto (see d'Herbelot). [We have seen p. 246 that this is not Tibet.]

of God's earth, permission was given[1]. Leaving the valley and travelling for a whole day they came to the city of SINDABIL[2], the capital of China, and where the king's palace is. They stopped the night at a mile from the city. Setting out in the early morning, and making the best of their way for a whole day[3], they reached the city at sunset. It is a great city, a day's journey in length, and having sixty straight streets radiating from the palace. The wall (of the palace ?) is ninety cubits high and ninety thick ; on the top of it is a stream of water throwing off sixty branches, one at every gate. Each branch flows down the street and back to the palace, so that every street has a double canal flowing this way and that. The one supplies water, the other acts as a drain[4]. There is a great temple inclosure, greater than that of Jerusalem, inside of which are images and a great pagoda[5]. The constitution of the government is very elaborate, and the laws are strict. No animals are slaughtered for food, and to kill them is a capital offence[6]. The traveller found the king most accomplished, intelligent, and benevolent, and enjoyed his hospitality until the terms of the marriage were settled, and the princess was then committed to the escort of two hundred slaves and three hundred handmaidens to be taken to Khorāsān to Noah Ben Naṣr.

Leaving Sindabil, the traveller proceeded to the sea-coast and halted at KALAH, the first city of India (from the east) and the extreme point made by ships going in that direction. If they go

[1] This part of the narrative has a kind of verisimilitude, and may be compared with that of Sháh Rukh's ambassadors, who were stopped and entertained for a day or two by the Chinese officials, after which they proceeded *through the desert* to the Great Wall, provisions of all sorts being supplied to them, etc. (See the abstract in Note XVII.)

[2] [Sandābil, Marquart, p. 85.—Ferrand, p. 219.]

[3] "*Per totam diem contendimus.*" I do not understand, unless it be meant that getting through the crowded population took them a whole day to move a mile ?

[4] This is all very obscure in the Latin. I have tried to interpret into consistent meaning. [" Sur le faîte du mur, se trouve un grand fleuve qui se divise en soixante bras. Chaque bras coule vers l'une des portes et rencontre un moulin qui déverse l'eau au-dessous, puis un autre moulin d'où l'eau coule sur le sol. Ensuite, la moitié de l'eau sort hors du mur et irrigue les jardins. L'autre moitié est dirigée vers la ville, fournit de l'eau aux habitants de la rue [dans laquelle elle passe] jusqu'au palais du gouvernement [auquel aboutit la rue]. Puis [l'eau] passe dans la rue opposée et sort [enfin] de la ville. Chaque rue a ainsi deux courants d'eau. Toute rue a deux courants d'eau coulant en sens inverse l'un de l'autre. Le courant qui coule dans le sens de l'extérieur de la ville vers l'intérieur, fournit de l'eau potable ; celui qui coule dans le sens de l'intérieur de la ville vers l'extérieur, emporte les immondices [des habitants]." Ferrand, p. 219.]

[5] [A great Buddha, Ferrand, p. 219.]

[6] [" Cette ville est en même temps la capitale de l'Inde et des Turks." Ferrand, p. 220.]

past it they are lost. This is a great city with high walls, gardens, and canals. Here are the mines of lead[1] called *Qala'i*, which is found in no part of the world except QALA'H[2]. Here also are made the swords of Qala'h, the best in India. The inhabitants rebel against their king or obey him, just as they please. Like the Chinese, they do not slaughter animals (*i.e.*, are Buddhists). The Chinese frontier is three hundred parasangs from their territory. Their money is of silver, worth three dirhems, and is called *Fahri*. Their king is under the King of the Chinese, and they pray for him and have a temple dedicated to him.

From Kalah Ibn Muhalhil proceeds to the PEPPER COUNTRY, by which name Malabar is often styled[3], and thence to the foot of Mount Káfúr, on which there are great cities, one of which is KAMRUN[4], from which comes the green wood called *Mandal Kamruni*[5]. There also is the city called SANF, which gives its name to the Sanfi aloes-wood. At another foot of the mountain towards the north is the city called SAIMUR, whose inhabitants are of great beauty, and said to be descended from Turks and Chinese. From this place also the SAIMURI[6] wood is named, though it is only brought thither for sale, etc.[7] After describing

[1] [Tin, Ferrand, p. 221.]

[2] This difference of spelling is in the original. Kalah or Kalah-bar is spoken of by the authors of the *Relation* as one month's voyage from Kaulam, and as midway between Oman and China, and as a great central point of trade in aloes, camphor, sandal, ivory, the lead called *al-qala'i*, ebony, brazil-wood, and spices, i.e. of the products of the Archipelago. Reinaud is very wild about the position of this *Kalah*, and whether he means it to be a port on the Coromandel coast, the Kalliana of Cosmas (*i.e.* a port on the West of India), or Pt. de Galle in Ceylon, is difficult to discern. It seems to me certain that it is a port of the Archipelago, representing in a general way the modern Singapore or Malacca, and very possibly identical with *Kadah* (*Quedah*) as M. Maury has suggested. M. Reinaud objects to "the lead called *al-qala'i*" being translated tin, though all the light he throws on it is a suggestion that it is the *brass* which Cosmas says was exported from Kalliana. Yet *qala'i* is the word universally used in Hindustani for the tinning of pots and pans, and I see F. Johnston's Persian Dictionary simply defines it as *tin*. This product sufficiently fixes Kalah as in or near the Malay Peninsula. Edrisi also places the mine of *qala'i* at that place.

I should not have enlarged on this if Sir E. Tennent had not in his *Ceylon* followed up and expanded the suggestion of Reinaud that Kalah was Pt. de Galle. He refers to the arguments of Dulaurier in the *Journ. Asiat.*, but there does not seem to be much force in them.

[3] *E.g.*, see Ibn Batuta, *infra*, Vol. IV, and Cosmas, *supra*, p. 226.

[4] [Kāmarūb (Ferrand) = Skr. *Kāmārupa* = Assam.]

[5] [Green aloes called *Mandal al-Kāmarūbī*. (Ferrand, p. 222.)]

[6] [Saymūr, Ferrand, p. 223.]

[7] This passage is a strange jumble, but it may be doubted whether the author has been fairly represented in the extracts. For in Gildemeister (p. 70) will be found a quotation from Kazwini which seems to represent the same passage, in which the cities named are Kamarún, Kumár, and Sanf, but nothing is said of Saimur *Kamrún* is generally

JAJALI[1], a city on a great mountain overlooking the sea, he goes to KASHMIR, where there is a great observatory made of Chinese iron which is indestructible[2]; thence to KABUL and its chief city THĀBAN (see *supra*, p. 242). He then returns rapidly to the shore of the India Sea, and describes the city called MANDURAFIN[3] (or KIN), a place which has not been identified; and thence to KŪLAM, where grow teak, brazil, and bamboos, and respecting which various other perplexing particulars are stated. From the cities of the shore he visits MULTĀN, where he gives a romancing description of the great idol so celebrated among the early Arab invaders[4]. According to Abu Dulif it was a hundred cubits high,

understood to be intended for *Kamrûp* or Assam, though the notices of Abulfeda (*ib.*, p. 191) leave this very doubtful. *Sanf* is Champa, and Kumar will be spoken of in Vol. IV, Ibn Batuta, *infra*. *Saimur* was the name of a seaport not far from Bombay, the exact site of which has not been ascertained. [Yule has written since (*M. Polo*, ii, p. 367 *n.*): "Saimur (the modern Chaul, as I believe").] According to Reinaud it is the Simylla of Ptolemy and the Periplus, and perhaps the Chimolo of Hiuen Tsang (*Vie de H. T.*, p. 420). It seems to be called by Al-Birúni Jaimur. He puts it south of Tana in the country of *Lárán* (see Reinaud's *Mém. sur l'Inde* in *Mém. Acad.*, p. 220, and his extracts in *J. As.*, sér. iv, tom. iv, pp. 263–4). Putting all these forms of the name together, and looking to the approximate position, it seems likely that the old name was something like *Chaimul* or *Chánwul*, and that the port was no other than CHAUL, some thirty miles south of Bombay, which continued to be a noted port down to the seventeenth century. [Chaul is a town in the Alībāg *tāluka* or Kolāba district, Bombay, 30 miles south of Bombay, and on the right bank of the Kundalika river, or Roha creek. "Chaul is a place of great antiquity. Under the names of Champāvati and Revatikshetra, local Hindu traditions trace it to the times when Krishna reigned in Gujarāt. It seems probable that Chaul or Cheul is Ptolemy's (A.D. 150) headland and emporium of Symulla or Timulla; and it has a special interest, as Ptolemy mentions that he gained information about Western India from people who had come from Symulla to Alexandria. About a hundred years later (A.D. 247) it appears in the *Periplus* of the Erythraean Sea as Semulla, the first local mart south of Kalliena; and in 642 it is called Chimolo by Hiuen Tsang. Chaul next appears under the names Saimur and Jaimur in the writings of the Arab travellers of the tenth, eleventh, and twelfth centuries. Early in the fourteenth century it is mentioned as one of the centres of Yādava power in the Konkan. The Russian traveller Athanasius Nikitin (1470) calls it Chivil. Thirty-five years later (1505) the Portuguese first appeared at Chaul." *Imperial Gazet. India.*]

[1] [Jājullā, Ferrand, p. 223.]

[2] Compare Pliny at p. 17, as to Seric iron.

[3] [Mandura-patan, Ferrand, p. 225.]

[4] According to Edrisi the image was mounted on a throne of plastered brick. The temple was in the form of a dome (probably the Hindu bulging pyramidal spire) which was gilt; the walls were painted. When Multān was taken in the time of the Khalif Walid by Muhammad bin Kāsim [712], he left the temple of the idol standing, but hung a piece of beef round the neck of the latter. (Edrisi, i, 167; Reinaud, *Mém.*, p. 185.)

and hung suspended in air, without support, a hundred cubits from the ground. Thence he goes to MANSŪRA and DÁBIL[1], etc.[2]

On the whole the impression gathered is, that the author's work (like that of some more modern travellers) contained genuine matter in an arrangement that was not genuine[3]; but that some at least of the perplexities found in it are due to the manner in which its fragments have been preserved and joined together.

NOTE XIII.

EXTRACTS REGARDING CHINA FROM ABULFEDA[4].

(A.D. 1273–1331.)

"China is bounded on the west by the lands[5] between India and China; on the south, by the sea; on the east, by the Eastern Atlantic[6]; on the north by the lands of Gog [Yâdjûdj] and Magog [Mâdjûdj], and other regions respecting which we have no information. Writers on the customs and kingdoms of the world have in their works mentioned many provinces and places and rivers as existing in China under the different climates, but the names have not reached us with any exactness, nor have we any certain information as to their circumstances. Thus they are as good as unknown to us; there being few travellers who arrive from those parts, such as might furnish us with intelligence (respecting those places), and for this reason we forbear to detail them.

1° "Some places, however, are named by persons who come

[1] [Daybul, Ferrand, p. 229.]

[2] As to Daibal see p. 85 *supra*. Mansūra, the capital of the Musulman conquerors of Sind, was two parasangs from the old Hindu city of Bahmanabad; and this lay on an old channel forty-three miles to the north-west of Haidarabad. (See *Proc. R. G. S.*, vol. x, p. 131.)

[3] [Marquart who quotes these lines writes, p. 83: "Schon aus dem Bisherigen erhellt, dass die Berichte des Abū Dulaf, ehe sie verwertet werden können, erst auf ihre Quellen zurückgeführt werden müssen, dass aber aus der Reihenfolge, in welcher die Völker bei ihm stehen, noch keineswegs auf geographische Nachbarschaft geschlossen werden darf."]

[4] My friend Mr. Badger was kind enough to make a literal translation of these extracts for me. I have slightly smoothed the ruggedness of a literal version from Arabic, whilst trying not to affect the sense.

It is to be lamented that M. Reinaud has left his version of Abulfeda's Geography unfinished for some eighteen years. There is a Latin translation by Reiske in Büsching's *Magazine*, but I have no access to it. [The translation left unfinished by Reinaud was completed by the late Prof. Stanislas Guyard in 1883; I have revised Yule's text with Guyard's translation and added the end of Abulfeda's chapter concerning China (*Sîn*), *i.e.*, Sila, Jankût, Khâju, Sankjû. H. C.]

[5] [Desert.—Guyard.]

[6] [Eastern Surrounding Sea.—Guyard.]

from those parts, and of these one is [Khânqû, *read*] KHÂNFÛ[1], which is known in our day as KHANSÂ, and on the north side of which is a lake of fresh water called SÎKHÛ about half-a-day's journey in circumference[2].

"It is also stated that SHANJÛ [Shinjû], known in our time as ZAITÚN, is one of the ports of China, and with them the ports are also the places of customs[3].

"[Khânqû, *read*] Khânfû is one of the gates of China, and is situated on the river, as it is stated in the *Qánún*[4]. Ibn Sa'id says it is mentioned in books, and is situated on the east of the River of Khamdán. Ibn Khurdádhbah says it is the greatest commercial port of China, and abounds in fruit, vegetables, wheat, barley, rice, and sugar-cane.

2° "KHÂNJÛ is, according to the *Qánún*, one of the gates of China, situated on the river. Ibn Sa'id states that it is the chief of the gates of China, and is fortified with masonry....To the east of it is the city of TÂJAH [Tai chau]. Ibn Sa'id adds: It[5] is the capital of China where the Baghbúr their great king resides[6].

3° "YANJÛ, the residence of their king. The *Qánún* states that *this* is the abode of the Fághfúr of China, who is called Tamghâj Khân, and is their Great King, etc. (see *supra*, p. 33)[7]. The *Qánún* also states that the city of KAZQÛ in China is greater than the above-named Yanjû....Some who have seen Yanjû describe it as in a temperate part of the earth, with gardens and a ruined wall[8]. It is two days from the sea, and between it and Khansâ is

[1] The word is written as in Jaubert's Edrisi, *Khánkú*, but I believe there can be no doubt as to the right reading. See above, pp. 89, 129, 135.

[2] The *Si-hu* or Western Lake of Hang chau. Its mention here is no doubt a part of Abulfeda's scanty recent information, as well as the next paragraph.

[3] [" Both places (Khânfû and Shinjû) are *bandars* of China. Now the word *bandar* means a port, in China." Guyard.]

[4] The *Qánún* is I believe the lost work of Al-Birúni upon Geography. The "Gates of China" appears to have been a sort of technical expression for the chief ports of China, connected with the view of the access to that country conveyed in the *Relations* and in Edrisi. In approaching China ships find a series of mountainous islands or promontories. Between these are narrow channels, through which the ships pass to the various ports of the Empire, and these passages are called the *Gates of China* (Reinaud, *Relations*, i, 19; Edrisi, i, 90).

[5] *I.e.* as I apprehend *Tájah*, the *Bájah* of Jaubert's Edrisi (*supra*, p. 143). *Khânjû* is perhaps *Kwang chau* or Canton.

[6] [This last sentence is not given in Guyard's translation.]

[7] [" According to the Chronicle of Al-Niswy (Nasawi), which includes a history of the Kings of Khwarizm and of the Tartars: the Capital of the King of the Tartars in China is called Tûghâj." Guyard.]

[8] [" Its inhabitants drink water from wells." Guyard.

a distance of five days. Yanjû is to the north and west of Khansâ, and is smaller in size[1].

4° "ZAITÚN, *i.e.* Shanjû[2], is a haven of China, and, according to the accounts of merchants who have travelled to those parts, is a city of mark. It is situated on a marine estuary which ships enter from the China Sea. The estuary extends fifteen miles, and there is a river at the head of it. According to some who have seen the place the tide flows (at Zaitún). It is half-a-day from the sea, and the channel by which ships come up from the sea is of fresh water. It is smaller in size than Hamath[3], and has the remains of a wall which was destroyed by the Tartars. The people drink water from the channel and also from wells[4].

5° "KHANSÂ, *i.e.* Khânfû. According to some travellers Khânfû is at the present time the greatest port of China, and is that which is made by voyagers from our own country. According to some who have seen it, it is east and south of Zaitún, and is half-a-day from the sea. It is a very large city and lies in a temperate part of the earth. In the middle of the city are some four small hills. The people drink from wells. There are pleasant gardens about it. The mountains are more than two days distant from it.

[6° "SÎLA[5] or SÎLÂ is situated east at the top of China. Those who travel by sea do not often visit it. It is one of the islands of the Eastern Sea which is the counterpart of the Eternal and Fortunate Islands in the Western Sea; but these are cultivated and wealthy; it is the reverse with the islands of the Eastern Sea.

7° "JAMKÛT is the farthest inhabited eastern land; it is at the extreme eastern limit, just like the Eternal Islands which are

[1] Yanjû is evidently from name and position *Yang chau* (see Odoric, ii, p. 209; *Marco Polo*, ii, pp. 154 *seq.*). But it never was the capital of China. I do not know what *Kazku* is; but no doubt the name is corrupt. It is perhaps *Fuchau* in some form.

[2] ["Lorsqu'Abu'l-Fidā remarque que Zaitūn est identique à *Shindjū* (le *ū* de *ch'uān* semble se retrouver dans le son du *i*), il veut dire qu'on connaissait de son temps cette ville en occident sous son nom chinois (je pense que *Zaitūn* est une déformation de celui-ci: *zai* ou *zī* correspond à *ch'uān*, et *tūn* fut ajouté par jeu pour former un mot arabe connu de chaque musulman (Kur'ān, 95, 1)." (*Encyclop. de l'Islam*, *s.v. Chine*, par Martin Hartmann.)]

[3] Hamath was Abulfeda's own city. We may strongly doubt the accuracy of his information as to the comparative size of Zaitún.

[4] On Zaitún or Chin chan see note to Odoric, ii, p. 183, and to Ibn Batuta, Vol. iv. [M. Ferrand remarks that *Tze-tung* = زيتون, *zītūn* in Arabic, inexactly read *Zaytūn*, on account of its similitude with its homonym زيتون, *zaytūn*, olive. (*Relat. de Voy.*, i, p. 11.)]

[5] [During the first centuries of the Christian Era, Korea was divided into three kingdoms (*Sam kuk*): to the N. and N.E., Ko ku rye (Kau li); to the W., Paik tjyei (Pe tsi), and to the S.E. Sin ra (Sin la); in 660 Pe tsi, in 668 Kau li were divided between the T'ang and Sin ra. Kao li and Si la of Abulfeda are the Ko ku rye and Sin ra of Korea.]

stated to be at the extreme western limit. East of JAMKÛT, no habitable land is to be found. Persians call this country Jamâkûd. This country is on the equator and has no latitude.

8° "KHÂJÛ. A person who has seen Khâjû states that it is a great city, one of the capitals of China called *Sing*, and is fifteen days from Khân Bâliq. It is situated between Khaṭâ and Kao-li.

9° "SAUKJÛ. A person who visited it states that it is as great as Emese; that it is situated in a plain and is surrounded with small streams coming from a spring spouting out of the neighbouring mountains; that it has orchards; and finally, that it is four days from Qamjû[1].'']

NOTE XIV.

EXTRACT FROM THE HISTORY OF HAYTON THE ARMENIAN.

(Written in 1307.)

"*Of the Kingdom of Cathay.*

"The empire of Cathay is the greatest that you will find on the face of the earth, and it abounds with population, and has wealth without end. It is situated on the shore of the Ocean Sea. And there are in that quarter so many islands in the sea that there is no knowing their number. For no man is to be found in existence who shall venture to say that he hath seen all those islands. But such of them as are attainable are found to have an infinite store of riches.

"That which is reckoned well-nigh the most costly article that you can purchase in those parts is oil of olive, and when any such oil finds its way thither by any means the kings and nobles treasure it with the greatest care as if it were some princely salve.

"There are in that kingdom of Cathay more marvellous and singular things than in any other kingdom of the world. The people of the country are exceedingly full of shrewdness and sagacity, and hold in contempt the performances of other nations in every kind of art and science. They have indeed a saying to the effect that they alone see with two eyes, whilst the Latins see with one, and all other nations are blind! By this you may

1 ["Je remarque ici que les autres informations d'Abu'l-Fidā sur la Chine dénotent une certaine confusion; c'est ainsi qu'il confond Canton avec Hang-chou fou, car son 'al Khansā identique à Khānku (lisez Khānfū)' réunit les deux villes; il ne cite Khamdān et Khanbāliķ que dans les 'Notices,' et il n'a pas reconnu que son Khānkū (ii, 122–3) confond deux villes: le Khānbaliķ du nord (=Peking; voy. Ibn Batuta, ici) et le Canton du sud, le vrai Khānfu." (*Encycl. de l'Islam, s.v. Chine*, par Martin Hartmann.)]

easily gather that they look on all other nations as quite uncivilised in comparison with themselves. And in good sooth there is such a vast variety of articles of marvellous and unspeakable delicacy and elaboration of workmanship brought from those parts, that there is really no other people that can be compared with them in such matters.

"All the people of that empire are called Cathayans, but they have also other names according to the special nation to which they belong. You will find many among them, both men and women, who are very handsome, but as a general rule they have all small eyes, and nature gives them no beard. These Cathayans have a very elegant written character, which in beauty in some sort resembles the Latin letters. It were hard to enumerate all the sects of Gentiles in that empire, for there be some who worship idols of metal; others who worship oxen, because these plough the ground which produces wheat and the other fruits of the earth; others who worship great trees of different kinds; some who devote themselves to astronomy and the worship of nature; others who adore the sun or the moon; and others again who have neither creed nor laws but lead a mere animal life like brute beasts. And though these people have the acutest intelligence in all matters wherein material things are concerned, yet you shall never find among them any knowledge or perception of spiritual things.

"The people of that country are not courageous, but stand in greater fear of death than at all befits those who carry arms. Yet being full of caution and address they have almost always come off victorious over their enemies both by land and by sea. They have many kinds of arms which are not found among other people.

"The money which is current in those parts is made of paper in a square form, and sealed with the king's seal; and according to the marks which it bears this paper has a greater or less value. And if perchance it begins to wear from long usage the owner thereof shall carry it to a royal office, and they give him new paper in exchange. They do not use gold and other metals except for plate and other purposes of show.

"'Tis said of that empire of Cathay that it forms the eastern extremity of the world, and that no nation dwells beyond it. Towards the west it hath upon its frontier the kingdom of TARSE, and towards the north the Desert of BELGIAN, whilst towards the south it hath the Islands of the Sea, whereof we have spoken above."

FRENCH TEXT.

DU ROIAUME DE CATHAY.

Le roiaume de Cathay est tenu por le plus noble roiaume e por le plus riche qui soit eu monde, e est sur le rivage de la mer Occeane. Tantes isles y a de mer que l'om n'en poet bien savoir le nombre. La gent qui habitent en celui roiaume sunt apellez Cathaïns. E se trovent entre eaus meints beaus homes et fames, selonc luer nacion, mès touz ont les oils molt petiz, e ont poi de barbe. Cele gens ont letres qui de beautey resemblent à letres latines, e parlent une lengue qui molt est diverse des autres lengues du monde. La creance de ceste gent est molt diverse, car aucuns croient ès ydoles de metal, autres croient en le solail, autres en la lune, autres ès esteiles, autres ès natures, au feu, autres à l'éve, autres as arbres, autres as bues, por ce que laborent la terre dont il vivent; e aucuns ne ont point de loi, ne de creance, ains vivent come bestes. Cestes gens, qui tant sont simples en lur creance e ès choses espiriteus, sont plus sages e plus sotils que totes autres gens ès euvres corporels. E dient les Cataïns que il sont ceus qui voient de II oils, e des Latins disent q'il voient d'un oil, mès les autres nacions dient que sont avuegles. E por ce puet om entendre que il tienent les autres gens de gros entendement. E verraiement l'om voit venir de celui païs tantes choses estranges e merveilloses, e de sotil labour, que bien semblent estre la plus soutils gens du monde d'art e de labour de mains. Les homes de celui païs ne sont vigoros as armes, mès il sont molt sotils e engignous, dont sovent ont desconfit luer enamis par luer engins. E ont diverses manieres d'armes e d'engins, lesquels ne ont les autres nacions. En celui païs se despent monoie faite de papier en forme quarrée, signé du seignal du signor, e selonc ce que est signée vaut ou plus ou meins. E de cele monoie achatent e vendent toutes choses. E quant cele monoie enpire par veillesce ou autrement, celui qui l'aura la rendra à la cort du seignor, e em prenra de nueve. En celui païs l'oïle d'olive est tenue à molt chiere chose; e quant les rois e les seignors en poent trover, à grant chierté e por grant merveille le font garder. A ceste terre de Cathay, ne marchit nule terre, fors que le roiaume de Tarse, devers occident, car de toutes les autres parties le roiaume de Cathaï est environnés ou de desert ou de la mer Occeane." (Pages 121–2, *Recueil des Historiens des Croisades, Documents Arméniens*, II.—*Doc. latins et français relatifs à l'Arménie*, Paris, 1906, fol.)

This is the original text; the Latin text has been revised and added to.

LATIN TEXT.

DE REGNO CATAY.

Regnum Cathay est majus regnum quod in orbe valeat inveniri et est repletum gentibus et diviciis infinitis et in maris Occeani littore habet situm. Tot enim sunt ibidem maris insule quod numerus nullatenus potest sciri. Nam nullus penitus invenitur qui omnes illas insulas asserat se vidisse. Ille vero insule que calcari possunt inveniuntur innumerabilibus divitiis habundantes, et illud fere quod in illis partibus carius emitur et habetur est oleum olivarum, quoniam reges et magnates illud, quando modo aliquo reperitur, quasi precipuum medicamen cum magna diligentia faciunt custodiri. In ipso eciam regno Cathaï plura sunt mirabilia monstruosa quam in aliquo alio regno mundi. Homines vero illius patrie sunt sagacissimi et omni calliditate repleti et ideo in omni arte et scientia vilipendunt alias nationes et dicunt quod ipsi soli sunt qui duobus oculis respiciunt, Latini vero uno lumine tantum vident, sed omnes alias naciones asserunt esse cecas, et per hoc certissime demonstratur quod omnes alios reputant esse rudes. Et vere tot res diverse et mirabiles et ineffabilis subtilitatis et laboris manuum ex illis partibus deferuntur, quod non videtur esse aliquis qui in talibus eis valeat comparari. Omnes illi de illo regno Catayni vocantur et juxta naciones suas multi tam homines quam femine reperiuntur pulcerrimi; tamen omnes communiter parvos habent oculos et naturaliter barba carent. Isti Catayni valde pulcras litteras habent, que latinis litteris in pulcritudine quodam modo similantur. Secta vero gentium illius regni vix posset modo aliquo enumerari, quoniam quidam sunt qui colunt ydola de metallo, alii vero boves adorant, quia laborant terram de qua crescunt frumenta et alia nutritiva, alii colunt magnas arbores et diversas, alii secuntur naturalia et [alii] astronomiam, alii adorant solem, alii vero lunam, alii quidem nullam habent fidem vel legem, sed sicut bruta animalia ducunt bestialiter vitam suam, et licet sint perspicacissimi ingenii ad omnia opera corporalia exercenda, nulla tamen inter eos spiritualium noticia sive sciencia invenitur. Homines illius patrie non sunt audaces, sed sunt mortis timidi plus satis quam armigeros esse decet. Multum tamen sunt cauti et ingeniosi et propterea tam per terram quam per mare victoriam de inimicis suis sepius reportarunt. Multa habent armorum genera que non inveniuntur inter alias naciones. Moneta vero que in illis partibus expenditur fit de papiro in forma quadrata et est regali signo signata; et secundum signum illa moneta est majoris precii vel minoris. Et si forte illa moneta propter vetustatem incipiat devastari, ille qui illam habuerit ad regalem curiam deportabit et pro illa dabitur sibi nova. De auro vero et aliis metallis vasa fiunt et alia ornamenta. De isto regno Catay dicitur quod est in principio mundi, in oriente ab uno capite, et ex parte illa nulla est ulterius habitatio gentium, et ex parte occidentis suos habet confines cum regno Tarse, et ex parte septemtrionis cum deserto de Belgian, et ex parte meridiei sunt insule maris superius nominate." (Pages 261–2, *Recueil des Histor. des Croisades, Documents Arméniens*, II.—*Doc. latins et français relatifs à l'Arménie*, Paris, 1906, fol.)

NOTE XIV BIS.

LETTER OF SEMPAD (1243).

A très haut et puissant houme monseigneur Henry [Henri de Lusignan], par la grace de Die roy de Chipre, et a sa chiere suer Enmeline la royne, et a noble houme Jehan de Hibelin son frere, li connoitables de Ermenie salut et amour. Sachiés que aussi comme je me esmui la ou vous savés pour Dieu et pour le profit de la foy crestienne, tout aussinc Nostres Sires ma conduit sain et sauf jusques a une ville que on appelle Sautequant; mout terres estranges ay veues en la voie. Ynde lessames derrier nous; par le royaume de Baudas passames, et meimes II. moys a passer toute la terre de ce royaume; moult de citez veimes que li Tartarin avoient gastees, desqueles nus ne pourroit dire la grandesse ne la richesse dont eles estoient plainnes. Nous veimes aucunes villes grans par lespasse de III. journees, et plus de C. monciaus[1] grans et mervellieus des os de ceus que li Tartarin avoient ocis et tués; et se la grace de Dieu neust amené les Tartarins pour ocirre les paiens, il eussent destruit, si comme nous pouons veoir, la terre toute deça la mer. Nous trespassames I. grant fleuve qui vient de paradis terrestre, ca non Gyon, duquel les arenes durent dune part et dautre par lespasse dune grant journee. Si sachiés que des Tartarins est si grant plentez, que il ne pueent estre nombrez par homme; il sont bon archier, et ont laides faces et diverses; ne je ne vous pourroie dire ne descrire la maniere dont il sont. Bien a passé VIII. moys que nous finames derrer par nuit, et encore ne soumes pas ou milieu de la terre Cham le grant roi des Tartarins. Si avons entendu pour certaine choze, que puisque Cham li roys des Tartarins, peres di celui Cham qui regne maintenant, fu trespassez, que li baron et les chevaliers des Tartarins qui estoient par divers lieus, mistrent bien par lespasse de V. ans a assambler pour couronner le roy Cham qui maintenant regne, et apainnes porent estre assamblé en I. lieu.

[1] Another MS has: "et plus de cent mille monceaus."

Aucuns de eulz estoient en Inde et en Chatha, et li autre en Roussie et en la terre de Cascat[1], qui est la terre dont li roy furent qui vindrent en Jherusalem aourer Nostre Seigneur ; et sont les gens de celle terre crestiens. Je fui en leur eglizes, et vi la figure de Jhesu Crist paint, comme li troy roy li offrirent or, mirre et encens. Par ces trois roys tindrent et orent prumierement cil de Tangat la foy crestienne, et par aulz sont maintenant Cham[2] li roys des Tartarins et sa gent. Devant leur portes sont les eglizes, la ou on sonne les cloches selonc les Latins, et tables selonc la maniere des Grieus ; et va on prumierement saluer Nostre Seigneur au matin, puis après Cham en son palais. Nous avons trouvé moult de crestiens dispers et espandus par la terre d'Orient, et moult de eglizes hautes et beles, anciennes, qui ont esté gastees par les Tartarins avant quil feussent crestien ; dont il est avené que li crestien d'Orient, qui estoient espandu par divers lieues, sont venu au roy Cham des Tartarins qui maintenant regne, et a painnes porent estre assamblé en un lieu, lesquels il a receu a grant honneur et leur a donné franchize, et fait crier partout que nulz ne soit si hardis qui les courouce, ne de fait, ne de paroles. Et pourceque Nostre Sires Jhesu Crist navoit en ces parties qui prestast pour lui son non, il meismes par ces saintes vertus que il a demonstré et preschié en tele maniere que les gens croient en lui. En la terre dInde que saint Thoumas converti a la foy crestienne, avoit I. roy crestien entre les autres Sarrasins, que li Sarrasin avoient moult de maus fays et de griés, juques a tant que Tartarin vindrent qui pristrent sa terre en leur main, et en fu leur hons [vassal] ; il assambla son ost avec lost des Tartarins, et entra en Inde contre les Sarrasins, et conquit tant que toute sa terre est plainne desclaves et de gens indes ; et de ces esclaves je vis plus de V. C. mil, que li roys commanda a vendre. Si sachiés que li papes a envoyé au roy Cham des Tartarins, messages pour savoir se il estoit crestiens, et pourquoy il avoit envoié sa gent pour ocirre et tuer les crestiens et le peuple. A ce respondi li roys Cham, que nostre Sires Diex avoit mandé à ses devanciers ayeulz et bezaieulz, quil envoiassent leur gens pour occirre et pour destruire les mauvaizes gens. Et a ce qui li papes li manda se il estoit crestiens, il respondi que ce savoit Diex ; et se li papes le vouloit savoir, se venit en sa terre et veit et seut comment il est des Tartarins. (*Recueil des Hist. des Gaules et de la France*, xx, Paris, 1840, *Guillaume de Nangis*, pp. 361–3.)

---

[1] Another MS has : " estoient en Ynde et en la terre de Chata, li autre en Roussie et en la terre de Chastac et de Tangat."

[2] Another MS : " Et par euls sont maintenant crestiens Cham."

NOTE XIV TER.

EXTRACTS REGARDING CATHAY, FROM THE NARRATIVE OF RUY GONZALEZ DE CLAVIJO, AMBASSADOR TO THE COURT OF TIMUR.

(1403–6.)

"The ambassadors were then taken to a room, on the right-hand side of the place where the lord sat; and the Meerzas, who held them by the arms, made them sit below an ambassador, whom the emperor Chayscan, lord of Cathay, had sent to Timour Beg to demand the yearly tribute which was formerly paid. When the lord saw the ambassadors seated below the ambassador from the lord of Cathay, he sent to order that they should sit above him, and he below them. As soon as they were seated, one of the Meerzas of the lord came and said to the ambassador of Cathay, that the lord had ordered that those who were ambassadors from the king of Spain, his son and friend, should sit above him; and that he who was the ambassador from a thief and a bad man, his enemy, should sit below them; and from that time, at the feasts and entertainments given by the lord, they always sat in that order. The Meerza then ordered the interpreter to tell the ambassadors what the lord had done for them.

"This emperor of Cathay is called Chuyscan, which means nine empires; but the Zagatays called him Taugas, which means 'pig emperor.' He is the lord of a great country, and Timour Beg used to pay him tribute, but he refuses to do so now." (Pp. 133–4.)

"The city [of Samarcand] is also very rich in merchandize which comes from other parts. Russia and Tartary send linen and skins; China sends silks, which are the best in the world, (more especially the satins), and musk, which is found in no other part of the world, rubies and diamonds, pearls and rhubarb, and many other things. The merchandize which comes from China is the best and most precious which comes to this city, and they say that the people of China are the most skilful workmen in the world. They say themselves that they have two eyes, the Franks one, and that the Moors are blind, so that they have the advantage of every other nation in the world. From India come spices, such as nutmegs, cloves, mace, cinnamon, ginger, and many others which do not reach Alexandria." (P. 171.)

"When the lord returned to the city [from the war against the Turk], the ambassadors from Cathay arrived, with others to say that the lord held that land, subject to the emperor of Cathay, and to demand the payment of tribute every year, as it was seven years since any had been paid. The lord answered that this was true, but that he would not pay it. This tribute had not been paid for nearly eight years, nor had the emperor of Cathay sent for it, and the reason why he did not send for it, was this.

"The emperor of Cathay died, leaving three sons, to whom he bequeathed his territories. The eldest son wished to take the shares of the other two. He killed the youngest, but the middle one fought with the eldest, and defeated him, and he, from despair at the consequences which he dreaded would follow his treatment of his youngest brother, set fire to his palace, and perished with many of his followers. The middle brother, therefore, reigned alone. As soon as he was quietly established in his own empire, he sent these ambassadors to Timour Beg, to demand the tribute which was formerly paid to his father, but we did not hear whether he resented the answer which was given by Timour.

"From Samarcand to the chief city of the empire of Cathay, called Cambalu, is a journey of six months, two of which are passed in crossing an uninhabited land, never visited by anyone but shepherds, who wander with their flocks, in search of pasture. In this year as many as eight hundred camels, laden with merchandize, came from Cambalu to this city of Samarcand, in the month of June. When Timour Beg heard what the ambassadors from Cathay had demanded, he ordered these camels to be detained, and we saw the men who came with the camels. They related wonderful things, concerning the great power of the lord of Cathay: we especially spoke to one of these men, who had been six months in the city of Cambalu, which he said was near the sea, and twenty times as large as Tabreez. The city of Cambalu is the largest in the world, because Tabreez is a good league in length, so that Cambalu must be twenty leagues in extent. He also said that the lord of Cathay had so vast an army that, when he collected troops to march beyond his own territory, not counting those who thus departed with him, four hundred thousand cavalry and more were left to guard the land; he added that it was the custom of this lord of Cathay not to allow any man to mount a horse, unless he had a thousand followers; and he told many other wonders concerning this city of Cambalu, and the land of Cathay.

"This emperor of Cathay used to be a gentile, but he was converted to the faith of the Christians.

* * * * * * * * * * *

"Fifteen days journey from the city of Samarcand, in the direction of China, there is a land inhabited by Amazons, and to this day they continue the custom of having no men with them, except at one time of the year; when they are permitted, by their leaders, to go with their daughters to the nearest settlements, and have communication with men, each taking the one who pleases her most, with whom they live, and eat, and drink, after which they return to their own land. If they bring forth daughters afterwards, they keep them; but they send the sons to their fathers. These women are subject to Timour Beg; they used to be under the emperor of Cathay, and they are Christians of the Greek Church. They are of the lineage of the Amazons who were at Troy, when it was destroyed by the Greeks." (Pp. 172–5, *Narrative of the Embassy of Ruy Gonzalez de Clavijo to the Court of Timour, at Samarcand,* A.D. 1403–6. Translated...by Clements R. Markham. London, Hakluyt Society, 1859, 8vo.)

NOTE XIV QUATER.

EXTRACTS FROM THE TRAVELS OF NICOLÒ CONTI (1438)[1].

"Beyond this province of Macinus is one which is superior to all others in the world, and is named Cathay. The lord of this country is called the Great Khan, which in the language of the inhabitants means emperor. The principal city is called Cambaleschia. It is built in the form of a quadrangle, and is twenty-eight miles in circumference. In the centre is a very handsome and strong fortress, in which is situated the King's palace. In each of the four angles there is constructed a circular fortress for defence, and the circuit of each of these is four miles. In these fortresses are deposited military arms of all sorts, and machines for war and the storming of cities. From the royal palace a vaulted wall extends through the city to each of the said four fortresses, by which, in the event of the people rising against the King, he can retire into the fortresses at his pleasure. Fifteen days distant from this city there is another, very large, called Nemptai, which has been built by this King. It is thirty miles in circumference, and more populous than the others. In these two cities, according to the statement of Nicolò, the houses and palaces and other ornaments are similar to those in Italy: the men, gentle and discreet, wise, and more wealthy than any that have been before mentioned.

"Afterwards he departed from Ava and proceeded towards the sea, and at the expiration of seventeen days he arrived at the

[1] The Travels of Nicolò Conti in the East, in the early part of the fifteenth century, as related by Poggio Bracciolini, in his work entitled "Historia de Varietate Fortunae," Lib. IV. (39 Pages in *India in the Fifteenth Century*...Edited, with an Introduction by R. H. Major... London, Hakluyt Society, 1857, 8vo.)

mouth of a moderately sized river, where there is a port called Xeythona; and having entered the river, at the end of ten days he arrived at a very populous city called Panconia, the circumference of which is twelve miles. He remained here for the space of four months. This is the only place in which vines are found, and here in very small quantity: for throughout all India there are no vines, neither is there any wine. And in this place they do not use the grape for the purpose of making wine. They have pine apples, oranges, chestnuts, melons, but small and green, white sandal wood, and camphor. The camphor is found within the tree, and if they do not sacrifice to the gods before they cut the bark, it disappears and is no more seen." (Pp. 14–15.)

NOTE XV.

EXTRACT FROM A LETTER OF PAOLO DAL POZZO TOSCANELLI TO FERNANDO MARTINEZ, CANON OF LISBON.

(Written 25th June, 1474.)

"And now to give you full information as to all those places which you so much desire to learn about, you must know that both the inhabitants and the visitors of all those islands are all traders, and that there are in those parts as great a multitude of ships and mariners and wares for sale, as in any part of the world, be the other what it may. And this is especially the case at a very noble port which is called ZAITÚN, where there load and discharge every year a hundred great pepper ships, besides a multitude of other vessels which take cargoes of other spices and the like[1]. The country in question is exceedingly populous, and there are in it many provinces and many kingdoms, and cities without number, all under the dominion of a certain sovereign who is called the Great Caan[2], a name which signifies the king of kings. The residence of this prince is chiefly in the province of CATHAY. His predecessors greatly desired to have intercourse and friendship with Christians, and some two hundred years since they sent

[1] Here Toscanelli is drawing from Marco Polo (i, ch. 81), as again below where he speaks of Quinsai.

[2] [The use of the title of Great Caan is no proof against the authenticity of the letter; though obsolete, since it disappeared with the Yuen Dynasty (1368), it was still in use among foreigners at the beginning of the sixteenth century to designate the sovereign of China. In a letter from Cochin, dated 15th November 1515, Giovanni da Empoli writes to Lopo Soares de Albergaria: "Spero...fare un salto là a vedere il Grand Cane che è il re, che si chiama il re de Cataio."]

ambassadors to the Pope, begging him to despatch a number of wise and learned teachers to instruct them in our faith. But on account of the hindrances which these ambassadors met with they turned back without reaching Rome. And in later times there came an ambassador to Pope Eugenius IV[1], who rehearsed to him the great friendship that those princes and their people bore towards Christians. And I myself discoursed at length with this ambassador on many subjects, as of the greatness of their royal buildings, and of the vastness of their rivers in length and breadth. And he told me many things that were wonderful as to the multitudes of cities and towns which are built on the banks of those rivers; as that upon one river alone are to be found two hundred cities, all of which have their marble bridges of great width and length, and adorned with a profusion of marble columns. The country indeed is as fine a country as has ever been discovered; and not only may one have great gain, and get many valuable wares by trading thither, but also they have gold and silver and precious stones, and great abundance of all kinds of spices such as are never brought into our part of the world. And it is a fact that they have many men of great acquirements in philosophy and astrology, and other persons of great knowledge in all the arts, and of the greatest capacity who are employed in the administration of that great territory, and in directing the ordering of battle.

"From the city of Lisbon going right to the westward there are in the map which I have mentioned twenty-six spaces, each containing two hundred and fifty miles, to the great and very noble city of QUINSAI, which has a circuit of one hundred miles or thirty-five leagues[2]."

---

[1] 1431–1447. [I believe that the story of the ambassador sent to Pope Eugenius IV is but a reminiscence of the arrival of Nicolò Conti; the embassies sent southward by the third Ming Emperor never came to Europe.]

[2] [The authenticity of Toscanelli's letter to F. Martins has been attacked by Henry Vignaud in *La Lettre et la Carte de Toscanelli sur la route des Indes par l'Ouest*. . . Paris, 1901, 8vo. A bibliography of the controversy that followed the publication of this book has been written by Vignaud and translated into Italian by G. Uzielli, Napoli, 1905. Cf. H. Cordier's *Bibliotheca Sinica*, col. 2054–7. I do not think this is the place to give the arguments against or in favour of the thesis of Mr. Vignaud, whose case is very strong in my opinion, in spite of the weakness of some of the arguments: for instance the use of the title Great Khan by the writer of the letter.]

NOTE XVI.

EXTRACTS REGARDING CATHAY FROM THE NARRATIVE OF SIGNOR JOSAFA BARBARO.

(Written about 1480, but the information acquired about 1436.)

"And in this same province of Zagatai is the very great and populous city of SANMARCANT, through which all those of CHINI and MACHINI pass to and fro, and also those of CATHAY, whether traders or travellers....I have not been further in this direction myself, but as I have heard it spoken of by many people, I will tell you that Chini and Machini are two very great provinces inhabited by idolaters. They are, in fact, the country in which they make plates and dishes of porcelain. And in those places there is great store of wares, especially of jewels and of fabrics of silk and other stuffs. And from those provinces you go on into that of Cathay, about which I will tell you what I learned from the Tartar's ambassador who arrived from those parts when I was at Tana. Being with him one day and our talk running on this Cathay, he told me that after passing the places that have been mentioned, as soon as he had entered the country of Cathay all his expenses were provided stage by stage until he arrived at a city called CAMBALU. And there he was honourably received, and had an apartment provided for him. And he said that all the merchants who go that way have their expenses provided in the same manner. He was then conducted to where the sovereign was, and when he came in front of the gate he was obliged to kneel down outside. The place was a level, very broad and long; and at the far end of it there was a stone pavement, on which the prince was seated on a chair with his back turned towards the gate. On the two sides there were four persons sitting with their faces towards the gate, and from the gate to the place where those four were there was on each side a row of mace bearers standing with silver sticks, leaving, as it were, a path between them, and all along this were interpreters sitting on their heels as the women do with us here. The ambassador accordingly having been brought to the gate, where he found things arranged as we have described, was desired to say what his object was. And so having delivered his message it was passed from hand to hand by the interpreters till the explanation reached the prince, or at least those four who sat at the top. Answer was then made that he was welcome, and that he might return to his quarters where the official reply would be delivered to him. And thus there was no more need for him to return to the prince, but only to confer with some of his people who were sent to the ambassador's house for the purpose; reference being made in this quarter or that, as occasion arose; and so the business was despatched in a very prompt and pleasant manner. One of the servants of this ambassador, and also a son of his, both of whom had been with him in Cathay, told me wonderful things of the justice that was done there....And they said that not only in the city but anywhere outside of it where travellers pass, if anything should be found under a stone or elsewhere that a traveller has dropt, no one would dare to take it up and appropriate it. And, moreover, if one going along the road is asked by some one whom he regards with suspicion, or does not put much trust in, where he is going; and if he go and make complaint of this question, then the person who put it must give some good and lawful reason for asking, otherwise he will be punished. And so you may easily perceive that this is a city of liberty and great justice.

"As regards the disposal of merchandise, I have heard that all the merchants who arrive in those parts carry their goods to certain *fonteghi*, and those whose duty it is then go and see them, and if there is anything that the sovereign would like to have they take it at their option, giving in exchange articles of greater value. The rest remains at the disposal of the merchant. For small dealings there they use money of paper, which is exchanged every year for other paper freshly stamped; the old money being taken at the new year to the mint, where the owners receive an equal amount of fine new paper, paying always a fee of two per cent. in good silver money, and the old (paper) money is thrown into the fire. Their silver is sold by weight, but they have also some metal coinage of a coarse description.

"I am of opinion that the religion of these Cathayans is paganism, although many people of Zagatai and other nations who have been there assert that they are Christians. And when I asked on what ground they judged them to be Christians, the answer was that they had images in their temples as we have. And it having chanced once when I was at Tana, and the ambassador aforesaid was standing with me, that there passed in front of us one Nicolas Diedo, an old Venetian of ours, who sometimes used to wear a coat of cloth quilted with taffetas, and with open sleeves (as used to be the fashion in Venice) over a jerkin of leather, with a hood on the back, and a straw hat on his head that might be worth four sous, as soon as the ambassador saw him he said with some surprise, 'That's the very dress that the Cathay people wear; they must be of the same religion with you, for they dress just like you!'

"In the country of which we are speaking there is no wine grown, for 'tis a mighty cold country, but of other necessaries of life they have good store." Ramusio, ii, f. 106 *v.* and 107.

NOTE XVII.

THE EMBASSY SENT BY SHÁH RUKH TO THE COURT OF CHINA.

A.D. 1419–1422.

Abstracted from Quatremère's Translation in NOTICES ET EXTRAITS xiv, Pt. 1, pp. 387 *et seq.; with Notes*[1].

The embassy embraced representatives not only of Sháh Rukh himself but of several princes of his family governing different provinces of the empire founded by Timur, and appears also, like the ordinary sham embassies which frequented China under the Ming dynasty, to have been accompanied by merchants bound on purely commercial objects. Shádi Khwája was the chief of Sháh Rukh's ambassadors, and Ghaiassuddin Nakkásh ("The Painter"), one of the envoys (sent by one of the king's sons, Mirza Baisangar), was the author of the narrative which has been preserved by Abdurrazzák; his master having enjoined on him to keep a full diary of everything worthy of note.

The party left Herat, the capital of Sháh Rukh, on the 16th of Dhu'lqādah A.H. 822 (4th December 1419[2]), and proceeded via Balkh to Samarkand[3]. The envoys [Sultán Sháh and Muhammad Bakhshi] of Mirzá Olugh Beg (the astronomer, and eldest son of Sháh Rukh), who governed there, had already started[4], but those

[1] [Cf. An Embassy to Khatá or China A.D. 1419. From the Appendix to the Rouzat-al-Ssafâ of Muhammad Khâvend Shâh or Mirkhond. Translated from the Persian by Edward Rehatsek. (*Indian Antiquary*, March 1873, pp. 75–83.)

This is the beginning of this translation: "In the year 820 (A.D. 1419), the pious defunct well-known king Mirzá Sháh Rokh sent an embassy to Khatá under the leadership and direction of Shády Khájah, who was accompanied by the royal prince Mirzá Báysangar Sultán Ahmad, and Khájah Ghayáth-ul-din, the painter, who was a clever artist; he ordered the first-mentioned Khájah that notes in writing should be taken, from the day of their starting from the capital of Herât till the day of their return, concerning everything they might experience; such as the adventures they should meet, the state of the roads, the laws of the countries, positions of towns, the state of buildings, the manners of kings, and other things of this kind, without adding or omitting anything.

"Khájah Ghayáth-ul-din obeyed the above orders, and, having consigned everything he saw to his itinerary, presented it on his return: the following account of the strange and wonderful events the envoys met with, and all they saw, has been extracted from his diary; but the responsibility rests with the travellers."]

[2] [3rd Dec., Rehatsek.]

[3] ["Arrived on the 9th Dhulhejjah (Dec. 27th) in Balkh, where they remained, on account of the great falling [of snow ?] and the severe cold, till the beginning of Muharram of 823, and arrived on the 22nd of that month (Feb. 7th) in Samarqand." Rehatsek.]

[4] A place called Sairam appears in some of our modern maps about one degree north of Tashkand. The Sairam of those days must, how-

deputed by other princes joined the mission here, and the whole party left Samarkand on the 10th Safar 823 (25th February 1420).

Passing by TASHKAND, SAIRAM, and ASHPARAH[1], they entered the Mongol territory on the 25th April, and were soon afterwards met by the venerable Amir Khudaidád (see *infra*, IV, Ibn Batuta, Goës). We cannot trace with certainty their course to YULDUZ, but it probably lay by the Issikul and the Ili River, crossing the T'ien Shan N.W. of YULDUZ[2].

From Yulduz they proceeded to TURFAN [arrived 11th July] (see *infra*, Vol. IV, Goës) where the people were mostly Buddhists, and had a great temple with a figure of Sakya Muni[3]. From Turfan [left 13th July] they reached KARAKHOJA [arrived 16th July] (*infra*, Vol. III) and five days beyond this they were met by Chinese officials, who took down the names of the envoys and the number of their suite. Seven days later they reached the town of ATASUFI (a name which does not seem to occur elsewhere), and in

ever, have been further east, for Húlakú on his march to Persia reached Sairam, the second day after passing TALAS. Rashid also speaks of *Kari-Sairam* near Talas as an ancient city of vast size, said to be a day's journey from one end to the other, and to have forty gates. (*Not. et Ex.*, xiii, 224.)

[1] Asparah was a place on the Mongol frontier, frequently mentioned in the wars of Timur's time. Its position does not seem to be known, but it certainly lay east of Talas, not far from Lake Issik Kul. It is perhaps the *Equius* of Rubruquis, a place that has been the subject of great difference of opinion. The idea that its odd name is the translation of *some* Persian word beginning with *Asp* (a horse), is due to Mr. Cooley in *Maritime and Inland Discovery*. There is another Asparah or Asfarah south of the Sihun, with which this is not to be confounded. (Rémusat, *Nouv. Mélanges*, i, 171 *seqq.*; *Not. et Extraits*, xii, 224, 228; *Hist. Univ.* (*Moderne*), iv, 139, 141; *Arabshah*, i, 219.) Some remarks on the topography of Rubruquis, including the position of Equius, will be found at the end of this paper [See note, p. 287.]

[" Having passed through Táshkant and Byrám, they entered among the A'yl of the Mughuls, and when they arrived the news came that A'wys Khán had attacked Shir Muhammad Oghllan, and that on that account disturbances had arisen among the A'lós, but that afterwards peace had been restored...On the 18th of Jomády the first (May 31st), they arrived in a place called Săluyú subject to the jurisdiction of Muhammad Beg....They started from that place on the 22nd (June 4th), and crossing the river Langar... ; and on the 28th of the same month (10th June) they entered the Jalgáh of Yaldúz and the A'yl of Shir Behrám, and in that desert they found solid ice of the thickness of two fingers, although the sun was in the sign of Cancer." Rehatsek.]

[2] The only places named between Asparah and Yulduz are *Bilugtu* and the river *Kankar* or Kangar; and they passed the latter five days before reaching the Yulduz territory, whilst in that journey they traversed a desert region so cold that water froze two inches thick, though it was nearly midsummer. The Kangar from these indications would seem to have been the Tekes or one of its branches; perhaps the *Kungis*. The cold region must have occurred in the passage of the T'ien Shan.

[3] [" They found that in that country most of the inhabitants were polytheists, and had large idol-houses, in the halls whereof they kept a tall idol." Rehatsek.]

two marches more KAMUL (*infra*, III, p. 265, IV, Goës), where they found a magnificent mosque and convent of Derwishes in juxtaposition with a fine Buddhist temple[1]. The envoy notes that at the gate of the latter were figures of two demons which seemed preparing to fly at one another; a correct enough description of the figures commonly called *warders* which are often found in pairs facing one another in the approaches to temples in Burma and other Buddhist countries.

Twenty-five days were then occupied in crossing the Great Desert. In the middle of the passage they fell in with a wild camel and a *Kutás*, or wild Yak[2].

On arriving [24th August] near the frontier of China Proper, Chinese officers again came to meet them, and one march further on they found a platform with awnings erected in the desert, and an elegant repast set out for them, such as many cities would have found it difficult to furnish. Provisions of all sorts were also supplied to every member of the party, with many polite forms. The envoys were then called on to subscribe a document declaring the number of persons in their service, and the *Dájís*[3] had to make affidavit that nothing but truth was stated. The merchants who had accompanied the embassy were counted among the servants, and to give a colour to this they employed themselves in waiting on the ambassadors. There were five hundred and ten souls in the party, without counting Mirzá Olugh Beg's envoys who had gone on before, and those of Mirzá Ibrahim Sultán not yet arrived.

On Aug. 26th they were invited to a feast of royal magnificence at the camp of the *Dangchi*[4] [*dangdji*] commanding on the frontier[5]. The envoys took their places at the left hand of the Dangchi, that being the position of honour in Cathay, "because the heart is on the left side." Before each of the envoys two tables were placed, on one of which were various dishes of meat and poultry

[1] ["Amir Fakhar-ul-din had built a high, very costly, and ornamented mosque, but near it the polytheists had constructed a large and a small temple with wonderful pictures." Rehatsek.]

[2] ["After leaving Qáyl, they travelled 25 stages, and obtained water every alternate day; and on the 12th (August 22nd) they met in that boundless desert a lion (which statement is however contrary to the assertion that none exist on the frontiers of Khatá) which had a horn on its head." Rehatsek.]

[3] It is not explained who the *Dájís* were, but the word seems to be a Tartar form of the Chinese *Ta jin*, "great man," a title still applied to certain officers on the Tartar frontiers. They must have been Chinese officials who had joined the mission party at an earlier date. [*Ta Jen* is the title applied to Chinese mandarins from the highest to the *Tao t'ai* included.]

[4] [Ankjy.—Rehatsek.]

[5] This perhaps represents the Chinese *Tsiang-shi*, a general. Pauthier however, I see, says it is in Chinese *Tangchi*, without further explanation (*M. Polo*, 166). [Possibly a *T'ung Che*, Sub-Prefect.]

and dried fruits ; on the other cake, excellent bread, and artificial bouquets made of paper and silk admirably wrought. The other guests had but one table apiece. Elevated before them there was a great royal drum, and in front of this a buffet on which were ranged flagons, cups, and goblets of silver and porcelain[1]. On either side of this was an elaborate orchestra, which played admirably. One of the great Chinese lords presented the cup to each guest in turn, and as he did so took a sprig from a basket of artificial flowers, and placed it in the other's cap, "so that the pavilion presented the appearance of a parterre of roses." Beautiful children also were in attendance carrying dishes filled with various relishes, such as filberts, jujubes, walnuts, pickles, etc., every kind being disposed on the plate in a separate compartment. When the amir presented the cup to any person of distinction one of these children also presented this plate that he might choose what pleased him. Dances were performed by young men in feminine costume[2], and by figures of animals made of pasteboard with men inside ; among others a perfect representation of a stork, which bobbed its head to the music, this way and that, to the admiration of the spectators. Altogether the first Chinese fête seems to have been regarded as a great success.

The following day [August 27th] they proceeded on their march through the desert. On their arrival at a strong castle called KARAUL[3], in a mountain defile, through the middle of which the road passed, the whole party was counted and their names registered before they were allowed to proceed. They then went

[1] See this feature in the receptions of the Turk and Tartar Khans, in the extracts from Menander (p. 209, *supra*, and note there).

[2] [" There were also handsome youths adorned like women with their faces painted red and white ; they wore earrings of pearls, and represented a theatrical performance." Rehatsek.]

[3] *Karául* [Qaráwul] means in Persian (probably of Turkish origin) a sentry, guard, or advanced post. The place here so designated is the fortified entrance of the Great Wall called *Kia-yü Kwan*, or Fort of the Jade-Gate, mentioned by Hiuen Tsang in the seventh century, and which was in the latter days of the Ming the actual limit of the Chinese power (see *supra*, p. 175).

[This is the first mention by a western writer of this line of defence built for the purpose " of closing the great Central-Asian trade route at a time when China had resumed its traditional attitude of seclusion from the barbarian West." (Stein, *Ruins of Desert Cathay*, ii, p. 282.) Stein writes (*l.c.*, p. 283) with regard to Sháh Rukh's ambassador's narrative : " An exactly similar account was given about 1560 by a Turkish Dervish to Gislen de Busbeck, Charles V's envoy at Constantinople. Starting from the Persian frontier, his caravan, after a fatiguing journey of many months, " came to a defile which forms, as it were, the barrier gate of Cathay. Here there was an inclosing chain of rugged and precipitous mountains, affording no passage except through a narrow strait in which a garrison was stationed on the king's part. There the question is put to the merchants, ' What they bring ? whence they come ? ' etc."]

on to SUKCHAU[1], where they were lodged in the great *Yam-Khaan* or Post-House, at the City Gate.

"Sukchau is a great city, with strong fortifications, in the form of a perfect square[2]. The bazars are without covering, and are fifty ells[3] in width, all kept well swept and watered. The people keep tame swine in their houses, and in the butchers' shops mutton and swine's flesh are hung up for sale side by side! In every street you see numerous edifices surmounted by handsome wooden spires, and with wooden battlements covered with lacquer of Cathay[4]. All along the rampart of the city, at intervals of twenty paces[5], you find towers with the tops roofed over. There are four gates, one in the middle of each of the four walls, so that one directly faces another, and as the streets are as straight as can be you would think in looking from one gate to the other that it is but a little way. And yet to go from the centre of the town to any one of the gates is really a considerable distance. Behind [over ?] each gate there is a two-storied pavilion with a high pitched roof in the Cathayan fashion, just such as you see in Mazanderan. Only in this latter province the walls are plastered with plain mud, whereas in Cathay they are covered with porcelain. In this city there are a variety of idol temples to be seen, some of which occupy a space of ten acres, and yet are kept as clean as possible. The area is paved with glazed tiles, which shine like polished marble."

From this time the party were supplied with everything by the Chinese authorities. They were lodged at the *Yams* or post-houses, of which there were ninety-nine between Sukchau and Khan baliq, and every night found not only provisions but servants, beds, night-clothes, etc., awaiting them[6]. At every *yam* they

[1] SUCHAU; see III, p. 126, IV, Goës, *infra*; also Hajji Mahomed in Note XVIII. [Bykjú.—Rehatsek.]

[2] A *square* is the typical form of royal fortified cities, both in China and in all the Indo-Chinese countries including Java. It is, I believe, a sacred Buddhist form.

[3] [50 statute cubits broad.—Rehatsek.]

[4] ["There are many bázars and thoroughfares, the latter being covered by extremely handsome pavilions with *Khatáy-Muqranus* (Domes)." Rehatsek.]

[5] Quatremère has "twenty feet," but this cannot be. The word is *Kadam*, which means sometimes a foot, sometimes a step or pace.

[6] ["Chaque *iam* se trouve situé vis-à-vis une ville ou un bourg; dans l'intervalle qui sépare les *iam* on compte plusieurs *kargou* et *kidifou*. On désigne par le mot *kargou* une maison qui s'élève à une hauteur de soixante *ghez*; deux hommes se tiennent constamment dans cet édifice; il est construit de manière que l'on peut apercevoir un autre *kargou*: lorsqu'il arrive un évènement, tel que l'approche d'une armée étrangère, aussitôt on allume du feu qui est aperçu de l'autre *kargou*, où l'on s'empresse d'en allumer un pareil. La chose a lieu de proche en proche, et, dans l'espace d'un jour et d'une nuit, une nouvelle est connue à une distance de trois mois de marches. Une

brought four hundred and fifty well caparisoned horses and donkeys for the use of the travellers, besides fifty or sixty vehicles. The description of these vehicles (*'Arábah*) is a little obscure, but they seem to have been palankins of some sort, and were carried by twelve men each. "The lads who have charge of the horses are called *Bá-fú* (*Má-fú*); those who look after the donkeys are called *Lú-fú*; and those attached to the vehicles are called *Chí-fú*. ...At every post-house the travellers were presented with sheep, geese, fowls, rice, flour, honey, *darásun*[1], arak, garlic, pickled onions and vegetables. At every city the ambassadors were invited to a banquet. The palace of the government is called *Duson*, and the banquet took place there." On these occasions there was always a vacant throne with a curtain hung before it, and a fine carpet spread in front. The Chinese officials and the ambassadors sat down upon this carpet whilst the rest of the company stood behind them in ranks, like Mahomedans at their public worship. A man standing beside the throne then proclaimed something in Chinese, and the mandarins proceeded to *Kotow* before the throne, in which the envoys were obliged to follow them.

The first city that they reached was KAMCHAU[2], nine yams from Suchau. The entertainment given by the Dangchi, whose seat was here, took place in Ramadhán [Sept. 20th], and the envoys were obliged to excuse themselves from eating. The Dangchi

dépêche arrive également sans interruption, car, d'un *kidi-fou* à l'autre, elle est transmise de main en main. On désigne par le mot *kidi-fou* une réunion de plusieurs individus placés dans une station, et dont voici les fonctions. Lorsqu'ils reçoivent une lettre ou une nouvelle, un d'entre eux, qui se tient tout prêt, part à l'instant, et porte la dépêche à un autre *kidi-fou*, et ainsi de suite, jusqu'à ce qu'elle parvienne au pied du trône impérial. D'un *kidi-fou* à un autre la distance est de 10 *mereh*; seize de ces mesures équivalent à une parasange. Les hommes qui occupent le *kargou*, et qui sont au nombre de dix, sont remplacés tous les dix jours, et, à l'arrivée des seconds, les premiers se retirent. Mais ceux qui occupent le *kidi-fou* y sont à demeure. Ils se construisent des maisons, et s'occupent de la culture et de l'ensemencement des terres." Quatremère, pp. 395–6.

With regard to *yams* and fire-signals, see Odoric, pp. 233–4 *n*. The use of fire-signals in China is very ancient. They are mentioned in the biography of Wu-ki, lord of Sin-ling, who died in B.C. 243; the day fire-signals were called *fung* and gave a good deal of smoke; the night fire-signals were called *sui* with a strong light; the soldiers of the western garrisons had to keep these signals lighted. Cf. Chavannes, *Documents chinois découverts par A. Stein*, p. xi.]

[1] The rice wine of the Chinese (*infra*, II, p. 199). Ysbrant Ides (quoted in Astley, iii, 567) says: "Their liquors are brandy, which they call *arakka*, and *tarasu*, a sort of wine they drink warm. This is a decoction of immature rice," etc. In Ssanang Ssetzen there is a legend telling how Chinghiz was sitting in his hall when a Jade cup of a delicious drink called *darassun* descended into his hand from the chimney, a token which was considered as a celestial recognition of his supremacy.

[2] KANCHAU, see III, p. 148, and IV, Benedict Goës, *infra*, and next note (XVIII).

took their excuses in good part, and sent all that had been prepared to their quarters.

"In this city of Kamchau[1] there is an idol temple five hundred cubits square. In the middle is an idol lying at length, which measures fifty paces. The sole of the foot is nine paces long, and the instep is twenty-one cubits in girth. Behind this image and overhead are other idols of a cubit (?) in height, besides figures of *Bakshis*[2] as large as life. The action of all is hit off so admirably that you would think they were alive. Against the wall also are other figures of perfect execution. The great sleeping idol has one hand under his head, and the other resting on his thigh. It is gilt all over and is known as *Shakamuni-fu*. The people of the country come in crowds to visit it, and bow to the very ground before this idol[3]....In the same city there is another temple held in great respect. At it you see a structure which the Mussulmans call the Celestial Sphere[4]. It has the form of an octagonal kiosque, and from top to bottom there are fifteen stories. Each story contains apartments decorated with lacquer in the Cathayan manner, with anterooms and verandas....Below the kiosque you see figures of demons which bear it on their shoulders[5]....It is entirely made of polished wood, and this again gilt so admirably that it seems to be of solid gold. There is a vault below it. An iron shaft fixed in the centre of the kiosque traverses it from bottom to top, and the lower end of this works in an iron plate, whilst the upper end bears on strong supports in the roof of the edifice which contains this pavilion. Thus a person in the vault can with a trifling exertion cause this great kiosque to revolve. All the carpenters, smiths, and painters in the world would learn something in their trades by coming here!"

1 [Kan chau is called Campichu by M. Polo. "Messer Maffeo and Messer Marco Polo dwelt a whole year in this city when on a mission." (*M. Polo*, i, p. 220.) It fell under the Tangut dominion in 1208. Polo, i, p. 219, says that "the Idolaters have many minsters and abbeys after their fashion. In these they have an enormous number of idols, both small and great, certain of the latter being a good ten paces in stature; some of them being of wood, others of clay, and others yet of stone. They are all highly polished, and then covered with gold. The great idols of which I speak lie at length. And around them there are other figures of considerable size, as if adoring and paying homage before them." See note, *l.c.*, p. 221.]

2 *I.e.*, Buddhist monks; see II, p. 250, and Ibn Batuta, *notes*.

3 This recumbent figure at Kanchau is mentioned also by Hajji Mahomed in Note XVIII. Such colossal sleeping figures, symbolising Sakya Muni in the state of *Nirwana*, are to be seen in Burma, Siam, and Ceylon to this day. Notices of them will be found in Tennent's *Ceylon*, ii, 597; *Mission to the Court of Ava* in 1855, p. 52; and Bowring's *Siam*. Hiuen Tsang speaks of one such in a convent at Bamian which was 1000 feet long! (*Vie de H. T.*, p. 70).

4 ["A sky-wheel." Rehatsek.]

5 The statement of the dimensions is corrupt and unintelligible.

All the baggage was deposited at Kanchau till their return, and the Chinese took over all the presents intended for the Emperor, with the exception of a lion sent by Mirzá Baisangar, which the athlete Salahuddin[1], the lion-keeper, retained charge of till they reached the capital.

Every day they halted at a *yam*, and every week they reached some city. On the 4th of Shawal, A.H. 823 (Oct. 12th, 1420), they were on the banks of the Karamuran, a river which in size might be classed with the Oxus. There was a bridge over it composed of twenty-three boats attached together by a chain as thick as a man's thigh, and this was moored on each side to an iron post as thick as a man's body, deeply planted in the ground[2]. On the other side of the river they found a great city with a splendid temple. This city was remarkable for the beauty of its women, insomuch that it was known as the City of Beauty (HUSNABAD)[3].

After thirty-seven days' journey they reached [Nov. 18th], we are told, another great river *twice* the size of the Oxus, and this they had to cross in boats (evidently the Hwang Ho again, where it divides the provinces of Shen si and Shan si); and twenty-three days later they reached a city which they call SADINFU, where there was a great idol of gilt bronze, fifty ells in height[4].

Eleven days after this (14th December) they arrived at the gates of Peking [Khan baliq] some time before dawn. The city had been recently re-occupied after the temporary transfer of the Court to Nan King, and the buildings were yet under reconstruction. The envoys were conducted straight to the palace, in an inner court of which they found a numerous assemblage of courtiers and officers waiting for the Emperor's appearance[5]. "Each held

[1] [Pehlván Ssulláh.—Rehatsek.]

[2] [These two iron posts were still in existence a few years ago and were seen by Prof. Pelliot.]

[3] They probably crossed the Karamuran or Hwang Ho opposite LAN CHAU, the present capital of the province of Kan Suh, and this is therefore most probably the Husnabad of the Persians.

[4] As they reached Peking in eleven days from Sadinfu, the latter city must be looked for about two thirds of the way between the Hwang Ho and the capital. Hereabouts we find the city of CH'ENG TING FU in Pe Che-li; and at that city accordingly, as the Chinese Imperial Geography tells us, there is a Buddhist temple called "the Monastery of the Great Fo," founded A.D. 586, which possesses a bronze statue of Buddha, seventy Chinese feet in height (*Chine Moderne*, p. 50).

[Rehatsek has "reaching Ssadyn-Qúr on the 27th of the same month (Dec. 3rd)." They had arrived near the river on the 11th Dhulqadah (Nov. 18th), *i.e.* sixteen days before, not twenty-three; in fact Quatremère like Rehatsek says they reached "Sadin-four" on the 27th of the same month.]

[5] ["They obtained sight of a very large and magnificent city entirely built of stone, but as the outer walls were still being built, a hundred thousand scaffoldings concealed them. When the ambassadors were taken from the tower, which was being constructed, to the city, they alighted near the entrance to the Emperor's palace, which was extremely

in his hand a tablet of a cubit in length and a quarter as much in breadth, on which he kept his eyes steadfastly fixed[1]. Behind these were troops in countless numbers, of spearmen and cuirassiers, a part of whom held drawn swords. All preserved the profoundest silence. You would have thought it an assembly of the dead." As "the Emperor came out of the women's apartments they set against the throne[2] a silver ladder of five steps, and placed a golden chair on the top of the throne. The Emperor mounted and took his seat upon this chair. He was a man of the middle height; his face neither very large nor very small, and not without some beard; indeed two or three hundred hairs of his beard were long enough to form three or four curls upon his chest. To right and left of the throne stood two young girls with faces like the moon, who had their hair drawn to a knot on the crown; their faces and necks were bare; they had large pearls in their ears; and they held paper and pen in their hands ready to take down the Emperor's orders. It is their duty to write down whatever falls from the Emperor's mouth. When he returns to the private apartments they submit this paper to him. Should he think proper to change any of the orders, a new document is executed, so that the members of his Council may have his mature decisions to follow.

"When the Emperor had taken his seat on the throne, and everybody was in place in the royal presence, they made the ambassadors come forward side by side with certain prisoners. The Emperor proceeded to examine the latter, who were some seven hundred in number. Some of them had a *doshákah* (or wooden yoke) on their necks; others had both necks and arms passed through a board; some five or ten were held together by one long piece of timber, through holes in which their heads protruded[3]. Each prisoner had a keeper by him who held him by the hair, waiting for the Emperor's sentence. Some were condemned to imprisonment, others to death. Throughout the Empire of Cathay no Amir or Governor has the right to put any person whatsoever to death. When a man has committed any crime the details of his guilt are written on a wooden board which is hung round the delinquent's neck, as well as a memorandum

large; up to this entrance they proceeded on foot by a pavement formed of cut-stone, about 700 paces in length. On coming close they saw five elephants standing on each side of the road with their trunks towards it; after passing between the trunks the ambassadors entered the palace, through a gate near which a crowd of about a hundred thousand men had assembled." Rehatsek.]

1 See allusion to these tablets by Odoric, *infra*, II, p. 237, and the note there.

2 By *throne* is to be understood an elevated ottoman or cushioned platform.

3 These are varieties of the portable pillory called by our travellers, after the Portuguese, *Cangue* [and by the Chinese *Kiă*].

indicating the punishment incurred according to the infidel law, and then with a wooden pillory on and a chain attached to him he is sent off to Khan baliq to the foot of the throne. Should he have a year's journey to get there still he must never be allowed to halt till he reaches the capital[1].

"At last the ambassadors were led in front of the throne and placed some fifteen ells from it. An Amir kneeling read a paper in the Cathayan language, stating all about the ambassadors to the following effect: 'Certain deputies, sent by his majesty Sháh Rukh and his sons, have come from a distant country with presents for the Emperor, and present themselves in order to strike the ground with their foreheads before him.' His worship Hajji Yusuf the Kazi, who was one of the Amirs of a tuman (or commandants of ten thousand) and one of the officers attached to the person of the Emperor, as well as chief of one of the twelve imperial councils, came forward accompanied by several Musulmans acquainted with the languages. They said to the ambassadors: 'First prostrate yourselves and then touch the ground three times with your heads.' Accordingly the envoys bent their heads, but without absolutely touching the ground; then raising both hands they presented the letters of his majesty Sháh Rukh, of his Highness Baisangar, and of the other princes and Amirs, each of which was folded in a piece of yellow satin. For it is a law among the people of Cathay that everything intended for the Emperor must be wrapt in a piece of some yellow stuff. His worship the Kazi advanced, took the letters, and handed them to an eunuch who stood before the throne; the eunuch carried them to the Emperor, who received them, opened them, and glanced at them, and then gave them back to the eunuch."

After some trivial questions the emperor remarked that they had had a long journey, and dismissed them to take some refreshments. After having done so in an adjoining court they were conducted to the Yamkhana or hostelry, where they found everything handsomely provided for them.

Next morning, *before daylight*, they were summoned by the officer called the *Sejnin* (or *Sekjin*)[2], who had charge of them, to get up and come in haste to the palace, as a banquet was to be

[1] This was no doubt a misunderstanding, but it is the Chinese law (not we may presume the practice, at least in troubled times) that every capital sentence must be confirmed by a special court at the capital, composed of members of the six great Boards of Administration and of three great Courts of Justice (see *Chine Moderne*, pp. 230, 256). The presentation of the ambassadors along with criminals for sentence was characteristic. In Burma, even the ambassadors of China are subjected to analogous slight. (See *Mission to Ava*, p. 76.)

[2] The former in Quatremère, the latter in Astley. The word is (Chin.) *Sse-jin*, "a Palace-man or Eunuch" (see *Journ. Asiat.*, s. iv, tom. ii, 435).

given them by the emperor; but this affords nothing of much interest.

"On the 17th of the month of Dhulhajja (23rd December, 1420), several criminals were sent to the place of execution. According to the practice among the infidels of Cathay, a formal record is made of the punishment inflicted for every crime, and they enter into very long details on this subject. But my pen refuses to expose particularly the (horrid) nature of these punishments. The people of Cathay in all that regards the treatment of criminals proceed with extreme caution. There are twelve courts of justice attached to the Emperor's administration; if an accused person has been found guilty before eleven of these, and the twelfth has not yet concurred in the condemnation, he may still have hopes of acquittal[1]. If a case requires a reference involving a six months' journey or even more, still as long as the matter is not perfectly clear the criminal is not put to death, but only kept in custody.

"The 27th day of Moharram His Worship the Kazi sent a message to the ambassadors: 'To-morrow is the New Year. The Emperor is going to visit his New Palace, and there is an order that none should wear white clothes' (for among these people white is the colour of mourning). The 28th, about midnight, the *Sekjin* arrived to conduct the ambassadors to the New Palace. This was a very lofty edifice which had only now been finished after nineteen years of work. This night in all the houses and shops there was such a lighting up of torches, candles, and lamps, that you would have thought the sun was risen already. That night the cold was much abated. Everybody was admitted into the New Palace, and the Emperor gave an entertainment to his great officers of state[2]....It would be impossible to give a just description of this edifice. From the gate of the hall of audience to the outer gate there is a distance of 1985[3] paces....To the right and left there is an uninterrupted succession of buildings, pavilions, and gardens. All the buildings are constructed of polished stone and glazed bricks of porcelain clay[4], which in lustre are quite like white marble. A space of two or three hundred cubits is paved with stones presenting not the very slightest deflexion or in-

[1] Here is doubtless some misapprehension. See preceding page.

[2] Astley's version has here a passage not found in Quatremère's: "They found at the palace one hundred thousand people who had come thither from all parts of Cathay, the countries of Tachin and Machin, Kalmak, Tibet, Kabul (read *Kamul*), Karakhoja, Jurga (*Churché?*), and the sea coasts." ["In that camp nearly one hundred thousand men from the countries of Chin, Khatá, Má-Chin, Qalmáq, Tibbet, and others had congregated." Rehatsek.]

[3] [1925 paces.—Rehatsek.]

[4] I suppose this meant by "bricks formed of Chinese earth." ["Stones and burnt bricks, the latter being made of China-earth." Rehatsek.]

equality, insomuch that you would think the joints had been ruled with a pen. In the arts of stone-polishing, cabinet-making, pottery, brick-making, there is nobody with us who can compare with the Chinese. If the cleverest of our workpeople were to see their performances they could not but acknowledge the superiority of these foreigners. Towards noon the banquet ended.

"On the 9th of Safar (13th February, 1421), in the morning, horses were sent for the ambassadors....Every year, according to a practice of theirs, the emperor passes several days without eating animal food, or entering his harem, or receiving anyone. He goes to a palace which contains no image or idol, and there, as he says, adores the God of Heaven. This was the day of his return, and he entered his harem again with immense pomp. Elephants walked in procession, handsomely caparisoned, and bearing on their backs a circular-gilded litter; then came flags of seven different colours, and men-at-arms, and then five more handsomely gilt litters carried by men on their shoulders. Musical instruments played the while in a manner of which it is impossible to give an idea. 50,000 men marched before and behind the emperor, keeping perfect step and cadence. Not a voice was heard; nothing but the sound of the music. As soon as the emperor had entered the harem everybody went away."

It was now the time of the Feast of Lanterns, but it was stripped of its ordinary splendours, of which the ambassadors had heard much, because the astrologers had predicted that the palace would catch fire[1].

"The 8th of Rabbi First (13th March), the monarch having sent for Ahmed Sháh and Bakhshi Malik, gave them what is called a *sankish* or present. He gave Sultán Sháh eight *balish* of silver[2], thirty dresses of royal magnificence, a mule, twenty-four pieces of *kala'í*[3], two horses, one of them caparisoned, a hundred cane

[1] ["At that season the feast of lanterns takes place, when for seven nights and days in the interior of the Emperor's palace a wooden ball is suspended from which numberless chandeliers branch out, so that it appears to be a mountain of emeralds; thousands of lamps are suspended from cords, mice are prepared of naphtha, so that when a lamp is kindled the mouse runs along these ropes and lights every lamp it touches, so that in a single moment all the lamps from the top to the bottom of the ball are kindled. At that time the people light many lamps in their shops and houses, and do not condemn any one during those seven days [the courts of justice closed ?]. The Emperor makes presents and liberates prisoners. That year, however, the Khatáy astrologers had ascertained that the house of the Emperor would be in danger of conflagration, and on that account no orders for illumination had been issued; nevertheless the amirs met according to ancient custom, and the Emperor gave them a banquet and made them presents." Rehatsek.]

[2] See II, p. 196, and Ibn Batuta, *infra*, IV.

[3] Tin? Quatremère does not translate it. Astley has "under petticoats"!

arrows, five three-sided *kaibars*[1], in the Cathayan fashion, and five thousand *chao*[2]. Bakhshi Malik received a similar present, only he had one *balish* less. The wives of the ambassadors received no silver, but were presented with pieces of stuffs....

"The 1st day of the Latter Rabbi (5th April[3]), news was brought that the emperor was on his way back from the hunting field, and that they were expected to meet him. The ambassadors were out riding when the news came, and as he was to arrive next day they returned home at once. The blue *Shonghár* belonging to Sultán Ahmed was dead[4]. The *Sekjin* visited them, and said: 'Take care to start to-night in order that you may be ready to be presented to the emperor the first thing in the morning.' So they mounted in haste, and when they arrived at the post-house they found His Worship the Kazi looking very much put out. Asking what made him so out of spirits, he answered in a low tone: 'The emperor during the chase has been thrown by one of the horses sent by His Majesty Sháh Rukh, which he was riding. He is tremendously enraged at this mishap, and has ordered the ambassadors to be put in irons and sent off to the eastern provinces of Cathay.' The envoys, deeply disturbed at the intelligence, got on their horses again at morning prayer-time. By the time half the forenoon was past they had ridden some twenty *marrah*[5], and reached the camp where the emperor had spent the night. This occupied an area of some five hundred feet square, round which they had built that same night a wall of four feet in thickness and ten cubits high. Such walls, built of *pisé*, are erected in Cathay with extraordinary celerity. There

[1] Quivers?—[Five Khatáy girls.—Rehatsek.]

[2] Bank notes (see II, p. 196; III, p. 149).

[3] [25th March.—Rehatsek.]

[4] The *shonghár* was a species of falcon monopolised by eastern royalty, and was, I believe, that of which Marco Polo speaks as the gerfalcon, which bred on the shores of the Arctic Ocean. They were sent in tribute to the Great Khan by the chiefs of the Northern Tartar Tribes. In a passage of the narrative which has been omitted, the emperor had presented several to the envoys for their respective princes, adding the brusque observation that they brought him screws of horses and carried off his good *shonghárs*. Pétis de la Croix says of the *shonghár*: "'Tis a mark of homage which the *Russians* and Crim-Tartars are bound by the last treaty to send annually to the Porte." (*H. de Timur Bec*, ii, 75.)

[5] In a previous passage it is said that "every sixteen *marrah* make a *farsang*" (or nearly three miles and a half). Astley's version has *six* to a farsang. The former estimate reduces the distance ridden in half the forenoon to less than five miles. The word *marrah* is perhaps that which Clavijo called *molé*, but he applies it to Timur's leagues, "equal to two leagues of Castille" (p. 106). This last definition, however, corresponds with that which Ssanang Ssetzen gives of the *Bără*, probably the same word. This makes it 16,000 ells, which will be about six miles, taking the ell at two feet (see Schmidt, p. 5).

were two gates left in it, and at the foot of the wall there was a ditch from which the earth had been dug for it.... Inside there was a pavilion of yellow satin, and an awning adorned with gems. Each of these was some twenty-five cubits square, and was supported by four pillars. All round were other tents of yellow satin embroidered with gold.

"When the ambassadors had arrived within five hundred paces of the imperial camp, His Worship the Kazi told them to dismount and stop where they were till the emperor should appear, whilst he himself went on. As soon as the emperor had returned to camp and dismounted, the *Li-daji* and the *Ján-daji*[1] (who in the Cathayan tongue are called *Serai-id* and *Jik-fú*) came and stood before him. The emperor then discussed the question of arresting the ambassadors. The *Li-daji*, the *Ján-daji*, and His Worship Yusuf the Kazi bowed their foreheads to the ground, and said: 'The envoys are in no way to blame. Their princes send good horses as presents doubtless, when they can meet with such; but in any case these persons have no authority over their sovereigns. If your Majesty has the envoys cut in pieces it won't hurt their kings, but the name of the emperor will be evil spoken of. People will not fail to say that the Emperor of China has used violence to ambassadors contrary to all the rules of justice.' The emperor took these judicious remonstrances in good part. His Worship the Kazi came in great glee to tell this news to the ambassadors, saying: 'The Most High has shown his mercy to these foreigners.' The emperor having thus decided on a merciful course, the dishes which he had sent were placed before the envoys; but as they consisted of swine's flesh and mutton the Musulmans declined to partake of them. The emperor then started, mounted on a black horse with white points which had been sent as a present by Mirzá Olugh Beg, and which had housings of yellow brocaded with gold. Two grooms ran alongside, each holding by one of the stirrups, and these also were dressed in gold brocade of a royal magnificence. The emperor had on a red mantle brocaded with gold, to which was stitched a pocket of black satin in which the imperial beard was cased. Seven small covered palankins were borne after him on men's shoulders; these contained young ladies of the emperor's family. There was also a great palankin carried by seventy men. Right and left of the emperor, at the interval of a bow-shot, were columns of horsemen who kept exactly abreast of him. These lines extended as far as the eye could reach, and there was a space of twenty paces between their ranks. They marched in this way, keeping exact alignment, to the gates of the city. The emperor rode in the middle, accompanied by the *Dah-daji*, whilst the Kazi rode with the Li-daji and the Ján-daji. The Kazi coming forward, said to the ambassadors:

[1] [Lillájy and Jan Wájy.—Rehatsek.—LI TA JEN and JAN TA JEN?]

'Dismount and touch the ground with your heads'; and so they did. The emperor then desired them to mount again, which they did, and joined the procession. The monarch began to reproach them, saying to Shádi Khwája: 'When horses or other objects of value are sent as presents to kings, they should be of the best, if they are meant to strengthen the bonds of friendship. Here, I mounted for the chase yesterday one of the horses which you brought me, and the beast, being excessively old, came down with me. My hand is much hurt and has become black and blue. It is only by applying gold in great quantities that the pain has abated a little.' Shádi Khwája, to put the best face on the matter, answered: 'The fact is, this horse belonged to the Great Amir, Amir Timúr Kurkán. His Majesty Sháh Rukh in sending the animal to you intended to give you a testimony of his highest consideration; indeed, he thought that in your dominions this horse would be regarded as a very pearl of horses[1].' This account of the matter satisfied the emperor who then treated the ambassadors with kindness."

After this one of the emperor's favourite wives died, and also a fire, occasioned by lightning, took place in the new palace, so that, "contrary to what usually happens," the diarist observes, "the prediction of the astrologers was completely verified." These misfortunes made the old emperor quite ill, and it was from his son that the ambassadors received their dismissal. During the days that they remained at Peking after this they no longer received the usual supplies.

On their return journey, however, they met with all the same attentions as on their way to court. They followed the same road as before, and quitting Khan baliq on the middle of Jumadah first (about 18th May 1421), they reached the city of Bíkan[2] on the first day of Rajab (2nd July). Here they were splendidly fêted; and on the fifth of Shaban (3rd October[3]) they recrossed

[1] As the Great Amir was dead *sixteen years* before, this pearl of horses must indeed have been a venerable animal.

[2] [Bangán.—Rehatsek.] The dates indicate the position as about one-third of the way from the capital to the passage of the Hwang Ho at Lan chau. This and the name probably point to Ping yang fu in the province of Shan si, one of the most ancient capitals of China. It is the *Pian*-fu of Polo, who says of it—"moult est grant citez et de grant vaillance; en laquelle a marchans assez qui vivent d'art et de marchandize. Et si font soie en grant habondance." (Pauthier's *Polo*, p. 354.)

I find that in the identification of the three cities named on the journey through China (Husnabad, Sadinfu, and Bikan) M. Reinaud has anticipated me in every case; but as my identifications were arrived at independently on the grounds assigned, this is a strong confirmation of their correctness (see his Introduction to Abulfeda, pp. ccclxxxv–vii).

[3] [5th August.—Rehatsek.]

the Karamuran. Nineteen days later[1] they arrived at Kanchau and took up their servants and baggage which had been left there[2]. But they had to halt here two months on account of the disturbed state of the Mongol country; and they were again detained at Suchau, so that they did not pass the frontier fortress till some days after the middle of Moharram 825[3] (about 9th January 1422). Here the whole party were again mustered and registered by the Chinese officials. The troubles in Mongolia induced the ambassadors now to take the unfrequented southern route through the desert. They reached KHOTAN on the 30th May, and KASHGAR on the 5th July. From this they passed the mountains by the defile of ANDIJAN, *i.e.* by the Terek Dawan, and there separated; one party taking the road to Samarkand, the other "preferring the route of Badakhshan" travelled to HISSAR SHADUMAN[4], and thence reached BALKH on the 18th August. Finally on the 1st September 1422 they kissed the feet of his majesty Sháh Rukh at Herat, and related their adventures[5].

---

[1] *Nine* days according to the date in Quatremère (14th Shaban), but thus seems much too short. Astley has 24th. [24th Shăbăn, 24th August.—Rehatsek.]

[2] ["In this town they remained during seventy-five days, and leaving it on the first day of Dhulhejjah (Nov. 27th), they arrived on the 17th (Dec. 3rd) in the town of Bokjú, in which place the ambassador of Mirzá Ebráhim Sultán, who had arrived from Shyráz, and the envoy of Mirzá Rustum, who was coming from Essfahán, met the ambassadors of His Majesty Sháh Rokh, and asked them for information concerning the manners and customs of the Khatáys, which was given to them." Rehatsek.]

[3] [The 1st Muharram fell on the 26th Dec. 1421.—Rehatsek.]

[4] The expression in the text seems to show that Badakhshan was sometimes used in a much larger sense than is now attached to it. But this brief indication of the route followed by the ambassadors from Kashgar to Balkh is particularly interesting, because it precisely retraces Ptolemy's caravan route across Imaus, on the supposition that the Stone Tower was in the vicinity of Ush or Andiján (Andiján = The Stone Tower; Hissar Shaduman = Ascent to Hill Country of the Komedi; Balkh = Bactra). And this is certainly an argument in favour of Ritter's view, for the route from Kashgar via Tashbaliq and Wakhsh to Hissar would have been vastly more direct, and there must have been ample reason for not adopting it, even in the height of summer, as on this occasion (see *ante*, p. 191, *seq.*).

[5] ["After they had been searched and examined, they left Qáyl, and selected the road through Chúl on account of the insecurity of the highways, and arrived after much trouble on the 9th of Jomády the first (May 1st) in the town of Khotán, after leaving which they passed on the 6th Rajab (June 26th) through Káshgar, and on the 21st (July 11th) they passed over the heights of Andagán, where some of the ambassadors selected the road through Khorasán and others through Samarqand; in the beginning of Ramazan (Aug. 19th) they arrived in Balkh, and on the 10th of the same month (Aug. 28th) they reached the capital city Herát, where they were admitted to the honour of kissing the carpet of His prosperous Majesty the Khagán Sháh Rokh

(may God increase his fame); and were made happy thereby."—Rehatsek.]

["Après une vérification exacte, les ambassadeurs partirent de Karaoul le dix-neuvième jour de moharrem. La crainte de l'ennemi les décida à préférer la route du désert; le dix-huitième jour de rebi-awal, ils franchirent, avec de grandes fatigues, ces chemins non frayés et dépourvus d'eau; le neuvième jour de djoumada second, ils arrivèrent à la ville de Khoten; ils en partirent, et, le seizième jour de redjeb, ils atteignirent Kaschgar; le vingt et unième jour du même mois, ils traversèrent le défilé d'Andegan. De là, une partie des ambassadeurs prit le chemin des Samarykand; les autres, ayant préféré la route de Badakhschan, arrivèrent, bien portants et joyeux, à Hisar-shaduman, le vingt et unième jour de Schaban. Ayant traversé le fleuve Amouïeh, ils arrivèrent à Balkh le premier jour de ramazan; de là, ils se dirigèrent vers Hérat. Le quinzième jour du même mois, ils furent admis à l'honneur de baiser les pieds de l'empereur Schah-rokh, et exposèrent à ce prince les détails de leur voyage." Quatremère, pp. 425–6.]

I will here insert some remarks on the topography of Rubruquis's travels, in connexion with the site of *Equius*, which I suppose to be the *Asparah* of these ambassadors (*supra*, p. 272).

Rubruquis, riding with Tartars and relays of horses, set out from the Volga on the 16th September 1253. The route lay straight east, or nearly so, through the country of the *Kangli* till the 31st October. They then bore a good deal south, passing through certain Alps (mountain pastures ?). On the 7th November they entered a plain irrigated like a garden, through which a large river flowed which entered no sea, but after forming swamps was absorbed by the earth. It flowed from very high mountains which were seen towards the south (east).

On the 8th November they entered the city of KENCHAC. They went from this *east* towards the mountains, and got among the mountain pastures, where the *Caracatai* formerly dwelt, a few days later. They found there a great river which they had to cross in a boat; they then turned into a valley where there were old intrenchments of earth over which the plough had passed, and came to a good town called EQUIUS, where the Mahomedan inhabitants spoke Persian.

Next day they passed the "Alps," which were spurs from the great mountains to the south, and entered an extensive and beautiful plain, which was copiously irrigated by the streams from the mountains. The mountains in question were to the right of the travellers, and to the left, beyond the plain, was a sea or great lake of twenty-five days' journey in compass.

There had formerly been many cities in this plain but the Tartars had destroyed them. They found, however, one great town called CAILAC, where they halted for twelve days.

The country in which they now were was called ORGONUM; and here Rubruquis first met with Buddhist temples.

They quitted Cailac on the 30th November (hence they must have reached it on the 18th or 19th), and four days later (3rd December) they came upon the head of the great lake. There was a great island in the lake. The water was brackish, but drinkable. A valley opened upon the head of the lake from the south-east, and up this valley among the mountains was another lake. Through this gorge at times such furious gusts of wind blew that riders were apt to be blown into the lake.

Passing this valley they went north towards great mountains covered with snow.

From December 6th they greatly increased the length of their journeys, doing two days' journey in one. On December 12th they passed a horrible rocky defile, said to be haunted by demons, etc.

They then entered the plains of the Naiman country. After this they again ascended a hill country, tending northward. On December 26th they entered a great flat plain like the sea, and next day reached the camp of Mangu Khan, apparently not far from KARAKORUM.

Now the points on this journey which we may consider ascertained (besides its departure from the Volga somewhere near SARAI, and its termination near Karakorum) are two.

The first is the city of KENCHAC. This is known to have been one of the cities of the valley of the Talas, near the city so called. (See Quatremère in *Notices et Extraits*, xiii, 224–5–6.)

The other is the site of the great rushing wind. This is described in Carpini's narrative in very similar terms (see p. 751). It is also spoken of by the diarist of Hulaku's march; and in modern times by a Russian traveller Poutimsteff (quoted in Malte Brun, *Précis de la Géog. Universelle*, ix, p. 208). These three latter accounts point, and the last indeed, which is singularly coincident with Carpini's, distinctly refers the scene of this phenomenon, to the lake called *Ala-kul*. Rubruquis had specified the island in the lake; Carpini says "several islands"; Poutimsteff says it contains "three great rocks of different colours," with which he connects its name. We now go back to trace the route of Rubruquis.

After riding for six weeks east, but not quite so *due* east as he imagines, leaving the Caspian and Aral on the right, about long. 67° he strikes south-east, crosses the "Alps" of the *Kara-tau* to the south-east of the modern town of Turkestan (in the medieval map south-east of Otrar) and enters the valley of the Talas, the river which, as he says, loses itself in swamps and enters no sea. Here he has to the south-east very lofty mountains, the branches of the T'ien Shan, or perhaps the great range itself.

Quitting Kenchak and the Talas, he goes east into the "Alps" that separate the Upper Talas from the Chu; the Chu is the river crossed in a boat. Beyond this is the valley with the remains of old intrenchments. These are noticed also by the Diarist of Hulaku's march. Four days before reaching Talas, this writer says, "they passed between the two mountains *Itu* (qu. the two parallel ranges called Ala-tagh?). The country is flat, well peopled and well watered; and there are many old ramparts and military structures, for it was formerly occupied by the *Khitan*" (the *Caracatai* of Rubruquis, see *infra*, III, p. 19). "Near this is a river called *Yi-yun*, very rapid, flowing from the east; the people of the country call it the Yellow river" (as to the muddy colour and great rapidity of the Chu, see *Russians in Central Asia*, p. 262).

Rubruquis then reaches *Equius*, or as I have supposed the *Asparah* of the Mahomedan writers, and we must therefore locate this north of the Chu, somewhere opposite the modern Russian posts of Pishpek or Tokmak.

[Rockhill, *Rubruck*, writes, p. 139 *n.*: "The identification of Rubruck's 'great river' with the Ili obliges us to reject Yule's identification of Equius with the *Aspareh* of Shah Rokh's mission, which was on the Chu, somewhere near the present Pishpek, or Tokmak."]

They then cross the "Alps" again; this time the branch of the Ala-Tau between Pishpek and Almaty, and emerge on the great plain stretching to the Balkash. It is true that towards the lake this is a barren steppe, but the tract along the spurs of the Northern Ala-Tau, which bounded the plain to the right of the traveller as he describes, is rich arable land, amply irrigated (see Semenov in *Petermann's Mittheilungen* for 1858, pp. 352–3).

Somewhere at the foot of those hills was CAILAC, doubtless the KAYALIQ of the historians of the Mongols. It must have been some distance north of the Ili, for the traveller reaches the Alakul from Cailac in four days. It may be placed near the modern Russian station of Kopal.

That it was not *on* the Ili, but some distance beyond it, is in some degree confirmed by the circumstance that, though a place of importance, it is not mentioned in the route either of Hulaku or of King Hethum, both of whom seem to have come down the Ili valley from ALMALIQ (near modern Kulja) and then passed to Talas by the route by which Rubruquis had come.

In Benedict Goës *infra* are quoted some passages relating, or supposed to relate, to Kayaliq or Cailac. Another may be cited as slightly favourable to the site indicated. We are told that Batu was on his way from his domain on the Volga to Karakorum, when "at the mountain Aladagh, seven days march from Kayaliq, he heard of the death of the Kaan" (*Kuyuk*), and turned back. Supposing this to be the Alatagh pass between the Chu and the Ili the distance would be appropriate to our position (see *D'Ohsson*, ii, 246).

The name *Orgonum*, which Rubruquis heard applied to the country, I have endeavoured to elucidate in the notes to Ibn Batuta.

It will be observed that Rubruquis, coming upon the Alakul, regarded it as the continuation and termination of the great lake which had occupied the distant horizon on his left for a good many days, an error which the map alone renders very conceivable to us, and which may then have had still more excuse, as all those lakes appear to be contracting. Indeed there seems to be no doubt that the Balkash and Alakul were formerly actually one, though they may not have been so in the days of Rubruquis. (See Semenov as above, p. 351; and in *J. R. G. S.*, xxxv, p. 213; also *Petermann* for 1863, p. 392.)

From the Alakul the mountains crossed to the north were apparently those above Tarbagatai. From this the route probably lay along the Upper Irtish and then along the Jabkan river.

On the return journey in summer Rubruquis passed to the *north* of the Balkash. The only part common to the two journeys was, he says, a fifteen days' ride along a river among mountains, where there was no grass except on the banks. This would seem to have been the Jabkan.

I discern no real difficulty in the foregoing interpretation of the traveller except one, viz., the scanty time allowed between Kenchak in the Talas valley and the head of the Alakul. This distance is about five hundred miles without deviations of course, and the time according to the data (deducting the twelve days' halt at Cailac) is fourteen days, giving an average of more than thirty-five miles (crow-flight) daily, and much of it through hilly ground. It is true that the traveller says that they rode daily as far as from Paris to Orleans, say sixty miles; but the measurement of his first long stretch from the Volga to Talas gives only about twenty-seven miles a day as the crow flies. If we can venture to suppose that the halt at Cailac was written vii days instead of xii, this would bring the marches between Talas and Alakul to about the same average.

The map in *Russians in Central Asia*, or some other embracing the recent Russian surveys, will be serviceable in following these remarks.

NOTE XVIII.

HAJJI MAHOMED'S ACCOUNT OF CATHAY, AS DELIVERED TO MESSER GIOV. BATTISTA RAMUSIO[1].

(Circa 1550.)

"In the thirty-eighth chapter of Messer Marco Polo's first book he treats of the rhubarb which is produced in the province of SUCCUIR, and is thence exported into these parts and all over the world. And it seems highly necessary that I should give a particular account of what I chanced to hear on this subject some years ago from a certain Persian of great judgment and intelligence; for the matter is well worthy of correct knowledge, seeing how universal the use of the article among sick people has become in our time, nor have I ever yet seen so much information regarding it in any book.

"The name of the narrator was Chaggi Memet, a native of the province of CHILAN on the shores of the Caspian Sea, and from a city called TABAS[2], and he had himself been to Succuir, coming afterwards, at the time I speak of, to Venice with a large quantity of the aforesaid rhubarb. Now it happened one day that I had gone out of town to dine at Murano; a relaxation of business allowed me to get away from the city, and to enjoy it all the more I chanced to have in my party that excellent architect Messer Michele San Michele of Verona, and Messer Tommaso Giunti, both very dear friends of mine, besides this Persian[3]. So when dinner was over and the cloth was drawn, he began his narrative, and it was interpreted as he went along by Messer Michele Mambre, a man of great acquirements in the Arabic, Persian, and Turkish tongues, and a person of most agreeable manners, whose accomplishments have now obtained him the position of Turkish interpreter to this illustrious Signory. First

[1] [G. Uzielli and Amat di S. Filippo (*Studi biografici e bibliografici*, II, Roma, 1882, p. 246) mention under the name of Hagi Ahmed the following map of the world kept in the Library of St Mark, at Venice: "Mappamondo a forma di cuore, sopra legno intagliato per la stampa, o carta impressa col medesimo. È redatto in lingua turca. Comprende il mondo conosciuto. Scala e proiezione fantastiche." Would it not be possible that this Hagi Ahmed and our Hajji Mahomed are but one person?]

[2] I have not been able to find any place of this name in Ghilan. But Tabas in the Salt Desert north of Yezd is called in the Tables of Nasiruddín *Tabas Kili* or *Gili*, and this may be meant (see in Hudson, vol. iii).

[3] Sanmichele of Verona, the still celebrated architect and engineer of the Venetian Republic, and often called (though wrongly) the inventor of modern bastioned fortification. Giunti, the printer and publisher of Ramusio's great work, and editor of it after the author's death.

he told us that he had been at SUCCUIR[1] and CAMPION[2], cities of the province of TANGATH, at the commencement of the states of the Great Can, whose name he said was Daimir Can[3], and by whom rulers were sent to govern the said cities, the same that M. Marco speaks of in the thirty-eighth and thirty-ninth chapters of his first book. They are the first cities of idolaters that are met with in going from the Musulman territories; and he went thither with the caravan that goes with merchandise from Persia and the countries about the Caspian to the regions of CATHAY. And this caravan is not allowed to enter further into the country than Succuir and Campion; nor may any merchant belonging to it, unless he go as an ambassador to the Great Can[4].

"This city of Succuir is large and extremely populous, with very handsome houses built of brick after the Italian manner; and in it there are many great temples with idols carved in stone. It is situated in a plain, through which run an infinite number of streamlets, and abounds in all sorts of necessaries. They grow silk there in very great quantities, using the black-mulberry tree for the purpose. They have no wine grown there, but for their drink they make a kind of beer with honey. As regards fruit, the country is a cold one, so they have none but pears, apples, apricots, and peaches, melons, and grapes. Then he told us that the rhubarb grows over all that province, but much the best is got in a certain neighbouring range of lofty and rocky mountains, where there are many springs, with woods of sundry kinds of trees growing to a great height, and soil of a red colour, which, owing to the frequent rains and the springs which run in all directions, is almost always in a sloppy state. As regards the appearance of the root and its leaves it so chanced that the said merchant had brought a little picture with him from the country which appeared to be drawn with great care and skill, so he took it from his pocket and showed it us, saying that here we had the true and natural representation of the rhubarb....He said moreover...that in the Lands of Cathay they never used the rhubarb

[1] *Succuir*, or rather *Succiur* (*i.e.* Sukchúr) as Polo seems to have written it, is according to Pauthier a Mongol pronunciation of *Suh-chau-lu*, the Circuit of Suhchau (*Polo*, p. 164). On Suhchau or Suchau see *supra*, p. 275, and references there. [See on Suhchau my note, Vol. III, p. 126.]

[2] *Campicion* in most copies of Polo; well identified with *Kanchau*, though the form of the name has not been satisfactorily explained.

[3] *Daiming Khan* is the name by which the Emperor of China is called in Abdur Razzak's History introducing the narrative abstracted in the preceding note. It is, in fact, the name of the native *Dynasty* (*Ta-Ming*, "Great Light") usually called the Ming, which reigned from 1368 to 1644 (see *Chine Ancienne*, p. 389; *Atlas Sinensis* in Blaeu, p. 1; *Notices et Extraits*, xiv, pt. i, pp. 213 *seq.*; Schmidt, pp. 153, 211, 289).

[4] See the narrative of Goës *passim*.

for medicine as we do, but pounded it up and compounded it with some other odoriferous ingredients to burn as a perfume before their idols. And in some other places it is so abundant that they constantly use it for fuel, whilst others give it to their sick horses, so little esteem have they for this root in those regions of Cathay. But they have a much greater appreciation of another little root which grows in the mountains of Succuir where the rhubarb grows, and which they call *Mambroni Cini*. This is extremely dear, and is used in most of their ailments, but especially where the eyes are affected. They grind it on a stone with rose-water, and anoint the eyes with it. The result is wonderfully beneficial. He did not believe that this root was imported into these parts, and he was not able to describe it[1]. Then seeing the great pleasure that I beyond the rest of the company took in his stories, he told me that over all the country of Cathay they made use of another plant, or rather of its leaves. This is called by those people *Chiai Catai*[2], and grows in the district of Cathay, which is called CACIANFU[3]. This is commonly used and much esteemed over all those countries. They take of that herb whether dry or fresh, and boil it well in water. One or two cups of this decoction taken on an empty stomach removes fever, head-ache, stomach-ache, pain in the side or in the joints, and it should be taken as hot as you can bear it. He said besides that it was good for no end of other ailments which he could not then remember, but gout was one of them. And if it happens that one feels incommoded in the stomach from having eaten too much, one has but to take a little of this decoction and in a short time all will be digested. And it is so highly valued and esteemed that every one going on a journey takes it with him, and those people would gladly give (as he expressed it) a sack of rhubarb for an ounce of *Chiai Catai*. And those people of Cathay do say that if in our

[1] *Mambroni Cini* is, I suppose, *Mámirán-i-Chíní*; the first word of which is explained by F. Johnson as "swallow-wort." Bernier also mentions *Mamiron* as a little root very good for eye ailments, which used to be brought with rhubarb to Kashmir by caravans from China (in *H. Gén. des Voyages*, tom. 37, p. 335). It is possibly the *Jinseng* or "Man-Root" (from its forked radish shape), so much prized by the Chinese as a tonic, etc., and which used to sell for three times its weight in silver. Another root, called by the Chinese *Foling*, comes from the rhubarb region in question, and was formerly well known in European pharmacy under the name *Radix China*. This, however, was not a "little root." [See *Mamiran* in *Hobson-Jobson*: *Curcuma longa*, *Mamira* of the old Arabs; *Thalictrum foliosum*, *Mamira* of Punjab.]

[2] (Pers.) *Chá-i-Khitai*, "Tea of China." Here and in some other words in this narrative the *ch* must be sounded soft, and not as usual in Italian. I do not know of any earlier mention of tea in an European book. [See *Hobson-Jobson*, s.v. *Tea*.]

[3] *Cachanfu* is probably Kanjanfu, *i.e.* Si ngan fu (see *infra*, II, p. 246). Tea would come to the frontier from that quarter, whether it *grows* there or not.

parts of the world, in Persia and the country of the Franks, people only knew of it there is no doubt that the merchants would cease altogether to buy *Ravend Cini* as they call rhubarb in those parts[1]....I asked him what route he had followed in returning from Campion and Succuir on his way to Constantinople, if he were able to tell it me. He answered by Mambre our interpreter that he would tell me the whole gladly. So he began by saying that he had not returned by precisely the same way that he had taken with the caravan in going, for at the time that he wanted to start it happened that those Tartar chiefs of the Green caps, whom they call *Iescilbas*, were sending an ambassador of theirs with a great company by way of the Desert of Tartary to the north of the Caspian Sea to the Grand Turk at Constantinople in order to make a league with him for a joint attack on their common enemy the *Soffi*....And so he travelled with them as far as CAFFA. But he would willingly detail to me the route as it would have been had he returned by the same that he followed in going. And it would stand thus: Leaving the city of Campion you come to GAUTA[2], which is a six days' journey. Every day's journey is reckoned at so many *farsenc*, and one Persian *farsenc* is three of our miles. And a day's journey may be taken at eight farsencs, but in case of deserts and mountains they will not do half as much, so days made in the desert must be reckoned at half ordinary journeys. From Gauta you come to Succuir in five days, and from Succuir to CAMUL[3] in fifteen. Here the Musulmans begin; all having been idolaters hitherto. From Camul to TURFON thirteen; and after Turfon you pass three cities, the first of which is CHIALIS, ten days, then CHUCHE ten more, and then AQSU twenty days[4]. From Aqsu to CASCAR is twenty days more of the wildest desert, the journey hitherto having been through inhabited country. From Cascar to SAMARCAND twenty-five days, from Samarcand to BOCHARA in CORASSAM, five; from Bochara to ERI[5], twenty; and thence you get to VEREMI in fifteen days[6]; then CASBIN in six, from Casbin to SOLTANIA in four, and from Soltania to the great city of TAURIS in six. Thus much I drew

[1] Pers. *Râwand-i-Chini*, "China Rhubarb."

[2] *Kao-t'ai*, between Kanchau and Suchau.

[3] *Supra*, p. 273, *infra*, III, p. 265, and Goës, Vol. IV.

[4] On these places see Goës, *infra*, Vol. IV.

[5] HERAT.

[6] VERAMIN was a great town two marches east of Tehràn, close to the site of ancient Rai, "to which it succeeded as Tehràn has succeeded to Veramin." (Ritter, viii, 450.) It is mentioned also by Clavijo, who on his return, after passing Damghan, Perescote (*Firuz-koh*), and Cenan (*Semnan*), "came to a great city called *Vatami*" (read VARAMI) "which was nearly depopulated and without any wall, and they call this land the Land of Rei." (Markham's *Clavijo*, p. 182; see also Pétis de la Croix, *H. de Timur Bec*, ii, 181, 401.)

from that Persian merchant. And the detail of his route was all the more interesting to me because I recognised with great satisfaction the names of many cities and of several provinces which are written in the first book of the travels of M. Marco Polo. And on that account it seemed to me in a measure necessary to give the statement here.

"It seems also expedient to add here a brief summary, which was drawn up for me by the said Chaggi Memet the Persian merchant before his departure from this city, giving some particulars regarding the city of Campion, and the people of those parts. And these I shall repeat for the benefit and advantage of all my gentle readers in few words and under various heads just as he set them down.

"The city of Campion. . . . The people here go dressed in cotton stuff of a black colour, which in winter the poor have lined with wolf-skins and sheep-skins, and the rich with costly sables and martens. They wear black caps coming to a point like sugar-loaves. The men are short rather than tall. They wear their beard as we do, and especially at a certain time of the year.

"Their houses are built after our fashion with brick and cut stone, two or three stories high, with ceilings painted in various colours and patterns. There are no end of painters there; and one street in the city is entirely occupied by painters.

"The princes of that country to exhibit their pomp and grandeur have a great platform made, over which are stretched two canopies of silk embroidered with gold and silver, and with many pearls and other gems; and on this they and their friends take their places, and forty or fifty slaves take up the whole and carry them about the city for recreation. Ordinary noblemen go about in a simple open litter without ornament carried by four to six men.

"Their temples are made after the fashion of our churches with columns from end to end; and they are enormous things, fit to hold four or five thousand people. There are also in that city two remarkable statues, one of a man, the other of a woman, each of them forty feet in length and represented extended on the ground[1]; each figure is of one solid piece, and they are gilt all over. There are first-rate sculptors in stone there.

"They get their blocks of stone sometimes from a distance of two or three months' journey, conveying them on carts that have some forty very high wheels with iron tires; and these shall be drawn by five or six hundred horses or mules.

"There are other statues of smaller size that have six or seven heads and ten hands, each hand grasping a different article, as if (for example) one should hold a serpent, a second a bird, a third a flower, and so on.

[1] See preceding note, p. 277.

"They have also certain monasteries where many men dwell leading the most holy life possible. For they have the doors of their chambers walled up so they can never get forth again as long as they live. People come every day with food for them.

"There are also no end of the same class who go about the town just like our friars.

"Their custom is, when anyone of their kin shall die, to wear white clothes for many days, that is to say of cotton cloth. Their clothes are made after the same fashion as ours, reaching to the ground, and with large sleeves like those of ours at Venice which we call *a gomedo*[1].

"They have the art of printing in that country, and their books are printed. And as I wanted to be clear on the point whether their manner of printing was the same as our own, I took the Persian one day to see the printing office of M. Thomaso Giunti at San Giuliano: and when he saw the tin types and the screwpresses with which they print, he said that they seemed to him to be very much like the other[2].

"Their city is fortified by a thick wall, filled with earth inside, so that four carriages can go abreast upon it. There are great towers on the walls and artillery planted as thickly as on the Grand Turk's. There is a great ditch which is dry, but can be filled with water at pleasure.

"They have a kind of oxen of great size, and which have long hair extremely fine and white[3].

"The Cathayan people and pagans generally are prohibited from leaving their native country and going about the world as traders.

"On the other side of the desert north of Corassam as far as Samarcand, the *Iescilbas* or people of the green caps have sway. Those Green-caps are a certain race of Mahomedan Tartars[4] who wear conical caps of green felt, and give themselves that name to distinguish themselves from the followers of the *Sofi*, their deadly enemies, who are the rulers of Persia, who are also Mahomedans and wear red caps[5]. And these Green-caps and Red-caps are continually at most cruel war with one another on account of

1 "Utrisque (viris et feminis) manicæ laxiores longioresque communes sunt, quales in Italiâ Venetorum esse solent." (Trigautius, b. i, c. 8.)

2 The Hajji's observation must have been superficial, at least as regards the metal types. Printing with movable types (made of *terra cotta*) was invented in China by a smith named Pishing before the middle of the eleventh century, but the invention does not seem to have been followed up. Wood printing was known at least as early as A.D. 581; and about 904 engraving on stone for the press was introduced. (Julien in *Jour. Asiat.*, sér. iv, tom. ix, 509, 513; *Chine Moderne*, pp. 626 *seqq.*)

3 The Yak.

4 Uzbeks.

5 The *Kizil-bâsh*.

certain religious differences and frontier disputes. Among the cities that the Green-caps have under their rule are among others at present Bochara and Samarcand, each of which has a prince of its own.

"Those people have their peculiar sciences which they call respectively *Chimia*, that which we call alchemy, *Limia* or the science of attracting love, and *Simia*, or that of illusion[1]. They have no coined money, but every gentleman or merchant has his gold or silver made into small rods, and these are divided into small fragments for spending, and this is the practice of all the inhabitants of Campion and Succuir.

"On the public square at Campion every day there gather a number of charlatans who practise the art of *Simia*, and by means of it, in the middle of crowds of people, they will exhibit all sorts of wonders; for example they will take a man who accompanies them and cleave him through with a sword, or cut his arm off, and you'll see him all streaming with blood, and so forth[2]." (From the "*Espositione* of *M. Giov. Batt. Ramusio*, prefixed to the travels of Marco Polo, in the second vol. of the *Navigationi e Viaggi*," f. 14 *vers.* to f. 16 *vers.*)

NOTE XIX.

ACCOUNT OF CATHAY BY A TURKISH DERVISH, AS RELATED TO AUGER GISLEN DE BUSBECK.

(Circa 1560.)

"Now let me tell you what I heard about the city and country of CATHAY from a certain Turkish vagabond. He was one of that kind of sect whose devotion consists in wandering into the most distant countries, and in worshipping God in the loftiest mountains and in the wildest deserts. This fellow had rambled over well-nigh the whole Eastern World, and among other things he mentioned that he had come across the Portuguese. Then he was seized with a strong desire to see the city and kingdom of Cathay, and for that purpose attached himself to a company of merchants who were going thither. For it is their custom to join

[1] *Kimia* (Ar.) Alchemy; *Simia* (Pers.) Enchantment or fascination. *Limia* is probably a factitious word made on the jingling principle spoken of in note at p. 151.

D'Herbelot says, however, that *Simia* is that part of chemistry which refers to the preparation of metals and minerals, and that *Kimia Simia* is used to express chemistry in general. There is another *Simia*, he adds, which has for its subject a sort of divination by names and numbers; the word being connected with *ism*, a name.

[2] See Ibn Batuta, *infra*, Vol. IV.

together in large numbers, and to travel to the frontiers of that empire in a company. There is no passage for a small party that way, or at least it is very unsafe; for there are a number of treacherous tribes upon the way whose attacks the travellers have to dread at every moment. When they have got some distance from the Persian frontier they come to the cities of SAMMARCAND, BORCHARA, TASCHAN, and other places occupied by the successors of Demirlan[1]. After these there are extensive deserts and inhabited countries, some occupied by savage and inhospitable tribes, others by people of more civilised character, but everywhere scantily supplied with food and forage, so that everyone has to take his victuals and other necessaries along with him, and this involves a large number of camels to carry the loads. Such large companies of men and beasts they call *caravans*. After a fatiguing journey of many months they came to a defile which forms, as it were, the barrier gate of Cathay. For a great part of that empire consists of inland country, and here there was an inclosing chain of rugged and precipitous mountains, affording no passage except through a narrow strait in which a garrison was stationed on the king's part[2]. There the question is put to the merchants, 'What they bring, whence they come, and how many of them are there?' The answer being given, the king's guards pass it by signal—by smoke if in daylight, by fire if by night—to the next watch-tower; they to the next, and so on, till in a few hours the message reaches the king at Cathay: a thing which would by any other communication require many days[3]. The king sends back his orders in the same manner and with equal rapidity, saying whether all shall be admitted, or only a part, or the whole put off. If they are allowed to enter they proceed under charge of certain leaders, finding halting-places arranged at proper distances where everything needed for food or clothing is to be had at reasonable rates, until they reach Cathay itself. On arriving there they have each to declare what they bring, and then they make a complimentary present to the king, as each thinks fit. He, however, is accustomed to pay for what he wants at a fair price[4]. The rest of their goods they sell or barter, a day being appointed for their return, up to which they have full liberty to do business. For the people of Cathay do not approve of the prolonged stay of foreigners among them, lest their indigenous manners should be corrupted by some foreign infection. And so the merchants are sent back stage by stage along the same road that they followed in coming.

"This wanderer stated that they were a people of extraordinary accomplishments, highly civilised and polite in their mode of living, and had a religion of their own, which was neither Christian, Jewish, nor Mahomedan, but except as regards ceremonies came

[1] *Bokhara; Tashkand; Tamerlane.* [2] *Supra*, p. 274.
[3] *Infra*, II, pp. 233–4. [4] *Supra*, p. 130.

nearest to the Jewish. For many centuries past the art of printing has been in use among them, and books printed with types, which he had seen there, sufficiently proved the fact. For this they made use of paper made from the slough and envelopes of silkworms, which was so thin that it bore the impression of the types on one side only, whilst the other side was left blank[1].

"There were many taverns in that city....[2] The odour of the perfume called musk, which is the exudation of a certain little animal about as big as a kid. Nothing fetched so great a price among them as a lion; for this beast does not occur in those countries, and they look on it with immense admiration, and give any price for it.

"So much for the kingdom of Cathay, as I heard told by that vagabond; let him answer for its truth. For it might easily be that whilst my questions referred to Cathay, his answers referred to some other country thereabouts, and in fact that we were playing at cross purposes. But when I had heard so much, I thought I would ask if he had not brought back from his travels any curious kind of a root or fruit or pebble or what not? 'Nothing whatever,' he said, 'except this little root that I carry about with me, and if I am knocked up with fatigue or cold, by chewing and swallowing a tiny morsel of it, I feel quite warmed and stimulated[3].' And so saying, he gave it me to taste, telling me to be careful to take but the smallest quantity. My doctor William (who was alive then) tasted it, and got his mouth into a state of inflammation from its burning quality. He declared it to be regular wolfsbane." (From *Busbequii Epistolæ*, Amsterdam, 1661, pp. 326–330.)

---

[1] This is well known as a characteristic of Chinese printing. Paper in China is made from bamboo, from the bark of mulberry, of a *hibiscus* (*Rosa Sinensis*), and of a tree called *chu* (*Broussonetia Papyrifera*). "All bark paper is strong and tough; it has rays crossing it, so that when torn you would think it was made of silk fibres. This is why it is called *Mien-chi* or silk paper" (Chinese author translated by Julien—see *Chine Moderne*, pp. 622 *seqq.*). Duhalde, however, does mention a kind of paper made from "the cods the silk-worms spin" (ext. in Astley, iv, p. 158). [It is also made from cotton. See a paper in *T'oung pao*, 1908, p. 589.]

[2] An unindicated hiatus in the original.

[3] This was certainly *Jinseng* (*supra*, p. 292).

NOTE XX.

ON THE MAPS IN THIS WORK.

I. MAP OF ASIA IN THE FIRST HALF OF THE FOURTEENTH CENTURY.

This is intended to elucidate the narrative of the fourteenth century travellers, from John of Monte Corvino to Ibn Batuta, as far as was possible without attempting greater detail than my time or knowledge would permit. The basis is a trace from Keith Johnston's Map in the Royal Atlas; substituting for present political divisions the chief of those which existed at the period in question, and inserting (in general) only those names of places which occur in the narratives and notes of this collection. Before preparing the map, I had at different times consulted maps of the period by Klaproth (in *Tableaux Historiques de l'Asie*), D'Ohsson, and Sprüner (*Historical Atlas*, German), and at a later date the map attached to Pauthier's Marco Polo; but latterly none of these, except the last, have been within reach, and the map has in the main been compiled gradually along with the matter which it illustrates. The theory of the indications was to show all political divisions, and all names still extant, in *black*; obsolete names used by European writers in *red*; and obsolete names only used by Asiatics in *red* also, but with the slope of the letters *reversed*. I am afraid, however, that these minutiæ have sometimes been overlooked by myself.

II. CATALAN MAP OF 1375.

It occurred to me that an acceptable pendant to the map last noticed would be a copy of one showing the geography of the same period as it was conceived by the people of the time. The *Carta Catalana* of 1375, in the Imperial Library at Paris, as lithographed in vol. xiv, part II, of the *Notices et Extraits*, with a description by MM. Buchon and Tastu, was the only model accessible; but at the same time it is probably the best that could have been taken for the purpose. The original, as shown in the lithographed facsimiles, is complicated and perplexed with many radiations of *roses des Vents* and other geometrical lines, with numerous rude drawings and long rubrics, and by the fact that to read half the names and inscriptions you have to turn the map upside down. All this, together with the character of the writing, renders the map as published difficult to appreciate without considerable study, and it is trusted that the trouble taken to present its geographical substance here in a more lucid and compact form will not have been thrown away[1].

[1] [The original Catalan Map of 1375 from the Library of King Charles V of France is now kept in the Mazarine Gallery, at the Bibliothèque nationale, Paris (No. 119 of Morel-Fatio's Catalogue of Spanish

Those sheets of the map which pertain to Asia have alone been copied. The scale is one-fourth that of the original. All the embellishments, geometrical lines, and long rubrics, have been omitted, preserving the essential points of the latter, where it has been possible to do so in few words. On the shores of the Mediterranean and Black Sea, which are thickly studded with names in the original, only a few have been selected, but in the remainder of the map scarcely any have been intentionally omitted except a few on the Caspian. In deciphering the names the printed transcripts of the French editors have been consulted, but not servilely followed[1].

It may be observed that in the original facsimiles the sheets do not fit to one another properly. This is especially the case with sheets III and IV, and is obvious even in my reduction, as may be seen in the fragment shown of the Arctic Sea, and in the faulty junction of the coast lines of the Peninsula of India. We find also a pair of duplicate names occurring in these two sheets (*Chabol* and *Camar*), besides other instances of apparent duplication in sheet IV. This is probably the result of inexpert compilation from different authorities, and I have seen the same thing in modern published maps of some pretension.

The date of the map has been fixed, on sufficient grounds I believe, to 1375; but the data from which it has been constructed are naturally not all of one period. Thus CATHAY is represented as the Empire of the Great Can HOLUBEIM[2]; *i.e.*, not *Olug Beig*,

MSS). Buchon made a preparatory study of this document for the *Notices et Extraits*, Vol. xiii, part II, but only a few copies were struck off; later Buchon, with the help of Tastu, resumed the work, which finally appeared in Vol. xiv, part II, of the same collection, with a very poor lithographic reproduction. Viscount de Santarem in his magnificent collection of maps reproduced in colour the Catalan Map (1841); again Léopold Delisle in his *Choix de documents géographiques* (Paris, 1883) gave a faithful reproduction of the map in heliogravure. I have myself given a good phototypic reproduction of two sheets from the original map in my paper *L'Extrême-Orient dans l'Atlas catalan de Charles V roi de France* (Ext. du *Bull. de géog. hist. et descriptive*, 1895), Paris, 1895, 8vo.]

[1] In the names extracted below there are I think scarcely any variations from the French readings, though corrections of the *original* have been suggested occasionally. But in Central Asia there are several open to amendment, as where they read *Fista* and *Evi* for *Sistā* and *Eri*, thus obscuring the otherwise obvious identification of the places *Seistan* and *Heri* or Herat.

[2] [This is the text concerning the Great Khan :

Lo maior princeps de tots los Tartres
ha nom holubeim | q̇ uol dir gran Ca |
A quest emperador es molt pus rich
de tots los altres emperadors de tot lo
mon | aquest emꝑador guardeñ XII *mil*
caualles | z han IIIJ. *capitans | aquels ab*
XII. *millia caualles | e cascu capitan va*
en la cort absa copayā per IIJ *meses*
de l'any | e axi dels altres per orda.]

SERIES II. VOL. 38. 1915.

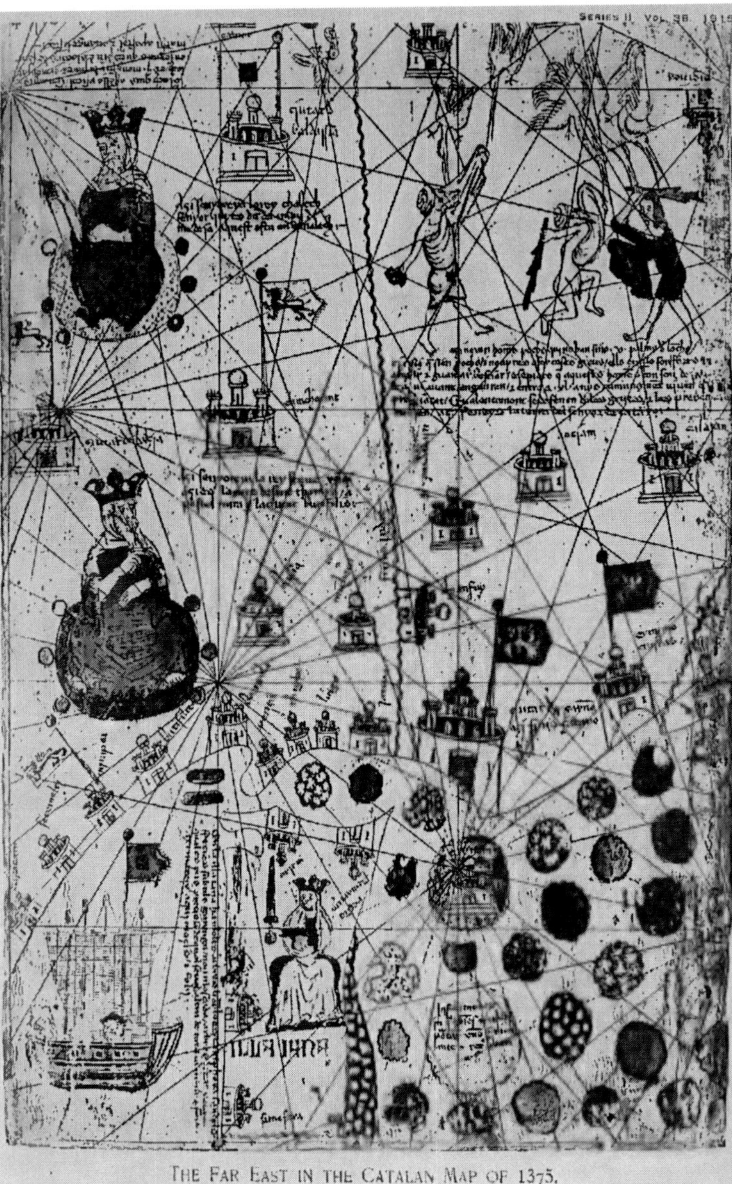

THE FAR EAST IN THE CATALAN MAP OF 1375.

Western portion. Part of Section 7 of the whole

Reproduced for the Hakluyt Society by Donald Macbeth, London.

To face page 310

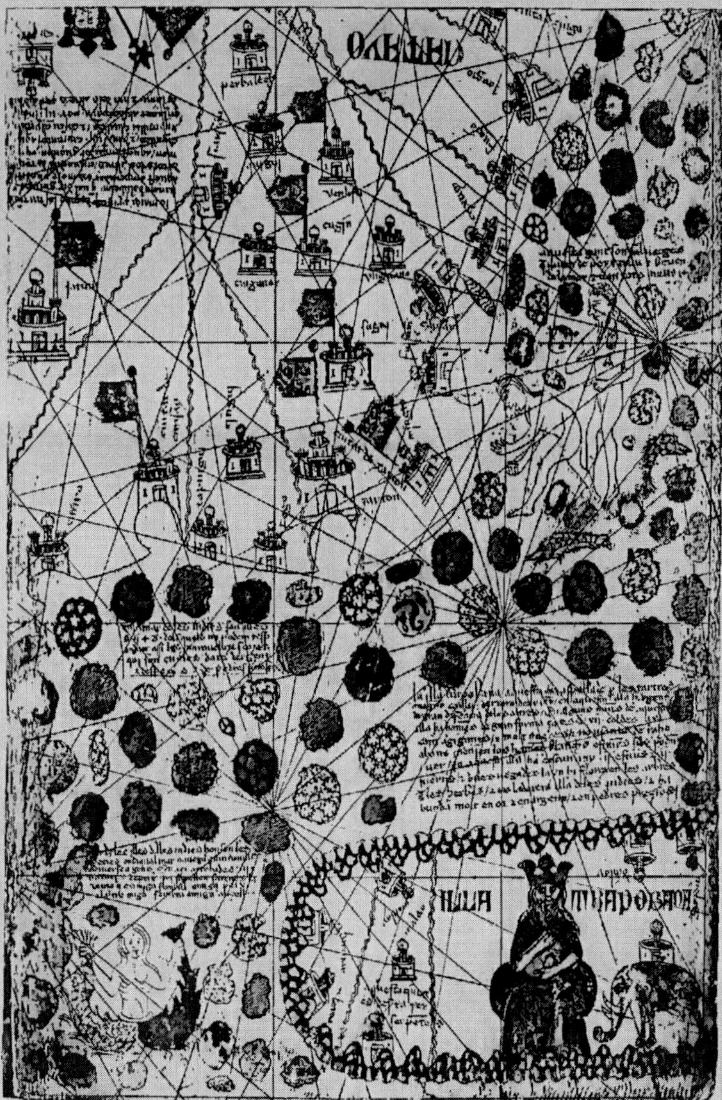

THE FAR EAST IN THE CATALAN MAP OF 1375.

Eastern portion. Part of Section 8 of the whole

as the French editors say (a Great Khan not known to history), but *Kúbláí*, who died in 1294[1]; MEDEIA or the Middle Empire of the Tartars is shown as ruled by King CHABECH; *i.e.*, *Guebek* or *Kapak*, who reigned some time between 1310 and 1320; and SARRA or Kipchak is under the Lord JANIBECH; *i.e.*, *Janibeg*, the son of Mahomed Uzbek, who reigned 1342–56.

One of the aids in compiling this map was almost certainly the Portulano Mediceo, now in the Laurentian Library, or perhaps it would be more safe to say that both copied from some common source. That they did so to a certain extent will be evident from a comparison of the coasts of Arabia and Persia and the west coast of India with the names entered, as they are on this map and on the map from the Portulano engraved by Baldello Boni in the Atlas to his *Il Milione*[2].

For Cathay and the countries adjoining[3] it we can trace Marco Polo as one of the authorities, and perhaps Odoric as another. To the former certainly belong Calajan (*i.e. Carazan*), Vociam, Zardandan, Michem (*Mien*), Penta (*Pentam*), and many more names found here; to the latter perhaps Zayton and Fozo. Cincolam and Mingio are found in Odoric and not in Polo, but they are located here with a correctness which seems to imply independent knowledge.

Much cannot be said, however, for correctness of detail in Cathay. We have a good approximation to its general form and position in the map of Asia; Chanbalech is placed correctly at the northern extremity of the empire[4], and Cincolam and Caynam (*Hainan*) at the southern, whilst Zayton and Mingio (Ningpo)

[1] Kúbláí is called *Quolibey* in Wadding's version of Pope Nicholas III's letter to the Khan of 1278 (*infra*, III, p. 5).

[2] Baldello's is not a perfect representation of the original, which contains half effaced traces of a good deal that he has not copied.

[3] [We find also Japan:

Japan insula, à M. Paulo
Veneto zipangri dicta,
olim Chrijse, a Magno
Cham olim bello petita
sed frustra]

[4] [*Cjuitas de*
chanbalech magni
canis catdyo.]

[This is the text concerning Chambalech:
Sapiats q́ de costa la ciutat de chambalech auja vna gran ciutat antigamēt q́ auja nota guaribalu | elo grā cha troba ꝑ lestornomia q́ a questa ciutat se deuja reuelar cōtra el axi q́ feula desabitare feu fer aqui esta ciutat de Chabalech. E a enuirō aquesta ciutat XXIIIJ. *legues | e es molt ben murada e es a cayre si qā cascun | cayre ha.* V̄J. *legues | e ha dalt* XX *passes. e* X *passes de gros | E ay* XII. *portes e ay* I *gran tora*
en q́ sta vn seyn q́ sona aꝑ u son o abans | axi pus
ha sonat no gossa anar negu ꝑ villa | e a cascuna
porta guarden mill homēs no ꝑ temēssa
mas ꝑ honor ꝑ d'l Senyor.]

appropriately occupy intermediate positions. Vociam and Zardandan are rightly placed on the south-west frontier towards Michem (Ava), and Cansio (*Kanchau*) properly stands on the north-west frontier towards the desert. But in the rest of the details we have confusion or darkness. Many of the names in the interior can be recognised but doubtfully or not at all. I suspect, however, that most of them are from corrupt copies of Marco Polo. And it may be added that the representation of China and Cathay in the geography of Magini at the end of the sixteenth century is decidedly less correct in general position and almost as wild in details as this. [Yule has written since in *Marco Polo*, i, p. *134*: "In this map it seems to me Marco Polo's influence, I will not say on geography, but on map-making, is seen to the greatest advantage. His Book is the basis of the Map as regards Central and Further Asia, and partially as regards India. His names are often sadly perverted, and it is not always easy to understand the view that the compiler took of his itineraries. Still we have Cathay admirably placed in the true position of China, as a great Empire filling the south-east of Asia. The Eastern Peninsula of India is indeed absent altogether, but the Peninsula of Hither India is for the first time in the History of Geography represented with a fair approximation to its correct form and position, and Sumatra also (*Jaua*) is not badly placed. Carajan, Vocian, Mien, and Bangala, are located with a happy conception of their relation to Cathay and to India. Many details in India foreign to Polo's book, and some in Cathay (as well as in Turkestan and Siberia, which have been entirely derived from other sources) have been embodied in the Map. But the study of his Book has, I conceive, been essentially the basis of those great portions which I have specified, and the additional matter has not been in mass sufficient to perplex the compiler. Hence we really see in this Map something like the idea of Asia that the Traveller himself would have presented, had he bequeathed a Map to us." In my study of the Far East in the Catalan Map, I have come to the conclusion that the cartographer's knowledge of Eastern Asia is drawn entirely from Marco Polo. It is worthy of notice that *Manzi* does not appear in the Catalan Map. H. C.]

The 7548 islands ascribed to the Eastern Archipelago are certainly derived from Polo[1].

As in the geographical ideas of Ibn Batuta, and it would seem

[1] Murray's *Polo* (ii, c. 4) has 7448 islands; Pauthier's (p. 250) 7459. [This is the text concerning these islands:

En la mar de les indies son illes
7 5 4 8. delsquals no podem resp
ondre assi les marauelozes cozas
quj son en eles d'or z dergent
z despecies z de pedres p'ec'oses.]

of Abulfeda, one great river with its radiating branches extends all over Cathay.

The eastern peninsula of India is omitted altogether, or confused with the Island of Java (probably Sumatra)[1]. In the extreme south-east is a great Island of TAPROBANE. It exhibits a number of cities, the names of which seem to be imaginary, and it is stated in the rubric to be the remotest island of the east called by the Tartars GREAT KAULI. Kao li was the Chinese and Tartar name for Corea[2], and this great Taprobane is perhaps a jumble of Corea and Japan[3].

The great river which separates India from China, rising in the mountains of BALDASSIA (*Badakhshan*), and flowing into the Bay of Bengal, appears to be a confusion between Indus and Ganges, a confusion still more elaborately developed in the map of Fra Mauro. BENGALA itself is placed with admirable correctness.

The width of the Great Desert of Central Asia is greatly over-

[1] In the facsimile the name is written *Jana*. The same clerical error occurs in Jordanus (p. 30), and perhaps he was one of the authorities used. For near it we have also the Island of the Naked Folk which that friar mentions. In *Jana* also the map shows us the *Regio Feminarum*, which Polo, Conti, Jordanus, and Hiuen Tsang all concur in placing in the western part of the *Indian* Ocean. But a Chinese authority quoted by Pauthier places it in the immediate vicinity of Java (*Polo*, iii, ch. 33; *Conti*, p. 20; *Jordanus*, p. 44; *Vie de H. Thsang*, p. 208; Pauthier's *Polo*, p. 559).

[This is the text concerning Jana:

"*En la illa Iana ha molts arbres leny ayloes, camphora, sandels, species subtils, garenga, nou moscada, arbres de canyela, laqual es pus preciosa de qual se vol altra de tota la India; e son axi mateix aqui maçis e folii.*"]

[This is the text concerning the Naked Folk south of Caynam:

*Insula nudo*ꝝ
in qª hoĩes z muliẽrs
portãt vñũ folũm
ante z retº alium.

Another text refers to the north of Taprobana:

Aquesta gent son saluaiges
ǭ uien de peyx cruu z beuen
de la mar | z van tots nuus.]

[On the Kingdom of Women [*Niu kwo*], see G. Schlegel, *Problèmes géographiques, T'oung pao*, III, 1892.]

[2] V. *infra*, III, pp. 113, 125.

[3] [This is the text concerning this island of Taprobana:

La illa trapobana | aquesta es appellade ꝑ los tartres
magno caulij derrera de oriẽt | en aquesta illa ha gens
de gran difeʼncia de les altres | En alguns mũts de aquesta
illa ha homẽs de gran forma, ço es de XII. *coldes | axi*
com ꝺ gigants | z molt negres | z no usants de raho
abans menjen los homẽs blanchs estrayṡ sils podñ
auer | In aquesta illa ha cascun any. IJ *estius z* IJ
juerns | z dues uegades layn hi florexen les arbres
z les herbes | z es la derera illa de les indies | z ha
bunda molt en or z en argent | z en pedres preçioses.]

estimated, and this has the effect of shoving up KAMUL and other cities of Eastern Turkestan into immediate contact with Siberia and the Eastern Volga regions.

In the extreme north-east of Asia we have the nations of Gog and Magog, shut up within mountains by Alexander the Great to await the latter days[1].

The Orontes is represented as a branch diverging from Euphrates; and in this we are again reminded of a similar error of Ibn Batuta's[2]. The Tigris is connected with the Euphrates by a branch or canal (the traces of which seem really to exist) near Baghdad (BALDACH), but flows into the sea by a separate mouth. Another great river, a duplicate of Tigris, having no prototype in nature, but perhaps an amalgamation of the two Zabs and other rivers east of Tigris, flows from the seas of ARGIS and MARGA (Lakes Van and Urmia), and enters the Persian Gulf to the eastward.

The Oxus flows into the Caspian in the latitude of Urganj after passing that city (ORGANCI). There is no indication of the Aral[3].

Notwithstanding these and many other errors the map is a remarkable production for the age. The general form of Asia is fairly conceived; the Peninsula of India is shown I believe for the first time with some correctness of form and direction. In these respects the map is greatly superior to the more ambitious work of Fra Mauro in the following century. The Catalan geographer was probably more of a practical man, and did not perplex himself and distort his geography with theories about the circular form of the inhabited earth. Unluckily, however, he seems to have allowed his topography towards the north and south to be compressed, by no theories indeed, but by the limits of his parchment!

The following is an orderly list of the names shown on our

[1] The name given to the mountains (*Caspis*) shows the curious jumble between the Wall of Derbend and the Wall of China, between the Caucasian nations, the Tartars, and the Gog Magog of Ezekiel and the Apocalypse, which was involved in this legend. It is very old, for it is found in the Pseudo-Callisthenes edited by Müller (pp. 139, 143). [See *Marco Polo*, i, p. 56.] It seems that a prince of the Shut-Up Nations found his way out in the sixteenth century, but he had better have stayed where he was: "It is reported by certain writers that the King of Tabor came from those parts to seek Francis I of France and Charles V the Emperor, and other Christian princes, in order to gain them secretly over to Judaism. But by the command of Charles V at Mantua in 1540 *his temerity was punished in the fire.*" (Magini, *Geografia*, Venet., 1598, f. 171, *v*.)

[2] *Infra*, Ibn Batuta, Vol. IV.

[3] In the map of Marino Sanudo dating from the beginning of the fourteenth century, besides the Caspian, which he calls *M. Yrcanum*, we have a smaller sea in the position of the Aral called *M. Caspium*, and then yet another and still smaller into which the *Gyon* flows.

reduction of the map in some of its most interesting portions, with as many identifications as I have been able to suggest[1].

IN SHEET IV *bis*[2].

Countries North of the Black Sea.

"ROSSIA, BURGARIA, CUMANIA, GATZARIA, ALLANIA."

R. Tiulo . .	The Dniester; ancient *Tyras*[3]; *Turlú* of the Mahomedans.
R. Lussom . .	The Dnieper. Sharifuddín calls the Dnieper *Uzi*[4], which is perhaps the name here (*L'Uzi*).
R. Tanay . .	The *Don* (*Tanais*).
Torachi . .	*Torshok* N.W. of Tver.
Rostaor . .	*Rostov*.
Tifer . .	*Tver*.
Perum . .	Novgorod? where there was a great idol called Perum[5].
Baltachinta . .	*Poltava?* Timur returning from the sack of Moscov took guides to travel across the steppes by way of *Balchimkin* (P. de la Croix, ii, 365). That translator gives as explanation of the name "les Palus Meotides"; but this is probably one of his random shots.
Branchicha . .	Somewhere near Czernikov, where we hear of a great forest of *Branki* (*Magini*). There was also a city *Bransko* in the same quarter.
Chiva . .	*Kiev*.
Canada . .	*Caminietz?*
Calamit . .	Eupatoria? on *Kalamita* Bay.
Cembaro . .	Balaclava (see III, p. 14).
Soldaya . .	*Sudak*.
CAFFA.	
Porto Pisano .	Taganrog.
Tana . .	Azov.

[1] A few of these identifications only are given by the French editors. M. Elie de la Primaudaie, in his *Etudes sur le Commerce au Moyen Age*, has identified nearly all the names on the Black Sea and Caspian Coasts. These I have not repeated here.

[2] Sheets of L. Delisle's collection.

[3] "Nullo tardior amne Tyras" (Ovid, *Epist. ex Pont.*, iv, 10). For Turlu, see *Not. et Extraits*, xiii, 274.

[4] Pétis de la Croix, ii, 360.

[5] Gwagnini, *Sarmatia Europ. descripta*, Moscovia, f. 8–9.

Egypt.

Larissa .	. *El-Arish.*
Damiyat .	. *Damietta.*
Casar Bochir	. *Abukir.*
ALEXANDRIA.	
Chayre .	. *Cairo.*
Babillonia .	. Old Cairo (III, p. 263).
Bussi .	. *Búsh*, near Beni Suef (see Ibn Bat., II, 95).
Mijnere .	. *Minieh.*
Ieuch (read Seuth)	. *Siút.*
Chossa .	. *Kús* (see Ibn Batuta, IV).
Tegia .	. ? near Luqsor. Possibly should read *Begia*, a station of the Bejah tribes of the Red Sea desert who held the emerald mines of Berenice; see quotation from Mas'ūdī, *supra*, p. 230.
Ansee .	. *Esneh.*
Lialeyse (read S—)	. *Silsilah.*
Sohan .	. *Assuan.*
Hurma .	. *Darmut?*
DONCOLA .	. (Old Donkola.) The Dominican Bartholomew of Tivoli was made Missionary Bishop of Donkola in 1330 (Le Quien, iii, 1414).
Coale .	. *Ghalwa* of Edrisi (i, 33).
Dobaha .	. Al-*Dabah*, above Donkola.
Sobaha .	. *Sobah*, the ruins of which are near Khartum?
Ciutat Sioene Insula Meroe	.} .} From the ancients.
Ciutat de Nubia	. *Nuábah* of Edrisi, i, 25.
Al-Bayadi .	. Little Oasis?
Desert de Gipte	. Libyan Desert.

Coast of Red Sea.

Mns. of Barchium.	
Meda .	. Suakin?
Lidebo .	. *Aidháb.*
Chos .	. *Kosseir.*
Aydip .	. A double of Aidhab.
ELIIM .	. *Exodus* (xv, 27).
ESSIONGEBER	. (*Deut.* ii, 8; I *Kings* ix, 26).
Guidè .	. *Jiddah.*
Semin .	. *Zabíd?*

Armenia, the Euphrates, and Interior Syria.

Poperti	*Baiburt.*
Savast	*Sivas* (*Sebaste*).
Scisia	*Sis* (III, p. 139).
Malmistra	*Mississa* (*Mopsuestia*).
Layazo	*Aias* (III, p. 139).
G. of Caramela	(Read *Cannamela*) G. of Scanderún. The castle Cannamella between Scanderún and Malmistra is mentioned by Wilibrand of Oldenburg, xi.
Malasia	*Malatia.*
Brisom	Castle of *Parshiam ?* see Ritter, x, 866, 868.
Benzab	*Membaj* or *Benbij ?*
Tira	(Read *Bira*) *Bir.*
Serug	*Seruj* or *Sarug*, S.W. of Urfa.
Domasch	*Damascus.*
Mt. Ermon	*Hermon.*
,, Sanir	*Shenir* of *Deuter.* iii; *Sanyr* of Friar Burchard iii, 7, 8, for the S. part of Hermon; see also *Prairies d'Or*, iv, 87.
,, Jilahd	*Gilead.*
,, PISGA.	
,, *Abari*	*Abarim*, see *Numb.* xxvii, 12, and *Deut.* xxxii, 49.
,, NEBO.	
,, de Rubeo	?
Sea of Gamora	Dead Sea.

IN SHEET V.

Country North of the Caspian.

EMPIRE OF SARRAY.

R. Edil	The *Athil* or Volga.
COSTRAMA.	
Borgar	City of *Bolgár* (see IV, Ibn Batuta).
Jorman	*Julman* of Rashíd and *Masálak-al-absár*, supposed the country on the Kama, asserted to be called also R. *Cholma* (see *Not. et Extr.*, xiii, 274). The Maps still show a place on the Viatka, tributary of the Kama, called *Churmansk.*
Pascherti	*Bashkird.*
Fachatim	*Viatka ?*
Sebur	*Sibir*, ancient city near Tobolsk.

City of Marmorea .	Mercator and Hondius (10th Ed., 1630) and N. Sanson (1650) show *Jorman* on the south of the Kama R., *Pascherti* in the position of Ufa, the present head-quarter of the Bashkirs, *Sagatin* (= *Fachatim* of the text) at the head of the Ufa River, *Marmorea* on the Bielaya south of Ufa. Blaeu (1662) has these, similarly placed, except Jorman. He has, however, *Iurmen* as a tract between Astracan and the Iaik. I suspect these names in the main were mere traditions from old maps like the Catalana.
Mns. of Sebur .	Altai and T'ien Shan.
Zizera . .	The *Jazirah* or Island on the Volga (nr. Zaritzin).
Berchimam . .	Probably the Upper City of Sarai.
City of Sarra. .	Or Sarai (see III, p. 82).
Agitarchan . .	*Astracan.*

Countries South of the Caspian.

"ARMENIA MAJOR, KINGDOM OF TAURIS AND CHALDÆA."

Three Churches .	Echmiazin ? or Uch Kilisi (see III, p. 163).
Malascorti . .	*Malasjerda.*
Pasalain . .	Read *Rasalain*, the ancient Callirrhoe, on the Khabur.
Zizera . .	*Jazirah* on the Tigris.
Arbo [Orbo] .	*Harba* (see Ibn Bat., II, 132, and *J.R.G.S.*, ix, 445).
C. of Baldach .	*Baghdad.*
Tauris . .	*Tabriz.*
Sodania . .	*Sultania.*
Sea of Argis .	L. Van.
Argis . .	*Arjish.*
Capreri . .	?
Sea of Marga .	L. Urumia.
Marga . .	*Maragha.*
Ormi . .	*Urumia.*
Cremi . .	*Karmisin* is mentioned by Ibn Khallikan as a place in Kurdistan. (See Quatremère's *Rashid*, p. 266.) *Kirmesin* was a city from whose ruins arose Kermanshah (see Rawlinson in *J.R.G.S.*, ix, 42).
Cade . .	*Hadith ?* at the confluence of the Gr. Zab and Tigris (see Assemani, p. 752).
Chesi . .	*Khuzistan.*

Rey .	. *Rai.*
Siras .	. *Shiraz.*
Abdeni .	. *Abadan*, on Island in mouth of Tigris.
Bassora .	. *Basra.*
Taiwust .	. *Wasit ?* called Madína*ta Wásit* (" The Two Cities Wasit," see Edrisi, i, 367).

Coast of Persia and India.

Serans or Seam	. Siraf ? But the Mediceo has *Sustar, i.e.* Shustar.
Ussn .	. *Husn Amárat ?* (see Edri., i, 379). Any castle is *Husn.*
Creman .	. *Kirman.*
I. of Chis .	. *Kish.*
I. of Ormis .	. *Hormuz.*
Hormisiom .	. Old *Hormuz* on the Continent.
Nocran .	. *Mekran.*
Chesimo .	. *Kij. Mediceo* has *Chechi.*
Damonela .	. *Daibul.*
Femenat .	. *Somnath.*
Goga .	. *Gogo.*
BAROCHE.	
Canbetum .	. *Cambay.*
Cocintaya .	. *Med.* has *Cocintana :* the *Kokan-Tana* of Ibn Batuta (III, 335)[1]; the city of Tana (see II, p. 113), capital of Konkan.
Paychinor .	. *Faknur* of Ibn Batuta (see Vol. IV); Bakanur, but out of place a little.
Chintabor .	. *Sandábúr*, Goa (see IV, Ibn Batuta).
Nandor (Nanaor ?)	. *Honore ? Med.* has *Niandor.*
Pescamor .	. Perhaps Barçelor.
Manganor .	. *Mangalore.*
Elly .	. *Hili* (see IV, Ibn Batuta, Note D).
Columbo .	. *Kaulam*, but on the wrong side of the Peninsula.
Carocam .	. *Karikal ?*
Setemelti .	. Seven Pagodas ? (see *supra*, p. 81).
Mirapor .	. *Mailapúr ;* Madras.
Butifilis .	. *Mutfili* of Polo (see III, p. 70); but by a misunderstanding the author puts St. Thomas's tomb here.
BENGALA .	. (See IV, Ibn Batuta.)

[1] Where Elliot, quoting Rashíd, has " Guzerat, which is a great country, in which are Cambay, Súmnáth, *Konkan, Tana,* and several other towns and cities "; and again: " Beyond Guzerat are *Konkan and Tana,*" probably the original will be found to read as here, " *Konkan-Tana* " (p. 42; I quote an extract in Pauthier's *Polo*, p. 663, not having the passage in my own notes).

Interior of India.

Bijder .	. *Bidr.*
Diogil .	. *Deogiri* or Daulatabad.
Jaleym .	. *Jálna ?*
DELLY. .	
Neruala .	. *Anhilwara.*
Hocibelch .	. ?
Bargelidoa .	. ?
MOLTAN.	

III. SKETCH MAP TO ILLUSTRATE TRAVELS OF IBN BATUTA IN BENGAL.

This is little more than a diagram, for no accurate map of Bengal east of the old Brahmaputra has yet been published. Two or three of the positions wanted in the Silhet district are, however, given by Rennell's and other maps, and others have been inserted from the information quoted in Note E, Ibn Batuta, IV, to give an idea of the localities.

IV. MAP IN ILLUSTRATION OF THE JOURNEY OF GOËS.

The following maps have been used or studied in the compilation of the map in question :

1. Wood's and other British surveys Kabul and on the Oxus, as embodied in a map by Mr John Walker (title and date missing in my copy).
2. Kiepert's large map of Asia, Weimar, 1864.
3. Tracing of part of a map of Central Asia, by Col. G. T. Walker, R.E. of the G. Trig. Survey of India.
4. Veniùkov's Sketch of the Bolor, as given in *Petermann*, for 1861 (plate 10).
5. Extract of Schlagintweit's General Map, as given in the same place.
6. Kashmir, in *Petermann* for 1861, p. 1.
7. Tracing of Gen. Court's Map (*Itinéraire d'Afghanistan*), in vol. viii of the *J. As. Soc. Bengal.*
8. Austin's Map of Balti, etc., in *J. R. G. S.* for 1864.
9. Tracing of a map by Masson, from his Travels.
10. Map of the Scene of the Umbeyla Campaign, from a Parliamentary Report.
11. Macartney's Map in Elphinstone's *Caubul.*
12. Arrowsmith's Map to Burnes's *Travels.*
13. Map in the *Russians in Central Asia* (by Stanford apparently).
14. Keith Johnston's Map of India, extracted from his *Royal Atlas.*

I have also derived from Leech's *Reports on the Passes of the Hindu Kush*, and still more from Wood's *Journey*, names and indications that do not appear in any of the maps named ; a chief object having been to make that part of the map which relates to the Hindu Kush and Badakhshan as complete as possible.

I have not been able to see a translation of Veniukov's paper on the Bolor (referred to in the Introductory Notice of Benedict Goës, Vol. IV, *infra*), excepting as regards some extracts from the journal of the anonymous German traveller, which have been kindly made for me by Mr. Moukhine, the Consul General of Russia in Sicily. Sir H. Rawlinson appears, however, to have completely demolished the claims of the German narrative to genuineness. We have seen such strange mystifications of a somewhat similar kind in our own day that it would be rash perhaps to say that the journey, or a part of it, was never made, but till the matter be more thoroughly investigated, none of his statements can be built upon[1]. Even if the German's MS prove entirely worthless, the Chinese itinerary referred to by Veniukov should be of great value.

How uncertain is still the basis of any map connecting the regions on the different sides of the Bolor, Karakorum, and T'ien Shan Ranges may be judged from the following statement of the longitudes assigned in the maps before me to some of the chief points, to which are added the data for the same as given by the Chinese missionary surveyors, and those of some of them deduced by Captain Montgomerie from the papers of his Múnshí Mahomed Hamid.

	Ilchi (Khotan)	Yarkand	Kashgar	Aqsu	Issikul (W. End)	Sirikul (W. End)
Chinese Tables .	80° 21′	76° 3′	73° 48′	78° 58′	78° 12′[2]	...
Veniukov . .	...	76° 10′	73° 58′	...	...	73° 38′
Kiepert . .	79° 12′	74° 56′	72° 53′	78° 20′	77° 30′	73° 5′
Colonel Walker .	79° 13′	76° 24′	73° 58′	79° 40′	...	73° 30′
John Walker (*Wood*)	...	...	...	...	...	73° 33′
Schlagintweit .	78° 20′	73° 58′	71° 50′	76° 27′	74° 6′	71° 28′
Golobev . .	...	...	...	...	76° 17′	...
Montgomerie .	79° 0′	77° 30′	75° 20′	...	...	...
Greatest Differences	2° 1′	3° 32′	3° 30′	3° 13′	4° 6′	2° 10′

It will be seen that the geographers who deviate most widely from all the rest are the Schlagintweits, who carry the whole of

[1] After this had gone to press I received a copy of Sir H. Rawlinson's remarks on the German narrative, and as M. Khanikov is stated to have taken up the defence, the question will doubtless be thoroughly discussed. A few memoranda that occur to me on the subject will be found at the end of this note.

[2] Only an approximate deduction from other data in the tables. I take them as given in the *Russians in Central Asia*, pp. 522–3. [I may note the following longitudes east of Paris for Khotan: Dutreuil de Rhins, 77° 37′ 5; Pievtsov, 77° 33′ 6.]

Turkestan from 2° to 3° further west than the Chinese tables. I have not seen any statement of the grounds on which this great change is based. It is certainly a bold one, for it throws over not merely the Chinese tables entirely, but the positions assigned by the Russians, north of the T'ien Shan, and by the British travellers on the Oxus. Our last intelligence affords no corroboration of this revolutionary map-making. On the contrary, Captain Montgomerie's data carry the position of Yarkand one degree more to the *east* than any previous map[1]. And it is not merely as regards calculations of longitude that the Schlagintweits reject the results of the British journeys on the Oxus. Captain Wood's latitude of Sirikul is treated with equal contempt; nor does that distinguished traveller seem to be considered competent even to take a compass bearing. For the Upper Oxus, the river which he represents himself as having travelled along for many days, and which his map shows as flowing from north-east by east to south-west by south, is made by Schlagintweit to flow from south by east to north by west. And the lake itself which Wood imagined that he saw lying east and west, is made by Schlagintweit to lie south-east and north-west.

The chief difficulty found in adjusting the longitude of the cities of Chinese Turkestan, in accordance with Captain Montgomerie's approximate determination of Yarkand, arises from the impossibility of reconciling this with the *difference* between Ilchi and Yarkand in the Jesuit Tables. This amounts in those Tables to 4° 18'; whilst the collation of Montgomerie's position of Yarkand with the Jesuit position of Ilchi reduces it to 2° 51', and with the position which the former's own data induced him to assign to Ilchi it comes down to 1° 30'. It had indeed long been pretty certain that the Jesuit position of Ilchi was too far east; and a communication, for which I have had to thank Captain Montgomerie since this went to press, reports later data obtained by Colonel Walker (who will no doubt publish them in detail) as fixing Ilchi approximately to longitude 79° 25' and latitude 37° 8'. This longitude I have adopted in my map, whilst in regard to Yarkand I have stretched Captain Montgomerie's data *westward* as far as their circumstances seemed to justify (perhaps further than he would admit), assigning to it a longitude of 77°. This is still 36' *further east* than the assignment of any previous map, whilst it *reduces* the discrepancy from the Jesuit data in relation to Ilchi, though still leaving it inevitably large.

Next to this general uncertainty about the longitudes the

[1] The map had been finished when I saw in the *Times* the account of my brother officer Captain Montgomerie's paper, read at the R. Geog. Society in May 1866. I have since re-cast the part affected by that information, and I have to thank him for his kind readiness in answering questions which I sent him. But I have not seen Capt. Montgomerie's full paper, or his map.

great geographical puzzle about this region appears to be the identity of the main source of the Oxus. In addition to Wood's River, which he traced to the Sirikul Lake, most maps represent another, a longer and therefore perhaps greater, feeder from a more northern source, under the name of the River of Bolor or Wakhsh. Nor has the narrative of Wood's journey through the district of Wakhán yet displaced from our maps another position assigned to Wakhán or Vokhán upon this northern river.

Wood unluckily never treats these questions at all. Finding Wakhán upon the Panja, just where Macartney's map led him to expect it, he notices no other place of the name, nor does he allude to any other great branch of the river. And it may well be doubted if there is in truth any other Wakhán than that which Wood passed through[1]. The position assigned to the northern Vokhán of the maps is due I believe to an entry in the Chinese tables. But it seems to be very doubtful if the Jesuit observers in person actually crossed the mountains[2]. This Northern Wakhán, if not a mere displacement, I suspect to represent *Wakhsh* or the Wakhshjird of the old Arab geographers.

The existence of a place called Bolor stands on better evidence; at least there is or has been a State so called, the chief inhabited place of which would appropriate the name in the talk of foreigners, according to a well-known Asiatic practice, whether rightly or not. It appears to be mentioned as a kingdom by Hiuen Tsang (*Pololo*)[3]; it is spoken of by Polo as the name of a province; it

[1] Edrisi speaks of Wakhán as the region in which the Jihun rises, lying towards Tibet. Abdul Razzak speaks of Mirza Ibrahim during a campaign in Badakhshan as advancing into *Saqndn, Ghand* (which Quatremère proposes to read *Waghand* or Wakhán), and *Bamir*, the exact order of Shagnán, Wakhán, and Pamir, as reported by Wood. Macartney's map, drawn up most carefully from information, many years before Wood's journey, gives Darwáz, Shagnán, Wakhán, exactly in Wood's order. Burnes, a few years before Wood, does the same. (Edrisi, i, 472; *Not. et Extraits*, xiv, 491.)

[2] [Felix da Rocha, named in Chinese *Fu Tso-lin*, a Jesuit, born at Lisbon on the 31st August 1713; entered the S.J. on the 1st May 1728; arrived in China in 1738; was vice-provincial, 1754–7, 1762; Superior at Peking, where he died on the 22nd May 1781. He was sent with the Chinese Armies to Central Asia in 1756. Da Rocha was accompanied in Central Asia by Father Joseph d'Espinha, another Portuguese Jesuit (died at Peking 10 July 1788), and four Chinese Geographers. See *Positions géog. déterminées par deux missionnaires jésuites dans le Turkestan oriental et la Dzoungarie en 1756...par* le P. Brucker, Lyon, 1880.]

[3] [" South of the valley of Pamir, and beyond a mountain range, is the Kingdom of *Po-lo-lo*, BOLOR, where is got much gold and silver, and which had been visited by the traveller [Hiuen Tsang] on his zigzag route when first entering India. It was then reached by him in five marches from *Talilo* or DARAIL (*Cunningham*); it had a circuit of forty days' journey (4000 *li*), being much longer from east to west than from north to south, etc. The particulars previously given, as well as the position now indicated, are in entire accordance with

appears as a geographical position in the tables of Nasiruddín, and reappears in the Chinese tables of the last century with exactly the same latitude. It is also mentioned in the *Tárikh Rashidi* of the sixteenth century[1]; and its prince appears as a tributary to China in the Chinese annals of some seventy years back[2].

But is there a great Wakhsh branch of the Oxus coming from those regions, and if so where does it join the Panja or river of the Sirikul? To the first question I would answer in the affirmative. The very name *Wakhsh* appears to be that from which the classical and Chinese names of the combined stream (*Oxus*, and *Potsu* or *Fatsu*) are derived. It is also spoken of both by Hiuen Tsang and by Edrisi, and by the latter is described as a very great river, though he evidently regards the Panja of Wood as the chief source.

Hiuen Tsang on the other hand appears to have regarded the Wakhsh branch as the main Potsu or Oxus. For after describing the Lake of Pamir, apparently the Sirikul of Wood, he says: "This lake discharges to the westward; for a river issues from it which runs west to the eastern frontier of the kingdom of *Tamositieti*, and *then joins the River Potsu;* their waters flow westward and are discharged into the sea[3]."

The following extracts show what Edrisi says on the subject:

"The Jihun takes its rise in the country of WAKHÁN[4] on the frontier of BADAKHSHAN, and there it bears the name of

Cunningham's view, that the country intended is BALTI, which he states to be still called *Bolor* by the Dard tribes. But doubtless, as he also remarks, the territory included Gilghit and Kanjút, the latter famous for its gold produce." Yule, *Notes on Hwen Thsang's Account of Tokhdristán*, p. 117.]

[1] "*Malaur* is a country with few level spots. It has a circuit of four months' march. The eastern frontier borders on Kashgar and Yarkand; it has Badakhshan to the north, Kabul to the west, and Kashmir to the south," etc. (*Not. et Extraits*, xiv, 492). ["Baluristán is bounded on the east by the provinces of Káshgar and Yarkand; on the north by Badakhshán; on the west by Kábul and Lumghán; and on the south by the dependencies of Káshmir. It is four months' journey in circumference." *Tarikh-i-Rashidi*... transl. by E. D. Ross, 1895, p. 385.—On *Bolor*, see Yule-Cordier's *Marco Polo*, i, p. 178 *n.* "It can, I think, be demonstrated that Bolor, or Bilaur, was the name applied throughout the Middle Ages to the elongated belt of mountain country south of the main range of the Hindu Kush, including the valleys of Kafiristan, Upper Chitral, Yasin, Gilgit, and Hunza-Nagar (and in the pages of some writers having an even wider application)." Curzon, *The Pamirs*, p. 70.]

[2] See Pauthier's *Polo*, p. 133.

[3] *Vie de H. T.*, p. 272.

[4] Jaubert has *Ujdn*, or rather (as his transcription of the Arabic shows) *Wajdn*, an obvious misreading for *Wakhán*. I regret that I cannot show these corrections (without which it is useless to quote the French Edrisi) in Arabic letters, which would carry conviction of their fairness, but at my distance from the press it gives too much trouble to the printer.

Khari-ab[1]. It receives five considerable tributaries which come from the countries of KHUTL[2] and WAKSH. Then it becomes a river surpassing all the rivers in the world as regards volume, depth and breadth of channel.

"The Khariab receives the waters of a river called *Akhsua* or *Mank*[3], those of *Than*[4] or *Balian*, of *Farghan* (or *Faughán*), of *Anjára* (or *Andijára*'), of WAKHSH-AB with a great number of affluents coming from the mountains of BOTM: (it also receives) other rivers such as those of *Sághanián*[5], and *Kawádián*[6], which all join in the province of the latter name and discharge into the Jihun.

"The Wakhsh-ab takes its rise in the country of the Turks; after arriving in the country of Wakhsh it loses itself under a high mountain, where it may be crossed as over a bridge. The length of its subterranean course is not known; finally, however, it issues from the mountain, runs along the frontier of the country of Balkh and reaches Tarmedh. The bridge of which we have spoken serves as a boundary between Khutl and Wakhshjird.

"The river having passed to Tarmedh flows on to Kilif, to Zam, to Amol, and finally discharges its waters into the Lake of Khwarizm (the Aral).

"Badakhshan is built on the west bank of the Khariab, the most considerable of the rivers that fall into the Jihun[7]. They bring to Badakhshan the musk of the regions of Tibet adjoining Wakhán. Badakhshan has on its frontier *Kanauj*, a dependency of India[8].

"The two provinces which you reach first beyond the Jihun are Khutl and Wakhsh. Although distinct and separate provinces they are under the same government. They lie between the Khariab and the Wakhsh-ab, the first of which rivers bathes the eastern part of Khutl, and the other the country of Wakhsh, of which we have spoken....Khutl is a province everywhere very

[1] This *Khari* is perhaps the *Icarus* of which Pliny speaks, on the authority of Varro (vi, 19).

[2] Jaubert throughout has *Jíl*, a name that seems totally unknown hereabouts (*Jíl* is another name for *Gilan*). There can be little doubt that it is misread for *Khutl* (sometimes called *Khutlán*), a province frequently mentioned as lying north to the Oxus towards Karategin. It is probably the *Kotulo* of Hiuen Tsang.

[3] Mank is afterwards described as a dependency of Jíl (Khutl).

[4] Afterwards apparently written Tha'lán (beginning with the fourth Arabic letter), and I believe a misreading for *Baghlán*.

[5] Apparently the Kafirnihan of the maps.

[6] Perhaps the Tupalak of the maps.

[7] This does not answer to the position of Faizabad, the capital of Badakhshan, abandoned in Wood's time, but reoccupied by Mír Shah, the chief, in 1866.

[8] *Kanauj* is absurd. I suspect it should be read *Mastauj*.

mountainous except near Wakhsh and the country of *Akjar* which borders on Mank, a dependency of Khutl[1]."

Further on, in giving a route from Sághánián (*Cheghánián*) to Wasjird (*Wakhshjird*) he mentions that the road comes upon the Wakhshab between nine miles and thirty miles from the former place, and that the river has here a breadth of *three miles*.... "From Wakhshjird to the place where the Wakhshab loses itself under a mountain is one short day....

"On the borders of Wakhsh and Khutl are Wakhán and Saknia, dependencies of the Turks' country. From Wakhán to Tibet is eighteen days. Wakhán possesses very rich silver mines, producing ore of excellent quality. Gold is found in the valleys when the torrents have been in flood[2]....Musk and slaves are also exported. Saknia is a town in dependence on the Khizilji Turks. It is five days from Wakhán, and its territories border on the possessions of China[3]."

In spite of the obscurities of these passages we can gather that the feeder of the Oxus which Edrisi's authorities regarded as the main one came from Wakhán, a country lying in the direction of Tibet, but that it received somewhere before reaching Tarmedh another great branch called the Wakhshab, so great as to be reported in one part of its course to have a channel three miles wide, and which rose in the Turks' country, *i.e.* at least as far off as the main chain of the Bolor; also that between those two great branches lay the provinces of Wakhsh and Khutl.

But where do these two streams join? Wood, the most competent to have settled the question, *in his book*, as we have seen, takes no notice of the Wakhshab at all. Nor is there any distinct trace of it in Macartney's map, though a tributary of the Oxus which he represents under the name of the *Surkháb* or R. of Karategín, entering the main stream a short distance above its

[1] *Mank* is perhaps the *Mungkien* (or Munkan) of Hiuen Tsang (see *Vie de H. T.*, pp. 269, 422).

[2] Wood mentions a torrent in Wakhán called *Zerzumen*, probably *Zar-Zamin*, "Gold-ground." He also says all the tributaries of the Oxus are fertile in gold (p. 382).

[3] This *Saknia* does not seem to be the Shagnán of Wood, which is below Wakhán. It appears to correspond to the *Shikini* of Hiuen Tsang.

["Northward across high mountains from *Tamosit'ieti* or Wakhán was *Shikhini*, having a circuit of twenty days' journey (2000 *li*). It consisted of a succession of mountains, valleys, and steppes covered with sand and stones. Much pulse and corn were grown, but little rice. The climate was very cold, and the people brutal, etc. Their written character resembled that of Tukhára, but their spoken language was different.

"Cunningham identifies this with Shighnán (or Shagnán) and there can be no doubt about it. The form *Shighnán* is no doubt a plural; the gentile adjective is *Shighni*, with which the Chinese form is identical." Yule, *Notes on Hwen Thsang's Account of the Principalities of Tokháristán*, p. 113.]

confluence with the Kokcha, has by later geographers (*e.g.* by the author of the map to *Russians in Central Asia*) been expanded into identity with the great Bolor-Wakhsh branch. But as Wood in his journey from Kila'h-Chap to Jan-Kila'h and Sayad *twice* passed the mouth of this Surkhab, so good an observer would scarcely have omitted to notice the confluence of a rival Oxus.

The gallant seaman is still more slightingly treated by Kiepert in his map of Asia. That geographer denies entirely the identity of the river which Wood ascended for thirty miles (as has just been mentioned) from the Kokcha confluence at Kila'h-Chap to Sayad, with that river which the same traveller had previously tracked from near the Ruby-Mines up to the Sirikul. The former river is conjured by Kiepert from the east to the west of the town of Sayad, and identified by him with the Bolor-Wakhsh River: the latter, under a new name, *Duwán*, due to the anonymous German, occupies quite a subordinate position, and is introduced into the Kokcha about half-way between Faizabád and Kila'h-Chap; a clandestine union surely! at a spot within a few miles of which Wood passed twice without being aware of it, and within five and twenty miles of which he lived for several weeks. Veniukov's treatment of this admirable traveller is equally violent, and we have already seen how he fares at the hands of the Schlagintweits. Surely this is geography run mad.

Perhaps Wood's own map suggests the real point of union, though without recognising its importance. In J. Walker's map of Wood's surveys we find the *Wagish* River indicated as entering the Oxus some twelve or thirteen miles to the *west* of Hazrat Imám, at a point of the river's course yet visited by no modern traveller. In my map I have assumed this to be the real Wakhshab, a hypothesis which has at least the advantage of not flying in the face of an honest and able traveller. [We have no room to discuss here anew the Oxus question; we refer the reader to our *Marco Polo*, to Yule's Introduction to the new edition of Wood's *Oxus*, 1872, and to G. N. Curzon's *The Pamirs and the Source of the Oxus*, 1896.]

Another vexed question embraced in this field is the course of the main feeder of the Yarkand river. According to Moorcroft's information, probably derived from Izzetoollah' (see *J.R.G.S.*, vol. i, p. 245), this rises in the north face of the Karakorum Pass, and flows in a northerly (north-westerly) direction to a point where it receives drainage from the (Eastern) Sarikul, and the Bolor Mountains, and then turns east (north-east) towards Yarkand. But, according to the best interpretation I can put upon the Chinese Hydrography translated by Julien (*N. Ann. des Voyages*, 1846, iii, 23 *seqq.*), the river rising in Karakorum, which I take to be that there termed *Tingdsapuho*, only joins the stream from Karchu and Sarikul *below* Yarkand. In the map I have hypothetically adopted the latter view, but with no great confidence.

I may add that both the authorities just cited illustrate the name given by Goës to the mountain between Sarikul and Yanghi-Hisar (Chechalith, no doubt misread for *Chechalich*)[1], the Chinese terming it *Tsitsikling*, and Moorcroft *Chechuklik* or "Place of Flowers."

Before concluding, I venture to contribute two or three remarks in aid of the discussion regarding the anonymous German Traveller.

Abdul Medjid, the British messenger in 1860, made *nineteen* long marches from Faizabad to the Karakul. The German is only *eleven* days, less some days' halt, say only eight days, from Karakul to Badakhshan (Faizabad).

The German represents the city just named as on the *south* side of the river on which it stands. We know from Wood that it is on the *north* side.

But on the other hand the German narrative, whether fictitious or no, contains indications of special sources of knowledge. For example, the name *Chakheraller*, which it applies to a mountain north of the Karakul, will be found in the Chinese Hydrography recently quoted, applied in the same way. The German speaks of the *Duvan*, by which the main Oxus of Wood seems meant, as crossed by a bridge to the north of Badakhshan. Wood tells us (p. 398) that it is bridged in that quarter. And the German speaks of the river of Vokhan passing underground at a spot on the frontier of the district of Vokhan, a remarkable coincidence with the statement of Edrisi quoted at p. 315.

I would suggest to any one trying to settle the question about this narrative a careful comparison of its indications with the map which Klaproth published of Central Asia. To this I have no access. [Recent voyages, especially those made by Sir Aurel Stein and Prof. Pelliot, have thrown a good deal of new light on the roads of Central Asia, and we have made use of the information in the revision of the itinerary of Goës; we had access also to the more recent Russian Maps.]

[1] See Vol. IV, *Journey of Benedict Goës*.

Cambridge:
PRINTED BY JOHN CLAY, M.A.
AT THE UNIVERSITY PRESS

The Hakluyt Society.

(Founded 1846.)

1915.

President.

ALBERT GRAY, Esq., K.C.

Vice-Presidents.

The Right Hon. The Lord BELHAVEN and STENTON.

Sir CLEMENTS MARKHAM, K.C.B., F.R.S., Ex.-Pres. R.G.S.

The Right Hon. The Lord PECKOVER of WISBECH.

Treasurer.

EDWARD HEAWOOD, Esq.

Council.

Admiral Sir LEWIS BEAUMONT, G.C.B., K.C.M.G.

Sir THOMAS B. BOWRING.

BOLTON GLANVILL CORNEY, Esq., I.S.O.

WILLIAM FOSTER, Esq., C.I.E.

F. H. H. GUILLEMARD, Esq., M.D.

Sir EVERARD IM THURN, K.C.M.G., C.B.

JOHN SCOTT KELTIE, Esq., LL.D.

Sir FREDERIC G. KENYON, K.C.B., F.B.A., Litt. D.

Sir CHARLES LUCAS, K.C.B., K.C.M.G.

Admiral Sir ALBERT HASTINGS MARKHAM, K.C.B.

ALFRED P. MAUDSLAY, Esq.

Lt.-Col. Sir MATTHEW NATHAN, G.C.M.G., R.E.

Admiral of the Fleet The Right Hon. Sir EDWARD HOBART SEYMOUR, G.C.B., O.M., G.C.V.O., LL.D.

H. R. TEDDER, Esq.

Lieut.-Col. Sir RICHARD CARNAC TEMPLE, Bart., C.I.E.

BASIL HOME THOMSON, Esq.

Hon. Secretary.

J. A. J. de VILLIERS, Esq.,
British Museum, W.C.

Clerk and Assistant Treasurer.

Mr. SAMUEL JOHN EVIS,
Royal Geographical Society, Kensington Gore, S.W.

Bankers in London.

Messrs. BARCLAY & Co., Ltd., 1, Pall Mall East, S.W.

Bankers in New York.

THE GUARANTY TRUST COMPANY OF NEW YORK, 140, Broadway.

Agent for Distribution and Sale of Volumes.

Mr. BERNARD QUARITCH, 11, Grafton Street, New Bond Street, W.

Annual Subscription.—One and a-half Guinea (in America, eight dollars).

The Hakluyt Society, established in 1846, has for its object the printing of rare and valuable Voyages, Travels, Naval Expeditions, and other geographical records. Books of this class are of the highest interest to students of history, geography, navigation, and ethnology; and many of them, especially the original narratives and translations of the Elizabethan and Stuart periods, are admirable examples of English prose at the stage of its most robust development.

The Society has not confined its selection to the books of English travellers, to a particular age, or to particular regions. Where the original is foreign, the work is given in English, fresh translations being made, except where it is possible to utilise the spirited renderings of the sixteenth or seventeenth century. The works selected for reproduction are printed (with rare exceptions) at full length. Each volume is placed in the charge of an editor especially competent—in many cases from personal acquaintance with the countries described—to give the reader such assistance as he needs for the elucidation of the text. As these editorial services are rendered gratuitously, *the whole of the amount received from subscribers is expended in the preparation of the Society's publications*.

One hundred volumes (forming Series I., see pages iv. to xiv.) were issued from 1846 to 1898; thirty-six volumes of Series II. (see pages xv. to xvii.) have been issued in the sixteen years ending 1914. A brief index to these is given on pages xix. to xxiv., and a list of works in preparation on page xviii.

THE Annual Subscription of ONE AND A-HALF GUINEA—entitling the member to the year's publications—is due on January 1, and may be paid to

Messrs. BARCLAY and Co., 1, Pall Mall East, London, S.W.;
The GUARANTY TRUST Co., 140, Broadway, New York.

Members have the sole privilege of purchasing back or current issues of the Society; these tend to rise in value, and those which are out of print are now only to be obtained at high prices.

The present scale of charges is as follows:—

FIRST SERIES,	*Sets*, omitting Nos. 1 to 14, 16, 17, 19, 22, 25, 32, 36, 37, and 42 (77 vols)	£40 0s. 0d.
Single Copies.—	Nos. 29, 31, 34, 46, 47, 51, 53, 55, 56, 58, 60 to 73, 77, 79, 80, 82 to 87, 90 to 94, 96, 97, 98, at	10s. 6d.
	Nos. 28, 30, 41, 45, 48, 49, 50, 57, 74, 76, 78, 81, 88, 89, 95, 100, at	15s. 0d.
	Nos. 20, 21, 23, 26, 27, 33, 35, 38, 40, 43, 44, 54, 59, 75, 99, at	25s. 0d.
SECOND SERIES,	Nos. 11 to 22, 28, 29, 31, 35, at	10s. 6d.
	Nos. 23, 24, 25, 26, 27, 30, 32, 37, at	15s. 0d.
	Nos. 33, 34, at	20s. 0d.
	Nos. 3, 6, at	25s. 0d.

All other issues of this Series are out of print.

Gentlemen desiring to be enrolled as members should send their names to the Hon. Secretary, with the form of Banker's Order enclosed in this Prospectus. Applications for back volumes should be addressed to the Society's Agent, MR. QUARITCH, 11, Grafton Street, New Bond Street, London, W.

WORKS ALREADY ISSUED.

FIRST SERIES.

1847-1898.

1—The Observations of Sir Richard Hawkins, Knt.,

In his Voyage into the South Sea in 1593. Reprinted from the edition of 1622, and edited by ADMIRAL CHARLES RAMSAY DRINKWATER BETHUNE, C.B. pp. xvi. 246. Index.

(First Edition out of print. See No. 57.*) Issued for* 1847.

2—Select Letters of Christopher Columbus,

With Original Documents relating to the Discovery of the New World. Translated and Edited by RICHARD HENRY MAJOR, F.S.A., Keeper of Maps, British Museum, Sec. R.G.S. pp. xc. 240. Index.

(First Edition out of print. See No. 43. Two copies only were printed on vellum, one of which is in the British Museum, C. 29. k. 14.)

Issued for 1847.

3—The Discovery of the Large, Rich, & Beautiful Empire of Guiana,

With a relation of the great and golden City of Manoa (which the Spaniards call El Dorado), &c., performed in the year 1595 by SIR WALTER RALEGH, Knt. . . . Reprinted from the edition of 1596. With some unpublished Documents relative to that country. Edited with copious explanatory Notes and a biographical Memoir by SIR ROBERT HERMANN SCHOMBURGK, Ph. D. pp. lxxv. xv. 1 Map. Index.

(Out of print. Second Edition in preparation.) Issued for 1848.

4—Sir Francis Drake his Voyage, 1595,

By THOMAS MAYNARDE, together with the Spanish Account of Drake's attack on Puerto Rico. Edited from the original MSS. by WILLIAM DESBOROUGH COOLEY. pp. viii. 65. *(Out of print.) Issued for* 1848.

5—Narratives of Voyages towards the North-West,

In search of a Passage to Cathay & India, 1496 to 1631. With selections from the early Records of . . . the East India Company and from MSS. in the British Museum. Edited by THOMAS RUNDALL. pp. xx. 259. 2 Maps.

(Out of print.) Issued for 1849.

6—The Historie of Travaile into Virginia Britannia,

Expressing the Cosmographie and Commodities of the Country, together with the manners and customs of the people, gathered and observed as well by those who went first thither as collected by WILLIAM STRACHEY, Gent., the first Secretary of the Colony. Now first edited from the original MS. in the British Museum by RICHARD HENRY MAJOR, F.S.A., Keeper of Maps, British Museum, Sec. R.G.S. pp. xxxvi. 203. 1 Map. 6 Illus. Glossary. Index.

(Out of print.) Issued for 1849.

7—Divers Voyages touching the Discovery of America

And the Islands adjacent, collected and published by RICHARD HAKLUYT, Prebendary of Bristol, in the year 1582. Edited, with notes & an introduction by JOHN WINTER JONES, Principal Librarian of the British Museum. pp. xci. 171. 6. 2 Maps. 1 Illus. Index. *(Out of print.) Issued for* 1850.

8—Memorials of the Empire of Japon.

In the Sixteenth and Seventeenth Centuries. (The Kingdome of Japonia. Harl. MSS. 6249.—The Letters of Wm. Adams, 1611 to 1617.) With a Commentary by THOMAS RUNDALL. pp. xxxviii. 186. 1 Map. 5 Illus.
(Out of print.) Issued for 1850.

9—The Discovery and Conquest of Terra Florida,

By Don Ferdinando de Soto, & six hundred Spaniards his followers. Written by a Gentleman of Elvas, employed in all the action, and translated out of Portuguese by RICHARD HAKLUYT. Reprinted from the edition of 1611. Edited with Notes & an Introduction, & a Translation of a Narrative of the Expedition by LUIS HERNANDEZ DE BIEDMA, Factor to the same, by WILLIAM BRENCHLEY RYE, Keeper of Printed Books, British Museum. pp. lxvii. 200. v. 1 Map. Index. *(Out of print.) Issued for* 1851.

10—Notes upon Russia,

Being a Translation from the Earliest Account of that Country, entitled Rerum Muscoviticarum Commentarii, by the BARON SIGISMUND VON HERBERSTEIN, Ambassador from the Court of Germany to the Grand Prince Vasiley Ivanovich, in the years 1517 and 1526. Translated and Edited with Notes & an Introduction, by RICHARD HENRY MAJOR, F.S.A., Keeper of Maps, British Museum, Sec. R.G.S. Vol. 1. pp. clxii. 116. 2 Illus.
(Vol. 2 = No. 12.) *(Out of print.) Issued for* 1851.

11—The Geography of Hudson's Bay,

Being the Remarks of Captain W. COATS, in many Voyages to that locality, between the years 1727 and 1751. With an Appendix containing Extracts from the Log of Captain MIDDLETON on his Voyage for the Discovery of the North-west Passage, in H.M.S. "Furnace," in 1741-3. Edited by JOHN BARROW, F.R.S., F.S.A. pp. x. 147. Index.
(Out of print.) Issued for 1852.

12—Notes upon Russia.

(Vol. I. = No. 10.) Vol. 2. pp. iv. 266. 2 Maps. 1 Illus. Index.
(Out of print.) Issued for 1852.

13—A True Description of Three Voyages by the North-East,

Towards Cathay and China, undertaken by the Dutch in the years 1594, 1595 and 1596, with their Discovery of Spitzbergen, their residence of ten months in Novaya Zemlya, and their safe return in two open boats. By GERRIT DE VEER. Published at Amsterdam in 1598, & in 1609 translated into English by WILLIAM PHILIP. Edited by CHARLES TILSTONE BEKE, Ph.D., F.S.A. pp. cxlii 291. 4 Maps. 12 Illus. Index.
(Out of print. See also No. 54.) Issued for 1853.

14-15—The History of the Great and Mighty Kingdom of China and the Situation Thereof.

Compiled by the Padre JUAN GONZALEZ DE MENDOZA, & now reprinted from the Early Translation of R. Parke. Edited by SIR GEORGE THOMAS STAUNTON, Bart., M.P., F.R.S. With an Introduction by RICHARD HENRY MAJOR, F.S.A., Keeper of Maps, British Museum, Sec. R.G.S., 2 vols. Index. *(Vol. 14 out of print.) Issued for* 1854.

16—The World Encompassed by Sir Francis Drake.

Being his next Voyage to that to Nombre de Dios. [By SIR FRANCIS DRAKE, the Younger.] Collated with an unpublished Manuscript of Francis Fletcher, Chaplain to the Expedition. With Appendices illustrative of the same Voyage, and Introduction, by WILLIAM SANDYS WRIGHT VAUX, F.R.S., Keeper of Coins, British Museum. pp. xl. 295. 1 Map. Index. *(Out of print.) Issued for* 1855.

17—The History of the Two Tartar Conquerors of China,

Including the two Journeys into Tartary of Father Ferdinand Verbiest, in the suite of the Emperor Kang-Hi. From the French of Père PIERRE JOSEPH D'ORLÉANS, of the Company of Jesus, 1688. To which is added Father Pereira's Journey into Tartary in the suite of the same Emperor. From the Dutch of NICOLAAS WITSEN. Translated and Edited by the EARL OF ELLESMERE. With an Introduction by RICHARD HENRY MAJOR, F.S.A., Keeper of Maps, British Museum, Sec. R.G.S. pp. xv. vi. 153. Index.
(Out of print.) *Issued for* 1855.

18—A Collection of Documents on Spitzbergen and Greenland,

Comprising a Translation from F. MARTENS' Voyage to Spitzbergen, 1671 ; a Translation from ISAAC DE LA PEYRÈRE'S Histoire du Groenland, 1663, and God's Power and Providence in the Preservation of Eight Men in Greenland Nine Moneths and Twelve Dayes. 1630. Edited by ADAM WHITE, of the British Museum. pp. xvi. 288. 2 Maps. Index. *Issued for* 1856.

19—The Voyage of Sir Henry Middleton to Bantam and the Maluco Islands,

Being the Second Voyage set forth by the Governor and Company of Merchants of London trading into the East Indies. From the (rare) Edition of 1606. Annotated and Edited by BOLTON CORNEY, M.R.S.L. pp. xi. 83. 52. viii. 3 Maps. 3 Illus. Bibliography. Index.
(Out of print). *Issued for* 1856.

20—Russia at the Close of the Sixteenth Century.

Comprising the Treatise, "The Russe Commonwealth" by Dr. GILES FLETCHER, and the Travels of SIR JEROME HORSEY, Knt., now for the first time printed entire from his own MS. Edited by SIR EDWARD AUGUSTUS BOND, K.C.B., Principal Librarian of the British Museum. pp. cxxxiv. 392. Index. *Issued for* 1857.

21—History of the New World. By Girolamo Benzoni, of Milan.

Showing his Travels in America, from A.D. 1541 to 1556. with some particulars of the Island of Canary. Now first Translated and Edited by ADMIRAL WILLIAM HENRY SMYTH, K.S.F., F.R.S., D.C.L. pp. iv. 280. 19 Illus. Index. *Issued for* 1857.

22—India in the Fifteenth Century.

Being a Collection of Narratives of Voyages to India in the century preceding the Portuguese discovery of the Cape of Good Hope ; from Latin, Persian, Russian, and Italian Sources. Now first Translated into English. Edited with an Introduction by RICHARD HENRY MAJOR, F.S.A., Keeper of Maps, British Museum. pp. xc. 49. 39. 32. 10. Index.
(Out of print.) *Issued for* 1858.

23—Narrative of a Voyage to the West Indies and Mexico,

In the years 1599-1602, with 4 Maps and 5 Illustrations. By SAMUEL CHAMPLAIN. Translated from the original and unpublished Manuscript, with a Biographical Notice and Notes by ALICE WILMERE. Edited by NORTON SHAW. pp. xcix. 48. *Issued for* 1858.

24—Expeditions into the Valley of the Amazons, 1539, 1540, 1639,

Containing the Journey of GONZALO PIZARRO, from the Royal Commentaries of Garcilasso Inca de la Vega ; the Voyage of Francisco de Orellana, from the General History of Herrera ; and the Voyage of Cristoval de Acuña. Translated and Edited by SIR CLEMENTS R. MARKHAM, K.C.B., F.R.S., ex-Pres. R.G.S. pp. lxiv. 190. 1 Map. List of Tribes in the Valley of the Amazons. *Issued for* 1859.

25—Early Voyages to Terra Australis,

Now called Australia. A Collection of documents, and extracts from early MS. Maps, illustrative of the history of discovery on the coasts of that vast Island, from the beginning of the Sixteenth Century to the time of Captain Cook. Edited with an Introduction by RICHARD HENRY MAJOR, F.S.A., Keeper of Maps, British Museum, Sec. R.G.S. pp. cxix. 200. 13. 5 Maps. Index. (*Out of print.*) *Issued for* 1859

26—Narrative of the Embassy of Ruy Gonzalez de Clavijo to the Court of Timour, at Samarcand, A.D., 1403-6.

Translated for the first time with Notes, a Preface, & an introductory Life of Timour Beg, by SIR CLEMENTS R. MARKHAM, K.C.B., F.R.S., ex-Pres. R.G.S. pp. lvi. 200. 1 Map. *Issued for* 1860

27—Henry Hudson the Navigator, 1607-13.

The Original Documents in which his career is recorded. Collected, partly Translated, & annotated with an Introduction by GEORGE MICHAEL ASHER, LL.D. pp. ccxviii. 292. 2 Maps. Bibliography. Index. *Issued for* 1860.

28—The Expedition of Pedro de Ursua and Lope de Aguirre,

In search of El Dorado and Omagua, in 1560-61. Translated from Fray PEDRO SIMON'S "Sixth Historical Notice of the Conquest of Tierra Firme," 1627, by WILLIAM BOLLAERT, F.R.G.S. With an Introduction by SIR CLEMENTS R. MARKHAM, K.C.B., F.R.S., ex-Pres. R.G.S. pp. lii. 237. 1 Map. *Issued for* 1861.

29—The Life and Acts of Don Alonzo Enriquez de Guzman,

A Knight of Seville, of the Order of Santiago, A.D. 1518 to 1543. Translated from an original & inedited MS. in the National Library at Madrid. With Notes and an Introduction by SIR CLEMENTS R. MARKHAM, K.C.B., F.R.S., ex-Pres. R.G.S. pp. xxxv. 168. 1 Illus. *Issued for* 1862.

30—The Discoveries of the World

From their first original unto the year of our Lord 1555. By ANTONIO GALVANO, Governor of Ternate. [Edited by F. DE SOUSA TAVARES.] Corrected, quoted, & published in England by RICHARD HAKLUYT, 1601. Now reprinted, with the original Portuguese text (1563), and edited by ADMIRAL CHARLES RAMSAY DRINKWATER BETHUNE, C.B. pp. iv. viiii. 242. *Issued for* 1862.

31—Mirabilia Descripta. The Wonders of the East.

By FRIAR JORDANUS, of the Order of Preachers & Bishop of Columbum in India the Greater, *circa* 1330. Translated from the Latin Original, as published at Paris in 1839, in the *Recueil de Voyages et de Mémoires*, of the Societé de Géographie. With the addition of a Commentary, by COL. SIR HENRY YULE, K.C.S.I., R.E., C.B. pp. iv. xviii. 68. Index. *Issued for* 1863.

32—The Travels of Ludovico di Varthema

In Egypt, Syria, Arabia, Persia, India, & Ethiopia, A.D. 1503 to 1508. Translated from the original Italian edition of 1510, with a Preface, by JOHN WINTER JONES, F.S.A., Principal Librarian of the British Museum, & Edited, with Notes & an Introduction, by the REV. GEORGE PERCY BADGER. pp. cxxi. 321. 1 Map. Index. (*Out of print.*) *Issued for* 1863.

33—The Travels of Pedro de Cieza de Leon, A.D. 1532-50,

From the Gulf of Darien to the City of La Plata, contained in the first part of his Chronicle of Peru (Antwerp, 1554). Translated & Edited, with Notes & an Introduction, by SIR CLEMENTS R. MARKHAM, K.C.B., F.R.S., ex-Pres. R.G.S. pp. xvi. lvii. 438. Index.
(Vol. 2 = No. 68.) *Issued for* 1864.

34—Narrative of the Proceedings of Pedrarias Davila

In the Provinces of Tierra Firme or Castilla del Oro, & of the discovery of the South Sea and the Coasts of Peru and Nicaragua. Written by the Adelantado Pascual de Andagoya. Translated and Edited, with Notes & an Introduction, by SIR CLEMENTS R. MARKHAM, K.C.B., F.R.S., ex-Pres. R.G.S. pp. xxix. 88. 1 Map. Index. *Issued for* 1865.

35—A Description of the Coasts of East Africa and Malabar

In the beginning of the Sixteenth Century, by DUARTE BARBOSA, a Portuguese. Translated from an early Spanish manuscript in the Barcelona Library, with Notes & a Preface, by LORD STANLEY OF ALDERLEY. pp. xi. 336. 2 Illus. Index. *Issued for* 1865.

36-37—Cathay and the Way Thither.

Being a Collection of mediæval notices of China, previous to the Sixteenth Century. Translated and Edited by COLONEL SIR HENRY YULE, K.C.S.I., R.E., C.B. With a preliminary Essay on the intercourse between China & the Western Nations previous to the discovery of the Cape Route. 2 vols. 3 Maps. 2 Illus. Bibliography. Index.
(*Out of print ; see also Ser. II., Vol.* 33.) *Issued for* 1866.

38—The Three Voyages of Sir Martin Frobisher,

In search of a Passage to Cathaia & India by the North-West, A.D. 1576-8. By GEORGE BEST. Reprinted from the First Edition of HAKLUYT'S Voyages. With Selections from MS. Documents in the British Museum & State Paper Office. Edited by ADMIRAL SIR RICHARD COLLINSON, K.C.B. pp. xxvi. 376. 2 Maps. 1 Illus. Index. *Issued for* 1867.

39—The Philippine Islands,

Moluccas, Siam, Cambodia, Japan, and China, at the close of the 16th Century. By ANTONIO DE MORGA, 1609. Translated from the Spanish, with Notes & a Preface, and a Letter from Luis Vaez de Torres, describing his Voyage through the Torres Straits, by LORD STANLEY OF ALDERLEY. pp. xxiv. 431. 2 Illus. Index. *Issued for* 1868.

40—The Fifth Letter of Hernan Cortes

To the Emperor Charles V., containing an Account of his Expedition to Honduras in 1525-26. Translated from the original Spanish by DON PASCUAL DE GAYANGOS. pp. xvi. 156. Index. *Issued for* 1868.

41—The Royal Commentaries of the Yncas.

By the YNCA GARCILASSO DE LA VEGA. Translated and Edited, with Notes & an Introduction, by SIR CLEMENTS R. MARKHAM, K.C.B. F.R.S., ex-Pres. R.G.S. Vol. 1. (Books I.-IV.) pp. xi. 359. 1 Map. Index.
(Vol. 2. = No. 45.) *Issued for* 1869.

42—The Three Voyages of Vasco da Gama,

And his Viceroyalty, from the Lendas da India of GASPAR CORREA ; accompanied by original documents. Translated from the Portuguese, with Notes & an Introduction, by LORD STANLEY OF ALDERLEY. pp. lxxvii. 430. xxxv. 3 Illus. Index. (*Out of print.*) *Issued for* 1869.

43—Select Letters of Christopher Columbus,

With other Original Documents relating to his Four Voyages to the New World. Translated and Edited by RICHARD HENRY MAJOR, F.S.A., Keeper of Maps, British Museum, Sec. R.G.S. Second Edition. pp. iv. 142. 3 Maps. 1 Illus. Index.
(First Edition = No. 2.) *Issued for* 1870.

44—History of the Imâms and Seyyids of 'Omân,

By SALÎL-IBN-RAZÎK, from A.D. 661-1856. Translated from the original Arabic, and Edited, with a continuation of the History down to 1870, by the REV. GEORGE PERCY BADGER, F.R.G.S. pp. cxxviii. 435. 1 Map. Bibliography. Index. *Issued for* 1870.

45—The Royal Commentaries of the Yncas.

By the YNCA GARCILASSO DE LA VEGA. Translated & Edited with Notes, an Introduction, & an Analytical Index, by SIR CLEMENTS R. MARKHAM, K.C.B., F.R.S., ex-Pres. R.G.S. Vol. II. (Books V.-IX.) pp. 553.
(Vol. 1. = No. 41.) *Issued for* 1871.

46—The Canarian,

Or Book of the Conquest and Conversion of the Canarians in the year 1402, by Messire JEAN DE BÉTHENCOURT, Kt. Composed by Pierre Bontier and Jean le Verrier. Translated and Edited by RICHARD HENRY MAJOR, F.S.A., Keeper of Maps, British Museum, Sec. R.G.S. pp. lv. 229. 1 Map. 2 Illus. Index. *Issued for* 1871.

47—Reports on the Discovery of Peru.

I. Report of FRANCISCO DE XERES, Secretary to Francisco Pizarro. II. Report of MIGUEL DE ASTETE on the Expedition to Pachacamac. III. Letter of HERNANDO PIZARRO to the Royal Audience of Santo Domingo. IV. Report of PEDRO SANCHO on the Partition of the Ransom of Atahuallpa. Translated and Edited, with Notes & an Introduction, by SIR CLEMENTS R. MARKHAM, K.C.B., F.R.S., ex-Pres. R.G.S. pp. xxii. 143. 1 Map. *Issued for* 1872.

48—Narratives of the Rites and Laws of the Yncas.

Translated from the original Spanish MSS., & Edited, with Notes and an Introduction, by SIR CLEMENTS R. MARKHAM, K.C.B., F.R.S., ex-Pres. R.G.S. pp. xx. 220. Index. *Issued for* 1872.

49—Travels to Tana and Persia,

By JOSAFA BARBARO and AMBROGIO CONTARINI. Translated from the Italian by WILLIAM THOMAS, Clerk of the Council to Edward VI., and by E. A. ROY, and Edited, with an Introduction, by LORD STANLEY OF ALDERLEY. pp. xi. 175. Index. A Narrative of Italian Travels in Persia, in the Fifteenth and Sixteenth centuries. Translated and Edited by CHARLES GREY. pp. xvii. 231. Index. *Issued for* 1873.

50—The Voyages of the Venetian Brothers, Nicolo & Antonio Zeno,

To the Northern Seas in the Fourteenth century. Comprising the latest known accounts of the Lost Colony of Greenland, & of the Northmen in America before Columbus. Translated & Edited, with Notes and Introduction, by RICHARD HENRY MAJOR, F.S.A., Keeper of Maps, British Museum, Sec. R.G.S. pp. ciii. 64. 2 Maps. Index. *Issued for* 1873.

51—The Captivity of Hans Stade of Hesse in 1547-55,

Among the Wild Tribes of Eastern Brazil. Translated by ALBERT TOOTAL, of Rio de Janiero, and annotated by SIR RICHARD FRANCIS BURTON, K.C.M.G. pp. xcvi. 169. Bibliography. *Issued for* 1874.

52—The First Voyage Round the World by Magellan. 1518-1521.
Translated from the Accounts of PIGAFETTA and other contemporary writers. Accompanied by original Documents, with Notes & an Introduction, by LORD STANLEY OF ALDERLEY. pp. lx. 257. xx. 2 Maps. 5 Illus. Index.
Issued for 1874.

53—The Commentaries of the Great Afonso Dalboquerque,
Second Viceroy of India. Translated from the Portuguese Edition of 1774, and Edited by WALTER DE GRAY BIRCH, F.R.S.L., of the British Museum. Vol. 1. pp. lx. 256. 2 Maps. 1 Illus. (Index in No. 69.)
(Vol. 2=No. 55. Vol. 3=No. 62. Vol. 4=No. 69.) *Issued for* 1875.

54—The Three Voyages of William Barents to the Arctic Regions, in 1594, 1595, & 1596.
By GERRIT DE VEER. Edited, with an Introduction, by Lieut. KOOLEMANS BEYNEN, of the Royal Netherlands Navy. Second Edition. pp. clxxiv. 289. 2 Maps. 12 Illus. *Issued for* 1876.
(First Edition=No. 13.)

55—The Commentaries of the Great Afonso Dalboquerque,
Second Viceroy of India. Translated from the Portuguese Edition of 1774, with Notes and an Introduction, by WALTER DE GRAY BIRCH, F.R.S.L., of the British Museum. Vol. 2. pp. cxxxiv. 242. 2 Maps 2 Illus. (Index in No. 69.) *Issued for* 1875.
(Vol. 1=No. 53. Vol. 3=No. 62. Vol. 4=No. 69.)

56—The Voyages of Sir James Lancaster, Knt., to the East Indies,
With Abstracts of Journals of Voyages to the East Indies, during the Seventeenth century, preserved in the India Office, & the Voyage of Captain JOHN KNIGHT, 1606, to seek the North-West Passage. Edited by SIR CLEMENTS R. MARKHAM, K.C.B., F R.S., ex-Pres. R.G.S. pp. xxii. 314 Index.
Issued for 1877.

57—The Hawkins' Voyages
During the reigns of Henry VIII, Queen Elizabeth, and James I. [Second edition of No. 1.] Edited by SIR CLEMENTS R. MARKHAM, K.C.B., F.R.S., ex-Pres. R.G.S. pp. lii. 453. 1 Illus. Index. *Issued for* 1877.
(First Edition=No. 1).

58—The Bondage and Travels of Johann Schiltberger, a Native of Bavaria, in Europe, Asia, & Africa.
From his capture at the battle of Nicopolis in 1396 to his escape and return to Europe in 1427. Translated from the Heidelberg MS., Edited in 1859 by Professor KARL FR. NEUMANN, by Commander JOHN BUCHAN TELFER, R.N.; F.S.A. With Notes by Professor P. BRUUN, & a Preface, Introduction, & Notes by the Translator & Editor. pp. xxxii. 263. 1 Map. Bibliography. Index. *Issued for* 1878.

59—The Voyages and Works of John Davis the Navigator.
Edited by ADMIRAL SIR ALBERT HASTINGS MARKHAM, K.C.B. pp. xcv. 392. 2 Maps. 15 Illus. Bibliography. Index. *Issued for* 1878.

The Map of the World, A.D. 1600.
Called by Shakspere "The New Map, with the Augmentation of the Indies." To illustrate the Voyages of John Davis. *Issued for* 1878.

60-61—The Natural & Moral History of the Indies.

By Father JOSEPH DE ACOSTA. Reprinted from the English Translated Edition of Edward Grimston, 1604; and Edited by SIR CLEMENTS R. MARKHAM, K.C.B., F.R.S., ex-Pres. R.G.S. Vol. 1, The Natural History Books, I.-IV. pp. xlv. 295. Vol. 2, The Moral History Books, V.-VII. pp. xiii. 295-551. Index. *Issued for* 1879.

Map of Peru.

To Illustrate Nos. 33, 41, 45, 60, and 61. *Issued for* 1879.

62—The Commentaries of the Great Afonso Dalboquerque,

Second Viceroy of India. Translated from the Portuguese Edition of 1774, with Notes & an Introduction, by WALTER DE GRAY BIRCH, F.S.A., of the British Museum. Vol. 3. pp. xliv. 308. 3 Maps. 3 Illus. (Index in No. 69.) *Issued for* 1880.

63—The Voyages of William Baffin, 1612-1622.

Edited, with Notes & an Introduction, by SIR CLEMENTS R. MARKHAM, K.C.B., F.R.S., ex-Pres. R.G.S. pp. lix. 192. 8 Maps. 1 Illus. Index. *Issued for* 1880.

64—Narrative of the Portuguese Embassy to Abyssinia

During the years 1520-1527. By Father FRANCISCO ALVAREZ. Translated from the Portuguese & Edited, with Notes & an Introduction, by LORD STANLEY OF ALDERLEY. pp. xxvii. 416 Index. *Issued for* 1881.

65—The History of the Bermudas or Summer Islands.

Attributed to Captain NATHANIEL BUTLER. Edited from a MS. in the Sloane Collection, British Museum, by General SIR JOHN HENRY LEFROY, R.A., K.C.M.G., C.B., F.R.S. pp. xii. 327. 1 Map. 3 Illus. Glossary. Index. *Issued for* 1881.

66-67—The Diary of Richard Cocks,

Cape-Merchant in the English Factory in Japan, 1615-1622, with Correspondence (Add. MSS. 31,300-1, British Museum). Edited by SIR EDWARD MAUNDE THOMPSON, K.C.B., Director of the British Museum. Vol. 1. pp. liv. 349. Vol. 2, pp. 368. Index. *Issued for* 1882.

68—The Second Part of the Chronicle of Peru, 1532-1550

By PEDRO DE CIEZA DE LEON. 1554. Translated and Edited, with Notes & an Introduction, by SIR CLEMENTS R. MARKHAM, K.C.B, F.R.S., ex-Pres. R.G.S. pp. lx. 247. Index. *Issued for* 1883.
(Vol. 1=No. 33.)

69—The Commentaries of the Great Afonso Dalboquerque,

Second Viceroy of India. Translated from the Portuguese Edition of 1774, with Notes & an Introduction, by WALTER DE GRAY BIRCH, F.S.A., of the British Museum. Vol. 4. pp. xxxv. 324. 2 Maps. 2 Illus. Index to the 4 vols. *Issued for* 1883.
(Vol. 1=No. 53. Vol. 2=No. 55. Vol. 3=No. 62.)

70-71—The Voyage of John Huyghen van Linschoten to the East Indies.

From the Old English Translation of 1598. The First Book, containing his Description of the East. In Two Volumes, Edited, the First Volume, by the late ARTHUR COKE BURNELL, Ph.D., C.I.E., Madras C. S.; the Second Volume, by PIETER ANTON TIELE, of Utrecht. Vol 1. pp. lii. 307. Vol. 2. pp. xv. 341. Index. *Issued for* 1884.

72-73—Early Voyages and Travels to Russia and Persia,

By ANTHONY JENKINSON and other Englishmen, with some account of the first Intercourse of the English with Russia and Central Asia by way of the Caspian Sea. Edited by EDWARD DELMAR MORGAN, and CHARLES HENRY COOTE, of the British Museum. Vol. 1. pp. clxii. 176. 2 Maps. 2 Illus. Vol. 2. pp. 177-496. 2 Maps. 1 Illus. Index. *Issued for* 1885.

74-75—The Diary of William Hedges, Esq.,

Afterwards SIR WILLIAM HEDGES, during his Agency in Bengal; as well as on his Voyage out and Return Overland (1681-1687). Transcribed for the Press, with Introductory Notes, etc., by R. BARLOW, and Illustrated by copious Extracts from Unpublished Records, etc., by Col. Sir HENRY YULE, K.C.S.I., R.E., C.B., LL.D. Vol. 1. The Diary, with Index. pp. xii. 265. Vol. 2. Notices regarding Sir William Hedges, Documentary Memoirs of Job Charnock, and other Biographical & Miscellaneous Illustrations of the time in India. pp. ccclx. 287. 18 Illus. *Issued for* 1886.
(Vol. 3=No. 78.)

76-77—The Voyage of François Pyrard, of Laval, to the East Indies,

The Maldives, the Moluccas and Brazil. Translated into English from the Third French Edition of 1619, and Edited, with Notes, by ALBERT GRAY, K.C., assisted by HARRY CHARLES PURVIS BELL, Ceylon C. S. Vol. 1. pp. lviii. 1 Map. 11 Illus. Vol. 2. Part I. pp. xlvii. 287. 7 Illus.
(Vol. 2. Part II.=No. 80.) *Issued for* 1887.

78—The Diary of William Hedges, Esq.

Vol. 3. Documentary Contributions to a Biography of Thomas Pitt, Governor of Fort St. George, with Collections on the Early History of the Company's Settlement in Bengal, & on Early Charts and Topography of the Húglí River. pp. cclxii. 1 Map. 8 Illus. Index to Vols. 2, 3. *Issued for* 1888.
(Vols. 1, 2=Nos. 74, 75.)

79—Tractatus de Globis, et eorum usu.

A Treatise descriptive of the Globes constructed by Emery Molyneux, and Published in 1592. By ROBERT HUES. Edited, with annotated Indices & an Introduction, by SIR CLEMENTS R. MARKHAM, K.C.B., F.R.S., ex-Pres. R.G.S. To which is appended,

Sailing Directions for the Circumnavigation of England,

And for a Voyage to the Straits of Gibraltar. From a Fifteenth Century MS. Edited, with an Account of the MS., by JAMES GAIRDNER, of the Public Record Office; with a Glossary by EDWARD DELMAR MORGAN. pp. l. 229. 37. 1 Illus. 1 Map. *Issued for* 1888.

80—The Voyage of François Pyrard, of Laval, to the East Indies, the Maldives, the Moluccas, and Brazil.

Translated into English from the Third French Edition of 1619, and Edited, with Notes, by ALBERT GRAY, K.C., assisted by HARRY CHARLES PURVIS BELL, Ceylon Civil Service. Vol 2. Pt. II. pp. xii. 289-572. 2 Maps. Index.
(Vol 1. Vol. 2. Pt. I.=Nos. 76, 77.) *Issued for* 1889.

81—The Conquest of La Plata, 1535-1555.

I.—Voyage of ULRICH SCHMIDT to the Rivers La Plata and Paraguai, from the original German edition, 1567. II. The Commentaries of Alvar Nuñez Cabeza de Vaca. From the original Spanish Edition, 1555. Translated, with Notes and an Introduction, by H. E. DON LUIS L. DOMINGUEZ, Minister Plenipotentiary of the Argentine Republic. pp. xlvi. 282. 1 Map, Bibliography. Index. *Issued for* 1889.

82-83—The Voyage of François Leguat, of Bresse, 1690-98.

To Rodriguez, Mauritius, Java, and the Cape of Good Hope. Transcribed from the First English Edition, 1708. Edited and Annotated by Capt. SAMUEL PASFIELD OLIVER, (late) R.A. Vol 1. pp. lxxxviii. 137. 1 Illus. 6 Maps. Bibliography. Vol. 2. pp. xviii. 433. 5 Illus. 5 Maps. Index.

Issued for 1890.

84-85—The Travels of Pietro della Valle to India.

From the Old English Translation of 1664, by G. HAVERS. Edited, with a Life of the Author, an Introduction & Notes by EDWARD GREY, late Bengal C. S. Vol. 1. pp. lvi. 192. 2 Maps. 2 Illus. Bibliography. Vol. 2. pp. xii. 193-456. Index. *Issued for* 1891.

86—The Journal of Christopher Columbus

During his First Voyage (1492-93), and Documents relating to the Voyages of JOHN CABOT and GASPAR CORTE REAL. Translated, with Notes & an Introduction, by SIR CLEMENTS R. MARKHAM, K.C.B., F.R.S., ex-Pres. R.G.S. pp. liv. 259. 3 Maps. 1 Illus. Index. *Issued for* 1892.

87—Early Voyages and Travels in the Levant.

I.—The Diary of Master THOMAS DALLAM, 1599-1600. II.—Extracts from the Diaries of Dr. JOHN COVEL, 1670-1679. With some Account of the Levant Company of Turkey Merchants. Edited by JAMES THEODORE BENT, F.S.A., F.R.G.S. pp. xlv. 305. Illus. Index.

Issued for 1892.

88-89—The Voyages of Captain Luke Foxe, of Hull, and Captain Thomas James, of Bristol,

In Search of a N.-W. Passage, 1631-32; with Narratives of the Earlier North-West Voyages of Frobisher, Davis, Weymouth, Hall, Knight, Hudson, Button, Gibbons, Bylot, Baffin, Hawkridge, & others. Edited, with Notes & an Introduction, by ROBERT MILLER CHRISTY, F.L.S. Vol. 1. pp. ccxxxi. 259. 2 Maps. 2 Illus. Vol. 2. pp. viii. 261-681. 3 Maps. 1 Illus. Index.

Issued for 1893.

90—The Letters of Amerigo Vespucci

And other Documents illustrative of his Career. Translated, with Notes & an Introduction, by SIR CLEMENTS R. MARKHAM, K.C.B., F.R.S., ex-Pres. R.G.S. pp. xliv. 121. 1 Map. Index.

Issued for 1894.

91—Narratives of the Voyages of Pedro Sarmiento de Gamboa to the Straits of Magellan, 1579-80.

Translated and Edited, with Illustrative Documents and Introduction, by SIR CLEMENTS R. MARKHAM, K.C.B., F.R.S., ex-Pres. R.G.S. pp. xxx. 401. 1 Map. Index.

Issued for 1894.

92-93-94—The History and Description of Africa,

And of the Notable Things Therein Contained. Written by AL-HASSAN IBN-MOHAMMED AL-WEZAZ AL-FASI, a Moor, baptized as GIOVANNI LEONE, but better known as LEO AFRICANUS. Done into English in the year 1600 by John Pory, and now edited with an Introduction & Notes, by Dr. ROBERT BROWN. In 3 Vols. Vol. 1. pp. viii. cxi. 224. 4 Maps. Vol. 2. pp. 225-698. Vol. 3. pp. 699-1119. Index.

Issued for 1895.

95—The Chronicle of the Discovery and Conquest of Guinea.

Written by GOMES EANNES DE AZURARA. Now first done into English and Edited by CHARLES RAYMOND BEAZLEY, M.A., F.R.G.S., and EDGAR PRESTAGE, B.A. Vol. 1. (Ch. i.—xl.) With Introduction on the Life & Writings of the Chronicler. pp. lxvii. 127. 3 Maps. 1 Illus.
(Vol. 2=No. 100.) *Issued for* 1896.

96-97—Danish Arctic Expeditions, 1605 to 1620. In Two Books.

Book 1. The Danish Expeditions to Greenland, 1605-07; to which is added Captain JAMES HALL'S Voyage to Greenland in 1612. Edited by CHRISTIAN CARL AUGUST GOSCH. pp. xvi. cxvii. 205. 10 Maps. Index.
Issued for 1896.

Book 2. The Expedition of Captain JENS MUNK to Hudson's Bay in search of a North-West Passage in 1619-20. Edited by CHRISTIAN CARL AUGUST GOSCH. pp. cxviii. 187. 4 Maps. 2 Illus. Index. *Issued for* 1897.

98—The Topographia Christiana of Cosmas Indicopleustes, an Egyptian Monk.

Translated from the Greek and Edited by JOHN WATSON MCCRINDLE, LL.D., M.R.A.S. pp. xii. xxvii. 398. 4 Illus. Index. *Issued for* 1897.

99—A Journal of the First Voyage of Vasco da Gama, 1497-1499.

By an unknown writer. Translated from the Portuguese, with an Introduction and Notes, by ERNEST GEORGE RAVENSTEIN, F.R.G.S. pp. xxxvi. 250. 8 Maps. 23 Illus. Index. *Issued for* 1898.

100—The Chronicle of the Discovery and Conquest of Guinea.

Written by GOMES EANNES DE AZURARA. Now first done into English and Edited by CHARLES RAYMOND BEAZLEY, M.A., F.R.G.S., and EDGAR PRESTAGE, B.A. Vol. 2. (Ch. xli.—xcvii.) With an Introduction on the Early History of African Exploration, Cartography, &c. pp. cl. 362. 3 Maps. 2 Illus. Index. *Issued for* 1898.
(Vol. 1=No. 95.)

WORKS ALREADY ISSUED.

SECOND SERIES, 1899, etc.

1-2—The Embassy of Sir Thomas Roe to the Court of the Great Mogul, 1615-19.

Edited from Contemporary Records by WILLIAM FOSTER, B.A., of the India Office. 2 vols. Portrait, 2 Maps, & 6 Illus. Index.
(*Out of print.*) *Issued for* 1899.

3—The Voyage of Sir Robert Dudley to the West Indies and Guiana in 1594.

Edited by GEORGE FREDERIC WARNER, Litt.D., F.S.A., Keeper of Manuscripts, British Museum. pp. lxvi. 104. Portrait, Map, & 1 Illus. Index. *Issued for* 1899.

4—The Journeys of William of Rubruck and John of Pian de Carpine

To Tartary in the 13th century. Translated and Edited by H. E. the Hon. WM. WOODVILLE ROCKHILL. pp. lvi. 304. Bibliography. Index.
(*Out of print.*) *Issued for* 1900.

5—The Voyage of Captain John Saris to Japan in 1613.

Edited by H. E. SIR ERNEST MASON SATOW, G.C.M.G. pp. lxxxvii. 242. Map, & 5 Illus. Index. *Issued for* 1900.

6—The Strange Adventures of Andrew Battell of Leigh in Essex.

Edited by ERNEST GEORGE RAVENSTEIN, F.R.G.S. pp. xx. 210. 2 Maps. Bibliography. Index. *Issued for* 1900.

7-8—The Voyage of Mendaña to the Solomon Islands in 1568.

Edited by the LORD AMHERST OF HACKNEY and BASIL THOMSON. 2 vols. 5 Maps, & 33 Illus. Index. (*Out of print.*) *Issued for* 1901.

9—The Journey of Pedro Teixeira from India to Italy by land, 1604-05;

With his Chronicle of the Kings of Ormus. Translated and Edited by WILLIAM FREDERIC SINCLAIR, late Bombay C. S., with additional Notes, &c., by DONALD WILLIAM FERGUSON. pp. cvii. 292. Index.
(*Out of print.*) *Issued for* 1901.

10—The Portuguese Expedition to Abyssinia in 1541, as narrated by

CASTANHOSO and BERMUDEZ. Edited by RICHARD STEPHEN WHITEWAY, late I.C.S. With a Bibliography, by BASIL H. SOULSBY, F.S.A., Superintendent of the Map Department, British Museum. pp. cxxxii. 296. Map, & 2 Illus. Bibliography. Index. (*Out of print.*) . *Issued for* 1902.

11—Early Dutch and English Voyages to Spitzbergen in the Seventeenth Century,

Including HESSEL GERRITSZ. "Histoire du Pays nommé Spitsberghe," 1613, translated into English, for the first time, by BASIL H. SOULSBY, F.S.A., of the British Museum: and JACOB SEGERSZ. van der Brugge, "Journael of Dagh Register," Amsterdam, 1634, translated into English, for the first time, by J. A. J. DE VILLIERS, of the British Museum. Edited, with introductions and notes by SIR MARTIN CONWAY. pp. xvi. 191. 3 Maps, & 3 Illus. Bibliography. Index. *Issued for* 1902.

12—The Countries round the Bay of Bengal.

Edited, from an unpublished MS., 1669-79, by THOMAS BOWREY, by Col. SIR RICHARD CARNAC TEMPLE, Bart., C.I.E. pp. lvi. 387. 19 Illus. & 1 Chart. Bibliography. Index. *Issued for* 1903.

13—The Voyage of Captain Don Felipe Gonzalez

in the Ship of the Line San Lorenzo, with the Frigate Santa Rosalia in company, to Easter Island, in 1770-1771. Preceded by an Extract from Mynheer JACOB ROGGEVEEN's Official Log of his Discovery of and Visit to

Easter Island in 1722. Translated, Annotated, and Edited by BOLTON GLANVILL CORNEY, Companion of the Imperial Service Order. With a Preface by Admiral SIR CYPRIAN BRIDGE, G.C.B. 3 Maps & 4 Illus. Bibliography. Index. pp. lxxvii. 176. *Issued for* 1903.

14, 15—The Voyages of Pedro Fernandez de Quiros, 1595 to 1606.
Translated and Edited by SIR CLEMENTS MARKHAM, K.C.B., Pres. R.G.S., President of the Hakluyt Society. With a Note on the Cartography of the Southern Continent, and a Bibliography, by BASIL H. SOULSBY, F.S.A., Superintendent of the Map Department, British Museum. 2 vols. 3 Maps. Bibliography. Index. *Issued for* 1904.

16—John Jourdain's Journal of a Voyage to the East Indies, 1608-1617.
(Sloane MS. 858, British Museum). Edited by WILLIAM FOSTER, B.A., of the India Office. pp. lxxxii. 394. With Appendices, A—F, and a Bibliography, by BASIL H. SOULSBY, F.S.A. 4 Maps. Index. *Issued for* 1905.

17—The Travels of Peter Mundy in Europe and Asia, 1608-1667.
(Bodleian Library. Rawl. MSS. A. 315.) Vol. I. Travels in Europe, 1608-1628. Edited by Lieut.-Col. SIR RICHARD CARNAC TEMPLE, Bart., C.I.E., Editor of "A Geographical Account of Countries round the Bay of Bengal." 3 Maps & 3 Illus. With a Bibliography, alphabetically arranged. Index. pp. lxiii. 284. *Issued for* 1905.

18—East and West Indian Mirror.
By JORIS VAN SPEILBERGEN. An Account of his Voyage Round the World in the years 1614 to 1617, including the Australian Navigations of JACOB LE MAIRE. Translated from the Dutch edition, "Oost ende West-Indische Spiegel, &c.," *Nicolaes van Geelkercken: Leyden*, 1619, with Notes and an Introduction, by JOHN A. J. DE VILLIERS, of the British Museum. With a Bibliography & Index by BASIL H. SOULSBY, F.S.A. 26 Illus. & Maps. Index. pp. lxi. 272. *Issued for* 1906.

19, 20.—A New Account of East India and Persia.
In eight Letters, being Nine Years' Travels, begun 1672, and finished 1681. By JOHN FRYER, M.D., Cantabrig., and Fellow of the Royal Society. *Printed by R. R. for Ri. Chiswell; at the Rose and Crown in St. Paul's Churchyard, London, 1698.* Fol. Edited, with Notes and an Introduction, by WILLIAM CROOKE, B.A., Bengal Civil Service (retired), Editor of "Hobson Jobson," &c., &c. Vol. I-II. (Vol. I) Map & 6 Illus. pp. xxxviii. 353; (Vol. II) Map. pp. 371. *Issued for* 1909 and 1912.

21—The Guanches of Tenerife, The Holy Image of Our Lady of Candelaria.
With the Spanish Conquest and Settlement. By the FRIAR ALONSO DE ESPINOSA, of the Order of Preachers. 1594. Translated and Edited, with Notes and an Introduction, by SIR CLEMENTS MARKHAM, K.C.B., President of the Hakluyt Society. With a Bibliography of the Canary Islands, A.D. 1341-1907, chronologically arranged, with the British Museum press-marks, and an alphabetical list of authors, editors, and titles. 2 Maps, by SIR CLEMENTS MARKHAM, and 4 Illus. Index. pp. xxvi. 221. *Issued for* 1907.

22—History of the Incas.
By PEDRO SARMIENTO DE GAMBOA. 1572. From the MS. sent to King Philip II. of Spain, and now in the Göttingen University Library. And The Execution of the Inca Tupac Amaru. 1571. By Captain BALTASAR DE OCAMPO. 1610. (British Museum Add. MSS. 17, 585.) Translated and Edited, with Notes and an Introduction, by SIR CLEMENTS MARKHAM, K.C.B. 2 Maps and 10 Illus. Index. pp. xxii. 395.

——— Supplement. A Narrative of the Vice-Regal Embassy to Vilcabambal 1571, and of the Execution of the Inca Tupac Amaru, Dec. 1571. By FRIAR GABRIEL DE OVIEDO, of Cuzco, 1573. Translated by SIR CLEMENTS MARKHAM, K.C.B. Index. pp. 397-412. *Issued for* 1907.

23, 24, 25—Conquest of New Spain.

The True History of the Conquest of New Spain. By BERNAL DÍAZ DEL CASTILLO, one of its Conquerors. From the only exact copy made of the Original Manuscript. Edited and published in Mexico, by GENARO GARCÍA, 1904. Translated into English, with Introduction and Notes, by ALFRED PERCIVAL MAUDSLAY, M.A., Hon. Professor of Archæology, National Museum, Mexico. Vols. I-III. (Vol. I) pp. lxv. 396. 3 Maps. 15 Illus.; (Vol. II) pp. xvi. 343. Map and 13 Panoramas and Illus.; (Vol. III) pp. 38. 8 Maps and Plans in 12 sheets. *Issued for* 1908 *and* 1910.

(Vol. IV = No. 30.)

26, 27.—Storm van's Gravesande.

The Rise of British Guiana, compiled from his despatches, by C. A. HARRIS, C.B., C.M.G., Chief Clerk, Colonial Office, and J. A. J. DE VILLIERS, of the British Museum. 2 vols. pp. 372, 373-703. 3 Maps. 5 Illus. *Issued for* 1911.

28.—Magellan's Strait.

Early Spanish Voyages, edited, with Notes and Introduction, by Sir CLEMENTS R. MARKHAM, K.C.B. pp. viii. 288. 3 Maps. 9 Illus. *Issued for* 1911.

29.—Book of the Knowledge.

Book of the Knowledge of all the Kingdoms, Lands and Lordships that are in the World. . . . Written by a Spanish Franciscan in the Middle of the XIV Century; published for the first time, with Notes, by MARCOS JIMENEZ DE LA ESPADA. Translated and Edited by SIR CLEMENTS MARKHAM, K.C.B. With 20 Coloured Plates. pp. xiii. 85. *Issued for* 1912.

30.—Conquest of New Spain.

The True History of the Conquest of New Spain. By BERNAL DIAZ DEL CASTILLO. . . . Edited by GENARO GARCÍA. Translated, with Notes, by ALFRED P. MAUDSLAY, M.A., Hon. Professor of Archæology. Vol. IV. pp. xiv. 395. 3 Maps and Plan. 3 Illus. *Issued for* 1912.

(Vols. I-III = Nos. 23-25.)

31.—The War of Quito.

The War of Quito, by CIEZA DE LEON. Translated and Edited by SIR CLEMENTS MARKHAM, K.C.B. pp. xii. 212. *Issued for* 1913.

32.—The Quest and Occupation of Tahiti.

The Quest and Occupation of Tahiti by Emissaries of Spain during the years 1772-1776. Compiled, with Notes and an Introduction, by B. GLANVILL CORNEY, I.S.O. Vol. I. pp. lxxxviii. 363. 3 Charts, 8 Plans and Illus. *Issued for* 1913.

33.—Cathay and the Way Thither.

Cathay and the Way Thither. Being a Collection of Mediæval Notices of China. Translated and Edited by Colonel SIR HENRY YULE, K.C.S.I., R.E., C.B. New Edition, revised throughout by Professor HENRI CORDIER, de l'Institut de France. Vol. II. pp. xii. 367. Map & 6 Illus. *Issued for* 1913.

34—New Light on Drake.

New Light on Drake. Spanish and Portuguese Documents relating to the Circumnavigation Voyage. Discovered, translated, and annotated by Mrs. ZELIA NUTTALL. pp. lvi. 443. 3 Maps and 14 Illus. *Issued for* 1914.

35—The Travels of Peter Mundy.

The Travels of Peter Mundy in Europe and Asia, 1608-1667. Edited by SIR RICHARD CARNAC TEMPLE, Bart., C.I.E. Vol. II. pp. lxxix. 437. 2 Maps and 29 Illus. *Issued for* 1914.

37—Cathay and the Way Thither.

Cathay and the Way Thither. Being a Collection of Mediæval Notices of China previous to the XVIth century. Translated and edited by COLONEL SIR HENRY YULE, K.C.S.I., R.E., C.B. A new edition by PROFESSOR HENRI CORDIER, de l'Institut de France. Vol. III. pp. xv. 270. Map and Portrait. *Issued for* 1914.

EXTRA SERIES.

1-12—The Principal Navigations, Voyages, Traffiques, & Discoveries of the English Nation,

Made by Sea or Over-land to the remote and farthest distant quarters of the earth at any time within the compasse of these 1600 yeeres. By RICHARD HAKLUYT, Preacher, and sometime Student of Christ Church in Oxford. With an Essay on the English Voyages of the Sixteenth Century, by WALTER RALEIGH, Professor of the English Language in the University of Oxford. Index by Madame MARIE MICHON and Miss ELIZABETH CARMONT. 12 vols. James MacLehose & Sons: Glasgow, 1903-5. (*Out of print.*)

13—The Texts & Versions of John de Plano Carpini and William de Rubruquis.

As printed for the first time by HAKLUYT in 1598, together with some shorter pieces. Edited by CHARLES RAYMOND BEAZLEY, M.A., F.R.G.S. pp. xx. 345. Index. University Press: Cambridge, 1903. (*Out of print.*)

14-33—Hakluytus Posthumus or Purchas His Pilgrimes.

Contayning a History of the World in Sea Voyages and Lande Travells by Englishmen and others. By SAMUEL PURCHAS, B.D. 20 vols. Maps & Illus. With an Index by Madame MARIE MICHON. James MacLehose and Sons: Glasgow, 1905-7.

THE ISSUES FOR 1915 WILL BE:

SERIES II.

Vol. 36.—The Quest and Occupation of Tahiti. Edited by B. GLANVILL CORNEY, I.S.O. Vol. II.

Vol. 38.—Cathay and the Way Thither. Being a collection of mediæval notices of China previous to the XVIth century. Translated and edited by COLONEL SIR HENRY YULE, K.C.S.I., R.E., C.B. A new edition by PROFESSOR HENRI CORDIER, de l'Institut de France. Vol. I.

Vol. 39.—A New Account of East India and Persia. In eight Letters, being Nine Years' Travels, begun 1672, and finished 1681. By JOHN FRYER, M.D. Edited, with Notes and an Introduction, by WILLIAM CROOKE, B.A., Bengal Civil Service (retired). Vol. III and last.

OTHER VOLUMES IN ACTIVE PREPARATION ARE:

The True History of the Conquest of New Spain. By BERNAL DIAZ DEL CASTILLO. Translated, with Notes, by A. P. MAUDSLAY. Vol. V and last. [*In Press.*

Cathay and the Way Thither. New edition. Vol. IV and last. [*In Press.*

William Lockerby's Journal in Fiji, 1808. Edited by SIR EVERARD F. IM THURN, K.C.M.G., C.B., and L. C. WHARTON, B.A.

Jons Olafssonar Indiafara. An English Translation by MISS BERTHA PHILLPOTTS. Edited by SIR R. C. TEMPLE, Bart., C.I.E. Two Vols.

A Description of the Coasts of East Africa and Malabar in the beginning of the Sixteenth Century, by DUARTE BARBOSA, a Portuguese. A new translation by MR. LONGWORTH DAMES.

The Travels of Peter Mundy in Europe and Asia, 1608-1667. Edited by SIR RICHARD CARNAC TEMPLE, Bart., C.I.E. Vol. III and last.

INDEX

TO THE FIRST AND SECOND SERIES OF THE SOCIETY'S PUBLICATIONS, 1847-1913.

LAWS OF THE HAKLUYT SOCIETY.

I. The object of this Society shall be to print, for distribution among the members, rare and valuable Voyages, Travels, Naval Expeditions, and other geographical records.

II. The Annual Subscription shall be One and a-half Guinea (for America, eight dollars, U.S. currency), payable in advance on the 1st January.

III. Each member of the Society, having paid his Subscription, shall be entitled to a copy of every work produced by the Society, and to vote at the general meetings within the period subscribed for; and if he do not signify, before the close of the year, his wish to resign, he shall be considered as a member for the succeeding year.

IV. The management of the Society's affairs shall be vested in a Council consisting of twenty-two members, viz., a President, three Vice-Presidents, a Treasurer, a Secretary, and sixteen ordinary members, to be elected annually; but vacancies occurring between the general meetings shall be filled up by the Council.

V. A General Meeting of the Subscribers shall be held annually. The Secretary's Report on the condition and proceedings of the Society shall be then read, and the meeting shall proceed to elect the Council for the ensuing year.

VI. At each Annual Election, three of the old Council shall retire.

VII. The Council shall meet when necessary for the dispatch of business, three forming a quorum, including the Secretary; the Chairman having a casting vote.

VIII. Gentlemen preparing and editing works for the Society shall receive twenty-five copies of such works respectively.

LIST OF MEMBERS.—1915.*

Members are requested to inform the Hon. Secretary of any errors or alterations in this List.

1899 Aberdare, The Right Hon. Lord, 83, Eaton Square, S.W.
1847 Aberdeen University Library, Aberdeen.
1913 Abraham, H. C., Esq., c/o W. Abraham, Esq., 69, Tennyson Road, Portswood, Southampton.
1895 Adelaide Public Library, North Terrace, Adelaide, South Australia.
1847 Admiralty, The, Whitehall, S.W. [2 COPIES.]
1847 Advocates' Library, 11, Parliament Square, Edinburgh.
1899 Alexander, William Lindsay, Esq., Pinkieburn, Musselburgh, N.B.
1847 All Souls College, Oxford.
1847 American Geographical Society, 11, West 81st Street, New York City, U.S.A.
1906 Andrews, Michael C., Esq., 17, University Square, Belfast.
1847 Antiquaries, The Society of, Burlington House, Piccadilly, W.
1909 Armstrong, Capt. B. H. O., R.E.
1847 Army and Navy Club, 36, Pall Mall, S.W.
1847 Athenæum Club, Pall Mall, S.W.
1912 Aylward, R. M., Esq., 7ª Avenida Sur, No. 87, Guatemala.

1899 Baer, Joseph & Co., Messrs., Hochstrasse 6, Frankfort-on-Main, Germany.
1847 Bagram, John Ernest, Esq., 10, Old Post Office Street, Calcutta.
1912 Baird, H. A., Esq., West House, Bothwell, N.B.
1909 Baldwin, Stanley, Esq., M.P., Astley Hall, nr. Stourport.
1899 Ball, John B., Esq., Ashburton Cottage, Putney Heath, S.W.
1893 Barclay, Hugh Gurney. Esq., Colney Hall, Norwich.
1911 Barwick, G. F., Esq., British Museum.
1899 Basset, M. René, Directeur de l'Ecole Supérieure des Lettres d'Alger, Villa Louise, rue Denfert Rochereau, Algiers.
1894 Baxter, Hon. James Phinney, Esq., 61, Deering Street, Portland, Maine, U.S.A.
1896 Beaumont, Admiral Sir Lewis Anthony, G.C.B., K.C.M.G., St. Georges, Hurstpierpoint, Sussex.
1913 Beaumont, Lieut. H., Rhoscolyn, Holyhead, N. Wales.
1904 Beetem, Charles Gilbert, Esq., 110, South Hanover Street, Carlisle, Pa., U.S.A.
1899 Belfast Library and Society for Promoting Knowledge, Donegall Square North, Belfast.
1913 Belfield, T. Broom, Esq., 1905, Spring Garden Street, Philadelphia, Pa., U.S.A.
1896 Belhaven and Stenton, Col. The Right Hon. the Lord, R.E., 41, Lennox Gardens, S.W. (*Vice-President*).
1913 Bennett, Ira A. Esq., Editor *Washington Post*, Washington, D.C., U.S.A.
1847 Berlin Geographical Society (Gesellschaft für Erdkunde), Wilhelmstrasse 23, Berlin, S.W., 48.
1847 Berlin, the Royal Library of, Opernplatz, Berlin, W.
1847 Berlin University, Geographical Institute of, Georgenstrasse 34-36 Berlin N.W. 7.
1914 Bernice Pauahi Bishop Museum, Honolulu, Hawaii Island.
1913 Beuf, L., 6, Via Caroli, Genoa.

* *Sent to press, July 1st*, 1915.

1913 Bewsher, F. W., Esq., 25, Brook Green, W.
1911 Bingham, Professor Hiram, Yale University, New Haven, Connecticut.
1899 Birmingham Central Free Library, Ratcliff Place, Birmingham.
1847 Birmingham Old Library, The, Margaret Street, Birmingham.
1910 Birmingham University Library.
1899 Board of Education, The Keeper, Science Library, Science Museum, South Kensington, S.W.
1847 Bodleian Library, Oxford.
1894 Bonaparte, H. H. Prince Roland Napoléon, Avenue d'Jéna 10, Paris.
1847 Boston Athenæum Library, 10½, Beacon Street, Boston, Mass., U.S.A.
1847 Boston Public Library, Copley Square, Boston, Mass., U.S.A.
1912 Bourke, Hubert, Esq., Feltimores, Harlow, Essex.
1899 Bowdoin College, Brunswick, Maine, U.S.A.
1894 Bower, Major-General Hamilton, c/o Messrs. Cox and Co., 16, Charing Cross.
1896 Bowring, Sir Thomas B., 7, Palace Gate, Kensington, W.
1912 Boyd-Richardson, Lieutenant S. B., R.N., Wade Court, Havant, Hants
1914 Braislin, Dr. William C., 556, Washington Avenue, Brooklyn. U.S.A.
1906 Brereton, The Rev. William, The Rectory, Steeple Gidding, Peterboro'.
1893 Brighton Public Library, Royal Pavilion, Church Street, Brighton.
1890 British Guiana Royal Agricultural and Commercial Society, Georgetown, Demerara.
1847 British Museum, Department of British and Mediæval Antiquities.
1847 British Museum, Department of Printed Books.
1896 Brock, Henry G., Esq., 1612, Walnut Street, Philadelphia, Pa., U.S.A.
1909 Brooke, John Arthur, Esq., J.P., Fenay Hall, Huddersfield.
1899 Brookline Public Library, Boston, Mass., U.S.A.
1899 Brooklyn Mercantile Library, 197, Montague Street, Brooklyn, N.Y., U.S.A.
1899 Brown, Arthur William Whateley, Esq., 62, Carlisle Mansions, Carlisle Place, Victoria Street, S.W.
1896 Buda-Pesth, The Geographical Institute of the University of, Hungary.
1910 Buenos Aires, Biblioteca Nacional (c/o E. Terquem, 19, Rue Scribe, Paris).
1890 Burns, Capt. John William, Leesthorpe Hall, Melton Mowbray.
1914 Byers, Gerald, Esq., c/o Messrs. Butterfield and Swire, Shanghai.

1913 Cadogan, Lieut. Francis, R.N., H.M.S. "Argyll."
1903 California, University of, Berkeley, Cal., U.S.A.
1847 Cambridge University Library, Cambridge.
1911 Canada, Department of the Naval Service, Ottawa.
1847 Canada, The Parliament Library, Ottawa.
1896 Cardiff Public Library, Trinity Street, Cardiff.
1847 Carlisle, The Rt. Hon. the Earl of, Castle Howard, York.
1847 Carlton Club Library, 94, Pall Mall, S.W.
1899 Carnegie Library, Pittsburgh, Pa., U.S.A.
1914 Casserly, John Bernard, Esq., San Mateo, California, U.S.A.
1910 Cattarns, Richard, Esq., 7, Gloucester Terrace, Regent's Park, N.W.
1899 Chambers, Captain Bertram Mordaunt, R.N., c/o Messrs. Cocks, Biddulph and Co., 43, Charing Cross, S.W.
1910 Chapelot et Cie., 30, Rue et Passage Dauphine, Paris.
1913 Charleston Library, Charleston, U.S.A.
1910 Chicago, Geographical Society of, P.O. Box 223, Chicago.
1899 Chicago Public Library. Chicago, Ill., U.S.A.
1899 Chicago University Library, Chicago, Ill., U.S.A.
1896 Christ Church, Oxford.
1847 Christiania University Library, Christiania, Norway.
1913 Churchill, Arnold, Esq., Stone House, Broadstairs.
1899 Cincinnati Public Library, Ohio, U.S.A.

1907 Clark, Arthur H., Esq., Caxton Buildings, Cleveland, Ohio.
1913 Clark, James Cooper, Esq., Ladyhill House, Elgin, N.B.
1913 Clarke, Sir Rupert, Bart., Clarke Buildings, Bourke Street, Melbourne.
1903 Clay, John, Esq., University Press and Burrell's Corner, Cambridge.
1913 Coates, O. R., Esq., British Consulate-General, Shanghai.
1847 Colonial Office, The, Downing Street, S.W.
1899 Columbia University, Library of, New York, U.S.A.
1896 Conway, Sir William Martin, Allington Castle, Maidstone, Kent.
1903 Cooke, William Charles, Esq., Vailima, Bishopstown, Cork.
1847 Copenhagen Royal Library (Det Store Kongelige Bibliothek), Copenhagen.
1894 Cora, Professor Guido, M.A., Via Nazionale, 181, Rome.
1847 Cornell University, Ithaca, New York, U.S.A.
1903 Corney, Bolton Glanvill, Esq., I.S.O., c/o Royal Geographical Society, Kensington Gore, S.W.
1899 Corning, C. R., Esq., 36 Wall Street, New York.
1893 Cow, John, Esq., Elfinsward, Hayward's Heath, Sussex.
1902 Cox, Alexander G., Esq., Engineer-in-Chief's Office, Canton-Hankow Railway, Hankow, China.
1908 Crewdson, W., Esq., J.P., Southside, St Leonards-on-Sea.
1904 Croydon Public Libraries, Central Library, Town Hall, Croydon.
1893 Curzon of Kedleston, The Right Hon. Earl, G.M.S.I., G.M.I.E., 1, Carlton House Terrace, S.W.
1911 Cutting, Lady Sybil, c/o the Earl of Desart, 2, Rutland Gardens, S.W.

1913 Dalgliesh, Percy, Esq., Guatemala, C.A.
1847 Dalton, Rev. Canon John Neale, C.M.G., C.V.O., 4, The Cloisters, Windsor.
1913 Dames, Mansell Longworth, Esq., Crichmere, Edgeborough Road, Guildford.
1899 Dampier, Gerald Robert, Esq., I.C.S., Dehra Dun, N.W.P., India.
1847 Danish Royal Naval Library (Det Kongelige Danske Søkaart Archiv), Copenhagen.
1912 Dartmouth College Library, Hanover, N.H., U.S.A.
1908 Darwin, Major Leonard, late R.E., 12, Egerton Place, S.W.
1894 De Bertodano, Baldomero Hyacinth, Esq., Cowbridge House, Malmesbury, Wilts.
1911 Delbanco, D., Esq., 9, Mincing Lane, E.C.
1899 Detroit Public Library, Michigan, U.S.A.
1893 Dijon University Library, Rue Monge, Dijon, Côte d'Or, France.
1899 Dresden Geographical Society (Verein für Erdkunde), Kleine Brüdergasse 21II, Dresden.
1902 Dublin, Trinity College Library.
1910 Dunn, J. H., Esq., Coombe Cottage, Kingston Hill, S.W.

1899 École Française d'Extrême Orient, Hanoi, Indo-Chine Française.
1913 École des Langues Orientales Vivantes, Paris.
1892 Edinburgh Public Library, George IV. Bridge, Edinburgh.
1847 Edinburgh University Library, Edinburgh.
1847 Edwards, Francis, Esq., 83, High Street, Marylebone, W.
1913 Eliot, Sir Charles, K.C.M.G., C.B., The University, Hong Kong.
1906 Enoch Pratt Free Library, Baltimore, Md., U.S.A.
1912 Ewing, Arthur, Esq.

1910 Fairbrother, Colonel W. T., C.B., Indian Army, Bareilly, N.P., India.
1911 Fayal, The Most Noble the Marquis de, Lisbon.

1899 Fellowes Athenæum, 46, Millmont Street Boston, Mass., U.S.A.
1894 Fisher, Arthur, Esq., The Mazry, Tiverton, Devon.
1896 Fitzgerald, Major Edward Arthur, 5th Dragoon Guards.
1914 FitzGibbon, F. J., Esq., Casilla 106, La Paz, Bolivia.
1847 Foreign Office of Germany (Auswärtiges Amt), Wilhelmstrasse, Berlin, W.
1893 Forrest, George William, Esq., C.I.E., Rose Bank, Iffley, Oxford.
1902 Foster, Francis Apthorp, Esq., Edgartown, Mass., U.S.A.
1893 Foster, William, Esq., C.I.E., India Office, S.W.

1911 Garcia, Señor Genaro, Apartado 337, Mexico D.F.
1913 Gardner, Harry G., Esq., Hongkong and Shanghai Bank, Hankow, China.
1847 George, Charles William, Esq., 51, Hampton Road, Bristol.
1901 Gill, William Harrison, Esq., Marunouchi, Tokyo (c/o Messrs. Nichols, Ocean House, 24/5, Great Tower Street, E.C.
1847 Glasgow University Library, Glasgow.
1913 Glyn, The Hon. Mrs. Maurice, Albury Hall, Much Hadham.
1880 Godman, Frederick Du Cane, Esq., D.C.L., F.R.S., 45, Pont Street, S.W.
1905 Goldie, The Right. Hon. Sir George Taubman, K.C.M.G., F.R.S., Naval & Military Club, Piccadilly, W.
1847 Göttingen University Library, Göttingen, Germany.
1914 Gottschalk, Hon. A. L. M., American Consul-General, Rio de Janeiro, Brazil.
1877 Gray, Albert, Esq., K.C. (*President*), Catherine Lodge, Trafalgar Square, Chelsea, S.W.
1894 Gray, Matthew Hamilton, Esq., Lessness Park, Abbey Wood, Kent.
1903 Greenlee, William B., Esq., 130 Kenesaw Terrace. Chicago, Ill., U.S.A.
1899 Griffiths, John G., Esq., 4, Hyde Park Gardens, W.
1899 Grosvenor Library, Buffalo, N.Y., U.S.A.
1847 Guildhall Library, E.C.
1887 Guillemard, Francis Henry Hill, Esq., M.A., M.D., The Old Mill House, Trumpington, Cambridge.

1910 Hackley Public Library, Muskegon, Mich, U.S.A.
1847 Hamburg Commerz-Bibliothek, Hamburg, Germany.
1901 Hammersmith Public Libraries, Carnegie (Central) Library, Hammersmith, W.
1898 Hannen, The Hon. Henry Arthur, The Hall, West Farleigh, Kent.
1913 Hargreaves, Walter Ernest, Esq., Nazeing, Essex.
1906 Harrison, Carter H., Esq. (c/o Messrs. Stevens and Brown).
1913 Harrison, George L., Esq., 400, Chestnut Street, Philadelphia.
1905 Harrison, William P., Esq., 1021, Lawrence Avenue, Chicago, Ill., U.S.A.
1847 Harvard University, Cambridge, Mass., U.S.A.
1899 Harvie-Brown, John Alexander, Esq., Dunipace, Larbert, Stirlingshire.
1913 Hay, E. Alan, Esq., 14, Kensington Court, W.
1887 Heawood, Edward, Esq., M.A., Church Hill, Merstham, Surrey (*Treasurer*).
1899 Heidelberg University Library, Heidelberg (Koestersche Buchhandlung).
1904 Henderson, George, Esq., 13, Palace Court, W.
1915 Henderson, Capt. R. Ronald, Little Compton Manor, Moreton-in-Marsh.
1890 Hervey, Dudley Francis Amelius, Esq., C.M.G., Westfields, Aldeburgh, Suffolk.
1899 Hiersemann, Herr Karl Wilhelm, Königsstrasse, 3, Leipzig.
1874 Hippisley, Alfred Edward, Esq., 8, Herbert Crescent, Hans Place, W.
1904 Holdich, Colonel Sir Thomas Hungerford, K.C.M.G., K.C.I.E., C.B., R.E., 41, Courtfield Road, S.W.
1913 Holman, R. H., Esq., "Wynnstay," Putney Hill, S.W.
1913 Hong Kong University, c/o Messrs. Longmans & Co., 38, Paternoster Row, E.C.
1899 Hoover Herbert Clarke, Esq., The Red House, Hornton Street, Kensington, W.

1887 Horner, Sir John Francis Fortescue, K.C.V.O., Mells Park, Frome, Somerset.
1911 Hoskins, G. H., Esq., Sydney.
1915 Howland, S. S., Esq., c/o Messrs. N. M. Rothschild and Sons, New Court, St. Swithin's Lane, E.C.
1890 Hoyt Public Library, East Saginaw, Mich., U.S.A.
1909 Hubbard, H. M., Esq., H6, The Albany, Piccadilly, W.
1899 Hügel, Baron Anatole A. A. von, Curator, Museum of Archæology and Ethnology, Cambridge.
1913 Hughes, R H. Esq., 22, Sussex Mansions, Sussex Place, S.W.
1894 Hull Public Libraries, Baker Street, Hull.
1913 Humphreys, John, Esq., 26, Clarendon Road, Edgbaston, Birmingham.

1912 Illinois, University of, Urbana, Ill., U.S.A.
1899 Im Thurn, Sir Everard, K.C.M.G., C.B., 39, Lexham Gardens, W.
1847 India Office, Downing Street, S.W. [20 COPIES.]
1899 Ingle, William Bruncker, Esq., 4, Orchard Road, Blackheath, S.E.
1892 Inner Temple, Hon. Society of the, Temple, E.C.

1899 Jackson, Stewart Douglas, Esq., 61, St. Vincent Street, Glasgow.
1898 James, Arthur Curtiss, Esq., 92 Park Avenue, New York City, U.S.A.
1896 James, Walter B., Esq., M.D., 17, West 54th Street, New York City, U.S.A.
1912 Jenkins, Captain F. W. R., Apartado 331, Guatemala.
1907 Johannesburg Public Library, Johannesburg, South Africa.
1847 John Carter Brown Library, 357, Benefit Street, Providence, Rhode Island, U.S.A.
1847 John Rylands Library, Deansgate, Manchester.
1847 Johns Hopkins University, Baltimore, Md., U.S.A.
1899 Johnson, W. Morton, Esq., Woodleigh, Altrincham
1910 Jones, L. C., Esq., M.D.. Falmouth, Mass., U.S.A.
1914 Jones, Livingston E., Esq., Germantown, Pa., U.S.A.
1913 Jowett, The Rev. Hardy, Ping Kiang, Hunan, China.

1903 Kansas University Library, Lawrence, Kans.. U.S.A.
1887 Keltie, John Scott, Esq., LL.D., 1, Kensington Gore, S.W.
1909 Kesteven, C. H., Esq., 2, Hungerford Street, Calcutta.
1899 Kiel, Royal University of, Kiel, Schleswig-Holstein.
1907 Kindberg, Herrn Captain J. P., Göteborg, Sweden.
1898 Kinder, Claude William, Esq., C.M.G., Kelvin, Avondale Road, Fleet, Hants.
1890 King's Inns, The Hon. Society of the, Henrietta Street, Dublin.
1899 Kitching, John, Esq., Oaklands, Queen's Road, Kingston Hill, S.W.
1912 Koebel, W. H., Esq., Author's Club, 2, Whitehall Court, S.W.
1913 Koloniaal Instituut, Amsterdam.
1910 Koninklijk Instituut voor de Taal Land en Volkenkunde van Nederlandsch Indie. The Hague.

1899 Langton, J. J. P., Esq., 802, Spruce Street, St. Louis, Mo., U.S.A.
1899 Larchmont Yacht Club, Larchmont, N.Y., U.S.A.
1913 Laufer, Berthold, Esq., Field Museum of Natural History, Chicago.

1899 Leeds Library, 18, Commercial Street, Leeds.
1899 Lehigh University, South Bethlehem, Pa., U.S.A.
1893 Leipzig, Library of the University of Leipzig.
1912 Leland Stanford Junior University, Library of, Stanford University, Cal. U.S.A.
1899 Levy, Judah, Esq., 17, Greville Place, N.W.
1912 Lind, Walter, Esq., 1° Calle, Guatemala, C.A.
1899 Lindsay-Smith, Fred. Alex., Esq., J.P., 18, Sussex Place, Regent's Park.
1847 Liverpool Free Public Library, William Brown Street, Liverpool.
1896 Liverpool Geographical Society, 14, Hargreaves Buildings, Chapel Street, Liverpool.
1899 Liverpool, University of Liverpool.
1911 Loder, Gerald W. E., Esq., F.S.A., Wakehurst Place, Ardingly, Sussex.
1899 Loescher, Messrs. J., and Co., Via Due Macelli, 88, Rome.
1847 London Institution, 11, Finsbury Circus, E.C.
1847 London Library, 12, St. James's Square, S.W.
1899 London University, South Kensington, S.W.
1895 Long Island Historical Society, Pierrepont Street, Brooklyn, N.Y., U.S.A.
1899 Los Angeles Public Library, Los Angeles, Cal., U.S.A.
1899 Lowrey, Joseph, Esq., The Hermitage, Loughton, Essex.
1912 Luard, Major Charles Eckford, M.A., D.S.O., Indore, Central India.
1880 Lucas, Sir Charles Prestwood, K.C.B., K.C.M.G., 65, St. George's Square, S.W.
1895 Lucas, Frederic Wm., Esq., 21, Surrey Street, Strand, W.C.
1912 Lukach, H. C. Esq., M.A., Government House, Cyprus.
1898 Lydenberg, H. M., Esq., New York Public Library, Fifth Avenue and Forty-second Street, New York City, U.S.A.
1880 Lyons University Library, Lyon, France.
1899 Lyttleton-Annesley, Lieut.-General Sir Arthur Lyttelton, K.C.V.O., Templemere, Oatlands Park, Weybridge.

1910 MacDonald, The Right Hon. Sir Claude M., G.C.M.G., G.C.V.O., K.C.B., 46, Chester Square, S.W.
1899 Macrae, Charles Colin, Esq., 93, Onslow Gardens, S.W.
1908 Maggs Brothers, Messrs., 109, Strand, W.C.
1847 Manchester Public Free Libraries, King Street, Manchester.
1899 Manierre, George, Esq., 112w, Adams Street, Chicago, Ill., U.S.A.
1880 Markham, Admiral Sir Albert Hastings, K.C.B., Belmont Paddocks, Faversham.
1852 Markham, Sir Clements Robert, K.C.B., F.R.S., 21, Eccleston Square, S.W. (*Vice-President*).
1892 Marquand, Henry, Esq., Whitegates Farm, Bedford, New York, U.S.A.
1899 Martelli, Ernest Wynne, Esq., 4, New Square, Lincoln's Inn, W.C.
1847 Massachusetts Historical Society, 1154, Boylston Street, Boston, Mass., U.S.A.
1905 Maudslay, Alfred Percival, Esq., Morney Cross, Hereford.
1899 McClurg, Messrs. A. C., & Co., 215-221, Wabash Avenue, Chicago, Ill., U.S.A.
1914 Means, Philip A., Esq., 196, Beacon Street, Boston, Massachusetts, U.S.A.
1913 Mensing, A. W. M., Esq. (Frederik Muller and Co.), Amsterdam.
1901 Merriman, J. A., Esq., Standard Bank of South Africa, Durban.
1911 Messer, Allan E., Esq., 2, Lyall Street, Belgrave Square, S.W.
1913 Meyendorff, Baron de, Ambassade de Russie, Madrid.
1893 Michigan, University of, Ann Arbor, Mich., U.S.A.
1899 Middletown, Conn., Wesleyan University Library, U.S.A.
1904 Mikkelsen, Michael A., Esq., 610, South Fifth Avenue, Mt. Vernon, New York.
1847 Mills, Colonel Dudley Acland, R.E., Droaks, Beaulieu, Hants.

1912 Milward, Graham, Esq., 77, Colmore Row, Birmingham.
1896 Milwaukee Public Library, Milwaukee, Wisconsin, U.S.A.
1895 Minneapolis Athenæum, Minneapolis, Minn., U.S.A.
1899 Minnesota Historical Society, St. Paul, Minnesota, U.S.A.
1899 Mitchell Library, 21, Miller Street, Glasgow.
1899 Mitchell, Wm., Esq., 14, Forbesfield Road, Aberdeen.
1899 Monson, The Right Hon. Lord, C.V.O., Burton Hall, Lincoln.
1901 Moreno, Dr. Francisco J.,La Plata Museum, La Plata, Argentine Republic.
1893 Morris, Henry Cecil Low, Esq., M.D., The Steyne, Bognor, Sussex.
1899 Morrison, George Ernest, Esq., M.D., *Times* Correspondent, c/o H.B.M. Legation, Peking.
1911 Morrison, R.E., Esq., Ardoch, Partickhill, Glasgow.
1899 Morrisson, James W., Esq., 200-206, Randolph Street, Chicago, Ill., U.S.A.
1913 Moule, The Rev. A. C., Littlebredy, Dorchester.
1895 Moxon, Alfred Edward, Esq., c/o Mrs. Gough, The Lodge, Souldern, near Banbury.
1899 Mukhopadhyay, Hon. Sir Asutosh, Kt., C.S.I., D.Sc., LL.D., 77 Russa Road North, Bhowanipur, Calcutta.
1847 Munich Royal Library (Kgl. Hof u. Staats-Bibliothek), Munich, Germany.

1913 Natal Society's Library, Pietermaritzburg, S. Africa.
1899 Nathan, Lt.-Col. Sir Matthew, G.C.M.G., R.E., Brandon House, Kensington Palace Gardens, W.
1894 Naval and Military Club, 94, Piccadilly, W.
1909 Nebraska University Library, Lincoln, Nebraska, U.S.A.
1913 Needham, J. E., Esq., Bombay Club, Bombay.
1880 Netherlands, Royal Geographical Society of the (Koninklijk Nederlandsch Aardrijkskundig Genootschap), Singel 421, Amsterdam.
1899 Netherlands, Royal Library of the, The Hague.
1847 Newberry Library, The, Chicago, Ill., U.S.A.
1847 Newcastle-upon-Tyne Literary and Philosophical Society, Westgate Road, Newcastle on-Tyne.
1899 Newcastle-upon-Tyne Public Library, New Bridge Street, Newcastle-on-Tyne.
1894 New London Public Library, Conn., U.S.A.
1899 New South Wales, Public Library of, Sydney, N.S.W.
1899 New York Athletic Club, Central Park, South, New York City, U.S.A.
1895 New York Public Library, 40, Lafayette Place, New York City, U.S.A.
1847 New York State Library, Albany, New York, U.S.A.
1894 New York Yacht Club, 37 West 44 Street, New York City, U.S.A.
1897 New Zealand, The High Commissioner for, 13, Victoria Street, S.W.
1911 Nijhoff, Martinus, The Hague, Holland.
1896 North Adams Public Library, Massachusetts, U.S.A.
1893 Northcliffe, The Right Hon. Lord. Elmwood, St. Peter's, Thanet.
1899 Nottingham Public Library Sherwood Street, Nottingham.

1890 Oriental Club, 18, Hanover Square, W.
1902 Otani, Kozui, Esq., Nishi Honganji, Horikawa, Kyoto, Japan.
1899 Oxford and Cambridge Club, 71, Pall Mall, S.W.
1847 Oxford Union Society, Oxford.

1911 Pan-American Union, Washington, D.C., U.S.A.
1847 Paris, Bibliothèque Nationale, Rue de Richelieu, Paris.
1847 Paris, Institut de France, Quai de Conti 23, Paris.

1899 Parlett, Harold George, Esq., H.B.M. Consulate, Dairen, Japan.
1880 Peabody Institute, Baltimore, Md., U.S.A.
1908 Pearson, Dr. F. S., Coombe House, Kingston Hill, S.W.
1847 Peckover of Wisbech, The Right Hon. Lord, Bank House, Wisbech (*Vice-President*).
1893 Peek, Sir Wilfred, Bart., c/o Mr. Grover, Rousdon, Lyme Regis.
1911 Penrose, R. A. F., Esq., Bullitt Buildings, Philadelphia, U.S.A.
1899 Pequot Library, Southport, Conn., U.S.A.
1913 Petersen, V., Esq., Chinese Telegraph Administration, Peking, China.
1880 Petherick, Edward Augustus, Esq., Commonwealth Library, Melbourne, Australia.
1895 Philadelphia Free Library, Pa., U.S.A.
1899 Philadelphia, Library Company of, N.W. corner Juniper & Locust Streets, Philadelphia, Pa., U.S.A.
1899 Philadelphia, Union League Club, 8, Broad Street, Philadelphia, Pa., U.S.A.
1899 Philadelphia. University Club, 1510 Walnut Street, Philadelphia. Pa., U.S.A.
1909 Plymouth, Officers' Library, Royal Marine Barracks.
1899 Plymouth Proprietary and Cottonian Library, Cornwall Street, Plymouth.
1899 Portico Library, 57, Mosley Street, Manchester.
1912 Provincial Library of British Columbia, Victoria, British Columbia.
1911 Pykett, The Rev. G. F., Anglo-Chinese School, Methodist Epis. Mission, Penang.
1913 Pym, C. Guy, Esq., 35, Cranley Gardens, S.W.

1894 Quaritch, Bernard, Esq., 11, Grafton Street, New Bond Street, W. (12 COPIES).
1913 Queen's University, The, Kingston, Ontario, Canada.
1913 Quincey, Edmund de Q., Esq., Oakwood, Chislehurst.

1890 Raffles Museum and Library, Singapore.
1847 Reform Club, 104, Pall Mall, S.W.
1899 Reggio, André C., Esq., 43, Tremont Street, Boston, Mass., U.S.A.
1895 Rhodes, Josiah, Esq., The Elms, Lytham, Lancashire.
1907 Ricketts, D. P., Esq., Imperial Chinese Railways, Tientsin, China.
1882 Riggs, T. L., Esq., 1311, Mass. Avenue, Washington, D.C., U.S.A.
1911 Rio de Janeiro, Archivo Publico Nacional, Sa da Republica, No. 26.
1899 Rodd, H.E. The Right Hon. Sir James Rennell, G.C.V.O., K.C.M.G., C.B., British Embassy, Rome.
1906 Rotterdamsch Leeskabinet, Rotterdam.
1911 Royal Anthropological Institute, 50, Great Russell Street, W.C.
1893 Royal Artillery Institution, Woolwich.
1847 Royal Colonial Institute, Northumberland Avenue, W.C.
1896 Royal Cruising Club, 1, Bolton Street, Piccadilly, W.
1847 Royal Engineers' Institute, Chatham.
1847 Royal Geographical Society, Kensington Gore, W.
1890 Royal Scottish Geographical Society, Synod Hall, Castle Terrace, Edinburgh.
1897 Royal Societies Club, 63, St. James's Street, S.W.
1847 Royal United Service Institution, Whitehall, S.W.
1899 Runciman, The Right Hon. Walter, M.P., Doxford, Chathill, Northumberland.
1904 Ruxton, Captain Upton Fitz Herbert, Little Drove House, Singleton, Sussex.
1900 Ryley, John Horton, Esq., 8, Rue d'Auteuil, Paris.

1899 St. Andrews University, St. Andrews.
1899 St. Deiniol's Library, Hawarden, Flintshire, N. Wales.
1893 St. John's, New Brunswick, Free Public Library.
1890 St. Louis Mercantile Library, St. Louis, Mo., U.S.A.
1899 St. Martin's-in-the-Fields Free Public Library, 115, St. Martin s Lane, W.C.
1847 St. Petersburg University Library, St. Petersburg.
1894 St. Wladimir University, Kiew, Russia.
1911 Saise, Walter, Esq., D.Sc., M. Inst. C.E., Stapleton, Bristol.
1913 Salby, George, Esq., 65, Great Russell Street, W.C.
1899 San Francisco Public Library, San Francisco, Cal., U.S.A.
1899 Sclater, Dr. William Lutley, 10, Sloane Court, S.W.
1899 Seattle Public Library, Seattle, Washington, U.S.A.
1894 Seymour, Admiral of the Fleet the Right Hon. Sir Edward Hobart, G.C.B., O.M., G.C.V.O., LL.D., Queen Anne's Mansions, St. James's Park, S.W.
1898 Sheffield Free Public Libraries, Surrey Street, Sheffield.
1914 Sheppard, S. T., Esq., Byculla Club, Bombay, No. 8.
1847 Signet Library, 11, Parliament Square, Edinburgh.
1890 Sinclair, Mrs. William Frederic, 102, Cheyne Walk, Chelsea, S.W.
1910 Skimming, E. H. B., Esq., 6, Cleveland Terrace, W.
1913 Skinner, Major R. M., R. A. M. Corps, c/o Messrs. Holt and Co., 3, Whitehall Place, S.W.
1912 Skipper, Mervyn G., Esq., care of Eastern Extensions Tel. Co , Electra House, Finsbury Pavement, E.C.
1904 Smith, John Langford, Esq., H. B. M. Consular Service, China, c/o E. Greenwood, Esq., Frith Knowl, Elstree.
1906 Smith, J. de Berniere, Esq., 4, Gloucester Terrace, Regent's Park, N.W.
1913 Smith, The Right Hon. James Parker, Linburn, Kirknewton, Midlothian.
1896 Smithers, F. Oldershaw, Esq., Dashwood House, 9, New Broad Street, E.C.
1899 Societá Geografica Italiana, Via del Plebiscito 102, Rome.
1847 Société de Géographie, Boulevard St. Germain, 184, Paris.
1899 South African Public Library, Queen Victoria Street, Cape Town, South Africa.
1904 Stanton, John, Esq., High Street, Chorley, Lancashire.
1912 Stein, Herr Johann, K. Ungar. Universitäts - Buchhandlung, Kolozsvar, Hungary.
1847 Stevens, Son, and Stiles, Messrs. Henry, 39, Great Russell Street, W.C.
1847 Stockholm, Royal Library of (Kungl. Biblioteket), Sweden.
1895 Stockton Public Library, Stockton, Cal., U.S.A.
1905 Storer, Albert H., Esq., Ridgefield, Ct., U.S.A.
1890 Strachey, Lady, 67, Belsize Park Gardens, N.W.
1904 Suarez, Colonel Don Pedro (Bolivian Legation), Santa Cruz, 74, Compayne Gardens, N.W.
1909 Swan, J. D. C., Dr., 25, Ruthven Street, Glasgow.
1908 Sydney, University of, New South Wales.
1899 Sykes, Colonel Sir Percy Molesworth, K.C.I.E., C.M.G., Kashgar.

1914 Tamplen, Lewis H., Esq., c/o Messrs. Jardine, Matheson & Co., Ltd., Hong Kong.
1899 Tangye, Richard Trevithick Gilbertstone, Esq., LL.B., 40, Bramham Gardens, S.W.
1914 Taylor, Frederic W., Esq., 1529, Niagara Street, Denver, Colorado, U.S.A.
1910 Teleki, Count Paul, Joszef-tór., 7, Budapest V.
1899 Temple, Lieut.-Col. Sir Richard Carnac, Bart., C.I.E., The Nash, nr. Worcester.
1894 Thomson, Basil Home, Esq., 81, Victoria Road, Kensington, W.
1906 Thomson, Colonel Charles FitzGerald, late 7th Hussars, St. James's Club, 106, Piccadilly, W.
1913 Thurston, E. Coppée, Esq., Milnthorpe, St. John's Road, Harrow.

1904 Todd, Commander George James, R.N., The Manse, Kingsbarns, Fife.
1896 Toronto Public Library, Toronto, Ont., Canada.
1890 Toronto University, Toronto, Ont., Canada.
1911 Tower, Sir Reginald, K.C.M.G., C.V.O., 8, Baker Street, Portman Square, W.
1847 Travellers' Club, 106, Pall Mall, S.W.
1899 Trinder, Arnold, Esq., River House, Walton-on-Thames.
1913 Trinder, W. H., Esq., The Old Vicarage, Kingswood, Surrey.
1847 Trinity College, Cambridge.
1847 Trinity House, The Hon. Corporation of, Tower Hill, E.C.
1911 Tuckerman, Paul, Esq., 59, Wall Street, New York, U.S.A.
1890 Turnbull, Alexander H., Esq., Elibank, Wellington, New Zealand.
1902 Tweedy, Arthur H., Esq., Widmore Lodge, Widmore, Bromley, Kent.

1847 United States Congress, Library of, Washington, D.C., U.S.A.
1899 United States National Museum (Library of), Washington, D.C., U.S.A.
1847 United States Naval Academy Library, Annapolis, Md., U.S.A.
1847 Upsala University Library, Upsala, Sweden (c/o Simpkin, Marshall).

1911 Van Ortroy, Professor F., Université de Gand, Belgium.
1913 Vasquez, Señor Don Ricardo, Guatemala, C.A.
1899 Vernon, Roland Venables, Esq., Colonial Office, Downing Street, S.W.
1899 Victoria, Public Library, Museums, and National Gallery of, Melbourne, Australia.
1847 Vienna Imperial Library (K. K. Hof-Bibliothek), Vienna.
1905 Vienna, K. K. Geographische Gesellschaft, Wollzeile 33, Vienna.
1887 Vignaud, Henry, Esq., LL.D., 2, Rue de la Mairie, Bagneux (Seine), France.
1912 Villa, Dr. F. Luis de. Banco Colombiano, Guatemala, C.A.
1909 Villiers, J. A. J. de, Esq., British Museum (*Hon. Secretary*) (2).

1904 Wagner, Herrn H., and E. Debes, Geographische Anstalt, Brüderstrasse 23, Leipzig.
1902 War Office, Mobilisation and Intelligence Library, Whitehall, S.W.
1847 Washington, Department of State, D.C., U.S.A.
1847 Washington, Library of Navy Department, Washington, D.C., U.S.A.
1899 Watanabe, Chiharu, Esq., 4, Shimotakanawamachi, Shibaku, Tokyo, Japan.
1899 Watkinson Library, Hartford, Connecticut, U.S.A.
1899 Weld, Rev. George Francis, Hingham, Mass., U.S.A. (Weldwold, Santa Barbara, California).
1899 Westaway, Engineer Rear-Admiral Albert Ernest Luscombe, 36, Granada Road, Southsea.
1913 Western Reserve Historical Society, Cleveland, U.S.A.
1898 Westminster School, Dean's Yard, S.W.
1913 White, James, Esq., Commission of Conservation, Ottawa.
1914 White, John G., Williamson Building, Cleveland, Ohio, U.S.A.
1893 Whiteway, Richard Stephen, Esq., Brownscombe, Shottermill, Surrey.
1910 Wihlfahrt. E., Esq.
1914 Willard, A. F., Esq., Lloyd's Agency, Livingston, Guatemala.
1899 Williams, O. W., Esq., Fort Stockton, Texas, U.S.A.

1914 Williams, Sidney Herbert, Esq., 32, Warrior Square, St. Leonards-on-Sea.
1899 Wilmanns, Frederick M., Esq., 89, Oneida Street, Milwaukee, Wisc., U.S.A.
1913 Wimble, John Bowring, Esq., 18, Westbourne Terrace, Hyde Park, W.
1895 Wisconsin, State Historical Society of, Madison, Wisc., U.S.A.
1913 Wood, Henry A. Wise, Esq., 1, Madison Avenue, New York.
1900 Woodford, Charles Morris, Esq., The Grinstead, Partridge Green, Sussex.
1907 Woolf, Leonard Sidney, Esq., 38, Brunswick Square, W.C.
1899 Worcester, Massachusetts, Free Library, Worcester, Mass., U.S.A.
1914 Wright, Dr. J. Farrall, 46, Derby Street, Bolton, Lancs.
1913 Wright, R., Esq., The Poplars, Worsley Road, Swinton, Lancs.

1847 Yale University, New Haven, Conn., U.S.A.
1894 Young, Alfales, Esq., Salt Lake City, Utah, U.S.A.

1847 Zürich, Stadtbibliothek, Zürich, Switzerland.